Women's history: Britain, 1850–1945

Women's History

General Editor
June Purvis
Professor of Sociology, University of Portsmouth

Published
Carol Dyhouse
No distinction of sex? Women in British universities, 1870-1939

Bridget Hill
Women, work and sexual politics in eighteenth-century England

Linda Mahood
Policing gender, class & family: Britain, 1850-1940

June Purvis (editor)
Women's history: Britain, 1850-1945

Forthcoming
Lynn Abrams and Elizabeth Harvey (editors)
Gender relations in German history

Shani D'Cruze
Sex, violence and working women in Victorian and Edwardian England

jay Dixon
The romantic fiction of Mills & Boon, 1909-95

Ralph Gibson
Women, faith and liberation: female religious orders in nineteenth-century France

Wendy Webster
Women in the 1950s

Barbara Winslow
Sylvia Pankhurst: a political biography

Women's history: Britain, 1850–1945

An introduction

Edited by

June Purvis

University of Portsmouth

UCL PRESS

First published in 1995 by UCL Press

UCL Press Limited
University College London
Gower Street
London WC1E 6BT

The name of University College London (UCL) is a registered trade mark used by UCL Press with the consent of the owner.

British Library Cataloguing in Publication Data
A catalogue record for this book is a available from the British Library.

ISBNs
1-85728-319-8 HB
1-85728-320-1 PB

Typeset in Garamond.
Printed and bound by
Page Bros (Norwich) Ltd, England

Contents

CONTENTS

Preface

In September 1973, Sheila Rowbotham's *Hidden from history: 300 years of women's oppression and the fight against it* was published. Its influence has been enormous in that it acted as a catalyst for the "taking off" of women's history in Britain. In the 1990s, publications in women's history are booming and there are now three specialised journals in the field: *Journal of Women's History*, *Gender and History*, and *Women's History Review*. Yet despite the output of researchers, few general textbooks have been published that attempt to provide an overview of women's lives in Britain from 1850 to 1945. The pathbreaking analysis offered by Jane Lewis in *Women in England, 1870-1950: sexual divisions and social change*, first published in 1984, covered mainly the family, marriage, motherhood and employment. But since that date, no other general accounts of the period have been published.

The aim of this book is to fill this gap. Specialists in the field have each written a chapter about a key aspect of women's lives in Britain, 1850-1945, an analysis that is preceded by a discussion about the nature of women's history itself, from the nineteenth century to the present day. We hope that the book will be especially useful to undergraduate and postgraduate students on history, sociology, cultural studies and women's studies courses and, above all, that it will promote discussion and stimulate further research and reinterpretation. The field of women's history is exciting and challenging. If this book contributes in some small way to that debate, it will be more than sufficient justification for our efforts.

June Purvis

Notes on contributors

Shani D'Cruze is History Subject Leader at Crewe and Alsager Faculty, Manchester Metropolitan University. She has published articles on eighteenth-century urban history, women, gender and the household economy, and on the history of sexual violence. She is currently writing a full-length study of Victorian working-class women and sexual assault.

June Hannam teaches labour history and women's studies at the University of the West of England, Bristol, where she is head of history. Her publications include *Isabella Ford, 1855-1924*, "Women and the ILP, 1890-1914" in *The centennial history of the Independent Labour Party* (eds D. James et al.), and "Women, history and protest" in *Introducing women's studies* (eds D. Richardson and V. Robinson). She is currently working on a study of women in Bristol politics, 1830-1939 and researching into Dorothy Jewson and the politics of gender in the ILP in the 1920s.

Barbara Harrison is Reader in the Sociology of Health and Illness at NESCOT, Epsom's Higher and Further Education College, and has taught historical aspects of health and welfare, and the area of women's health, for a number of years. Her own research has been concerned with women and occupational ill-health in late-nineteenth- and early-twentieth-century Britain. She is the author of a forthcoming book *Not only the dangerous trades: women and occupational ill-health, 1880-1914*.

Sandra Stanley Holton is an Australian Research Fellow at the University of Adelaide. She has recently completed a full-length history of the suffrage movement from the 1860s to the 1920s. She is currently working on a biography of Alice Clark, the pioneer woman industrialist and suffragist.

Pat Hudson is Professor of Economic and Social History at the University of Liverpool. Her research has concentrated on the process and impact of industrialization in Britain, with particular emphasis on proto-industrialization, capital accumulation, regional specialization and the family economy. Her publications include *The genesis of industrial capital* and *The industrial revolution*, and she was co-editor of *Women's work and the family economy in historical perspective*. Together with Dr Pamela Sharpe, she is currently preparing a volume on industrialization in Britain, which attempts to integrate women's history and challenges the sources, methods and terms of mainstream arguments and debates.

Jane Humphries is Lecturer in Economics at the University of Cambridge and a Fellow of Newnham College, Cambridge. She is the author of numerous articles on the history of women's work and family lives. Most recently, with Sara Horrell, she has been working on a project funded by the Leverhulme Trust on family living standards in the British Industrial Revolution. She is currently working, with Jill Rubery, on an edited volume of essays on the economics of equal opportunities for the Equal Opportunities Commission.

Sheila Jeffreys teaches sexual politics and lesbian and gay politics in the department of political science at the University of Melbourne, Australia. She is the author of several books on the history and politics of sexuality: *The spinster and her enemies*, *Anticlimax* and *The lesbian heresy*. She is currently working on the development of the idea of prostitution in the twentieth century.

Jane McDermid teaches women's history and European history in the department of historical and political studies at LSU College, Southampton. She has published articles on Russian and Scottish women, and on literature and women's history. Current research projects include a prosopographical study of Russian revolutionary women, and an examination of the relationship between women and the Scottish educational tradition in the nineteenth century.

Clare Midgley is Senior Lecturer in History at Staffordshire University. She is the author of *Women against slavery: the British campaigns, 1780-1870*, and is currently preparing an edited collection of essays on the theme of gender and imperialism.

June Purvis is Professor of Sociology at the University of Portsmouth, where she teaches courses in women's studies and women's history. She is the author of *Hard lessons: the lives and education of working-class women in nineteenth century England* and *A history of women's education in England*, as well as being co-editor of a number of volumes, the latest being (with Mary Maynard) *Researching women's lives from a feminist perspective*. She is the founding and managing editor of *Women's History Review* and is currently researching the suffragette movement in Edwardian Britain, in particular the life of Christabel Pankhurst.

NOTES ON CONTRIBUTORS

Penny Summerfield is Professor of Women's History at Lancaster University. She is the author of *Women workers in the Second World War* and co-author of *Out of the cage: women's experiences in two world wars.* She has also published numerous articles on women, war and social change, and on gender, class and schooling in the twentieth century.

Penny Tinkler is a lecturer in the department of sociology at the University of Manchester. She has written articles on adolescent girlhood, leisure and popular culture between 1900 and 1950. She is the author of *Constructing girlhood: magazine representations of adolescent girlhood and femininity, 1920-50.*

For my beloved daughter, Catherine Malvina

Chapter One

✍

From "women worthies" to poststructuralism? Debate and controversy in women's history in Britain[1]

June Purvis

Introduction

In 1929, the well-known English essayist and novelist Virginia Woolf lamented the fact that so few histories of women had been written:

> The history of England is the history of the male line, not of the female. Of our fathers we know always some fact, some distinction. They were soldiers or they were sailors; they filled that office or they made that law. But of our mothers, our grandmothers, our great-grandmothers, what remains? . . . We know nothing of their marriages and the number of children they bore.[2]

The printed works on women that Woolf might have consulted were few, despite the fact that in the nineteenth and early twentieth centuries in particular, there were a number of writers researching women's past.[3] Indeed, it was not until the 1970s that publications in women's history became more numerous, and since then they have proliferated into a booming publishing field. My aim in this chapter is to offer a brief overview of the development of women's history in Britain, from the nineteenth century to the 1990s, highlighting key concerns, debates and controversies.

Early work

It would appear that before the professionalisation of history in the nineteenth century, there were at least two main (and often overlapping) strands of women's history - the lives of "women worthies" and the biography of an individual woman, often a political or religious figure of some importance. As Natalie Zemon Davis observes, the "women worthies" tradition had a polemical purpose, namely to reveal the range of women's capacity, to provide exemplars for female readers, to argue from what some women had done to what "all could do, if given the chance and the education".[4] Not unexpectedly, this tradition often intertwined with the individual biography approach that focused much more on a woman within her society and culture, although even here the author did not necessarily seek to explain how her subject's sex and gender as a woman might shape her expectations and public role.[5]

One such prominent nineteenth-century temperance writer and lecturer was Mrs Clara Lucas Balfour, who published a number of works with titles such as *Working women of the last half century: the lessons of their lives* and *Women worth emulating*.[6] In her preface to the latter, she claimed that emulation was the spirit "most desirable to arouse in the young". That which we approve and admire, she coaxed her readers, we are led to emulate: "The sterling qualities which made a character excellent, still more than the mental powers which made it remarkable, convey lessons for instruction and encouragement that all can apply".[7] It was with this purpose in mind that she selected various women of "womanly worth and wisdom" for the young of her own sex "in the hope that studious habits, intellectual pursuits, domestic industry, and sound religious principles, may be promoted and confirmed by such examples".[8] The women whose biographies she discussed include the scientist Mary Somerville, the astronomer Caroline Herschel, the hymn writer Charlotte Elliott, the authoress Amelia Opie and the philanthropic prison visitor Sarah Martin. What distinguished these women for Mrs Balfour was their humility and the acceptance of "traditional" feminine qualities, such as self-sacrifice. Sarah Martin, for example, although a "humble seamstress",[9] wished to be useful to God and became a well-known prison visitor in her home town of Great Yarmouth. "All workers in the Lord's vineyard," entreated Mrs Balfour, "can emulate her self-sacrifice, her diligence, her faith, her love, and thus live blessing and blessed".[10]

Another prolific nineteenth-century writer in this genre was William H. Davenport Adams, producing books with such titles as *Stories of the lives of noble women, Celebrated women travellers of the nineteenth century*, and *Some historic women or, biographical studies of women who have made history*.[11] In the latter, he claimed to bring together "a group of Celebrated Women, who might fairly be considered representative of the higher qualities of Womanhood, – such qualities as patriotism, religious enthusiasm, fidelity, moral courage, fortitude, devotion, and the capacity of governing".[12] Such qualities were frequently stressed in the many biographies of well-known women, such as the upper-middle-class spinster Florence Nightingale who, as Superintendent of the female nursing establishment in the Crimea War, drastically reduced the death rate of British soldiers.[13] These accounts, however, presented Miss Nightingale as the self-sacrificing "Lady with the Lamp", mopping the brow of sick soldiers and overcoming the barriers of her "ladylike" status to nurse men who were her social inferiors. No mention is made of her ambition, ruthlessness and iron determination since, as Vicinus observes, such characteristics did not fit public expectations about middle-class women.[14]

Many of these studies were, therefore, celebratory; in addition, they rarely cited sources for assumptions or generalizations made. But other biographies of well-known women, such as the 12 volumes by Agnes and Elizabeth Strickland on the *Lives of the queens of England from the Norman Conquest*, first published 1840–48 and then reprinted in a widely read, cheap and popular edition in 1864–5, were based on careful research.[15] As Thirsk notes, these first of the nineteenth-century women historians were at the forefront of historical research since they searched out original documents, letting them "speak for themselves".[16] Working at a time before the calendaring of state papers and private archives began in the 1860s, the Strickland sisters often had to fight to gain access to such sources. Nevertheless, they were successful in their endeavours and gained entry to the State Paper Office, the British Museum and the Bodleian Library, as well as many private collections. A well-known contemporary of theirs, Mary Anne Everett Green, similarly made extensive use of primary sources. From 1849 to 1855 she published a series of volumes on the *Lives of the princesses of England*, dating from the Norman Conquest of 1066 to the end of Charles II's reign in the seventeenth century.[17]

Other histories about women, published in the nineteenth century, were often written by feminists active in various campaigns, such as women's right to higher education and to the franchise. The women's educational reform movement seems to have begun almost abruptly in the late 1840s and to have gathered momentum in the 1850s and 1860s, with London University, in 1878, being the first university to award women degrees on equal terms with men.[18] Charlotte Carmichael Stopes, the first woman in Scotland to take a university certificate, was one of this new generation of university educated women who combined her feminist activities with a keen interest in women's history. She campaigned for women's suffrage and participation in local government, and was also a member of the Rational Dress Society that was critical of the corsets, flannel petticoats and flounced skirts that "feminine" Victorian ladies were supposed to wear, and advocated instead the wearing of "sensible" clothes.[19] In 1894, Stopes' *British freewomen, their historical privileges* first appeared, in which she investigated the ancient rights of women through an analysis of state papers, parliamentary writs, journals of the House of Commons, and works on law, history and archaeology.[20] Two years later, another book was published by a supporter of women's suffrage, namely *Women in English life from medieval to modern times* by Georgina Hill. Hill contested the common assumption of male historians who, adopting a Whiggish interpretation of the past, suggested that "mankind" was moving toward a better world. Thus she contended that the position of women in England "cannot be regarded as an orderly evolution. It does not show unvarying progress from age to age. In one direction there has been improvement, in another deterioration".[21]

Hill gave some consideration to the everyday lives of "ordinary" as opposed to "great" women, a topic that began to attract the attention of academic historians in the 1890s as they researched a new field of enquiry, namely the social and economic life of the nation.[22] Since working-class women as well as their menfolk had always been involved in paid work, whether as single women, wives or mothers, their contribution to the economy now came under scholarly scrutiny. At the newly established London School of Economics (LSE), for example, associated with the Fabians Sidney and Beatrice Webb, the history of women especially focused on the period 1760 to 1900 and with women's part in the agricultural and industrial revolutions.[23] Elizabeth Leigh Hutchins, a founder member of the Fabian Society's Women's Group, registered at the LSE between 1896 and 1906 for several lecture courses and then published *Women in modern industry* in 1915. In this book, she suggested that although the Industrial Revolution had increased employment opportunities for women, the expansion was largely in unskilled and poorly paid work which not only restricted women's employment opportunities but also made them financially dependent on fathers or husbands or, if a widow or wife of an unemployed man, condemned to a life of poverty.[24]

Two other students at the LSE, Alice Clark and Ivy Pinchbeck, also went on to write books in women's history that have similarly become classics. Clark, a socially and politically conscious daughter of a prominent liberal Quaker manufacturing family in Somerset, had joined in 1912 the National Union of Women's Suffrage Societies (NUWSS), the non-militant wing of the women's suffrage movement led by Millicent Garrett Fawcett.[25] The following year she began research at the LSE which led eventually to the publication in 1919 of her book *Working life of women in the seventeenth century*, in which she argued that capitalism had eroded the status of women, which had been higher in pre-capitalist and pre-industrialist times.[26] Clark's supervisor was Lilian Knowles, who inspired and encouraged another LSE student, Ivy Pinchbeck. In *Women workers and the Industrial Revolution*, first published in 1930, Pinchbeck contended, contrary to Clark, that industrialization brought about changes that were largely beneficial for both single and married women.[27] By the 1930s, then, women's changing role in the economic life of the nation, especially with industrialization, was a relatively well researched theme. Indeed, Erickson claims that in early-twentieth-century Britain more women academics were active in the field of economic history than at any time since.[28]

Despite the importance of this early work, it was rarely given extended coverage in subsequent mainstream general histories. "History" had been professionalized as a discipline by white, heterosexual, middle-class men who taught the subject in British universities and shaped it in particular ways. The field was defined as "man's truth" so that women were "outside" of history, the unhistorical other, different from men in that they were identified with social life.[29] Mainstream history was thus largely written not only by men but also about men's activities in wars, politics, business and administration. Women's history was largely invisible or, if represented, belittled in some way or located within sex-stereotypical discussions about the family or the effect of women's paid work on their family roles. George Dangerfield's influential *The strange death of liberal England*, first published in 1935 and reprinted at least up to 1972, devoted one whole chapter to the women's suffrage movement, but treated the Women's Social Political Union (WSPU), the main militant wing of the movement, lead by Mrs Emmeline Pankhurst and her eldest daughter, Christabel, as a "brutal comedy", where the spectacle of women attacking men produced "even in this day, an outrageous, an unprincipled laughter".[30] In Dangerfield's view, militant women have no place in the male sphere of politics, especially when setting fire to empty buildings:

> when a scene as ordinary as English politics is suddenly disturbed with the swish of long skirts, the violent assault of feathered hats, the impenetrable, advancing phalanx of corseted bosoms – when, around the smoking ruins of some house or church, there is discovered the dread evidence of a few hairpins or a feminine galosh – then the amazing, the ludicrous appearance of the whole thing is almost irresistible.[31]

As the first "historian", that is *male* historian, to devote one whole chapter to the women's movement, Dangerfield's powerful narrative created a plot from which, as Jane Marcus observes, future male historians have seldom been able to break free, since it served a "public (or patriarchal) need to label a serious women's politics as 'hysterical'".[32]

In other instances, women, when present in mainstream history books, were presented in sex-stereotypical ways. Harold Perkin's key text *The origins of modern English society 1780–1880*, first published in 1969, has no entry for women in the index but, predictably, women are to be found in the 12 pages devoted to the section "Industrialism and the family".[33] Overall, he concluded that the Industrial Revolution, "if only indirectly", brought about "the emancipation of women", a claim which many feminists today would dispute.[34] Accounts such as those by Dangerfield and Perkin reveal vividly the politics of history writing, something that is not confined to such texts but found in all histories, including, as we shall now see, the "new" women's history.

The "new" feminist women's history

By 1969, the so-called "second wave" of the organized women's movement in Western Europe and the USA had begun, and sparked off renewed interest in women's history. As feminists in the late 1960s and early 1970s met in women's consciousness-raising groups, they discussed and analyzed the subordination, oppression and inequalities that they felt and experienced as "women". In particular, in Britain, many feminists involved in left wing politics were disillusioned with the way they were treated by the male left and with the male bias of Socialism/Marxism. Juliet Mitchell epitomized this feeling of discontent in her widely read essay, "Women: the longest revolution" – "In the Marxist meetings on the politics of the Third World, in the University common rooms I frequent, where were the women? Absent in the practices and in the theories".[35] The invisibility generally of women in history, whether written from a socialist, liberal or mainstream perspective, was highlighted in Sheila Rowbotham's influential text *Hidden from history: 300 years of women's oppression and the fight against it.*[36] Published in 1973, this book is regarded as the "taking-off point" for women's history in Britain.[37] Feminists "set the pace" of this development, defining the field of activity and mapping out the main directions of research.[38] Women's history thus developed separately from mainstream history as taught in higher education, and still has an indirect relationship with it today. In particular, some scholars will not accept the academic status of women's history. Professor Geoffrey Elton, for example, refers to the "non-existent" history of ethnic entities and women; Ronald Hyman in *Empire and sexuality, the British experience*, speaks of "the poverty of feminism" for historical work, asserting that feminist scholars display both a "hostility to sex" and a "dogma about the supposedly 'pervasive violence against women by men'", views which he labels "sour and immature" and "feminist hysterics".[39] By 1986 and 1990 respectively, when these male historians made those remarks, the division between women's history and feminist history was well marked, a development that was becoming evident in the 1970s.

Generally, *women's history* takes women as its subject matter and may be written by men (who cannot be feminists but may be sympathetic to, and supportive of, the women's cause) and women, alike.[40] Women's history is not, therefore, necessarily feminist history, despite the fact that the links between the two have been strong.[41] Indeed, some men writing women's history are decidedly anti-feminist. For example, David Mitchell's biography of Christabel Pankhurst, a leader, as we mentioned earlier, of the WSPU in Edwardian Britain, is renowned for its misogyny. His final chapter, where he compares Christabel's feminism with "the wilder rantings" of well-known feminists of the 1970s such as Kate Millet, Ti-Grace Atkinson and Germaine Greer is even titled "Bitch power".[42] Furthermore, some women writing women's history, such as Elizabeth Roberts, wish to distance themselves from the label "feminist". Roberts, in an oral history of the daily lives of working-class women in three Lancashire towns in the late-nineteenth and early-twentieth centuries, explored a number of key themes – youth, work and leisure; marriage; women as housewives and managers; and families and neighbours. She stressed, however, that although she began and ended her research "as a feminist", some feminists may be disturbed to find that her study does not seek to investigate patriarchy or male oppression of women.[43] "The patriarchal model tends to stress the negative aspects of women's lives," she asserted, "and thus, I believe, distorts the true picture at least in the area I studied".[44] Consequently, Roberts does not see her book as "an obviously feminist history".[45]

As these examples illustrate, the terms, "women's history" and "feminist history" are not interchangeable. Feminist history is history that is informed by the ideas and theories of feminism[46] and when the subject of study is women we should strictly use the term *feminist women's history*. However, feminists also research other topics, such as men, masculinity and the male world; when this is the case, the more general term *feminist history* should be used. However, not all writers follow these strict conventions, and so one frequently finds these terms used interchangeably with *women's history* and with each other.

In Britain, then, the growth of feminist women's history in the 1970s was intertwined with the politics of the women's liberation movement, and especially with socialist feminist historians such as Sheila Rowbotham, Sally Alexander, Anna Davin, Barbara Taylor, Jill Norris and Jill Liddington, who at that time were not employed full time in higher education and were connected with the socialist publication *History Workshop Journal* (HWJ). That the "marriage" between Socialism and feminism was not very satisfactory was evident in the first issue of HWJ, where an editorial on "Feminist history" pointed out that as recently as 1971, when the suggestion had been made at a History Workshop meeting, that people working on women's issues should meet later in the day, there was a roar of laughter. "We know that women's history still has to be argued for," it was tactfully pointed out by Alexander and Davin.[47] Furthermore, they went on to define feminist women's history from a socialist perspective:

> feminism not only demands a history of the family but also seeks to explain why women's work as the reproducers of labour power, and their servicing of labour power in the home, has remained invisible for so long. By bringing women into the foreground of historical enquiry our knowledge of production, of working class politics and culture, of class struggle, of the welfare state, will be transformed. Men and women *do* inhabit different worlds, with boundaries which have been defined (and from time to time re-arranged) for them by the capitalist mode of production as it has made use of and strengthened the sexual division of

labour and patriarchal authority. It is the relationships like that between the two worlds, between the sexual division of labour and class struggle, home and work, or the private sector and the public, the social relationships between men and women, which form the substance of feminist history, and will enrich all socialist history.[48]

As this quotation makes clear, socialist feminist historians at this time were working within paradigms constructed by influential male socialist historians, such as E. P. Thompson, who wished to write a "history from below" rather than a history of elites and of constitutional matters.[49] This orientation therefore encouraged a particular range of historical issues to be investigated, and especially the way in which women in the past had been affected by the development of a capitalist mode of production. A concern with writing a "history from the bottom up" led to a focus on the lives of working-class rather than middle-class women, and with an analysis that attempted to integrate both social class and gender divisions. However, although "patriarchal authority" is mentioned in the above quotation, there was much debate about the term, and whether it was useful in historical analysis.

"Patriarchy", which usually referred to male domination and to the power relationships by which men dominated women, was criticised by Rowbotham as a term that implied a universal, transhistorical, fixed structure rooted in biological differences between men and women, suggesting a single determining cause of women's subordination.[50] Alexander and Taylor, on the other hand, defended its usefulness, especially as a theoretical tool for explaining women's oppression.[51] Indeed, Taylor later illustrated, in her brilliant study of the tensions between Socialism and feminism in early-nineteenth-century England, how a socialist feminist might intertwine successfully patriarchy with class analysis. Combing various sources where the voices of working-class women might be found, such as in letters published in the radical press of the 1830s, she cites many examples of working-class women who felt that their own menfolk, even the trade unionists, were no better than their male employers. Thus a tailoress, writing under the pen name of "A Woman" in a letter in *The Pioneer* on 12 April 1834, complained that "In these days, when servants are rising up against their masters, and claiming equal privileges with their employers, why should the spirit of tyranny still reside in the very servants themselves? . . . the men are as bad as their masters".[52]

The dominance of the socialist feminist voice within feminist women's history in Britain has led to a forging of strong links, not necessarily integrative, between the field and with socialist and labour history. *History Workshop Journal*, for example, in an editorial in its Spring issue in 1982 announced that from then on its subtitle would be changed from "'a journal of socialist historians' to a 'journal of socialist *and* feminist historians'" (my emphasis). However, women's history is usually confined to specific articles –

like a separate sections slot – that cover a wide range of themes including imperialism and motherhood in early-twentieth-century Britain, misogyny and English women's experiences in the brewing industry between c1300 and c1700, Mary Wollstonecraft (whose *Vindication of the rights of woman*, first published in 1792, is usually regarded as the founding text of Anglo-American feminism), women's work and the Industrial Revolution, and the influence of Marie Stopes' birth control clinics on the lives of working-class women in the interwar years in twentieth-century Britain.[53]

Strong links with socialist history are also evident in the specialized journal, *Gender and History*, which, as its name implies, takes "gender" rather than "women" as its key focus of analysis. Whereas "sex" refers to the biological differences between men and women, "gender" commonly refers to the socially conditioned behaviour of men and women, and the ways in which "masculinity" and "femininity" are socially and culturally constructed (this broad distinction is usually upheld in the social sciences although "sex", "gender" and "sexuality" interact in complex ways). It is this broad meaning of gender that *Gender and History* upholds, since in the editorial of its first issue, in the Spring of 1989, the Anglo-American Collective state:

> we seek to examine all historical social relations from a feminist perspective, to construct a comprehensive analysis of all institutions that take their gender-specific characters into account. In addressing men and masculinity as well as women and femininity, the journal will illuminate the ways in which societies have been shaped by the relations of power between women and men . . . Our subjects of study will include traditionally male institutions as well as those defined commonly as female.[54]

This emphasis on putting gender at the centre of the historical agenda holds important implications for the way feminist history is written (about which I shall say more later), and also for feminist politics. In regard to the latter, *Gender and History*, like *History Workshop Journal*, not only publishes articles on men's history, but also includes men on its editorial board.

Socialist feminism, however, was not the only feminist voice shaping and influencing the growth of feminist women's history in Britain, although it is often presented as such.[55] A broadly based group of women, working much more within an egalitarian or liberal feminist paradigm, also made a major contribution through studies on such themes as the history of feminism and women and the family.[56] However, it was especially radical feminist writers who offered the major challenge in interpretation to the dominant socialist feminist historiography.

Unlike socialist feminist historians in the 1970s and 1980s, radical feminist writers in Britain researching women's past often came from disciplines other than history, such as education and sociology, and were working within a women-centred paradigm derived from the emerging, multidisciplinary field of women's studies. Women's studies, like the "new" feminist women's history, grew out of the second wave women's movement, and developed in the 1970s as a "recuperative action" to challenge the silencing, stereotyping, marginalization and misrepresentation of women prevalent in malestream academic fields.[57] Key figures in Britain in radical feminist women's history during the 1980s were Dale Spender, Elizabeth Sarah and Sheila Jeffreys, for whom patriarchy and sexual politics, rather than capitalism and class relations, were the key sources of women's oppression. Spender, in her edited book *Feminist theorists*, pointed out that men, as the gatekeepers of knowledge, presented women of ideas in particular ways, in order to exclude them from entry in the "worthwhile" history. Thus Aphra Behn, a seventeeth-century feminist playwright, is represented as "a whore" rather than as a creative thinker.[58] Jeffreys, in her study of feminism and sexuality in England from 1880 to 1930, claimed that:

> male sexual control is of enormous importance in maintaining women's subordination. It is clear that we must look at the area of sexuality, not as merely a sphere of personal fulfilment, but as a battleground; an arena of struggle and power relationships between the sexes.[59]

As the above statements suggest, radical feminists tend to investigate in history a different range of issues from those studied by socialist feminists, namely men's control over the production of knowledge; men's control over women's bodies; male violence towards women; personal relationships between men and women in courtship, in marriage and in parenthood; women's friendships; and sexuality. Yet radical feminism remained very much a "minority voice" in feminist women's history in Britain,[60] despite its much more pervasive influence within the broader field of women's studies.

It was partly for this reason that I decided to launch in 1992 the new journal *Women's History Review*, since, as I stated in the editorial of our first issue, I hoped to attract "a range of feminist perspectives", including the more radical.[61] Thus we have published a number of articles written by radical feminists, such as Rosemary Auchmuty, Sheila Jeffreys and Elaine Miller, on lesbian and gay history: Liz Stanley on researching lesbian history and biography, and Emma Donaghue on lesbians and hermaphrodites, 1671–1766, as well as essays by those much more firmly within a socialist feminist paradigm, such as Eileen Janes Yeo, on social motherhood and the sexual communion of labour in British social science, 1850-1950.[62] And the debate over male power and patriarchy, so prominent in feminist debates in Britain in the 1970s and 80s, is yet again being aired in the pages of *Women's History Review*. Bridget Hill, a well-known socialist feminist historian, argued in 1993:

> the belief in the supremacy of patriarchy over all other factors in women's history . . . promises to be an arid study . . . As a thesis that emphasises the continued oppression of women by men as of central – and supreme – importance to women's history it may well alienate the

very allies - and there are many - we have won in the years since the 1960s . . . As women we will never achieve real equality and the enrichment that quality could bring to relationships without carrying men with us.[63]

Judith Bennett, in a thoughtful, nuanced reply to Hill, defended the historical study of patriarchy and pointed out that within any group - whether structured by commonalities of race, class, sexuality, or whatever - "Women as a group are disempowered compared to *men of their group*".[64] Patriarchy is not a static force, she insisted, but exists in many forms and varieties, so that its history will be a history of many different historical patriarchies, e.g. feudal patriarchy, capitalist patriarchy and socialist patriarchy.

The way in which feminist women's history in Britain was formed and shaped by some of the key concerns outlined here was not, of course, divorced from debates and issues within the women's movement generally. And as that movement in Britain became more fragmented during the 1980s, awareness grew of how the divisions between the usual "big three" feminist perspectives of socialist, radical and liberal feminism, excluded other feminisms.[65] In particular, black and lesbian feminists raised key questions about racism and heterosexuality, pointing out how their experiences as women had been marginalized in both feminist theory and practice. At the same time that this fragmentation was taking place, women's studies was becoming a major growth area in higher education - although women's history was much less rarely taught, and often located within women's studies and sociology rather than in history departments.[66] But as the differences between women began to be voiced, women's studies and women's history became much more separate from feminist political struggles than had been the case earlier, when the commonalities that all women shared were emphasized. Indeed, fears were expressed that with the "institutionalization" of women's studies, feminist knowledge was being tamed and incorporated within essentially unchanged systems.[67]

Such debates were not impervious to developments in women's history in the USA, which had always had a much stronger foothold in higher education than in Britain - even though in both societies, knowledge about women's lives in the past was rarely integrated into mainstream history. During the 1960s and 1970s, feminist historians in the USA were at the forefront of the developing feminist studies and, on the whole, tended to be radical feminists, giving far less emphasis to social class differences between women than did their British counterparts. Bennett suggested, however, that by the 1990s, this history was less feminist and more descriptive, avoiding "the hard questions, analyses, and conclusions that a feminist history requires" and, in particular, "avoiding difficult questions about the sexual dynamics of power".[68] The reasons she advanced for this shift are many, not least being the decline of historical influence as the frameworks provided by feminist literary criticism now take on a leadership role. In particular, the work of the male philosopher and historian Michel Foucault, and the areas of thought defined (in various ways) as postmodernism and poststructuralism[69] have made a tremendous impact within the broad interdisciplinary field of women's studies as well as within women's history in the USA. In Britain, however, the influence has been less marked, especially within women's history, which has been strongly embedded within an empiricist tradition (which is a theoretical position in itself) rather than in theorising. Nevertheless, the challenges posed by poststructuralism (I shall use this term) for the writing of history (and other disciplines) are now being debated hotly in Britain too.

Feminist women's history and poststructuralism

In 1988, two influential books appeared which argued that a poststructuralist approach could transform feminist women's history through focusing on gender (defined in a different way from that which we have considered previously) rather than on women, and through deconstructing the term "women" and concentrating on the differences between women rather than what they have in common. Joan Scott's *Gender and the politics of history* emphasized the importance of studying the differing social meanings of gender through an analysis of language and discourse (ways of thinking and talking about the world) rather than the material reality that happens to people. The story, she asserted, is no longer "about the things that have happened to women and men and how they have related to them; instead it is about how the subjective and collective meanings of women and men as categories of identity have been constructed".[70] For Scott, then, gender in this poststructuralist sense refers to abstract representations of the differences between men and women created by society, representations we can find through studying texts. Later, Scott further elaborated on the term "experience", pointing out that although historians can never recapture it in the sense of lived reality, it is a word we cannot do without; however, the closest she came to defining "experience" was to say that it is a "linguistic event" that "doesn't happen outside established meanings"[71] – in other words, there is no experience outside the ways that language constructs it. Denise Riley, who worked with Scott as a postdoctoral research student, objected to what she saw as an unchanging essentialism in the category "women" across different historical epochs, as if it had a common meaning throughout history. She argued, instead, that we see "women" as a "volatile collectivity in which female persons can be very differently positioned, so that the apparent continuity of the subject of 'women' isn't to be relied on".[72]

Although I do not have the space to examine all the implications for feminist women's history of the poststructuralist arguments advanced by Scott and Riley, some general points may be made. First, Scott's emphasis on the study of gender in history, an emphasis that marked a shift from women's history to gender history that had been under way for some time in the USA,[73] decentres the study of women *as* women. In particular, to move from studying the causes of the social construction of gender in history to the meanings of gender, particularly its use in language and discourses as a metaphor for many human relations and activities is to run the risk, as Bennett points out, of intellectualizing and abstracting the inequalities between the sexes.[74] The material forces that shaped women's lives as wives, mothers, sisters, mistresses, lovers, employees, political activists and friends, receive little attention. "Flesh-and-blood women", as Joan Hoff comments, become "social constructs", with no physiological context except as a set of "symbolic meanings constructing sexual difference".[75] This "deconstructionist death of the subject", as it is commonly called, can also lead to a situation where women are no longer seen as agents in history, challenging and resisting some of the inequalities they have experienced and "making" history, even if it is not under conditions of their own choosing. Secondly, the emphasis on gender and history rather than women and history deradicalises what is taught, since we then adopt, I believe, "a more neutral stance where equal consideration is given to men and women and to issues around masculinity and femininity".[76] Generally, as Mary Evans has perceptively observed, "gender" is less threatening to the male establishment in higher education in Britain, since it encompasses the study of both men and women and seems to add "an aura of 'complexity' to what might otherwise be seen as a narrow or restricted field".[77] Thirdly, by emphasizing the importance of studying men and masculinity, as well as women and femininity, we leave less space for the study of women; we also run the risk of "women" being subsumed, yet again, within a dominant male frame of reference. Fourthly, gender history, under the impact of poststructuralism, encourages the growth of a new men's studies which, as Lois Banner has noted, focuses on male sensitivity and male persecution, and plays down male privilege and male power, seeing many "masculinities" and denying implicitly the existence of patriarchy.[78] Fifthly, the emphasis in Scott on how knowledge is produced plays down key concerns of feminist historians, namely to explain what the world was like for women and why is was that way. Sixthly, the deconstruction of the term "women" as a socially constructed category, advocated so readily by Riley, and the emphasis on the differences between women at the expense of what they have in common, denies the existence of women as a political category and as a subordinate class; it also denies women a position from which they can speak, based on their embodied experience of womanhood.[79] Lastly, the emphasis given to poststructural terminology and analysis by historians of women, especially in the USA, "distances" them from scholars in Western Europe who are ignoring poststructuralism or subjecting it to rigorous questioning – and from women in Eastern Europe and Third World countries who are just beginning to research their past, and who see much of this "trendy" theory as "irrelevant or even counterproductive".[80] Indeed, Hoff concludes generally that gender (in the poststructuralist sense) has now become a "postmodern category of paralysis" rather than, as Scott asserted, a "useful category of historical anlsysis".[81]

I am not denying, of course, that some gender history has made important contributions to our understanding of women in history. This is especially so in Britain, where the North American distinction between gender history and women's history is less well marked and where the term "gender" has been used more in the traditional social science sense.[82] But the gender historians making such a contribution tend to be grounded in feminist politics rather than abstract poststructural theorizing. As Catherine Hall, an eminent British gender historian, has commented, feminists do not need poststructuralism to develop gender as a category of analysis – it emerged out of years of work in consciousness-raising groups and out of years of studying malestream histories.[83] Neither can one deny, I would claim, the importance of studying different meanings of the term "women" in different historical epochs. However, poststructuralist feminists tend to ignore the fact that differences between women, especially of social class and marital status, have been researched by feminist historians for some years (as is evident in most of the chapters in this volume). To study women *as* women is not to claim, as poststructuralists assume, that all women's shared experiences have been experienced equally; as Liz Stanley, among others, has pointed out, the category "women" has a number of multiple fractures based on differentia-tion by "race", ethnicity, social class, marital status, sexual orientation, culture, religion, ablebodiedness and age.[84] What is important is for feminist women's historians to research and explore women's differences while also acknowledging and recognizing the common ground of these female genders against male genders.

Conclusion

This chapter has attempted to explore, albeit in a selective way, some of the main concerns, debates and controversies within the field of women's history in Britain, from the nineteenth century to the end of the twentieth. The growth of the field, especially since the early 1970s, has, however, been marked by "uneven developments".[85] Most of the research has focused on England, although new studies about Welsh and Scottish women have been published recently.[86] More attention has been given to the nineteenth and twentieth centuries than to earlier times.[87] And lesbian history and the history of black women are still in their infancy.[88] The problems of writing a "national" women's history that would also take into account the ways in which these social and cultural factors interact in complex ways is further complicated by Britain's entry into the European Union and the desire to place "British" women within a broader, European context.[89] The multiplicity of international perspectives on women's history illustrates also that the recovery of women's past worldwide does not fit neatly any one theoretical framework or approach[90]. Bolanle Awe, for example, warns that existing theories and methodologies that emanate from Western experience are "extremely limited" in accounting for the historical and cultural peculiarities of Nigerian societies.[91]

Awareness of these issues, while posing many difficulties for the individual researcher, has also created vigorous debate among those working within the field. While it is true that feminist women's history in Britain remains on the margins academically, it is a margin that is growing and evolving rather than shrinking and unchanging. Indeed, Carolyn Steedman asserts boldly that the influence of feminism in putting "women" and "gender" in the historical frame has been such that more women's and gender history is now taught outside conventional history courses – on interdisciplinary degrees, in cultural studies, in English and Sociology departments, in adult education, open studies and women's studies – than within them.[92] In such a time of expansion, it is critical that we keep "women" centre stage in the content of our courses. Unless we do so we run the risk of our past being pushed back into obscurity, yet again, and of being marginalized and distorted through a male lens.

Notes

1. Parts of this chapter are based on my article "Women's history in Britain: an overview", *European Journal of Women's History*, pp. 7-19, 1985.
2. V. Woolf, "Women and fiction", in V. Woolf, *Collected essays*, vol. 2 (London: Hogarth Press, 1966), p. 141. This essay was first published in *The Forum* (March 1929).
3. Much more research needs to be conducted into writings on women's history before the nineteenth century. For some interesting observations on this, see G. Pomata, "History, particular and universal: on reading some recent women's history textbooks", *Feminist Studies* 19 (1), pp. 7-50, Spring 1993.
4. N. Zemon Davis, "Women's history in transition: the European case", *Feminist Studies* p. 83, (1975-76).
5. Ibid, pp. 83-4. See also Zemon Davis, "Gender and genre: women as historical writers, 1400-1820", in *Beyond their sex: learned women of the European past*, P. H. Labalme ed. (New York and London: New York University Press).
6. Clara Lucas Balfour, *Working women of the last half century* (London: W. & F. G. Cash, 1854) and *Women worth emulating* (London, Sunday School Union, n.d. 1877?). J. Purvis, *Hard lessons: the lives and education of working-class women in nineteenth-century England* (Cambridge: Polity), p. 153 notes that Mrs Balfour was the key lecturer on topics about women within the mechanics' institute movement, the major adult education movement of nineteenth-century Britain.

7. Balfour, *Women worth emulating*, p. v.
8. *Ibid.*, pp. v–vi.
9. *Ibid.*, p. 93.
10. *Ibid.*, p. 100.
11. W. H. Davenport Adams, *Stories of the lives of noble women* (London: Nelson and Sons, 1882); *Celebrated women travellers of the nineteenth century* (London: Swan Sonnenschein & Co, 1882) and *Some historic women or, biographical studies of women who have made history* (London: John Hogg, n.d.).
12. *Ibid.*, p. v.
13. See, for example, E. F. Pollard, *Florence Nightingale, the wounded soldier's friend* (London: S. W. Partridge & Co., n.d.), S. A. Tooley, *The life of Florence Nightingale* (London: Cassell and Company n.d.) and A. Matheson, *Florence Nightingale, a biography* (London: Thomas Nelson and Sons, n.d.).
14. M. Vicinus, *Independent women, work and community for single women 1850–1920* (London: Virago Press), p. 21.
15. A. and E. Strickland, *Lives of the Queens of England from the Norman Conquest* (London: Bohn's Library, 6 vols, 1864–5).
16. J. Thirsk, "Foreword", in *Women in English society 1500–1800*, ed. M. Prior (London: Methuen) p. 3. Thirsk notes (p. 2) that the cheap edition sold over 11,000 copies.
17. Quoted in *ibid.*, p. 3.
18. J. Purvis, *A history of women's education in England* (Milton Keynes: Open University Press, 1991), p. 116.
19. J. Rose, *Marie Stopes and the sexual revolution* (London: Faber & Faber, 1992), p. 10; R. Hall, *Marie Stopes, a biography* (London: Andre Deutsch, 1977) pp. 15–16. Since Charlotte attended university before 1892, she could only be awarded a university certificate – the only qualification, according to Hall, open to women who, although taking the same examination papers as men, were not allowed to attend lectures or to be awarded a degree. This experience, claims Hall, contributed to her passionate advocacy of women's suffrage long before the movement became fashionable in the early twentieth century.
20. C. Carmichael Stopes, *British Freewomen, their historical privilege* (London: Swan Sonneschein, 1894).
21. G. Hill, *Women in English life from medieval to modern times*, vol. 1 (London: 1896), p. xiii.
22. Thirsk, "Foreword", p. 5.
23. *Ibid.*, p. 6
24. B. L. Hutchins, *Women in modern industry* (London: G. Bell and Sons Ltd, 1915).
25. M. Chaytor and J. Lewis, "Introduction", in *Working life of women in the seventeenth century*, 2nd edn, Alice Clark (London: Routledge, 1982) p. x; A. L. Erickson, "Introduction", *Working life*, 3rd edn, (London: Routledge, 1992), pp. xi–xii.
26. A. Clark, *Working life of women in the seventeenth century* (London: Routledge & Sons Ltd, 1919). The importance of Clark's book is reflected in the fact that it has been reprinted twice since it was first published and remains, according to Erickson, "Introduction", p. vii, the "leading exposition" of the pessimistic view that industrialization was a "bad thing" for women.
27. I. Pinchbeck, *Women workers and the Industrial Revolution 1750–1850* (London: Routledge & Sons Ltd, 1930) pp. 312–13. This work was reprinted in 1969 and a 3rd edn, with a new "Introduction" by Kerry Hamilton, published by Virago Press, 1981. J. Rendall, *Women in an industrialising society: England 1750–1880* (Oxford: Basil

Blackwell, 1990), p. 7, makes the point that although first written in 1930, Pinchbeck's book remains "the major survey of the impact of industrialisation on women workers in Britain".

28. Erickson, "Introduction", pp. xii–xiii.
29. C. Crosby, *The ends of history, Victorians and "the woman question"* (London: Routledge, 1991), pp. 1–2.
30. G. Dangerfield, *The strange death of liberal England* (London: Paladin, 1970; first published 1935) p. 145.
31. *Ibid.*, p. 145.
32. J. Marcus (ed) *Suffrage and the Pankhursts* (London: Routledge, 1987), p. 3.
33. H. Perkin, *The origins of modern English society 1780-1880* (London: Routledge, 1969), pp. 149–60.
34. *Ibid.*, p. 160.
35. J. Mitchell, "Women: the longest revolution", *New Left Review* **40**, pp. 17–18, 1966.
36. S. Rowbotham, *Hidden from history: 300 years of women's oppression and the fight against it* (London: Pluto Press, 1973).
37. J. Norris, "Women's history", *North-West Labour History Society Bulletin* **7** (1980-1), Special Issue *Women and the labour movement*, p. 10.
38. *Ibid.*, p. 7.
39. The Elton quote is made in D. Cannadine, "British history; past, present – and future?", *Past and Present* **116**, p. 188, 1987. The Hyman quotes come from H. Hyman, *Empire and sexuality: the British experience* (Manchester: Manchester University Press, 1990), p. 16; and from quotations highlighted in the review of his book, together with that of L. White, *The comforts of home: prostitution in colonial Nairobi* (Chicago: University of Chicago Press, 1990) and M. Strobel, "Sex and work in the British Empire", *Radical History Review* **54**, p. 178, 1992.
40. Many definitions of feminism have been offered, but at a most general level it may be defined as a political movement that seeks to eradicate the injustices that women experience because of their sex. Within this broad definition, one may identify various feminisms, each offering differing emphases for the causes of female oppression. Consciousness raising among women about injustices to their sex is a key method of feminism, and a feminist is a women who has experienced this. Indeed, since women's "experiences" are regarded as the cornerstone of feminist theory and politics, only women can be feminists. Not everyone, of course, will agree with this view – see, for example, B. Harrison, *Prudent revolutionaries, portraits of British feminists between the wars* (Oxford: Oxford University Press, 1987), where he includes two "male feminists", Henry Harben and Frederick Pethick-Lawrence, in his group biography. For a general overview of some of these issues, see A. Jardine & P. Smith (eds), *Men in feminism* (London: Methuen, 1987).
41. J. Bennett, "Feminism and history", *Gender & History* **1** (3), p. 253, Autumn 1989.
42. D. Mitchell, *Queen Christabel, a biography of Christabel Pankhurst* (London: MacDonald and Jane's, 1977), p. 319.
43. E. Roberts, *A women's place, an oral history of working-class women 1890-1940* (Oxford: Basil Blackwell, 1984), pp. 1–2.
44. *Ibid.*, pp. 2–3.
45. *Ibid.*, p. 1.
46. For a definition of feminism, see Note 40 above.
47. S. Alexander & A. Davin, "Feminist history", *History Workshop Journal* (HWJ), p. 4, Spring 1976.
48. *Ibid.*, p. 5.

49. E. P. Thompson is best known for his epoch-making tome, *The making of the English working-class* (London: Victor Gollancz, 1963).

50. S. Rowbotham, "The trouble with 'patriarchy'", reprinted in *People's history and socialist theory*, R. Samuel (ed.) (London: Routledge, 1981); first published in *New Statesman* (December 1981), pp. 364-6.

51. S. Alexander & B. Taylor, "In defence of 'patriarchy'", in *People's history and the socialist theory*, R. Samuel (ed.) (London: Routledge, 1981).

52. B. Taylor, *Eve and the new Jerusalem, Socialism and feminism in the nineteenth century* (London: Virago Press, 1983) p. 99.

53. A. Davin, "Imperialism and motherhood", HWJ **5**, pp. 9-65, Spring 1978; J. Bennett, "Misogyny, popular culture, and women's work", HWJ **31**, pp. 166-88, Spring 1991; B. Taylor, "Mary Wollstonecraft and the wild wish of early feminism", HWJ **35**, pp. 22-44, Spring 1993; and D. A. Cohen, "Private lives in public spaces: Marie Stopes, the Mothers' Clinics and the practice of contraception", HWJ **35**, pp. 95-116, Spring 1993.

54. Editorial; "Why gender and history?", *Gender and History* **1** (1), p. 1, Spring 1989.

55. See, for example, the absence in C. Hall, "Feminism and feminist history", in *White, male and middle class, explorations in feminism and history*, C. Hall (Cambridge: Polity, 1992) of any discussion of feminist groupings other than socialist feminists.

56. See, for example, O. Banks, *Faces of feminism, a study of feminism as a social movement* (Oxford: Martin Robertson, 1981); D. Gorham, *The Victorian girl and the feminine ideal* (London: Croom Helm, 1982); M. Forster, *Significant sisters, active feminism 1839-1939* (London: Secker and Warburg, 1984), and B. Caine, *Destined to be wives, the sisters of Beatrice Webb* (Oxford: Oxford University Press, 1986).

57. J. de Groot & M. Maynard, "Doing things differently? A context for women's studies in the next decade" in *Women's studies in the 1990s, doing things differently?* J. de Groot and M. Maynard (eds) (London: Macmillan, 1993), p. 2.

58. D. Spender, *Women of ideas and what men have done to them* (London: Routledge, 1982), p. 23.

59. S. Jeffreys, *The spinster and her enemies, feminism and sexuality 1880-1930* (London: Pandora Press, 1985), p. 3.

60. J. Rendall, "'Uneven developments: women's history, feminist history and gender history in Great Britain", in *Writing women's history, international perspectives*, K. Offen, R. Roach Pierson and J. Rendall (eds) (London: Macmillan, 1991), p. 48.

61. J. Purvis, Editorial, *Women's History Review* **1** (1) p. 7, (1992).

62. R. Auchmuty, S. Jeffreys, E. Miller, "Lesbian history and gay studies: keeping a feminist perspective", *Women's History Review* **1** (1), pp. 89-108; L. Stanley, "Romantic friendship? Some issues in researching lesbian history and biography", *Women's History Review* **1** (2), pp. 193-216; E. Donaghue, "Imagined more than women: lesbians as hermaphrodites, 1671-1766", *Women's History Review* **2** (2), pp. 199-216; and E. J. Yeo, "Social motherhood and the sexual communion of labour in British social science, 1850-1950", *Women's History Review* **1** (1), pp. 63-87, 1992.

63. B. Hill, "Women's history: a study in change, continuity or standing still?", *Women's History Review* **2** (1), p. 19, 1993.

64. J. M. Bennett, "Women's history: a study in continuity and change", *Women's History Review* **2** (2) p. 177, 1993, (author's emphasis).

65. H. Hinds, A. Phoenix, J. Stacey, "Introduction", in *Working out, new directions for women's studies* H. Hinds, A. Phoenix and J. Stacey (eds) (London: Taylor and Francis, 1992), pp. 6-9.

66. Hall, "Feminism and feminist history", p. 34, suggests that in the 1980s, it was in the polytechnic rather than the university sector in higher education in Britain that some feminist historians managed to gain a foothold. In 1991, the polytechnics became universities, thus ending what was called the "binary system" in higher education.

67. J. Aaron & S. Walby, "Introduction: towards a feminist intellectual space", in *Out of the margins, women's studies in the nineties*, J. Aaron and S. Walby (eds) (London: Taylor and Francis), p. 1.

68. Bennett, "Feminism and history", p. 254.

69. The details of the differences between postmodernism and poststructuralism are not important here, since both have now come together in social science theory to question and deconstruct (take apart) grand narratives that explain the social world. Their combined impact has been to shift the emphasis from accounts/stories about what is true to stories about how we produce "truths". A useful beginner's starting point in understanding the complexity of postmodernism/poststructuralism is to be found in S. Jackson, "The amazing deconstructing woman", *Trouble and Strife* 25, pp. 26-7, Winter 1992/3 where she suggests that the basic tenets include the following: 1. Language does not simply transmit thoughts or meaning - the latter are constructed through language, and there can be no meaning outside of language. Furthermore, meaning is relational, since any word, such as "woman", means something only in relation to other words, such as "man". Meaning, therefore, is never fixed or stable. 2. There is no essential, biologically given, fixed "self". Rather, subjectivity is produced through language and culture and is fragmented and always being constructed and negotiated. "Ain't I a fluctuating identity?" may sum this up. Women's experiences, therefore, regarded as the cornerstone of feminist politics and theory, cannot be taken as unproblematic, because there is no experience outside language and culture. 3. There is no possibility of objective scientific "truth" in history or any other discipline. Knowledges are "discursive constructs". Thus "discourses" (that is, ways of thinking and talking about the world) produce objects of knowledge. Both knowledge and discourses can be deconstructed to reveal that they are not objective truths but discourses produced by people who hold particular positions. See also C. Ramazanoglu (ed), *Up against Foucault, explorations of some tensions between Foucault and feminism* (London: Routledge, 1993); and J. Appleby, L. Hunt, M. Jacob, *Telling the truth about history* (New York and London, W. W. Norton & Co., 1994). Throughout the rest of this chapter I shall use the term "poststructuralism", since it is this variety of postmodernist thought with which I am most concerned.

70. J. Wallach Scott, *Gender and the politics of history* (New York: Columbia University Press, 1988), p. 6.

71. J. Scott, "The evidence of experience", *Critical Inquiry* 17, p. 793, Summer 1991.

72. D. Riley, *"Am I that name?" Feminism and the category of "women" in history* (London: Macmillan, 1988), p. 2.

73. K. Canning, "Feminist history after the linguistic turn: historicising discourse and experience", *Signs* 19, p. 372, Winter 1994.

74. Bennett, "Feminism and history", p. 258.

75. J. Hoff, "Gender as a postmodern category of paralysis", *Women's History Review* 3 (2), p. 159, 1994.

76. Purvis, "Editorial", p. 6.

77. M. Evans, "The problem of gender for women's studies", in Aaron and Walby (eds) *Out of the margins, women's studies in the nineties* (London: Taylor and Francis), p. 73.

78. L. W. Banner, "A reply to 'Culture et Pouvoir' from the perspective of United States women's history", *Journal of Women's History* **1** (1), p. 104, Spring 1989.
79. Jackson, "The amazing deconstructing woman", p. 31.
80. J. Hoff, "The pernicious effects of poststructuralism on women's history", *The Chronicle of Higher Education* (20 October 1993).
81. J. Hoff, "Gender as a postmodern category of paralysis", *Women's Studies International Forum* **17** (4), pp. 443-7, 1994; J Hoff, "Gender as a postmodern category of paralysis", *Women's History Review* **3** (2), pp. 149-68, 1994; and J. Wallach Scott, *Gender and the politics of history*, Ch. 2: "Gender as a useful category of historical analysis", pp. 28-50, orig. pub. in *American Historical Review* **19** (5), December 1986. For debate about the impact of poststructuralism on British History see especially the relevant articles in issues of 1991-3 of *Social History* and *Past and Present*.
82. Key texts in British gender history include L. Davidoff & C. Hall, *Family fortunes, men and women of the English middle class 1780-1850* (London: Hutchinson, 1987); and S. O. Rose, *Limited livelihoods, gender and class in nineteenth-century England* (London: Routledge, 1992). E. Gordon, *Women and the labour movement in Scotland 1850-1914* (Oxford: Oxford University Press, 1991) is a good example of the "integration" of women's history and gender history approach, especially common among socialist feminist historians in Britain.
83. C. Hall, "Politics, post-structuralism and feminist history", which reviews D. Riley, "*Am I that name?*"; and J. Wallach Scott, *Gender and the politics of history*, *Gender and History* **3** (2), p. 209, 1991.
84. L. Stanley, "British feminist histories, an editorial introduction", *Women's Studies International Forum*, "British Feminist Histories" L. Stanley (ed.) **13** (1/2), p. 4, Special Issue, 1990.
85. Rendall, "Uneven developments: women's history, feminist history and gender history in Great Britain".
86. See, for example, in regard to Scotland – E. Gordon & E. Breitenbach (eds), *The world is ill divided, women's work in Scotland in the nineteenth and twentieth centuries* (Edinburgh: Edinburgh University Press, 1990); E. Gordon, *Women and the Labour Movement in Scotland 1850-1914*; L. Leneman, *A guid cause, the women's suffrage movement in Scotland* (Aberdeen: Aberdeen University Press, 1991); E. Breitenbach & E. Gordon (eds), *Out of bounds, women in Scottish society 1800-1945* (Edinburgh: Edinburgh University Press, 1992); and E. King, *The hidden history of Glasgow's women, the Thenew factor* (Edinburgh: Mainstream Publishing Co., 1993). With regard to Wales, see A. John (ed.), *Our mother's land, chapters in Welsh women's history 1830-1939* (Cardiff: University of Wales Press, 1991); L. Verrill-Rhys & D. Beddoe (eds), *Parachutes and petticoats, Welsh women writing on the Second World War* (Dinas Powys: Honno, 1992); J. Aaron, T. Rees, S. Betts, and M. Bincentelli (eds), *Our sisters' land, the changing identities of women in Wales* (Cardiff: University of Wales Press, 1994).
87. More, however, has been published in recent years on the medieval and early modern periods – see, for example, L. Roper, *Oedipus and the devil, witchcraft, sexuality and religion in early modern Europe* (London: Routledge, 1994).
88. For lesbian history, see especially S. Jeffreys, *The spinster and her enemies, feminism and sexuality 1880-1930* (London: Pandora Press, 1985); London Lesbian Feminist Group, *Not a passing phase, reclaiming lesbians in history 1840-1985* (London: The Women's Press, 1989); and M. B. Duberman, M. Vicinus, G. Chauncey (eds), *Hidden from history, reclaiming the gay and lesbian past* (Harmondsworth: Penguin, 1991)

(first published in the USA in 1989). The history of black women in Britain has been particularly ignored, but see B. Bryan, S. Dadzie, S. Scafe, *The heart of the race, black women's lives in Britain* (London: Virago, 1985); Z. Alexander, "Let it lie on the table: the status of black women's biography in the UK", *Gender and History* 2 (1), pp. 22-39, Spring 1990; and the relevant sections in Clare Midgley's chapter in this volume (ch. 10).

89. For discussion of the term "British" women, see especially Clare Midgley in Chapter 10 of this volume. A "classic" reader on European women is R. Bridenthal, C. Koonz and S. Stuard (eds), *Becoming visible, women in European history*, 2nd edn (Boston, Mass.: Houghton Mifflin, 1987), 1st edn published (without S. Stuard as editor) in 1977.

90. See especially, S. Jay Kleinberg, *Retrieving women's history, changing perceptions of the role of women in politics and society* (Oxford: Berg, 1988); and Offen, Pierson and Rendall (eds), *Writing women's history, international perspectives*.

91. B. Awe, "Writing women into history: the Nigerian experience" in *Writing women's history, international perspectives*, Offen, Pierson and Rendall (eds), p. 213.

92. C. Steedman, "Bimbos from hell", *Social History* (January 1994), p. 89.

Suggestions for further reading

Overviews of the nature of women's history in Britain are to be found in J. Lewis, "Women lost and found: the impact of feminism on history", in *Men's studies modified, the impact of feminism on the academic disciplines*, D. Spender (ed.) (Oxford: Pergamon Press, 1981), pp. 55-77; and, more recently, J. Rendall, "Uneven developments: women's history, feminist history and gender history in Great Britain", in *Writing women's history, international perspectives*, K. Offen, R. Roach Pierson and J. Rendall (eds) (London: Macmillan, 1991), pp. 45-57; J. Lewis, "Women's history, gender history and feminist politics", in *The knowledge explosion, generations of feminist scholarship* C. Kramarae and D. Spender (eds) (Hemel Hempstead: Harvester Wheatsheaf, 1993), pp. 154-60; and J. Hannam, "Women, history and protest", in *Introducing women's studies*, D. Richardson & V. Robinson (eds) (London Macmillan, 1993), pp. 303-23. Other useful introductions to some of the debates about women's history/feminist history in Britain and elsewhere include "What is women's history?", *History Today* (June 1985), pp. 38-48; J. Wallach Scott, "Women's history and the rewriting of history", in *The impact of feminist research in the academy*, C. Farnham (ed.) (Indiana: Indiana University Press, 1987), pp. 34-50; K. Offen, R. Roach Pierson, J. Rendall (eds), *Writing women's history, international perspectives* (London: Macmillan, 1992); C. Hall, "Feminism and feminist history", Ch. 1 in her *White, male and middle class, explorations in feminism and history*, pp. 1-40 (Cambridge: Polity Press, 1992): D. Thom, "A lop-sided view: feminist history or the history of women?" in *Critical feminism: argument in the disciplines*, K. Campbell (ed.) (Milton Keynes: Open University Press, 1992), pp. 25-51; G. Bock, "Women's history and gender history: aspects of an international debate", *Gender and History* 1 (1) pp. 7–30, (1989); and J. Bennett, "Feminism and history", *Gender and History* 1 (3) pp. 251–72, (1989).

Discussions about the influence of postmodernism/poststructuralism on women's history are to be found in P. Burke (ed.) *New perspectives on historical writing*, (Cambridge: Polity, 1991), pp. 42–66; the review article by C. Hall, "Politics, post-structuralism and feminist history", *Gender and History* 3 (2), pp. 204–10, 1991 and J. Hoff, "Gender as a postmodern category of paralysis", *Women's History Review* 3 (2), pp. 439–62 1994; L. Newman, "Critical theory and the history of women: what's at stake in deconstructing women's history"; L. Vogel, "Telling tales: historians of our own lives", both in *Journal of Women's History* 2 (3), pp. 58–68 and pp. 89–101, Winter 1991 respectively; and the essays by S. Rose, K. Canning, A. Clark, M. Valverde in the section, "Dialogue: women's history/gender history: is feminist history losing its critical edge?", *Journal of Women's History* 5 (1), pp. 89–125, Spring 1993. The introduction by E. C. DuBois & V. L. Ruiz to their edited *Unequal sisters, a multi-cultural reader in US women's history* (London: Routledge, 1990) gives an introductory overview to the debate about "differences" between women in American women's history and the contents of the volume generally display the multicultural nature of that diversity. A revised and expanded second edition was published in 1994.

Perusal of the three specialized journals in the field - *Journal of Women's History* (US based, editors Christie Farnham & Joan Hoff, published by Indiana University Press, Bloomington, Indiana 47405, USA); *Gender and History* (editors Keith McClellant, UK, and Nancy Grey Osterud, USA, published by Basil Blackwell, 108 Cowley Road, Oxford OX4 1JF, UK); and *Women's History Review* (editors June Purvis, UK, and Phillipa Levine, USA, published by Triangle Journals, PO Box 65, Wallingford, Oxfordshire OX10 0YG, UK) - will give a "feel" for the current state of research, although most of the articles about women in Britain are to be found in *Women's History Review* and *History Workshop Journal*.

The Fawcett Library, Guildhall University, Old Castle Street, London E1 7NT, UK, is the key library for primary sources about British women's history. Demand is often heavy and visitors are advised to first contact the librarian, David Doughan. The local records office may house relevant sources too. For an introductory guide to help in finding and using such sources, see D. Beddoe, *Discovering women's history, a practical manual* (London: Pandora Press, 1983).

Chapter Two

ᴗᶳ

Women and industrialization[1]

Pat Hudson

The degree to which the process of industrialization was shaped by change in women's lives and gender attitudes has recently become a focus of debate.[2] Research on the subject has been slow to develop because of male bias in recording and ensuring the survival of documentary evidence, a relative lack of interest in the economic history of women and a failure to see the necessity of separating female from male experience in economic analysis. More has been written on the ways in which industrialization affected the economic and social status of women, but interpretations have been dominated by generalizations and an increasingly sterile debate between optimistic and pessimistic interpretations.[3] The time is ripe for a reassessment of both aspects of this subject, and of their interconnectedness, in the light of recent research. This chapter considers established views, highlights the innovativeness and importance of new research, and then covers a range of aspects of industrialization where our understanding of female experiences, and thus of the process of economic development itself, is currently improving and changing.

Old and new research

Most established accounts stress that industrialization in one way or another destroyed a family economy where work was centred on the home, carried out within domestic patriarchal social relations, and where men and women made a different yet equally indispensable contribution to household income and subsistence.[4] Some argue that this had a beneficial effect upon the economic and social status of women in the longer term, emphasizing the impact of female wage earning outside the home in changing established power relationships between husbands and wives, fathers and daughters. As women went out to work in greater numbers, daughters freed themselves from family constraints, marriage became a partnership, domestic work and childcare were shared increasingly, and affective individualism replaced broader family decisions about love and marriage.[5] It is also argued that female wage earning increased the power and influence of women in spending decisions and in underpinning the rise of a consumer society from the late eighteenth century.[6]

The pessimistic interpretation, by contrast, dwells on the creation of a reserve army of unemployed women following the destruction of household units of production, and stresses the rise of the male breadwinner wage norm, the growth of domestic ideology and the emergence of the housewife. By separating the public world of work from the private world of the household it is argued that industrialization curtailed the role of women in economic production, and the status of their economic contribution declined. The sexes were consigned to separate spheres, and the influence and power women once had by virtue of their productive role was reduced. Even though, in reality, most women continued to work both inside and outside the home, their role in the family economy was regarded increasingly as dispensable and supplementary; sex differentials in wages, even for similar work, both reflected and endorsed this.[7] Women's employment in factories has also been seen as replicating patriarchal relations in the home, increasing the opportunities for sexual abuse and harassment of female workers by men in positions of authority, and strengthening a sexual division of labour in which women's work was redefined continuously as inferior.[8]

Much socio-political history takes a pessimistic view of the relationship between industrialization and female oppression. The dominant assumption has therefore been that the reduced status of women in production contributed to an erosion of their influence and their role in political activity. This has become a part of the explanation for a perceived quiescence in mid-nineteenth-century political radicalism. A shift in the locus of protest from the community to the workplace, and from broader political issues to focus upon conditions of work and wages, is seen as having isolated women from politics.[9] But it is also argued that the withdrawal of middle-class women from business into lives of domesticity created the free time, the sociability and the resentments that gave rise to early feminism and the suffrage movement while philanthropic endeavour added to the confidence and public experience of middle-class women generally.[10]

The decline of the family economy as a unit of production, and the rise of individual wage earning, dominates both pessimistic and optimist perspectives and has been enshrined in some classic schematic accounts of the impact of industrialization.[11] This decline can be made to fit both pessimistic and optimistic interpretations because of the unreliability of statistical indicators of patterns of female employment and unemployment, both in pre-industrial times and in the nineteenth and twentieth centuries. The nineteenth-century census is particularly misleading in its coverage of women's occupations.[12] Most later records of formally declared employment are similarly wildly inaccurate, as much women's work was casual, informal and unregistered.[13] It is also important to note that both pessimistic and optimist interpretations of the decline of the family economy assume that the social prestige and political power of women can be related directly to changes in their labour market participation and waged work. In reality, many forces combined to structure and restructure the nature of patriarchy and female subordination over time.[14]

The decline of the family economy also underpins what little has been written, until very recently, about the role of women in shaping the industrialization process. Historians have acknowledged the extent to which the commercial employment of women in domestic proto-industries was vital in creating a range of cheap and successful consumer goods industries in the pre-factory period. It has also been suggested that women's networks of trade, mutuality, subsistence and credit were vital in underpinning proto-industrial putting-out networks and artisan businesses.[15] Although the important role of women in some centralized and factory sectors, particularly textiles, has always been acknowledged, this has been seen to have declined generally in the nineteenth century with the rise of new male dominated technologies, male trade unions and the ideology of the male breadwinner.[16] Some authors have stressed the importance for capitalist development of the creation of pools of unemployed and underemployed female labour: labour which can be employed in cyclical upswings, but which is easily and cheaply reabsorbed into the household and casual employment in recessions. Other research has demonstrated the continued importance and durability of domestic and workshop sweated trades alongside the factory: casual, low waged, largely employing women, and evading state regulation of wages and conditions of employment.[17] But because the sectors which have been seen as being at the forefront of British supremacy from the late nineteenth century – coal mining, iron and steel, shipbuilding, international trade and finance – employed relatively few women (with the exception of textiles), the role of women in the dynamics of economic change has been minimized and neglected. This neglect has been further promoted by an unwillingness to research the economics of the informal and casual sector, and of subsistence and household activities which absorbed most female labour.

Since the mid-1980s research on women and industrialization in Britain has accelerated and changed substantially in nature.[18] Earlier accounts were based on attempts to write a parallel history of women to match the mainstream narrative of male experience. These accounts were also influenced by the desire to seek the origins of contemporary gender attitudes and relationships, including the roots of female oppression in modern society and the rise of the women's movement. The resulting self-serving narratives provided a generalized linear and often schematic picture of radical change in women's lives, a picture in which regional, sectoral, class, ethnic and life cycle diversities of experience tended to be hidden, and in which the yardstick by which changes were assessed was one provided by mainstream, male orientated historiography. Older accounts were thus concerned exclusively with the formal (and more easily documented) economy of waged work, mostly outside the home, with production in the economy rather than with consumption or reproduction, with work rather than with leisure, and they were also unconcerned with the interface between the latter two. The influence of Marxism and structuralism in the social history produced during the postwar decades privileged change in production, and changes in the (largely male) labour process, in accounting for shifts in the socio-cultural and political climate. The importance of the private sphere of the family and of social life outside work, in neighbourhood and communal associations, in which women were as involved as men, was consistently played down.

This is now being superseded by attempts both to integrate women's experience into mainstream accounts and, more importantly, to question the terms and points of reference of the established male orientated historiography itself. Thus the chronologies and debates of mainstream economic and social history have started to be questioned on a range of issues central to the process of industrialization, from structural shifts in the economy to demographic and technological change, from changes in political and social consciousness to the foundations of imperialism.[19] And a new agenda is emerging which includes important links between industrialization and largely female concerns and activities such as neighbourhood and familial reciprocities, the informal economy, shopping, household budgeting, women's leisure, menarche and menopause, conception and breastfeeding.[20] These links cross the divide between everyday practices and the development of modern industrial society, between family life and the economy and between personal and political activities. They thus enlarge considerably the scope of historical enquiry, and challenge an earlier literature and set of interpretations based on a separation of private and public spheres of life, and on privileging the latter.

The family economy and women's waged work

One sacred cow of traditional historiography that has become a focus of criticism in the new wave of research has been the concept of radical change in the "family economy".[21] Proletarianization and urbanization were well advanced in Britain, and in many areas of western Europe, long before industrialization became widespread. In England by 1750 21 per cent of the population lived in towns (greater than 5,000) and a further third of the population was rural but non-agricultural.[22] The bulk of the population in the seventeenth and eighteenth centuries, even in the countryside, were not involved in family units of production but in families where there was a mix of subsistence and varied income-earning activities.[23] Female chain and nail makers of the Black Country were often the wives and daughters of ironworkers; female silk workers in the Warwickshire coalfield were commonly the wives of miners. In West Yorkshire, the vast majority of female domestic worsted spinners had husbands and fathers who were not involved in textile production. Later, female factory workers often had menfolk who were domestic outworkers, were unemployed or engaged in entirely different sectors of the economy, such as mining.[24] Much work was seasonal, depending on the state of trade, and changed over the family life cycle. Thus the pre-industrial family economy was most often nearer in type to the modern family wage economy model than most accounts of industrialization have suggested. Artisan families in the woollen sector in West Yorkshire provide a more classic example of integrated household production, but these households usually also contained journeymen, young male and female apprentices, and servants living away from their families.[25] In fact, the bulk of young unmarried people before industrialization, in agriculture and in industry, in towns and in the countryside, lived and worked not within their own family economy but in the houses of others as servants.[26] The social relations of employment (and in particular the opportunities for both accumulation and exploitation) experienced by young people living at home compared with those employed as residential servants has been hidden under the general label of the family or household economy, as have the very varied lives, employment structures and living arrangements of the multitude of widows, spinsters and single parents in early industrializing society. The number of *femmes soles* rose in the nineteenth century with the increasing surplus of women in the population (365,159 by 1851, over a million by 1914). These women sit uneasily alongside neat assumptions about nuclear family units of either production or wage earning.[27]

Several authors have identified a withdrawal of middle-class wives and daughters from active participation in family businesses and this has tended to influence our view of the breakdown of the family economy as a whole with industrialization.[28] But it is difficult to sustain the notion that most middle-class women were directly involved in family businesses in the pre-industrial period, particularly in manufacturing. Neither was there any sudden withdrawal. Historians have identified shifts in all periods from the late seventeenth to the early nineteenth century, but most of the evidence for withdrawal is unreliable as it comes from a literature campaigning against idleness and luxury and, later, extolling the social and moral virtues of the angel in the house. Furthermore, evidence is accumulating of a marked continuity of female involvement as entrepreneurs in manufacturing and commercial ventures well into the nineteenth century and beyond, especially in regions where small family businesses remained dominant.[29]

Our knowledge of the nature of female participation in the early modern period and of the status of female labour before the nineteenth century is perhaps too shaky to make major generalizations about the decline of women's participation in income earning and paid work. It is also the case that most established accounts have failed to acknowledge that economic change in the eighteenth and nineteenth centuries also swelled opportunities, in certain regions and sectors, particularly for women's work. Women were at the forefront of the expansion of commercially orientated manufacturing, certainly up to the 1830s and 1840s during the marked shift that was occurring from subsistence to the commercial production of many consumer goods. Proto-industrial and workshop trades employing women more than men flourished, both before and alongside factories. As well as in textiles, there was increasing involvement of women in most of the West Midlands trades, also in calico printing and the booming sweated trades. Female and child labour accounted for 75 per cent of the early factory workforce in wool textiles, and over half in the cotton sector. Almost half of the handloom weavers in the cotton sector were women by the early nineteenth century.[30]

More important numerically than all these areas of employment, and certainly more widespread geographically, was the huge expansion of women's work as domestic servants. Servants in husbandry may have been declining, but the huge growth of live-in (as well as underrecorded living-out) domestic service in urban households was a marked feature during and beyond the Industrial Revolution period, and it accounted for the bulk of formal female employment. By 1851 there were over 900,000 female domestic servants recorded in the census which compares with only 250,000 women in the cotton sector and half of that number in the wool textile industry.[31]

In addition, population growth, urbanization and male cyclical and technological unemployment combined to create an expansion of many female traditional activities tied to making ends meet: petty trading, neighbourhood services, back street brewing, nursing, laundering, childminding, and sweated homeworking organized on a putting-out basis for the production of things such as envelopes and boxes. Most of these occupations were ignored entirely by the census, and this has been partly responsible for a pervasive view that such sources of income earning were on the decline with industrialization.[32]

The fact is that when we come to consider the impact of industrialization on women's work and on the contribution of women to the family patchwork of survival, the evidence is varied and inconsistent, with enormous variations by region, sector and class.[33] Chronological and cyclical shifts are also apparent in women's labour force participation. In many sectors, expansion in the participation of women in the early nineteenth century was followed by a relative decline associated with the activities of male trade unions, state protective legislation and the strength of ideals about domesticity and fit and proper female work. It has been suggested that early industrialization itself, by expanding the opportunities for women's paid work outside the home, destabilized patriarchal society to a point at which reaction and retrenchment set in, characterized most obviously by the rise of the male breadwinner wage norm, which affected the attitudes, if not the realities, of all social classes.[34] Thus, whether we see industrialization reducing or increasing the sphere and status of women's paid work depends very much on the region and sector concerned, the dates we choose to compare, and whether we take a short-term or longer-term view. Linear generalizations will not do.

Female labour force participation also varied over different phases of industrialization in response to wage levels, gender differentials in wages, and other characteristics of often localized labour markets.[35] It is likely within a family economy that when men's wages were low and/or unemployment rates high, women would enter the labour force even at very low levels of pay. (This happened in the late-eighteenth and early-nineteenth centuries in many regions, in the interwar period in the twentieth century in some industries, and in the 1980s and 1990s.) The sustained growth of the economy in the later nineteenth century and increasing real wages, particularly men's wages, meant that, other things being equal, women (in nuclear families) would tend to withdraw from the labour market. This helps to explain a tendency for the labour force participation of married women to decline from the mid-nineteenth century until the interwar period and after in the twentieth century when changes in the economy both nationally and internationally brought new demands for female labour, new material incentives and (latterly) domestic innovations that might have influenced female labour supply.[36]

Thus new research and approaches have pointed the way forward for future investigation, highlighting the need to look at cyclical changes rather than linear developments, and to consider the range of factors, public and private, economic, ideological and personal, which influenced women's labour force participation in the process of industrialization. At the same time, research has also stressed important continuities. The vast bulk of women's work from the Middle Ages onwards has been casual, intermittent, low status, low paid and usually part of a patchwork of household subsistence and income. Recent studies of female employment in London in the eighteenth and nineteenth centuries show that casual and seasonal work, domestic service, domestic cleaning, laundry, nursing and needlework were the most common throughout.[37] It was probably much the same until at least 1914. These sorts of continuity make it difficult to link the changing economic and social status of women in modern society primarily to industrialization, certainly in terms of the influence of economic change on waged work.[38] The optimistic picture that relates (what must have been) increasing work loads for women to an elevation in their power and prestige is particularly suspect, as is the assumption that women's work and wages were perceived by them as a route to independence rather than as a necessary prop to family resources and an added burden.[39] Instead, new research points to a need to study the changing internal relations of household and family, and the interplay between familial, commercial/institutional and state sources of patriarchal authority. Clearly, these all changed with industrialization, but not at the same time nor in the same direction.

Agriculture and structural change

Agricultural change in many areas of the country appears to have had an impact earliest and hardest on the availability of work for women. Changes in farm size, in hiring practices and in cropping regimes, together with population growth and an increased supply of male workers, all contributed to a decline in the demand for female labour, especially of female farm servants. A tightening of restrictions on customary and common rights, and the effect of enclosure on women's agricultural sidelines further aggravated this trend.[40] In other regions, the problem of female unemployment was less acute. In the predominantly pastoral economies of the North and West of Britain women were less affected, although dairying was to become a more commercial and male dominated activity during the nineteenth century. In the North East, buoyant demand for male labour in heavy industries made agriculture more reliant on female work gangs, and near to many towns and cities female employment expanded in market gardening, poultry production, fruit, vegetable and hop cultivation.[41] On balance, female labour tended to be shaken out of farming by economic change, and female rural unemployment was only very partially and patchily absorbed by the expansion of rural domestic industries such as lace making and straw plaiting.[42] Thus a huge reserve of unemployed and underemployed women was created (more so than men). The migration of young women to towns in search of employment appears to have been more prominent than the movement of young men, indicating a gender imbalance in the release of labour from the land.[43] Female migration to towns obviously had an impact on the process of urbanization, urban sex ratios, the marriage market and demography in both towns and the countryside, as well as providing a supply side stimulus to the expansion of urban domestic service, centralized manufacturing and urban sweating. And yet women feature very little in established accounts of the process of proletarianization and structural change.

Estimating the extent of women's presence at the forefront of the great structural shift from rural/agrarian to urban/industrial employment (the hallmark of industrialization) is only just starting. But early signs are that this may well result in a re-evaluation of the mainsprings, nature and timing of that shift and its effect on the industrialization process.[44] There are two types of theory regarding the release of labour from the primary sector during industrialization. Dominant in much current and past literature (which concentrates on men and draws on male occupational ascriptions in parish registers and elsewhere) are supply side theories which imply that surplus labour from the agricultural sector will be absorbed automatically, and that in accordance with neoclassical economic theory, no significant structural unemployment will occur.[45] The second sort of theory revolves around labour demand, and concentrates on those factors that influence the rate of absorption of labour by industry. It is argued that a perfectly elastic labour supply characterises most underdeveloped economies: labour retained on small family farms, labour on the margins of petty retailing, domestic and farm servants, and women in general.[46] Concentrating on women (as much as men) in the process of structural change places renewed emphasis on this demand side theory of economic growth. It takes away some of the traditional stress on a chronologically distinct and labour releasing agricultural revolution (which historians have had difficulty in pinning down), fits with recent and contemporary arguments about agriculture acting as a brake on the economy, rather than as a stimulus, and dilutes some of the established emphasis on the importance and timing of demographic change (resulting in population rise and labour supply increase) as a supply side causal factor in industrialization.[47]

The "industrious revolution", consumption and living standards

Integrating women's history back into the mainstream of historical debate on industrialization also highlights the shortcomings of a hitherto dominant exclusive reliance on supply side analyses of the changing composition and increasing levels of manufactured output in the economy. Early work on proto-industrialization rightly emphasized the importance of the extension of manufacturing in the countryside in replacing the expensive and more regulated (largely male) labour of the towns with cheap, underemployed (often female) labour, possessing subsistence craft skills.[48] But an equally, if not more important, link between changes in women's lives in the proto-industrial period and beyond and the dynamics of economic growth, has recently been suggested. This lies in the demand as well as the supply implications of major shifts in the labour allocation of women between subsistence and commercial employment (the shift from home to commercially produced everyday items such as textiles, crockery, candles, butter and beer).[49] A shift of female labour from the production of subsistence goods to commercial manufacturing for wages altered simultaneously both the supply of marketed goods and labour, and the demand for market bought products. This shift may be the most important key to understanding the widespread expansion of consumer demand from the late-eighteenth century, alongside slow, if any, growth in real wages. Recent research has suggested that female earnings could balance out the vagaries of male incomes and increase the variation in family earnings across occupations, adding to growing inequalities in income distribution among wage earning families.[50] The "industrious revolution" clearly affected the level of demand for market-bought products in a differential manner, varying greatly by region, sector and lifecycle.

Supply and demand curves for labour and for manufactured goods were themselves the products of an evolving structure of economic and social forces, including gender relations within the home and family, which must now become an important focus for research: relations between men and women, husbands and wives, fathers and daughters. If many women subordinated time spent in domestic and reproductive activities increasingly to income-earning work in the eighteenth and nineteenth centuries, what economic and social effects did this have? This question is important because such subordination might have adverse effects on maternal and child health, childbearing and childrearing. Breastfeeding could also be affected, which in turn had an impact on infant health as well as fertility levels and family size. Clearly, research on women's labour allocation, both inside and outside the household, is important to our understanding of many aspects of industrialization: living standards, changes in the distribution of income in society, nutrition, demography, socialization and gender relations.

Demography

Demographic history is particularly important in identifying both the impact of industrialization on women, and women's role in economic change. The age and rate of marriage, family size, age of leaving home, and life expectancy are among the most vital variables in understanding changes in women's economic and personal lives, yet little demographic analysis has emphasized gender-specific connections of this kind. The dominant view of demographic change in England during industrialization is that population growth before the mid-nineteenth century was driven very largely by changes in the age and rate of marriage, and that these variables were in turn dependent on the long-run growth of real incomes. It is argued that higher incomes (as indicated by the movement of male adult real wages!) encouraged earlier and more universal marriage as the eighteenth century progressed.[51] There are several weaknesses in this thesis when one regards it from the perspective of research on the economic history of women. First, long-run correlations between male wages and marriage must be seen as being unreliable as a measure of the links between nuptiality and general income levels. As we have already seen, changes in female employment prospects differed from those of men, as did the movement of female wages, and there was commonly an inverse relationship between male wage levels and female labour supply. Secondly, generalizations about the motivations behind marriage decisions need to be questioned. It is just as likely that higher incomes and greater employment opportunities for women might delay the need to marry, especially as marriage was often regarded by women as an alternative to poverty. The decline of female farm service might have promoted earlier marriage to avoid poverty, but urban domestic service often played the same role as had earlier farm service in promoting the accumulation of pre-nuptial savings and possessions, but also in preventing as well as delaying marriage.[52]

Both illegitimacy and pre-nuptial conception increased markedly in eighteenth- and nineteenth-century Europe. This has been linked to a transformation in the sex lives of young people promoted by the decline of the peasant family, proletarianization, and the rise of independent income earning outside the home.[53] Once the role of women in the growth of new workshop and factory industries, in the rise of domestic service, in casual and informal activities, and in the migration of young people to towns is highlighted, arguments linking sexual behaviour with the greater freedom of young women, as well as men, from the older controls of family and community, appear more convincing. Furthermore some studies have shown rising illegitimacy unlinked to marriage plans. In the metal industries of the Birmingham area in the 1840s, parliamentary enquirers found that women workers achieved early economic independence, and some supported three or four illegitimate children with no contemplation of marriage.[54] In Culcheth, Lancashire, unmarried female handloom weavers commonly had children and remained as wage earners in their parents' households.[55] These developments must be seen in relation to the declining marriage age in the eighteenth century, from around 26 to 23 years on average.[56] This alone reduced the potential for a period of freedom and independent income-earning outside the claims of fathers or husbands. And the fact that illegitimacy rose at the same time as marriage ages fell suggests an explanation in terms of changes in sexual behaviour and attitudes.[57]

A greater understanding of the process and impact of migration and of the redistribution of population between countryside and towns (with their higher death rates) also points towards renewed interest in improvements in life expectancy that have been a hallmark of the industrialization process.[58] The subject of gender-specific mortality has scarcely been addressed by historians of the nineteenth century, although we do know that maternal mortality levels in childbirth were low and relatively stable over several centuries (but increasing somewhat in the nineteenth century with the intervention of male surgeons and the growth of puerperal fever).[59] The decline of infant mortality was a key variable in changes in life expectancy and intimately connected with breastfeeding, weaning, diet and childrearing – all largely dependent on changes in women's lives and attitudes.[60] Variations in women's work and domestic roles as well as localized customs and social class influenced patterns of breastfeeding. In Calverley, West Yorkshire, for example, breastfeeding appears to have declined with the increasing demands for female labour in the household production of textiles. This resulted in more frequent childbearing and larger family size in the late-eighteenth and early-nineteenth centuries and infant mortality remained very high.[61] In the pre-industrial period in localities where wet nursing for middle-class city dwellers was common, fertility remained lower than elsewhere, whereas middle-class wives who put children out to nurse had very high conception rates. The decline of wet nursing in the nineteenth century had obvious economic, demographic and social repercussions.[62] Here again, the personal lives of women were intimately linked, and in a reciprocal manner, with changes in economic life, and we cannot understand the latter without research that focuses on women.

Technological and organizational innovation

The role of women in technological innovation is only just starting to be explored, largely because the history of technology has concentrated on heroic accounts of major inventors and innovators of productive equipment. The importance of small-scale adaptations and tinkering, and of the flexibility of craft and artisan skills alongside major inventions have always been recognized, and recent renewed emphasis on this opens the door to a closer appreciation of the role of women in innovation, particularly as we know that some of the most dynamic sectors of the economy employed women increasingly as the major proportion of the workforce.[63] This was especially the case in consumer goods industries such as textiles, shoes, pottery, paper and ornamental ware. Incremental changes in style, colour and shape were crucial to the success of many industries employing a largely female workforce. These were achieved by on-the-spot changes in design, and by the flexibility of largely female work roles. In many sectors it is important to emphasize also that women were the major force behind those shifts in tastes and fashion that spurred continuous improvements and innovations in product design.[64]

Research has also highlighted the relationship between major waves of innovation in the organization and technology of manufacturing and the tertiary sector, and shifts in favour of the employment of women. This was sometimes associated with harnessing the indigenous skills and manual dexterity of female workers in producing those consumer goods previously made by women in the home for subsistence use. Many new work regimes and work disciplines, as well as new mechanical technologies, were experienced first by female and child workers, and receptivity to innovation was often encouraged by emphasizing the employment it would create for women and children.[65] Sometimes the substitution of female for male labour that often accompanied technological change appears to have been associated with a need to avoid the resistance of established male craft workers, as in power loom weaving and initially in power spinning. In the latter case, the jenny and frame were associated with female labour, but the more efficient long and double-hand mules rapidly became a male preserve. Thus, although women were associated with early technological shifts, the later changes of the nineteenth century were accompanied generally by reworking of the sexual division of labour such that men retained work of superior status, prestige and income earning, in addition to monopolizing many supervisory grades, which placed them in positions of power and authority over women.[66]

A struggle between male craft workers and deskilling machinery has dominated accounts of the speed of innovation. Variations in the collective resistance of different regions and different craft groups have been examined, with little attention being paid to those workers, many of whom were women, who had much to gain from technological change. Thus different regional and sectoral responses to new technology may best be explained not by concentrating on male solidarity or the ingredients of "class conscious" resistance, but by attending to gender relations, family and community, and the nature of alternative work opportunities for both women and men.[67] The relatively rapid pace of technological change in West Yorkshire compared with the West Country has been associated with the amenable and receptive structure of artisan small businesses, but some innovations met with great opposition: much depended on the extent to which specific innovations disrupted established patterns of family and gender-specific labour. Thus innovations in cropping and dressing, and later in powered weaving, met with focused opposition (as they affected hierarchies of male labour and undermined the basis of domestic outwork), while innovations in carding, scribbling and spinning were accepted more readily.[68]

Women, property, customary right and crime

Until recently it was assumed that women's property rights during industrialization were very limited and declined in social and economic importance, but research has undermined this by considering the types of property ownership that commonly involved women in the eighteenth and early nineteenth centuries: women as beneficiaries of wills, trustees, executors and widows. Detailed study of marriage settlements, probates and other sources has shown that there were many legal loopholes in the seventeenth and eighteenth centuries that allowed women considerable power in controlling capital, running businesses and making important decisions about the disposal of assets and the upbringing of children. Although these loopholes may gradually have closed during the eighteenth century, new work has also indicated that women, particularly widows administering trusts of various kinds, figured prominently in small-business management and ownership in Birmingham and Sheffield in the nineteenth century. In this, they were continuing a long tradition of active involvement, which contradicts our understanding (based largely on formal legal stipulations) of the level of female property and capital control, and of a shift in property rights occurring with industrialization.[69]

Much has also been written recently about the decline in customary rights and perquisites that appears to have accompanied industrialization in the eighteenth and nineteenth centuries. Attempts by employers to cut costs and waste by clamping down on previously accepted forms of appropriation, often by criminalizing these activities, have been documented, and a transition from custom to crime has been discussed. In employing a gender perspective, this issue comes into closer interpretive focus, because many forms of customary access to informal income earning were associated with women: from grazing and gathering on common land to gleaning after harvest, and including what came to be regarded increasingly as the embezzlement of raw materials in commercial domestic production.[70] The curtailment of customary rights and perquisites occurred alongside the reduction of women's employment opportunities on the land and the decline of byemployments in some areas of the country.[71] This fuels the negative perspective of the impact of industrialization on women's income earning. There is also an implication here for our understanding of crime: despite the decline of varied customary livelihoods, only a very small proportion of the increasing number prosecuted for property offences in the late-eighteenth and early-nineteenth centuries were women.[72] The idea of a 'custom-to-crime' shift, so central in the male orientated historiography, appears inappropriate for women.

Most explanations of changes in crime during industrialization stress unemployment, urbanization and poverty in addition to the curtailment of customary perquisites, with little analysis of why these factors appear to have had less effect on female than on male crime.[73] Looking at crime from the perspective of women's history points to links between crime and gender-specific changes in employment as well as incomes, the household division of labour, and changes in the law and in ideology concerning female deviance. There was a decline in female crime indictments in the later nineteenth century (excluding indictments for prostitution and drunkenness), which has generally been seen as reflecting a decline in female law breaking.[74] In one of the few studies to address female crime it has been argued that the ideology of femininity in Victorian England gave women an important moralizing role as guardians of respectability and virtue. Thus women's crimes were seen to offend not only the law but also the spiritual ideals of the role of wives and mothers. This double jeopardy may have acted as a deterrent to female law breaking, while the increasingly prevalent notion that women by nature were non-criminal may also have discouraged prosecutions. Concern for the moral deviance of fallen women helps to explain attitudes to, and prosecution of, prostitutes in the later nineteenth century. Together with renewed debate about sexual difference, female susceptibility and feeble mindedness, the treatment of prostitutes also throws light on gender-specific penal attitudes, which placed greater stress on reform for females compared with male criminals.[75]

It has also been argued that the decline of female crime indictments in the nineteenth century was related to industrialization and the shift to domesticity, separate spheres and more private forms of social control.[76] But, as we have already argued, the notion of separate spheres can be a very misleading guide to the realities of family life for most women, and particularly for those social groups most likely to offend. More important in the decline in female offenders may have been a reduction in the opportunities that women had for workplace appropriation compared with their situation in the proto-industrial period. This can, however, be overplayed. The massive growth of female domestic service and sweating does not appear to have ushered in a commensurate increase in female indictments for theft from their employers despite the opportunities these employments may have presented. Perhaps such transgressions were deterred privately by dismissals, or perhaps we need to consider the ways in which women, both in domestic service and in other new occupations as the nineteenth century progressed (governesses, shop and office workers, for example) were able to create new and accepted forms of perquisites.

Gender, class and social identity

Discussion of the nature of womanhood grew more common in the nineteenth century in political, religious and scientific writings as well as in art and literature, suggesting that the construction of gender was related to the quickening pace of economic and social change. Debate about sexuality, morality, prostitution, illegitimacy, the free lifestyles of factory girls and the impropriety of wearing hair ribbons and colourful dresses flourished.[77] Ideas about sexual differences were endorsed and extended by evangelical religion and by bio-medical theories. Evangelicalism stressed the importance of women in transforming national morality partly through the creation of well ordered domestic routines and partly through the philanthropic endeavour of middle-class women among the poor and the fallen. The tension between the moral and spiritual inspiration of women and their social subordination intensified. Scientific and medical theories suggested that women were mentally unstable and prone to insanity, especially at times of menarche and menopause, and that their mental evolution had been arrested to conserve their energies for childbirth and childrearing. It was thus argued that for the health of the race and for the future of the Empire, the range of women's activities outside reproduction should be curtailed severely.[78]

Middle class and professional views were important in the formation of gender ideology in the mass of the population through the influence of media, schools, temperance movements, domestic service and private charity. But the working-classes also had independent notions of proper gender roles and proclivities, derived particularly from Thomas Paine, John Locke and William Cobbett, who all placed women firmly in a position of domestic dependence.[79] Mary Wollstonecraft had raised the issue of sexual difference in the 1790s, but the only working-class movement of the nineteenth century to incorporate the idea that politics should be about gender as much as class was Owenite Socialism. Owenite analysis questioned all social relations including the institutions of marriage and the family, monogamy and heterosexuality.[80] But as radical working-class politics after the decline of Chartism revolved increasingly around issues of work and wages, it turned away from earlier Utopian influences and at the same time became more male orientated. Technological change and new methods and relations of production increased the tensions and antagonism between male and female workers, and in defending their place in the world of work and in labour hierarchies men could be as bad as their masters.[81] Trade unions in the nineteenth century seldom included women. Historians have usually seen this as an indication of the apolitical nature of women – sometimes this in turn is seen as a reflection of their withdrawal from the world of work.[82] But it is necessary to ask what attraction trade unions in the nineteenth century held for female members, given their very different interests in the labour market and in the home.[83] In some areas and industries, and for particular periods, it appears that solidarities of class overrode gender divisions. In the Lancashire weaving sector, for example, and in some coalmining areas, women worked alongside men for state regulation of labour, especially that of women and children in order to minimize exploitation.[84] In most occupations it is, however, likely that gender divisions undermined industrial solidarity and that employers were able to use this to their advantage. In some sectors and regions women formed their own unions and worked for their separate interests. In all sectors it is impossible to understand the impact of changes in the labour process on the formation of new solidarities and divisions without reference both to male and female workers.[85]

Just as the study of the growth of manufacturing, of consumption, demographic change and women's work in the different stages of industrialization involves breaking down the false divide between public and private, economic and non-economic, production and reproduction, so also our understanding of the changing nature of social identity and political consciousness needs to be re-examined in the light of female experience. The influence of Marxism and of male orientated labour history have together been responsible for a long-standing emphasis on the importance of new relations of production (often narrowly conceived as workplace relations) in the formation of social identity and political consciousness (often narrowly conceived as class and class consciousness) during industrialization. Research on women highlights the need to subject the importance of change in the social relations of the family and household (productive and reproductive), and broader changes in cultural forms and practices to the same sort of scrutiny reserved for the social relations of paid work outside the home.

Current debates in social and cultural history about the primacy of discourse create an opportunity to rethink the method of social and political history in new ways that incorporate the importance of women and gender. Attention to discourse raises our consciousness of the gendered nature of language.[86] The concept of class, for example (so bound up in its origins with our perception of the process of industrialization), is based on the idea and ideals of a shared masculinity. Thus male dominated, rational, secular politics is too often seen as being the only legitimate or genuine manifestation of class or political consciousness. Women's informal, often more Utopian, political activities have been ignored or undervalued in classic accounts of the making of class. In these accounts, domestic priorities and attachments are seen as removing women from full immersion in the economic relationships of exploitation that can give rise to political consciousness.[87] Their high profile in pre-industrial riots is acknowledged because, "Their role in winning the family subsistence gave them the status to join men in defending it". But in the nineteenth century, it is argued, women became "Marooned in a traditional form of protest while their brothers and fathers formed more modern, political and labour actions."[88]

Recent poststructural approaches and attention to discourse have freed the analysis of popular politics and social identity from a Marxian anticipation of Socialism and have cleared the ground for the expansion of research on social relations and political perspectives other than class narrowly defined, including those relating to gender and sexuality (as well as nationalism, race, ethnicity and localism).[89] Thus current trends augur well for our increased understanding of the social and political identity of women as well as men. And this will be further advanced if the British debate in the 1990s about language and texts is broadened to include a wider definition of discourse encompassing signs, symbols and everyday practices in private as well as in public life.[90]

Conclusion

Research on the pro-active role of women in agricultural change, demography, urbanization, technological innovation and the rise of a consumer society is in its infancy, but integrating women's history into mainstream debates is clearly set to shift both our interpretation of the industrialization process and many of the terms, sources, methods and assumptions of established accounts.

Most discussion of the impact of industrialization on women has until recently been concerned to detect economic and social improvement or deterioration over several centuries. One problem with this is that we know too little about the position of women and gender ideology in pre-industrial society to be sure whether industrialization represented any sort of watershed in attitudes. Too many of our accepted ideas about the family economy, women's work and the overlap between domestic, commercial and familial structures stand in need of revision. From the perspective of the late twentieth century, it appears most useful to look at cycles of demand for female labour, the economic conditions that create these (such as demand for manufactured goods, price competition, technological and organizational innovation and age structure of the population, for example) and the ways in which individuals, families, institutions and ideas shift to accommodate and in turn actively to modify the social and cultural impact of such cycles.

Domesticity for women was an ideal rather than a reality for most families. And the formal as well as informal income earning of wives and daughters (to say nothing of spinsters, widows, single parents and most men) overlapped so closely with subsistence, domestic, reproductive and leisure activities that it seems wise to consider social relations in the private and public spheres as being part of a seamless web of experience. The tradition of history which, through a male orientation has always separated and privileged the public over the private, and the formal over the informal, needs to be challenged because industrialization influenced private as well as public life directly, and was in turn itself affected by both. Shifts in emotional and family life, leisure, communal structures and institutions, were as much a part of industrialization as were changes in production, consumption and the formal economy. And the roots of social identity and political activity remained as much in the home and the neighbourhood as in the workplace.[91]

The integration of women's history into mainstream debates about industrialization is essential in order that they be fully addressed but only by questioning the validity, the terms and the language of such debates will feminist history be able to take its rightful and central place in *establishing* (as well as revising) mainstream historiographical priorities.

Notes

1. This chapter owes a great deal to discussions with many colleagues, but principally with Maxine Berg, Pamela Sharpe, Peter King, Jane Humphries and Osamu Saito, all of whom contributed to a session on "Women and Industrialization" organized by the author at the Economic History Society Conference, University of Nottingham in April 1994. New work by these scholars has been particularly important in the project of integrating women's history into mainstream accounts of the economic and social history of industrialization.

2. See, for example, M. Berg, "What difference did women's work make to the Industrial Revolution?", *History Workshop Journal* **35**, pp. 22-44, 1993; M. Berg, *The age of manufactures, 1700-1820. Industry, innovation and work in Britain*, 2nd edn (London: Routledge, 1994); L. Davidoff & C. Hall, *Family fortunes. Men and women of the English middle-class, 1780-1850* (London: Hutchinson, 1987); D. Levine, *Reproducing families: the political economy of English population history* (Cambridge: Cambridge University Press, 1987).

3. This debate and some of the problems surrounding it are surveyed in J. Thomas, "Women and capitalism:oppression or emancipation? A review article", *Comparative Studies in Society and History* **30**, pp. 534-49, 1988.

4. This view dominates several classic and more recent accounts: A. Clark, *Working lives of women in the seventeenth century* (London, 1919; reprinted London: Routledge, 1982, 1992). I. Pinchbeck, *Women workers and the Industrial Revolution, 1750-1850* (London: 1930; London: Virago, 1981); Davidoff and Hall, *Family fortunes*; L. Tilly & J. Scott, *Women, work and family* (New York: Holt, Rinehart and Winston, 1978); J. Rendall, *Women in an industrializing society, 1750-1880* (Oxford: Basil Blackwell, 1990); B. Hill, *Women, work and sexual politics in eighteenth century England* (Oxford: Basil Blackwell, 1989).

5. E. Shorter, *The making of the modern family*. See also W J. Goode, *World revolution and family patterns* (Glencoe, Illinois: Free Press, 1963); and M. Young & P. Wilmott, *The symmetrical family* (London: Pelican, 1973).

6. N. McKendrick, "Home demand and economic growth: a new view of the role of women and children in the Industrial Revolution", in *Historical Perspectives: studies in English thought and society*, N. McKendrick (ed.) (London: Europa, 1974), pp. 152-210.

7. S. Rowbotham, *Women's consciousness, man's world* (Harmondsworth: Penguin, 1973); T. McBride, "Women's work and industrialization", in *Becoming visible: women in European history* R. Bridenthal & C. Koonz (eds) (Boston, Mass.: Houghton Mifflin, 1977), reprinted in L. Berlanstein (ed.), *The Industrial Revolution and work in nineteenth century Europe* (London: Routledge, 1992); W. Seccombe, "The housewife and her labour under capitalism", *New Left Review* **94**, pp. 47-58, 1975; and "Patriarchy stabilised: the emergence of the male breadwinner wage norm in nineteenth century Britain", *Social History* **11**, 1986.

8. H. Bradley, *Men's work, women's work* (Cambridge: Polity Press, 1989); J. Lown, *Women and industrialization: gender at work in nineteenth century England* (Cambridge: Polity Press, 1990); A. Phillips & B. Taylor, "Sex and Skill: towards a feminist economics", *Feminist Review* **6**, pp. 79-88, 1980.

9. D. Thompson, "Women and nineteenth century radical politics: a lost dimension", in J. Mitchell & A. Oakley (eds), *The rights and wrongs of women* (Harmondsworth: 1976); J. Bohstedt, "Gender, household and community politics: women in English riots, 1790-1810", *Past and Present* **120**, 1988.

10. M. Vicinus, *Independent women: work and community for single women, 1850-1920* (London: Virago, 1985); M. Shanley, *Feminism, marriage and the law in Victorian England, 1850-1895* (Princeton, New Jersey, USA: Princeton University Press, 1989, 1989) pp. 6-7.

11. Most notably L. Tilly & J. Scott, *Women, work and family* (London: Methuen, 1989) (1st edn, New York: 1978). This work identified the passage from a pre-industrial family economy to a family wage economy and on to a family consumer economy in the twentieth century. For difficulties with this model, see A. Meyering, "La Petite Ouvrière surménée: family structure, family income and women's work in nineteenth century France", in P. Hudson & W. R. Lee (eds), *Women's work and the family economy in historical perspective* (Manchester: Manchester University Press, 1990).

12. For the pitfalls of pre-industrial figures, see M. Berg & P. Hudson, "Rehabilitating the Industrial Revolution", *Economic History Review* **45**, pp. 24-50, 1992. On the census, see E. Higgs, "Women, occupations and work in the nineteenth century censuses", *History Workshop Journal* **23**, 1987; and B. Hill, "Women, work and the census: a problem for historians of women", *History Workshop Journal* **35**, 1993. The problems of largely-unquestioned acceptance of the census figures of female employment are apparent in E. Richards, "Women in the British economy since about 1700: an interpretation", *History* **59**, pp. 337-47, 1974, which argues that women's employment was severely curtailed in the nineteenth century.

13. Circumscribed and male orientated definitions of work need to be considered in assessing the reliability of employment and unemployment statistics, which are too often assumed to be value free and objective. For the importance of a discursive approach to historical documents of this kind, and a warning against the privileging of male organizational categories and positivistic method, see J. Scott, *Gender and the politics of history*, esp. pp. 113-39. See also J. Allen, "Evidence and silence: feminism and the limits of history", in *Feminist challenges. Social and political theory*, C. Pateman & E. Gross (eds) (London: Allen & Unwin, 1986), pp. 173-89; L. Beneria, "Conceptualizing the labour force: the underestimation of women's economic activities", in R. E. Pahl (ed.), *On work: historical, comparative and theoretical approaches* (Oxford: Basil Blackwell, 1988) pp. 372-91.

14. For an introduction to debates about patriarchy and capitalism, see S. Walby, *Patriarchy at work* (Oxford: Blackwell, 1986), Chs 2 and 3.

15. The best survey of women's employment in England in the proto-industrial period is Berg, *Age of Manufactures*. For the importance of women in pre-industrial credit, see W. C. Jordan, *Women and credit in pre-industrial and developing societies* (Philadelphia, Pa.: University of Pennsylvania Press, 1993).

16. See, for example, M. Freifeld, "Technological change and the self-acting mule: a study of skill and the sexual division of labour", *Social History* **11**, 1986; S. Rose, "Gender antagonism and class conflict: exclusionary tactics of male trade unionists in nineteenth century Britain", *Social History* **13**, pp. 191-208, 1988; S. Rose, *Limited livelihoods: gender and class in nineteenth century England* (Berkeley, California: University of California Press, 1992). W. Seccombe, "Patriarchy stabilised: the construction of the male breadwinner wage norm in nineteenth century Britain", *Social History* **21**, 1986; E. Jordan, "The exclusion of women from industry in nineteenth century Britain", *Comparative Studies in Society and History* **31** (2), 1989; J. Mark-Lawson & A. Witz, "From 'family labour' to 'family wage'? The case of women's labour in nineteenth century coal mining", *Social History* **13** (2), 1988.

17. S. Alexander, "Women's work in early-nineteenth century London", in *The rights and wrongs of women*, A. Oakley & J. Mitchell (eds) (Harmondsworth: Penguin, 1976); J.

Schmiechen, *Sweated industries and sweated labour: the London clothing trades, 1860-1914* (Urbana, Illinois: University of Illinois, 1984); L. Davidoff, "The separation of home and work? Landladies and lodgers in nineteenth and twentieth century England", in *Fit work for women* S. Burman (ed.) (London: Croom Helm, 1979); A. V. John (ed.) *Unequal opportunities: women's employment in England 1800-1918* (Oxford: 1986).

18. Part of this shift in approach has been documented by J. Humphries, "'Lurking in the wings'. . .Women in the historiography of the Industrial Revolution", *Business and economic history* **20** (1991). Recent changes in approach are also explored in J. Scott, *Gender and the politics of history* (New York: Columbia University Press, 1988), pp. 15-52. For a review of recent research on changes in women's work, see P. Sharpe, "Continuity or change? Recent developments in the history of women's employment in the British Isles, 1700-1900", *Economic History Review* (forthcoming).

19. See, for example, Berg and Hudson, "Rehabilitating"; B. Hill, "The marriage age of women and the demographers", *History Workshop Journal* **28**, 1989. Berg, *Age of manufactures*; B. Taylor, *Eve and the new Jerusalem: Socialism and feminism in the nineteenth century* (London: Virago, 1983); J. Scott, "Women in the making of the English working-class, in *Gender and the politics of history*, J. Scott; R. Hyam, *Empire and sexuality: the British experience* (Manchester: Manchester University Press, 1990).

20. This agenda was reflected in the essays contained in J. Lewis (ed.) *Labour and love: women's experience of home and family, 1850-1940* (Oxford: Basil Blackwell, 1986). Also in P. Hudson & W. R. Lee (eds), *Women's work and the family economy in historical perspective* (Manchester: Manchester University Press, 1989), esp. essays by Lee and Ayres. For research on the twentieth century in this area, see E. Ross, "Survival networks: women's neighbourhood sharing in London before World War I", *History Workshop Journal* **15**, 1983; E. Ross, *Love and toil: motherhood in outcast London, 1870-1918* (Oxford: Oxford University Press, 1993); A. Davies, *Leisure, gender and poverty: working-class culture in Salford and Manchester, 1900-1939* (Milton Keynes: Open University Press, 1992).

21. A. Vickery, "The neglected century", *Gender and History* **32**, 1991 and "Golden age to separate spheres? a review of the categories and chronology of English women's history", *Historical Journal* **36** (2), 1993.

22. E. A. Wrigley, "Urban growth and agricultural change: England and the Continent in the early modern period", *Journal of Interdisciplinary History* **15**, 1985.

23. These economies of makeshift were very similar to those found in the nineteenth and twentieth centuries and cannot be used as a yardstick of change. See O. Hufton, "Women without men: widows and spinsters in Britain and France in the eighteenth century", *Journal of Family History* **8** (4), pp. 355-76, 1984. See also E. Roberts, "Working class standards of living in Barrow and Lancaster", *Economic History Review* **30**, 1977. P. Ayres, "The hidden economy of dockland families: Liverpool in the 1930s", in *Women's work and the family in historical perspective*, P. Hudson & W. R. Lee (eds), pp. 271-90.

24. Berg, "What difference did women's work make?", p. 39; R. Q. Gray, "Factory legislation and the gendering of jobs in the north of England, 1830-1860", *Gender and History* **5** (1), 1993; A. Vickery, "The neglected century", *Gender and History* **3** (2), pp. 211-19, 1991.

25. H. Heaton, *The Yorkshire woollen and worsted industries* (Oxford: 1920; reprinted Oxford: Clarendon Press, 1965), pp. 89-118. My own current work has added to our knowledge of these clothier households drawing evidence from apprenticeship indentures, legal records and household surveys.

26. A. Kussmaul, *Servants in husbandry in early modern England* (Cambridge: Cambridge University Press, 1981). P. Earle, "The female labour market in London in the late seventeenth and early eighteenth centuries", *Economic History Review* **42** pp. 328-53, (1989).

27. O. Hufton, "Women without men: widows and spinsters in Britain and France in the eighteenth century", *Journal of Family History* **9** (4), pp. 355-76, 1984; M. Vicinus, *Independent women*, p. 293; B. A. Holderness, "Widows in pre-industrial society; an essay on their economic functions", in *Land, kinship and life-cycle*, R. M. Smith (ed.) (Cambridge: Cambridge University Press, 1984) pp. 423-42.

28. A. Clark, *Working lives of women in the seventeenth century*; Davidoff and Hall, *Family fortunes*.

29. See, for example, M. Berg, "Women's property and the Industrial Revolution", *Journal of Interdisciplinary History* **24** (2), pp. 223-50, 1993.

30. M. Berg, "What difference did women's work make to the Industrial Revolution?", *History Workshop Journal* **35**, pp. 223-50, 1993; and "Women's work, mechanization and the early phases of industrialization in England", in *The historical meanings of work*, P. Joyce (ed.) (Cambridge: Cambridge University Press, 1987), pp. 64-98.

31. For the relative importance of domestic service in the formal employment of women in the nineteenth century see E. Roberts, *Women's work 1840-1940* (London: Macmillan, 1988); and J. Rendall, *Women in an industrializing society: England 1750-1880* (Oxford: Basil Blackwell, 1990).

32. Richards, "Women in the British economy". See Notes 11 and 12 above.

33. Some idea of these variations can be gained from John, *Unequal opportunities*; Berg, *Age of manufactures*; E. Roberts, *Women's work 1840-1940* (London: Macmillan, 1988).

34. Seccombe, "Patriarchy stabilised". See also references in Note 15 above.

35. O. Saito, "Labour supply behaviour of the poor in the English Industrial Revolution", *Journal of European Economic History* **10**, pp. 633-52, 1981.

36. Official labour force participation figures suggest that the major shift in the nature of twentieth-century female employment occurred after the Second World War, but as far as occupational distribution is concerned one can see that many postwar changes in women's employment stemmed from a restructuring well underway in the interwar years: M. Glucksman, *Women assemble: women workers and the new industries in interwar Britain* (London: Routledge, 1990).

37. P. Earle, "The female labour market in London in the late seventeenth and eighteenth centuries", *Economic History Review* **42**, pp. 328-53, 1989; L. D. Schwarz, *London in the age of industrialization: entrepreneurs, labour force and living conditions* (Cambridge: Cambridge University Press, 1992), pp. 14-22.

38. J. Bennett makes this point in "History that stands still: women's work in the European past", *Feminist Studies* **14**, pp. 269-83, 1988; see also her "Misogyny, popular culture and women's work", *History Workshop Journal* **31**, pp. 166-88, 1991.

39. That the latter was often the case is demonstrated by E. Roberts, *A woman's place: an oral history of working-class women, 1890-1940* (Oxford: Basil Blackwell, 1984).

40. K. D. M. Snell, *Annals of the labouring poor: social change and agrarian England 1660-1900* (Cambridge: Cambridge University Press, 1985). R. C. Allen, *Enclosure and the yeoman* (Oxford: Oxford University Press, 1992); J. A. Neeson, *Commoners: common right, enclosure and social change in England, 1700-1820* (Cambridge: Cambridge University Press 1993); J. Humphries, "Enclosures, common rights and

women: the proletarianization of families in the late-eighteenth and early-nineteenth centuries", *Journal of Economic History* **50**, pp. 17-42, 1990.

41. The influential work of Snell on the decline of women's employment on the land and the erosion of their status drew evidence only from the south and east of Britain and from a narrow range of sources, principally Settlement certificates and examinations. This has tended to obscure varieties of experience in other areas: Allen, *Enclosure and the yeoman*, p. 289; D. Valenze, "The art of women and the business of men: women's work and the dairy industry c. 1740-1840, *Past and Present* **130**, pp. 142-69, 1991; Pinchbeck, *Women workers*, pp. 59-65.

42. Allen, *Enclosure and the yeoman*. On straw plaiting, see P. Sharpe, "The women's harvest: straw plaiting and the representation of labouring women's employment c. 1793-1885", *Rural History* (1994).

43. David Souden, "East, west - home's best? Regional patterns in migration in early modern England", in *Migration in early modern England*, P. Clark & D. Souden (eds) (London: 1987) pp. 292-333; J. G. Williamson, *Coping with city growth during the Industrial Revolution* (Cambridge: Cambridge University Press, 1990).

44. Berg and Hudson, "Rehabilitating"; Berg, "What difference did women's work make?".

45. This is implicit in Crafts' model; see, N. F. R. Crafts, *British economic growth during the Industrial Revolution* (Oxford: Clarendon Press, 1985). See also J. D. Chambers, *Population, economy and society* (Oxford: Oxford University Press, 1972) p. 431.

46. W. A. Lewis, "Economic development with unlimited supplies of labour", in *The economics of underdevelopment*, A. N. Agarawala and S. P. Singh (eds) (Oxford: Oxford University Press, 1958), pp. 400-49; Allen, *Enclosure and the yeoman*.

47. For a survey of these arguments and debates, see P. Hudson, *The Industrial Revolution* (London: Edward Arnold, 1992), Ch. 3.

48. For a recent survey of the literature on proto-industrialization, see P. Hudson, "Proto-industrialization in England", in *Proto-industrialization in Europe*, M. Cerman & S. Ogilvie (eds) (Cambridge: Cambridge University Press, forthcoming). For material on women and proto-industrialization, see M. Berg, *The age of manufactures*, Chs 7 and 10-12.

49. J. de Vries, "Between purchasing power and the world of goods: understanding the household economy in early modern Europe", in *Consumption and the world of goods*, J. Brewer and R. Porter (eds) (London: Routledge, 1993), pp. 85-132; and "The Industrial Revolution and the industrious revolution", *Journal of Economic History* **54**, pp. 249-71, 1994.

50. S. Horrell and J. Humphries, "Old questions, new data, and alternative perspectives: families' living standards in the Industrial Revolution", *Journal of Economic History* **52** (4), pp. 849-80, 1992. See also J. Lyons, "Family response to economic decline: handloom weavers in early nineteenth century Lancashire", *Research in Economic and Social History* **12**, 1989, who argues that the tenacity of male hand weaving in the face of plummeting wages was aided by the subsidy to household income provided by women's and children's earnings.

51. E. A. Wrigley & R. Schofield, *The population history of England, 1541-1871* (London, 1981).

52. B. Hill, "The marriage age of women and the demographers", *History Workshop Journal* **28**, pp. 129-47, 1989; D. A. Kent, "Ubiquitous but invisible: female domestic servants in mid eighteenth century London", *History Workshop Journal* **28**, pp. 111-28, 1989.

53. E. Shorter, *The making of the modern family* (London: Collins, 1976) Ch. 3; D. Levine, *Reproducing families*.

54. Officials may have been emphasizing the atypical to make a point here: Pinchbeck, *Women workers*, p. 273.

55. Gandy, "Illegitimacy in a handloom weaving community", pp. 232-3 and 273-81; Hill, "Marriage age of women", p. 143. For a Scottish example of the prevalence of single parenting, see A. Blaikie, *Illegitimacy, sex and society: north east Scotland, 1750-1900* (Oxford: Oxford University Press, 1994).

56. E. A. Wrigley, "Population growth in eighteenth century England: a conundrum resolved", *Past & Present* **98**, pp. 121-50, 1983.

57. T. Laqueur, "Sex and desire in the Industrial Revolution", in *The Industrial Revolution and British society* (eds), P. O'Brien & R. Quinault (Cambridge: Cambridge University Press, 1993), pp. 100-23.

58. For an introduction to this subject that does not dwell on gender-specific aspects, see R. Woods, "The effects of population redistribution on the level of mortality in nineteenth century England and Wales", *Journal of Economic History* **45**, 1985.

59. For a collection of European studies on mortality and urbanization see M. C. Nelson and J. Rogers (eds), *Urbanization and the epidemiological transition* (Uppsala: Uppsala University Family History Group, 1985); P. Razzell, *Essays in English population history* (London: Caliban, 1994); A. Rubenstein, "Subtle poison: the puerperal fever controversy in Victorian Britain", *Historical Studies* **20** (1983); R. Schofield, "Did the mothers really die", in *The world we have gained*, L. Bonfield, R. Smith, K. Wrighton (eds) (Cambridge: Cambridge university Press, 1986), pp. 231-60.

60. P. Laxton & N. Williams, "Urbanization and infant mortality in England: a long term perspective and review", in Nelson and Rogers, *Urbanization*.

61. S. A. King, "The nature and causes of demographic change in an industrializing township: Calverley, West Yorkshire 1680-1820" (Unpublished Ph.D. thesis, University of Liverpool, 1993).

62. V. Fildes, *Wet nursing: a history from antiquity to the present* (Oxford: Basil Blackwell, 1988).

63. T. Griffiths, P. A. Hunt, P. K. O'Brien, "Inventive activity in the British textile industry, 1700-1800", *Journal of Economic History* **52**, pp. 881-906, 1992; Berg, *Age of manufactures*, esp. Chs 11 & 12; M. Berg, "Women's work, mechanization and the early phases of industrialization in England", in *The historical meanings of work*, P. Joyce (ed.) (Cambridge: Cambridge University Press, 1987).

64. On the importance of fashion changes, see N. McKendrick, J. Brewer, J. H. Plumb, *The birth of consumer society* (London: Hutchinson, 1983) On the influence of female tastes and fashion on the cotton industry see B. Lemire, *Fashion's favourite: the cotton trade and the consumer in Britain, 1660-1800* (Oxford: Basil Blackwell, 1991).

65. For this and other debates surrounding innovation in the early-nineteenth century see M. Berg, *The machinery question and the making of political economy, 1815-1848* (Cambridge: Cambridge University Press, 1980).

66. M. Freifeld, "Technological change and the self-acting mule: a study of skill and the sexual division of labour", *Social History* **1**, 1986; C. Cockburn, *Machinery of dominance: women, men and technical know how* (London: Pluto, 1985); C. Cockburn, *Brothers: male dominance and technological change* (London: Pluto, 1991).

67. Berg compares resistance in the West of England to the more flexible and inventive workshop culture of the West Midlands in *Age of manufactures*, p. 181.

68. A. Randall, "Work, culture and resistance to machinery in the West of England woollen industry", in *Regions and industries*, P. Hudson (ed.) pp. 175-200; P. Hudson, *The genesis of industrial capital: a study of the West Riding wool textile industry c. 1750-1850* (Cambridge: Cambridge University Press, 1986); E. P. Thompson, *The making of the English working-class* (London: Gollancz, 1963).

69. A. Erickson, *Women and property*; S. Staves, *Married women's separate property in England, 1660-1833* (Cambridge: Mass.: Harvard University Press, 1990); L. Holcome, *Wives and property: reform of the married women's property law in nineteenth century England* (Oxford: Oxford University Press, 1983); Berg, "Women's property and the Industrial Revolution", *Journal of Interdisciplinary History* 24 (2), pp. 223-50, 1993.

70. Neeson, *Commoners*; Humphries, "Enclosure"; J. Styles, "Embezzlement, industry and the law in England", in *Manufacture in town and country before the factory*, M. Berg, P. Hudson, M. Sonenscher (eds) (Cambridge: Cambridge University Press, 1983), pp. 173-208; P. King, "Customary rights and women's earnings: the importance of gleaning to the rural labouring poor 1750-1850", *Economic History Review* 44, pp. 461-76, 1991.

71. K. D. M. Snell, *Annals*; Allen, *Enclosure and the yeoman*.

72. Perhaps between 10 per cent and 17 per cent: L. Zedner, *Women, crime and custody in Victorian England* (Oxford: Oxford University Press, 1991), pp. 18-23.

73. The significant exception is Zedner, *Women, crime and custom*; see also F. Heidensohn, *Women and crime* (London: Macmillan, 1985). There is at the time of writing no major study of women and crime in the eighteenth century.

74. A longer-term decline in the proportion of indicted offenders who were female has also been suggested: see M. Feeley and D. Little, "The vanishing female: the decline of women in the criminal process 1687-1912", *Law and Society Review* 25 (4), pp. 719-57, 1991. Changes in recorded crime rates are, of course, difficult to interpret: they reflect changes in the law, in law enforcement and policing, and changes in gender-specific attitudes to law breaking as much as they tell us about the changing character of offenders, and this must be borne in mind.

75. Female criminals were most often regarded as being mad rather than bad: Zedner, *Women, crime and custody*, pp. 264-95. On attitudes to and prosecutions for prostitution, see J. R. Walkowitz, *Prostitution and Victorian society: women, class and the state* (Cambridge: Cambridge University Press, 1980).

76. Feeley and Little, "The vanishing female".

77. J. Rendall, *The origins of modern feminism: women in Britain, France and the United States 1780-1869* (London: Macmillan, 1985), Ch. 2; J. R. Walkowitz, *Prostitution and Victorian society* and *City of dreadful delight: narratives of sexual danger in late Victorian London* (London: Virago, 1992); Zedner, *Women, crime and custody*, pp. 11-91.

78. C. Hall, "The early formation of women's domestic ideology", in *Fit work for women*, S. Burman (ed.) (London: Croom Helm, 1979); J. Lewis, *Women in England, 1870-1950: sexual divisions and social change* (Brighton: Wheatsheaf, 1984); Davidoff and Hall, *Family fortunes*.

79. C. Hall, "The tale of Samuel and Jemima: gender and working-class culture in nineteenth century England", in *E. P. Thompson: critical perspectives*, H. Kay & K.

McClelland (eds) (Cambridge: Polity Press, 1990); Thompson, *The making of the English working-class*, pp. 84-203.

80. M. Wollstonecraft, *Vindication of the rights of woman* (Harmondsworth: Penguin, 1982 edn; first published 1792); B. Taylor, *Eve and the New Jerusalem: Socialism and feminism in the nineteenth century* (London: Virago, 1983).

81. Taylor, *Eve and the New Jerusalem*, Ch. 4; Hall, "Samuel and Jemima"; D. Thompson, "Women in radical politics: a lost dimension", in *The rights and wrongs of women*, J. Mitchell & A. Oakley (eds) (Harmondsworth: Penguin, 1976).

82. J. Bohstedt, "Gender, household and community politics: women in English riots, 1790-1810", *Past and Present* **120**, 1988.

83. This is explored by J. Bornat in "Lost leaders: women, trade unionism and the case of the General Union of Textile Workers, 1875-1914", in *Unequal opportunities*, A. V. John (ed.) (Oxford: Basil Blackwell, 1986), pp. 207-34.

84. C. E. Morgan, "Women, work and consciousness in the mid nineteenth century English cotton industry", *Social History* **17** (1), 1992; J. Humphries, "Class struggle and the persistence of the working-class family", *Cambridge Journal of Economics* **1**, 1977; J. Humphries, "Protective legislation, the capitalist state and working-class men. The case of the 1842 Mines Regulation Act", *Feminist Review* **7**, 1981.

85. S. O. Rose, "Gender antagonism and class conflict"; Rose, *Limited livelihoods*.

86. J. W. Scott, *Gender and the politics of history* (New York: Colombia University Press, 1988), esp. Chs 2-4.

87. Scott, *Gender and the politics of history*, pp. 68-90. For collected essays which frequently touch on these themes, see C. Hall, *White, male and middle-class: explorations in feminism and history* (Cambridge: Polity Press, 1992).

88. Bohstedt, "Gender, household and community politics", pp. 93-4. The quote is typical of a number of such interpretations.

89. See, for example, P. Joyce, *Visions of the people: industrial England and the question of class* (Cambridge: Cambridge University Press, 1991). There has been a very active debate about the impact of poststructuralism on British historiography, notably in *Social History* and in *Past and Present* issues of 1991-3.

90. The English debates about poststructuralism have been almost exclusively concerned with discourse as equated with the written and the spoken word, whereas, following earlier folklorist and anthropological traditions, continental discursiveness has involved a much wider set of concerns about the functions and symbols of everyday life. For an introduction to this, see G. Eley, "Labour history, social history, Alltagsgeschichte: experience, culture and the politics of the everyday - a new direction for German social history?", *Journal of Modern History* **61**, pp. 297-343, 1989.

91. See, for example, M. Savage, *The dynamics of working-class politics: the labour movement in Preston, 1880-1940* (Cambridge: Cambridge University Press, 1987).

Suggestions for further reading

Useful short surveys and introductions to the subject are J. Rendall, *Women in an industrializing society: England, 1750-1850* (Oxford: Basil Blackwell, 1990); P. Hudson, *The Industrial Revolution* (London: Edward Arnold, 1992), pp. 225-36; J. Thomas, "Women and capitalism: oppression or emancipation?", *Comparative Studies in Society and History* **30**, 1988; P.

Hudson & W. R. Lee (eds), *Women's work and the family economy in historical perspective* (Manchester: Manchester University Press, 1990). The following concentrate on changes in women's work and the first two have useful bibliographies: E. Roberts, *Women's work 1840-1940* (London: Macmillan, 1988); P. Sharpe, "Continuity or change? Recent developments in the economic history of women's employment in the British Isles", *Economic History Review* (forthcoming 1995); M. Berg, "What difference did women's work make to the Industrial Revolution?", *History Workshop Journal* **35,** 1993; J. M. Bennett, "History that stands still: women's work in the European past", *Feminist Studies* **14** (2), pp. 269-83, 1988. Various aspects of the subject can be explored further by using the references provided in the footnotes, especially S. Rose, *Limited livelihoods: gender and class in nineteenth century England* (Berkeley, California: California University Press, 1992); L. Zedner, *Women, crime and custody in Victorian England* (Oxford: Oxford University Press, 1991); C. Hall, *White, male and middle-class: explorations in feminism and history* (Cambridge: Polity Press, 1992); J. Scott, *Gender and the politics of history* (New York: Columbia University Press, 1988). Finally, much can still be learned from the classic works of Alice Clark, *Working lives of women in the seventeenth century* (London: 1919; reprinted London: Routledge, 1992); and Ivy Pinchbeck, *Women workers and the Industrial Revolution, 1750-1850* (London, 1930) (1981 edn.).

Future primary research in this area is likely to be based on detailed locality studies where a variety of sources (principally parish, probate and legal records) may be used (discursively) to integrate women's history into our larger understanding of the process and impact of industrialization.

Chapter Three

॥ऽ

Women and the family

Shani D'Cruze

Introduction

Histories of "the family" have generally agreed that the small, private, secular, nuclear family based on affective personal relationships has developed historically and can be associated with modern, industrial, urban society.[1] A great deal of women's history has in recent years begun to scrutinize in depth the historical changes in the family from a woman-centred perspective. Childbearing and childrearing have generally been a crucial determinant of women's life course, though once we begin to appreciate the family as being both socially-constructed and historically-located, it becomes apparent that there is nothing inevitable or unchanging about the ways that women have experienced family life. Furthermore, the history of women cannot be accounted for by the history of the family, not only because significant amounts of women's experience were located in the public sphere, but also because the ideologies that constructed the family as private were created publicly.

This chapter will survey broad currents of change that affected women's family life – principally through looking at ideological and structural developments. The diversity among and between families over time by class, by region, neighbourhood, occupational group and personal choice meant that such wider trends had their specific realizations. The family was (and is) a very flexible institution which has adapted within a broad normative framework to meet particular needs. By looking at different women's roles within their own families, not only change and diversity, but also continuities in strategies, practices and experience can be seen in such areas as household management, domestic work, maternity, childrearing, husband/wife relations, the extended family, social networks and neighbourhood.

Women's lives were coloured in different ways by their association with the family, and first and foremost, of course, in terms of their day-to-day experience of work, relationships, health, sociability and sexuality. One working-class wife in 1915 saw ten years of marriage, childbearing and childrearing as reducing her to "almost a mental and physical wreck".[2] For this woman, and many other women, family dominated the conditions of her life. However, daily life operated within family units whose structure was altering demographically through changes to women's own patterns of fertility and childbearing – changes in which they had at least some say, if only to keep their husbands under observation during intercourse and "push him out of the way when I think it's near".[3]

How things are experienced depends on social consciousness – how women understood and explained to themselves and each other the realities and possibilities of their lives. Many middle-class girls at this period were socialized within the family into a dependent, decorative, self-denying, feminine demeanour. Molly Hughes was reprimanded in the 1870s for wishing she was a boy. Her mother "did not give . . . [me] . . . a reason, but merely insisted that it was splendid to be a girl, and with such exuberant enthusiasm that I was quite convinced".[4] Middle-class women reaching adulthood in the early decades of the twentieth century often remained ambivalent about the family-centred roles they had learned as girls. Vera Brittain detested the role of faculty wife when she accompanied her husband to America and found the solution in a semi-detached marriage, living part of the year in London with her children and close friend Winifred Holtby.[5]

Although many working-class women, such as Hannah Mitchell and Ada Nield Chew, developed active careers, they still had to manage the difficulties this caused to their roles as wife and mother. Others perceived things differently. Margaret Llewelyn-Davies of the Women's Co-operative Guild commented on the "stoic resignation to fate" of so many working-class women at the turn of the twentieth century, a quality that could be interpreted by less sympathetic observers as stupidity or poor mothering. Not all women of the working-class were so resigned, however. Many, such as the women from Birmingham studied by Carl Chinn, used their role within the family as a basis for empowerment and self-assertion.[6]

Social consciousness is worked out through relationships of power. Dominant ideologies and discourses limit and structure consciousness, though this effect is always mediated by experience and challenged by resistance. The ideologies that associated women with the family and prescribed their life course within the domestic sphere were, as I have argued, very powerful. Yet, however frequently the cypher of a woman's place recurred, the discourses of domesticity changed substantially over time. Indeed, this discursive reworking developed with and through broader historical change, and enabled the ideologies that positioned women as family dependents to remain effective in a rapidly changing world.

Nineteenth-century ideologies and policies

The truism that "a woman's place is in the home" was repeated frequently in the century after 1850. Coventry Patmore's poem to the middle-class "angel in the house" defined the stereotype. The association was just as clear, though differently formulated, among the working-class. Working class activist and orator Mary Fletcher told striking Preston textile workers in 1853 that it was "a disgrace to an Englishman . . . to allow his wife to go out to work". Mary MacArthur, the Labour Party activist and trade unionist, said in 1917 that she was "sufficiently old fashioned to agree that there is something to be said" for the notion that women should be at home.[7] It is the recurrence of such ideas, across a century that saw far reaching change (including a major demographic shift, the spread of new levels of technology into everyday life and two world wars) that poses the most interesting historical questions. And they are questions that can only be answered historically by relating ideological and structural change to gender relationships and historical experience.

The middle of the nineteenth century was a time when the inevitability of industrial capitalism, its achievements and its ugliness, came home to roost. The anxieties and crises of early industrialisation: economic instability, political unrest and unprecedented urban growth, had been articulated in no small measure as a crisis of "the family". By mid-century, however, such phenomena had become more familiar, and the social and political confidence of the middle-classes and elites in managing industrial and urban problems had increased.[8]

"The family" had acquired particular meaning for the evolving middle-class well before 1850. Inspired and buttressed by evangelical or "serious" religion, the middle-class family home had become the affective and moral site of refuge from the harsh, industrializing world. Furthermore, in what was still a comparatively institution-poor society, the family was a vital source of business capital and personnel, of the investment required for professional training and education, and of social contacts and reputation. Middle-class women were central to this. It was often their inheritance or jointure that provided capital. Their role in the family linked husbands, kin or sons, who took on business or professional roles. Some middle-class women worked directly in family businesses earlier in the century. Women were vital in maintaining social contacts between business and professional families and established the credibility of the firm's reputation and credit through their genteel demeanour and social display.[9]

Deborah Gorham argues that middle-class ideologies of domesticity evolved to help "relieve the tension" between the moral imperatives of evangelical Christianity, which formed a vital shared cultural background for much of the evolving nineteenth-century middle class, and the hard-edged rationale of political economy, which was held to shape the destiny of industrial capitalism. Domesticity achieved "an efficient moral balance" between public and private in the early- and mid-nineteenth century. The maintenance of class status through mores of gentility contradicted directly the entrepreneurial ethos of the capitalist public sphere. It was to middle-class women that the job of maintaining genteel domesticity and thus the social status of the family – measured in both class and moral terms – was entrusted.[10] The legal doctrine of "couverture" subsumed married womens' legal identity within that of their husbands. Evangelical religion, law, literature and the discourses of the emergent social sciences all elaborated women's association with a separate private sphere. Excluded from paid work, middle-class and upper-class women were assigned the roles of angels in the house – seeing to the management of the household, supervising servants, socializing young children, establishing a genteel and advantageous social position, and maintaining a moral and respectable tone within the home. This role placed women in social and economic dependence on men, but at the same time gave them power as the moral arbiters of the domestic sphere.[11]

Middle-class domesticity required a material base, ideally the £300 per annum necessary to employ two household servants. The number of families whose incomes fell in the middle range of between £200 and £500 a year, and so could afford to keep one or two servants, doubled between 1851 and 1871, far in advance of the overall rate of population growth. The majority of these were at the lower end of the middle income bracket. Material affluence was used to establish formality, ritual and compartmentalization of domestic life.[12] Formality and ritual were in evidence: for example, at mealtimes with numerous courses and complex etiquette, in the family prayers with the servants on Sundays, and in the formal ordering of space and time by setting up daily timetables, and using different rooms for specific purposes. Nineteenth-century manuals of household management, such as the oft-reprinted Mrs Beeton's, were replete with elaborate timetables for both mistress and servants that borrowed notions of efficiency and order from the methods of industrial work discipline. The social interaction between households was also formalized. The ritual of morning calls (made in the afternoon after the household chores had been completed), of leaving cards and of dinner invitations was an endlessly time-consuming activity, resented by some women (and their adult daughters), but embraced by many others as a duty done on behalf of their families. Indeed, these social rituals were vital in establishing and maintaining the status and respectability of the family.[13]

Meeting the required standards of formalization, ritual and compartmentalization was a particularly onerous task for middle-class women whose families could not afford the two to three servants this ideally required. Mrs Gaskell gives a rather touching fictional example of tea parties at "Cranford" (modelled on the genteel small town of Knutsford, just south-west of Manchester), where the mistress would pretend she was surprised at the cakes the maid served, even though everyone knew she had spent the morning baking them. Middle-class women had to balance the appearance of a leisured lifestyle with the necessity of sharing at least some of the household work that had to be done to support it.[14]

Given the centrality of the family to the development of the middle-class, as well as the perceived social problems of fast-growing, unplanned, insanitary industrial cities, it is scarcely surprising that the domestic arrangements of the poor should provoke such a degree of anxiety or such a wide range of scrutiny and criticism. The middle-class ideology of the family as a prime maintainer of morals meant that attempts to discipline the moral inadequacies perceived in the poor should target the working-class family. The Victorian values enshrined in social policy, legislation, policing and a great deal of philanthropy, were frequently the values of the bourgeoise family stiffened by the harsher tones of political economy. A great deal of employment legislation, for instance, assumed the desirability of working-class women's economic dependence within the family. Therefore, while these laws removed working-class women from some of the hazards of industrial working conditions, they reinforced women's subordination in the workforce and reduced their ability to contribute to their families' subsistence. Consequently, ideologies which promoted the social and cultural identity of the middle-class as a *class*, were applied punitively to working-class women and, as mid-nineteenth-century feminists such as the Langham Place Group argued, also disadvantaged middle-class women as *women*.[15]

Changing fertility and family limitation

These ideologies of family and their translation into law and public policy took place in a period of marked demographic expansion in Britain. The period after 1870 saw a major change. The rapid population growth that had accompanied the earlier stages of industrialization began to tail off. The population still grew, but the rate of increase declined significantly. It is agreed by demographic historians generally that earlier marriage was the main cause of the population acceleration in the mid- to late-eighteenth century. Improved agricultural production meant that the multiplying mouths could be fed, and so the population continued to grow. Later in the nineteenth century, with industrialization and urbanization well established, people began to restrict their own fertility. The crude birthrate of around 35 per thousand of population between 1840 and 1880 had declined to 28.5 by 1901. Only 20 per cent of marriages made around 1860 resulted in fewer than three children, but this was the case for 67 per cent of marriages in 1925.[16]

Although the majority of women still married and had children, there were critical marginal changes. In the late-nineteenth century 88 per cent of women in their forties were, or had been married. Between 1921 and 1931, the comparable figure was 83 per cent. People (especially women) were marrying later, more people were not marrying at all, and both the married and the unmarried were having fewer children. Increased life expectancy also meant that marriages lasted longer and widowhood was more commonly the experience of old age. Of course, such changes meant significant differences in women's life experiences in comparison with earlier in the century.[17]

After 1871, the census showed that there were slightly more women than men in the population. This imbalance increased between 1871 and 1911 and was made still larger by the loss of male lives in the First World War. The question of what all these "surplus women" were to do with themselves exercised many minds. The issue centred on the middle and upper-classes, whose practices of domesticity and the need to prove gentility by female economic dependence were undermined by the necessity of providing for increasing numbers of spinster daughters, sisters and other relations. The opening up of respectable professional and white collar work for middle-class and lower middle-class women coincided with this. In terms of the family, it meant that many women did not realise their "biological destiny" as wives and mothers.[18] Some women emigrated, be it as a domestic servant or a doctor in Britain's colonial territories, but many more adopted the role of aunt or daughter-at-home. With later marriage, most middle-class daughters spent longer "at home" than had previous generations. Others established different domestic arrangements, either alone or with other women. Martha Vicinus has discussed how the settlement movement enabled respectable domesticity for single middle-class women. Vera Brittain combined marriage and children with a household shared with her close friend Winifred Holtby. All these arrangements meant a modification but not an abandonment of the nineteenth-century codes of middle-class domesticity.[19]

From the 1860s, sections of the middle-classes began to have fewer children.[20] By the 1930s, small families were the norm virtually throughout society. The reasons for this shift were a complex aggregate of the economic, social and cultural. It has been argued that codes of domesticity meant a heavier emotional and financial investment in parenting and education, initially for the middle and upper-classes. As I have argued, the need to support young adult children, especially daughters, was more pressing. People also came to value more companionship and closeness between husband and wife, on which large families intruded, even when a couple could afford paid domestic help. However, these changes came to be adopted more widely. Generalized emulation or diffusion models tend to miss the subtlety and complexity of what was a major social and cultural, as well as demographic, change, and need to be considered together with more materialist arguments based on specific economic and occupational circumstances.

The professional middle-class were the first to restrict their marital fertility. Many professional families did not have large capital assets, and the training and university education necessary to establish sons in a professional career was lengthy and expensive, particularly since at that period the professions were tightening up their organization and formalizing entry qualifications, so smaller families here seem to have been dictated by common sense. Other occupational groups can be argued to have an economic rationale for family limitation. Textile-working families had a low average of 3.19 children in 1911. Diana Gittins argues that paid mill work for women discouraged large families. In mining communities, where the average family size was 4.33 children in 1911, there was no available paid work for women and children. However, throughout the second half of the nineteenth century there was a high demand for adult male labour in mining, and reasonable security of income barring accident or ill health. Much the same could be said of agricultural communities, particularly in the South and East of Britain. Both these occupational groups maintained high fertility throughout the nineteenth century.[21] However, explanations based on occupational background alone cannot explain all the variations in the way fertility declined.

The widening income range and occupational base of the middle-class as the nineteenth century progressed also meant that more families sought to finance a middle-class lifestyle on a limited income. Marriage patterns among the upper-middle-class, however, show a heightened tendency to avoid "marrying beneath", to maintain social exclusiveness. At the same time, sections of the working-class, particularly the families of skilled workers, experienced comparatively greater stability of income later in the nineteenth century and could contemplate social mobility for their children, if not for themselves. More frequent marriages between lower middle-class and skilled working-class families blurred distinctions at this boundary, the crucial divide being that between the respectable and the non-respectable.[22] Changing labour market conditions made available more white collar and lower professional work such as elementary school teaching. The development of elementary education and the greater provision of industrial training and apprenticeships also combined to make aspirations of social mobility more realistic. The cost of supporting teenage children during education or training, as well as the desire for family betterment and respectability discouraged large families. Even when the numbers of people marrying increased again during the interwar period, family size still remained small. In the 1900s, 25 per cent of women had five or more children. By the 1940s, only 5 per cent of women had this many.[23]

Whatever the balance between economic interest and social aspiration or cultural norms that shaped an individual couple's decisions to have fewer children, two central questions remain: first, as Chapter 8 discusses, the issue of the power relations between a husband and wife, and secondly, is the methods adopted to avoid conception. Coitus interruptus and abstinence as a means of preventing pregnancy are the explanations most favoured by historians. The use of abortifacients as a contraceptive measure was well known and apparently widespread among working-class women. As well as gin, gunpowder or rat poison, lead-based "diachylon" compounds were fairly freely available. Newspapers advertised patent medicines such as Davies Emmenagogue Mixture which claimed to remove "all obstructions and irregularities". Many working-class women held it to be perfectly acceptable to end a pregnancy in its early stages before "quickening".[24] The increasing availability of cheap barrier contraceptives, particularly following the First World War, also played an important part in limiting marital and non-marital fertility. Fertility control was crucial to women's life experience. Fewer pregnancies and (arguably) less time spent in childcare had direct implications for maternal health and on women's other activities and occupations. As twentieth century studies demonstrate, smaller families were not the experience of very many working-class women until the interwar generation.

Maternity

Childbirth remained a potentially hazardous experience for women, and frequent pregnancy could affect the mother's health fundamentally, though in general these dangers varied inversely with income level. Poor living conditions among working-class women increased the risks, although the more sedentary lifestyles of affluent women, particularly at the beginning of the period, also had their dangers. Medical care in pregnancy and at childbirth was rationed by cost, although during the twentieth century some improvements were made. The 1918 Maternal and Child Welfare Act created powers for local government to provide health visitors, infant welfare centres and day nurseries, taking over from charitable foundations. After 1911, a state Maternity Benefit was available to women whose husbands were in the state National Insurance scheme, and antenatal and postnatal clinics slowly became more common. However, untreated (or badly treated) internal injuries following childbirth were not infrequent, affecting an estimated 10 per cent of all pregnant women as late as 1931. For many working-class women, the health consequences of poor nutrition, bad housing and a heavy workload further complicated pregnancy and made family limitation attractive.[25]

Despite falling mortality rates overall, infant and maternal mortality rates remained high. Infant mortality declined in the early twentieth century from 163 per thousand births in 1893 to below 100 in 1914, but maternal mortality rates increased between 1918 and 1934, to reach 4.66 per thousand live births. In depressed areas such as South Wales in the 1930s, maternal mortality was significantly higher. Rapidly increasing numbers of hospital births, from 15 per cent in 1927 to 54 per cent in 1954 did not reverse this trend immediately.[26]

Infant mortality was also closely correlated to poverty. In Birmingham in 1905, the figure in affluent Edgbaston and Harbourne was 131 per thousand live births, compared to 207 per thousand in a poor district.[27] Social commentators blamed poorer mothers for neglecting their children and leaving them in the care of inefficient childminders while they went out to work. Attention was drawn to the reduced infant mortality in Lancashire during the Cotton Famine in the 1860s. There was no work available for women when the mills closed, but more babies survived despite acute economic hardship. The evidence is, however, ambiguous. Infant mortality was high in Sunderland, where women did little paid work, and low in other towns where paid work was more common.[28]

Childminders and non-respectable working-class mothers were alleged to be a poor moral influence, to be ignorant of basic hygiene and nutrition, and to quieten the infants in their care with regular doses of opiates. Proprietory mixtures such as Godfrey's Cordial were cheap and easily available, and some women certainly made regular use of them to calm fractious or ill babies. Many babies and toddlers were fed largely on a diet of bread-and-water pap. However, this did not necessarily imply lack of care or neglect, since the regime of childcare then widely popular held that bland food and regular rest and sleep were necessary to promote growth.[29]

Affluent commentators overlooked the fact that middle-class and upper-class mothers also delegated much of the routine business of childcare to their own domestic servants, to governesses, and (particularly in the case of boys) to preparatory and public schools. Young children in affluent households spent most of their time in the nursery, away from adult members of the family. This segregation was part of the overall culture of domesticity. Often, late-nineteenth- and early-twentieth-century children of wealthy families only saw their parents for a short time each day, and oral history confirms that mothers could be perceived as distant and glamorous, if affectionate.[30] Such families were sufficiently well off to maintain the most elaborate codes of domesticity, and were slower to adopt practices of family privacy which accompanied family limitation in other social groups. Wealthy mothers spent little time caring directly for their children, but this does not necessarily mean that they lacked interest in them. Comparably, the lack of ready affection, the material hardship and often the harsh physical discipline in working-class homes could easily be misinterpreted.

In 1907, a Middlesborough mother whose baby had died told the social investigator, Lady Bell, that "it would not have mattered so much in another week, as by then the insurance would have come in".[31] This should not be interpreted as a cynical or uncaring remark. Many families took out burial policies on their children, which paid out only after the first few weeks of life, to discourage infanticide. The drain on health and resources of repeated childbearing meant that later births were not as celebrated as early ones. However, this Middlesborough woman told the simple truth. It *would* have been better if the insurance had paid out, since then she would not have had to find the money for the funeral from her housekeeping. The financial as well as the emotional costs of infant mortality were central to women's concerns as managers of their domestic economies.

Household management and family relationships

All married women of all classes were expected to manage their households. Of course, the duties this entailed varied according to class and income. The crucial divide was between those women who employed servants and those who were themselves responsible for all the household labour, though, as we have seen, this distinction was blurred for those who employed only a single maid-of-all-work, or later in the period a daily help, and would do at least part of the housework themselves. We shall look more closely in the next section at the processes of domestic work, the management of servants and the ways these changed over time. The management of money by working-class women will be reviewed here.

Money is, of course, easier to manage when it is plentiful. For working-class women, the chief *desideratum* in their attempt to sustain a viable family household was a regular and sufficient income. So many of them, however, did not have access to this. The irregularity of many working-class family incomes was, if anything, more difficult to cope with than their small size. This was not only the problem of the very poor. Although the wages of skilled workers did improve after 1850, illness or accident could strike, and most working-class wages were very low. As a Fabian Women's Group survey in Lambeth found in 1917, even respectable families living on a semi-skilled wage of "round about a pound a week" had almost no margin above basic subsistence.[32] The skills involved in stretching this level of household income to feed, house and clothe a family were legion, and this task was the virtually exclusive duty of a working-class wife.

If husbands were held to be responsible for bringing home the major part of the household's income, wives were expected to ensure that those monies provided for all the family's needs. This included an implicit duty to secure additional income if necessary. Although a husband generally retained a proportion of his wage for "spends" on beer, tobacco, fares, and often his own clothes, any money earned by wives was normally considered to be entirely part of the housekeeping. Married women tended not to work full time during the second half of the nineteenth century, though there were clear regional variations. They did, however, take on casual work of all kinds, including homework such as matchbox making, hawking and selling, or taking in lodgers to ensure that there was enough money coming into the household. For some women, paid work after marriage was a temporary expedient to tide the family over a crisis or to achieve a specific goal such as a child's education, though others, whose husbands' wages were very low or variable, worked regularly.[33]

Depending on the period and local codes of respectability, married women's paid work could be frowned upon. Some women hid their paid work from their husbands, as did one of Pat Ayers' respondents from a poor, dockland area of Liverpool in the 1930s. "He would have gone beserk", she said, "but I needed it".[34] It is fair to see married women's paid work throughout the whole period as just one economic strategy employed to make the household budget stretch. Poor relief or charity was another useful expedient, although depending on the neighbourhood acceptance of charity could compromise respectability. The mediators between charities and the working-class were very often middle-class women engaged in philanthropic work. Whether charities applied evangelical moral standards in deciding where to distribute aid or, as later, adopted a more scientific, casework rationale, it was generally the working-class wife and mother who met the visitor and convinced her that her family were properly respectable and deserving.[35] It is helpful to see the working-class domestic economy as an economy of expedients, and the household as a flexible and resilient social structure which enabled the subsistence of its members. Whether organising consumption or gaining resources by whatever means, women were the crucial figures in achieving this end.

Social relations between household members involved power differentials by both age and gender. Working-class parents claimed near absolute authority over their children. Obedience was expected and generally unquestioned. Physical punishment was widespread. In rural Essex in the 1900s, Clifford Hills' mother used a little cane. In the South London slums, Tommy Morgan's mother routinely hit her children. She and her husband were hard drinkers and the husband beat her, but she still had uncompromising standards for her children's behaviour and enforced them with physical punishment.[36] As the age of marriage rose in the later nineteenth century, it became accepted that children would remain in the parental household as young adults. Mothers claimed the greater part of their wage packets as contributions to the housekeeping. Many teenagers kept only a very small amount of pocket money, though boys were more often allowed to "board" for a fixed sum than were girls. Even after the advent of compulsory elementary schooling from the 1870s, many young children earned small sums, for example as half-timers in textile mills, or through doing casual chores such as cleaning doorsteps, childminding, working in shops, or hawking and selling. Very often these earnings were contributions to the housekeeping. Overall, mothers and children maintained a fierce sense of obligation to each other. Autobiographies and oral history evidence reiterate the importance of this bond. Children obeyed their mothers and contributed labour with household chores. Mothers provided for their children at whatever cost to themselves, nursed them through sickness or accident, and defended them unquestioningly if they found themselves in any kind of trouble.

If mothers had authority over children, their relationship with their husbands was one of qualified subordination. Not a few men enforced their superiority with violence, and many others assumed that they should be unquestionably masters of the house. A degree of male violence was tolerated, though a good husband was considered to be non-violent, sober and to regularly hand over the bulk of his wages as housekeeping. Because the structuring of labour markets was unequal and gendered, men were almost invariably able to earn far better wages than were women or children. It was in the whole household's interest to preserve a husband's capability to bring home this wage. This interest was combined with gendered assumptions about social roles, which ensured that in general husbands and fathers consumed as of right the largest share of the household's resources. As surveys such as those of Booth and Rowntree showed, for much of this period many working-class incomes were simply not sufficient to provide a good diet for the whole family. Where women and children lived chiefly on bread and margarine washed down with tea, men were provided with meat and other delicacies.[37]

A husband expected his "relishes" at tea or dinner – an egg, a chop or a kipper. Most mothers also aimed to provide a hot meal for themselves and their children once a day, usually something like suet pudding, vegetable stew or boiled potatoes. When money was tight, perhaps because a doctor's bill had to be paid or shoes repaired, bread was substituted for cooked food. "Pepper and salt slosh" (hot water poured over well-seasoned bread) was one mother's solution to this problem. This pattern, with its nutritionally-poor diet for women and children and far better food for the breadwinner, was strikingly persistent in the twentieth century, up to the interwar period at least, despite the enormous amount of social and economic change that took place and the slow but significant rise in real wages. By the 1920s, the families of better-paid men earning 30/- or more a week certainly experienced better nutrition and housing, but lower-earning families did not enjoy these improvements until after the Second World War.[38]

Overall, self-deprivation was the chief means that working-class wives used to make ends meet. Many women skipped meals to feed husbands and children. If necessary, children could go without before their father suffered. And many "good" husbands and fathers, tired and hungry no doubt after an arduous day's labour, accepted this situation. Often men had meals separately from the rest of the family, so it was comparatively simple to avoid knowing what the rest of the family ate or did not eat. This constructed blindness meant that many men were unaware of women's skills in household management and consequently undervalued them. Joseph Brooks, brought up in Lancashire by his grandparents, knew that "butties" doled out by grandfather were far larger and better spread than grandmother's wafer-thin slices. Maud Pember Reeves tells of a husband looking after the family while his wife was away. The margarine ran out because he made the mistake of giving all the children the amount he normally received. He overspent on fuel and had to contribute the full amount of his wages to the housekeeping, including his usual 4 shillings per week pocket money.[39]

Working-class men were not necessarily uncaring domestic tyrants. There is evidence of husbands and wives who were emotionally close, if often undemonstrative. Some men did help with the household chores. In places where there was comparatively well paid work for women, a more egalitarian sexual division of domestic labour was sometimes arrived at.

Many men were attached to their children and some played a part in childcare. Even where the sexual division of labour was absolute, men generally respected their wife's autonomy in the domestic sphere. In many ways, a husband was "mother's youngest child".[40] Her control of the household budget meant a wife often made decisions about where to live and when to move. More than one source gives examples of men who came home from work to find that the family had moved house during the day and had to ask neighbours where they had gone. Mothers not only claimed rights over their older children's wages, they also exercised sanctions over leisure activities and friends, particularly for daughters. Mothers used their social contacts to find employment for children. Rosemary Crooks argues that in the Rhondda of the 1930s, wives' involvement with the Chapel gave them cultural authority in the community. They could enforce their husbands' good behaviour in childminding duties at Sunday School outings.[41]

Women managed by depriving themselves of resources of all kinds. Repeated pregnancy and heavy household labour combined with an inadequate diet meant that many working-class women were in very poor health. Very few sought medical attention until the situation reached a crisis and they were physically unable to continue, by which time extensive and permanent damage was often likely. As well as doing without food and medical care, many women lacked decent clothing and especially footwear. The demands of household labour kept women indoors for much of their day, and the fact that many of them lacked boots was another reason to stay home. Many Birmingham women shopped late on a Saturday evening, not only because it was possible to buy cheap cuts of meat and bruised vegetables just before the shops shut, but also because they could then go out in their slippers under cover of darkness.[42]

There were, of course, more positive skills involved in household management. Shopping required a keen eye, plenty of local knowledge and a refusal to be fobbed off with second best. Making children's clothes, bedding, rugs and other household items required both skill and inventiveness. Very many women took pride in their housekeeping and in the cleanliness and neatness of their houses. Even more strove to educate and bring up their children, and were justly proud of their successes.

Very often women were of great assistance to each other in the task of making ends meet. The local focus of working-class women's lives – that of the neighbourhood and the street – enabled them to establish mutual social support networks. Extended families very often lived close to each other, and mothers, grandmothers and sisters maintained strong links. Neighbours also kept up regular contact, meeting in the street, at the shop, in each other's houses or chatting on the doorstep. There was a constant traffic between households of goods and services, all borrowed and strictly repaid. Much of this was short term and *ad hoc* – borrowing sixpence to buy the tea and repaying that evening when a child came home with some wages. Some of it was more regular – for example, arrangements for childcare if mothers or older siblings were working. Childcare arrangements in particular could be more extended, and some children lived for years with relations or neighbours. Where working-class incomes were uncertain and irregular, this kind of borrowing and lending was vital to smooth over the gaps. When a family met a major crisis such as illness, death or unemployment, neighbours and kin could be expected to provide immediate help and often more substantial assistance.[43]

Some neighbourhood assistance was organized on a cash basis. Young couples living with parents paid board and lodging. Regular childminding was often paid for, even when done by a family member. Whether arrangements involved cash payments depended on personal negotiation, but seem to have been related to the cash needs of each household. A married woman working, say, in the textile mills, introduced cash not only into her household economy but also into that of the woman who minded her children. The childminder provided a service for one or more other women and was able to earn income while remaining at home with her own children. Belinda Leach has argued that the outwork system in the Birmingham metal trades enabled a pragmatic reponse whereby women used their extended kin networks to earn income and find social support. The metalwork provided subsistence not only for Grandma Page but also for other extended family members at various times. The semi-casual work paid on piece rates meant that kin could use the work as a flexible expedient to provide those marginal yet crucial inputs of resources that women needed to sustain their household economies.[44]

Women also used commercial enterprises such as pawnshops and moneylenders that enabled them to even up the income flow without earning directly themselves. Every neighbourhood had one or more pawnshops, and women's use of them varied. Some would "pop" the Sunday best regularly on a Monday morning, redeeming it on Saturday when the wages arrived. Others tried hard to avoid the pawnshop, and some women made a small income delivering bundles on behalf of those who did not want to be seen in the queue. Local money lenders were often women who began lending for interest out of a small cash surplus or perhaps because their main wage arrived on a Thursday, and the rest of the street was not paid until Friday or Saturday. Money lenders charged very high rates of interest, not infrequently over 400 per cent as an annual rate. Although the fear of debt was widespread and could undermine respectability, local moneylenders and pawnshops nevertheless provided a much needed service in emergencies.[45]

As well as borrowing, pawning or exchanging services, women also saved. Some hid away money at home – others slept with their purse under their pillow. A smaller number used savings banks. Most working-class families paid burial insurance premiums for their children, and many paid the husband's "club". This was sickness and death insurance, generally provided by friendly societies, but increasingly by commercial insurers. The state then intervened with the 1911 National Insurance Act, which provided for free treatment by a GP and basic sick pay for employed men who contributed to the scheme. Many women found all kinds of systems of weekly payment useful. Shops organized clothing clubs, where the purchase of a weekly ticket including an interest payment enabled women to save up to buy children's clothes or boots. Roman Catholic parishes in Preston organized clothing clubs. Women also ran their own savings clubs. "Diddly clubs" operated over weeks or months. Groups of women paid weekly subscriptions beginning with a farthing (a quarter of an old penny) and increasing by a farthing a week. The club funds were then shared out, often at Christmas. Carl Chinn has noted that it was the trusted and powerful neighbourhood matriarchs who organized such clubs in Sparkbrook, Birmingham. Although very useful, such informal arrangements always ran the risk of embezzlement, or an absconding fundholder. Isabella Gardner and Ann Crabtree of Lancaster came to blows in 1875 over money that Ann allegedly owed to a clothing club. It is a measure of the effectiveness of women's social networks that such arrangements remained popular despite such risks.[46]

As Ellen Ross has authoritatively argued, women were crucial to the survival of working-class households in their role as household manager.[47] Their responsibility for the control of family consumption involved a wide range of skills and gave them a real level of authority in their household and neighbourhood. It provided the basis of a close emotional bond, particularly between mothers and children. Despite the formal status of the husband and his privileged access to food, pocket money and other resources, most men deferred to their wife's decision-making in domestic matters. Women used a range of strategies to make ends meet and to cope with the problems of scarce and fluctuating resources. As well as earning income themselves as and when necessary, shopping carefully, economizing and sometimes saving, their chief strategies were self-deprivation and the utilization of the support of children, kin and neighbourhood support networks.

Domestic labour

As well as managing their households, women were responsible for carrying out or supervising the housework. In the nineteenth century, domestic work was arduous, physically demanding and time consuming. This was true whether it was done by servants in a middle-class or upper-class household, or by wives, mothers and daughters without cash payment in working-class or lower middle-class homes. By the interwar period of the twentieth century, improvements in housing and amenities, and the manufacture and sale of consumer durables powered by gas or electricity, had gone some way to reduce the hard labour.

F. M. L. Thompson describes the Victorian middle-class as "the most home-centred group in British history".[48] The homes of the affluent were improved and modernized through the later nineteenth century to improve the "offices" which housed the infrastructure for the more formal elaboration of domestic life that genteel culture increasingly called for, and to establish a living space that was specialized, and segregated by both age and gender. The living environment created aimed to protect genteel women from "seeing or doing anything unseemly, unfitting or upsetting".[49] The labour of numbers of predominantly female servants were required to achieve this lifestyle. A formalized, segregated domestic environment on a more limited budget was attempted in the suburbs by the middle and lower middle-classes, through one or two specialized rooms (the master's study and the mistress's drawing room), and the apparently unceasing labour of a maid-of-all-work.

Among the lower middle-class and the respectable working-class, the maintenance of a separate best parlour for special occasions symbolized respectable domesticity: "It was class to have a parlour".[50] Working people who could afford it avoided slum areas, and even in very limited accommodation kept a special chair for father and maintained segregation at mealtimes by expecting children to eat standing, or in silence, or by the father having his meal separately. Even allowing for the autonomy of working-class respectable culture, the elements of formalization and segregation were present. Into the twentieth century, the development of working-class accommodation on housing estates provided bathrooms and more living space for better-off working people. These patterns of domestic culture depended crucially on household labour, mostly carried out by women. Notions of respectability, gentility, privacy and segregation structured and provided a rationale for a great deal of women's household labour.[51]

Within the home, cooking and lighting became rather easier with the introduction of gas as a domestic fuel in the late-nineteenth century. Most of the initial expansion of the gas industry was supported by the domestic market, which still accounted for 65 per cent of gas sales in 1939. Gas was marketed energetically by renting out appliances and installing slot meters. Electricity was initially very expensive compared to gas: only after the introduction of metal filament lamps and with improved distribution through a Central Electricity Board in 1926 did the price of domestic electricity fall, and its use for lighting, ironing or sometimes space heating became more common. In 1931, 32 per cent of English households had electricity, and 86 per cent in 1949. By 1948, 86 per cent of households had electric irons, 40 per cent had vacuum cleaners, 19 per cent cookers, 15 per cent electric water heaters, 4 per cent washing machines and 2 per cent fridges.[52] It was this change in technology that coincided with the reluctance of working-class women to work as domestic servants that emphasized the new ideologies and practices of housecraft as being a fit occupation for genteel and respectable married women whose access to the paid labour force was weakened by the introduction of the marriage bar towards the end of the nineteenth century, which required women to leave certain occupations when they married.

Despite these far-reaching changes, the benefits of improved housing and technological development were rationed by cost, and they varied regionally. Many poorer women saw little real benefit: the 1961 census showed that 22 per cent of the population of England and Wales did not have a hot tap in their home. For other women, these changes simply meant that increased standards of cleanliness and order became the norm. Before the nineteenth century, only a minority of people lived in large towns and cities. Most working people lived in thatched, dirt-floored cottages and even the middling sort had comparatively fewer domestic posessions and clothes than in subsequent periods. Fuel gathering, the collection of water, and tending animals designed for food were major components of domestic labour.[53] In the nineteenth century, the growth of the middle-class and the lifestyle that they evolved, saw the creation of fussy domestic interiors crammed with the icons of genteel living. All this meant that the nineteenth century historically was the period when cleaning came to be an important part of housework.

The proliferation of domestic possessions in middle-class households meant an elaboration in the kinds of cleaning technique that servants carried out. Dating from the beginning of our period, Hannah Cullwick's diaries relate the extent and the detail of scrubbing, sweeping, carpet beating, polishing, lifting and shifting that nineteenth-century housework required. Hannah may have been an exceptional general servant in the enthusiasm she had for her work – and in her eighteen-inch biceps. Nevertheless, many hundreds of thousands of Victorian women – entering domestic service in their adolescence – shouldered this kind of workload. And while servants were cheap and readily available, throughout the nineteenth century, changes in the basic processes of housework were not considered. Only in the twentieth century, when labour market change was offering alternative paid work to young working-class women, did the technology of housework begin to change on any appreciable scale.[54]

In very large establishments, much of the organization and control of domestic labour was delegated to senior servants, but middle-class women had to deal with their servants directly and frequently. The bourgeoise family was constructed as both moral and private, so the presence of a working-class outsider, however essential to keep the household functioning, was something of a contradiction. The middle-class attempted to overcome this difficulty by exacting the maximum possible control over the lives of their servants. The model of servants and tenants as dependants of a landed upper-class estate became transformed into a more familial model of authority and subordination in the middle-class home. Servants' working days were stretched to 18 hours, and time off was infrequent and hedged about with restrictions. Rules as to clothing, behaviour and followers (boyfriends) were strict.[55] The growing number of households on a lower income who kept servants also had every interest in getting as much work out of them as possible. The relationship between a mistress and her servants could never be reduced to simple labour hire. A mistress rooted her authority in her moral authority in the private sphere as well as her position as employer. Servants, of course, resisted these attempts to control and remoralize them, principally by moving regularly to a different position. Although some servants stayed in post for many years, most (especially those in one- or two-servant households) changed jobs about every 12 months.[56]

If middle-class women were able to distance themselves from the heavy labour of housework by employing servants, working-class women had to carry the burden unaided. The poor standards of housing available to working people presented women with an insoluble problem. Crumbling plaster, flagged or even earth floors, no piped water, shared privies, overcrowding, infestations of bugs and rats, inadequate storage for food and fuel, and a very constrained income, meant that high standards of cleanliness were impossible to achieve. At the same time, women were subject to pressure from middle-class "visitors", keen to educate and remoralize the "dirty" poor,[57] and, more importantly, had a clear motivation to preserve their family's dignity and respectability in their own eyes and those of their neighbours. Despite the odds, very many working-class and lower middle-class women toiled ceaselessly to achieve a clean and comfortable home.

In the mid-nineteenth century, heating and cooking were fuelled by coal, which, although it was delivered to affluent households who could afford to buy in bulk and store it it cellars, still had to be carried to the fireplaces and the ashes removed by servants. Coal is a more efficient fuel than wood or peat, but it is dirtier and leaves a thick dust over carpets, curtains, furniture and ornaments. As well as space heating, coal fuelled the kitchen range, "a dirty, inefficient, labour-making, fuel-devouring monster that made the place unbearable in hot weather".[58] Coal was also the chief fuel in the nineteenth-century working-class household, despite the dirt it made and its expense when purchased in the small quantities these women's budgets allowed. It was burned in a kitchen range or an open fire, which provided hot water, space heating and cooking. The limitations of inefficient ranges or open-fire cookery as well as scarce and poor utensils meant that food preparation needed to be kept simple, mostly frying or stewing. Middle-class advocacy of porridge as a cheap and nutritious meal, for example, fell on deaf ears, since it tasted foul without milk (too expensive for most budgets) and burnt over the unpredictable fire, ruining the pan. Bread was a far more convenient staple.

By contrast, the elaboration and ritual on which middle-class domesticity was based meant that food preparation became increasingly complex. Margaret Powell's description of her work as a kitchen maid at the beginning of the twentieth century, not only tending the range and scrubbing and cleaning the vast array of cooking utensils required to prepare an upper middle-class dinner, but also chopping endless vegetables into matchstick-sized pieces and sieving meat broth through muslin to make consommé, provides an illustration of what kind of labour and skill was involved.[59]

In the mid-nineteenth century, even modest middle-class homes had piped water and sewage systems, but servants still had to carry water upstairs for washing or bathing, and to heat all the domestic hot water on the kitchen range. Fetching and carrying water was also a time-consuming task in most working-class homes. In 1850 the government's General Board of Health estimated it would take two days' work per week to fetch the 20 pails (or 500 lbs) of water it considered necessary for a labouring family's sanitary needs. Mrs Pember Reeves found that in 1917 fetching water was still a heavy task for many women in Lambeth, particularly those that had upstairs lodgings. The weekly clothes wash took the whole of a long, exhausting day on a Monday or a Tuesday. Most British women continued to wash by hand throughout this period.[60]

Some provincial cities such as Manchester had provided internal water supplies for the majority of its houses by the later 1870s, but other areas lagged behind, and in the countryside, basic amenities took even longer to provide. In 1913, 62 per cent of rural houses in England lacked piped water, and even in 1951 the figure was 20 per cent for houses in England and Wales.[61] One of the chief "luxuries" provided by moving to a new council house in the 1920s was a hot water system. You "just open the tap and that was it. Smashing".[62] Elizabeth Roberts' investigation of Lancashire towns before the First World War shows that a shared outside tap was the majority experience. The communal tap met a variety of uses, including swilling out chamber pots in the morning.[63]

As well as communal water supplies, many working-class families before the First World War shared privies, middens and sometimes clothes-washing space with their neighbours. On washing day, backyards, courts and alleys were festooned with lines of drying washing.[64] Crowded living not only meant that this neighbourhood territory was the site of play, gossip and other social interaction; it also formed a necessarily public extension of women's household workspace and brought neighbours into close contact with each other. As I have argued this had effects in cementing the social relations that consolidated vital social support networks.

It could also generate conflict, as differential standards of respectability and of aspirations to domestic privacy were (sometimes literally) fought out by women. Local police courts teem with examples of such disputes. Three 1875 cases from Lancaster illustrate the point. Neighbours Emma Leake and Sarah Garrett came to blows because Garrett had allegedly left the communal water tap running. Elizabeth Ann Anderton and several neighbours were involved in a brawl which started because greengrocer Thomas Burrows could not load his cart in their shared yard because of all the washing hung out to dry. In the nearby town of Carnforth, William Willan, a railway worker, smashed the shared pump with an axe and assaulted his neighbour Elizabeth Dent who kept the key to the pump and would not let him use it.[65]

The demarcation of public and domestic space is inextricably bound up with that of establishing and maintaining respectability. The starched and spotless net curtains at the front window as well as the donkey-stoned or red-ochred front doorstep and flagstones on either side required women's intensive labour without making any material improvement to their family's domestic comfort. Other tasks such as black-leading the grate had the same, purely symbolic, effect. These icons of good housekeeping and domestic respectability not only proclaimed the family's status to the rest of the neighbourhood, they were also the means whereby working-class women negotiated the dilemma between the desire to demonstrate the excellence of their domestic skills and the intractable physical and environmental circumstances they had to cope with. As one woman said of Lancashire in the 1920s, "They were very houseproud, you know. They used to vie with each other who could have the nicest curtains".[66]

Although the 1930s saw depression and unemployment in areas of heavy industry, new light industries, particularly in the South and Midlands, provided alternative employment to domestic service for young working-class women. Live-in domestic servants were less freely available and, increasingly, middle-class families relied on daily helps. Wives and mothers took on more of the domestic tasks, assisted by the increasing number of domestic appliances (irons, vacuum cleaners, toasters, cookers and washing machines) coming on to the market. Much of the new light industry that produced these goods employed working-class women seeking better wages and conditions than they could obtain in domestic service.[67] Household management and mothercraft were presented as worthwhile career occupations for women below the upper middle class, when accomplished according to rigorous and scientific methods.

As middle-class wives and mothers became absorbed increasingly in housework, for them too, housework and the domestic role made the product of their own labour a direct expression of the family's gentility. Advice manuals of the 1930s directed the middle-class housewife in the minutiae of her duties. According to one advice manual, entitled *The marriage book for husbands and wives - and all who love children*, a wife should have all manner of skills and knowledge herself, as well as employing a servant or a daily help.[68] She was expected to be accomplished in cookery, household budgeting and accounts, table laying and decoration ("Glass birds or animals set on a piece of mirror glass form a bright decoration round a vase of glass flowers"), kitchen care and equipment ("All small tin utensils are all the better for a weekly boiling in soda water . . . but aluminium ware should, of course, never be washed with soda"), the care of the linen cupboard ("To most housewives the linen cupboard is the centre of their housewifely pride"), interior design, child development, and in maintaining a thriving emotional and sexual relationship with her husband. A suggested daily timetable for a mother of a small baby begins at 6 am and finishes with baby's last bottle at 9.55 pm. The husband presumably received attention thereafter.

Ideological reformulation and social change into the twentieth century

Advice manuals such as this aimed to dignify domestic labour by middle-class women with a sense of professionalism and purpose. They were a response to structural change and also to new ideas about women's domestic role that had become established during the interwar period. It is, however, a moot point whether the new ideologies of maternalism within the companionate family which highlighted family privacy, in fact raised women's status or whether they actively reinforced women's subordination. Family limitation coincided with a greater value being placed on family privacy, shared leisure and closer personal relationships. Despite the urgings of feminist intellectuals, however, the division of household labour remained substantially unchanged. Men's increased interest in family life, encouraged by patriarchal authority, could in some cases act to erode areas of female autonomy within the private sphere, such as having sole control of servants, or female-only leisure activities.[69]

The essence of genteel domesticity remained the economic dependence of women, despite the increasing acceptance of professional and white collar employment, or even academic study for unmarried adult daughters where the household income was insufficient to support them. However, apparent autonomy possible for genteel women through wage-earning remained subordinated to ideals of family domesticity.[70] Gendered labour market structures meant that women in paid work were always subject to patriarchal power hierarchies, and legal and other regulations, for their "protection". As Lown has argued, workplace relationships borrowed and reinforced familial models of authority. Many young women also found their freedom hedged about with reinforced codes of respectable behaviour and subject to familial

71

consent. Sophia Jex-Blake, for example, gained a lecturing post, and her father offered to increase her allowance if she did not take the job by the amount of salary she would have earned.[71] Philanthropic work or positions in local government (on School Boards, as Poor Law Guardians or as local councillors) could be interpreted as an extension of women's familial caring role and remained less prestigious than similar work done by men.[72] Of course, the subordination of genteel women's increasingly complex public role to domestic ideals was never complete. The progressive vision of the "new woman" in the early twentieth century, and the new-found freedom of many turn-of-the-century professional women would have been impossible if it had been.[73] However, the tensions and contradictions involved can perhaps explain the ambivalence and frustration of numbers of "new women" who have left accounts of their lives and feelings.

Beatrice Webb (social investigator and co-founder with her husband Sidney of the London School of Economics) found it personally and emotionally difficult to reconcile her professional life with her desire for marriage and domesticity. As a young woman, Beatrice chose the role of "glorified spinster" in preference to marriage to Joseph Chamberlain, and her decision later to marry Sidney Webb was by no means a straightforward one. Despite the challenges and satisfactions of paid, philanthropic or other work, the single life was not an easy choice. However, the alternative was also fraught with difficulty. Maria Sharpe, secretary of the Men's and Women's Club (a radical mixed-sex discussion group in 1880s London) married the club's founder, social Darwinist, Karl Pearson, in 1890. She had earlier maintained an intense emotional relationship with another Club member, Lina Eckstein. Although Maria spent the last thirty years of her life married to Pearson, devoting herself to their children and domestic life, she had agreed to the marriage only after a great emotional struggle at the prospect of her loss of independence. She had been a writer and a researcher but published almost nothing after the marriage and saw her maternal and domestic role as a duty. Many other less well-documented women must also have found it hard to reconcile their desire for a fulfilling emotional and sexual life with the social requirements of a married woman's role.[74]

The relationship between the apparent autonomy of the "new woman" and changing ideals of domesticity was therefore complex. The scientific authority of late-nineteenth and early-twentieth-century discourses of women's biological maternal destiny set the frame of discussion, even for supporters of the suffrage and of women's rights to employment. Eugenic ideas had made a very real impact on wide areas of philanthropy and public policy by the later-nineteenth century. These ideas reflected a concern to improve (or halt the decline in) the quality of the race.

Herbert Spencer and others writing from the 1870s sharpened Charles Darwin's ideas of sexual difference and of progress and social evolution.

Social Darwinists argued that women's individual development was arrested earlier in the life cycle than men's, to conserve energies for reproduction. The greater degree of racial advance, the better adapted were its women to reproduction, thus improving the quality of each succeeding generation. Racial development thus increased sexual differences. It was therefore widely argued that women's personal choices had to be subordinated to the scientifically and morally "higher" goal of racial advancement.[75]

Eugenicists focused on the declining fertility of the middle-class, on working-class infant welfare, and on the persistently high infant mortality rates. They too frequently blamed working-class mothers for the failure of their social and imperial duties to nurture the rising generation. Even Marie Stopes' mission to provide barrier contraception to the working-class in the 1920s was informed by notions of racial improvement. As Anna Davin has written, a great deal of social policy at the turn of the twentieth century was targeted on overcoming working-class women's perceived failure as mothers of an imperial nation. There were some practical benefits for working-class mothers in the measures that resulted from eugenic ideas – such as infant welfare clinics and more readily available barrier contraceptives – but there were other initiatives, such as domestic science in elementary schools, that had little relevance to their lives. Family-orientated social welfare policy in the early twentieth century was not intended primarily for the benefit of women. The goal was to achieve social reform through inculcation of a rational and energetic citizenship in individuals. Mothers were to be the agents of that change through their role in the family.[76]

Eugenics contributed to a major reformulation in ideologies of domesticity – a move away from explanations based in the moral discourse derived from evangelical religion and towards justifications for the separation of the private sphere and the economic and social dependence of women based in science and medicine. Although not all women were mothers, motherhood was clearly the manifest destiny of women. Increasingly, a distinction came to be drawn between what might be appropriate for single women, and their subsequent duties and role as mothers. These and other threads of public discourse all converged to underline a maternalistic view of the genteel woman, and overall by the end of the nineteenth century ideals of motherhood, its importance, its duties and, of course, its obligations, had been reinforced strongly. We have seen that declining marital fertility had been accompanied by changing notions of the obligations of parenthood. Fewer pregnancies combined with the ideological reinforcement of maternalism to channel women's energies into higher standards of domestic management, housework and childcare.[77]

By the turn of the century, however, ideologies of motherhood were reformulated in a more positive light. Eugenic concerns over the falling birthrate among educated women and the middle-classes more generally led to an increasing emphasis on the "importance of healthy and intelligent motherhood to an imperial nation".[78] Influential biologists Patrick Geddes and J. Arthur Thompson argued that sex roles were different but complementary, and that women should be educated, healthy and thus competent to choose eugenically sound mates. This new, more positive, role of motherhood combined with an increasing (if sometimes grudging) acceptance of respectable paid work, philanthropy or local government service for women, making use of their maternal qualities in the public sphere. This social maternalism had its feminist and non-feminist aspects.[79]

The popularization of Freudian ideas reinforced the notion of the non-maternal woman as deviant. The strong appeal of maternalist discourse eclipsed the distinctiveness of feminist argument in the interwar period. Many "new feminists" used maternalist arguments to achieve specific material gains for women. Eleanor Rathbone's persistent campaign for family allowances and the "new feminists" in the interwar Labour Party provide examples of this. A new emphasis on maternal competence provided some help and guidance for both working-class and middle-class mothers, but overall, maternal duties were elaborated and proliferated. Progressive views represented motherhood and domestic duties in the language of work, craft and skill. In the interwar period authorities on childcare such as Sir Frederick Truby King stipulated an organized, disciplined and timetabled regime. Too much physical contact and cuddling were discouraged because of anxieties about infection, and babies were to be fed only at four-hour intervals, however much they cried: to feed on demand would damage the digestion and produce a spoilt child. In the 1940s and 1950s the advice began to change, though a mother's duties remained just as onerous. Figures such as Donald Winnicott and John Bowlby argued that babies and young children needed their mother's attention continuously. Bowlby's widely-accepted theory of maternal deprivation made mothers alone responsible for their children's psychological development, and threatened dire consequences for cases of neglect.[80]

These changes in ideas reflected and interpreted social change. The marriage bar, which meant that women in the Civil Service, teaching and other occupations were required to leave work when they married, was introduced in the early twentieth century. Although debated in 1927, the legislation was not repealed until after the Second World War. The marriage bar admitted unmarried women into, but excluded married women from, the professional and white collar workforce. This legislation gave concrete effect to maternalist ideology in the lives of many middle-class and lower middle-class women. In 1901, 29.1 per cent of all women, including 6.3 per cent of married women, were in paid work. By 1931 the comparable figures were 29.7 per cent and 4.8 per cent.[81] Single women's paid work had increased at the expense of married women's.

Respectability, gentility, privacy and the companionate marriage

Although ideas of male superiority were not overturned in the hundred years before 1940, the character of idealized marital relationships underwent a clear change from the assumptions of thoroughgoing subordination typical of the mid-nineteenth century. The rather more positive image of the wife and mother reinforced by turn-of-the-century maternalism was accompanied by a view of marriage as a partnership. This did not mean any blurring of differential sex roles, nor of the sexual division of household labour – rather a complementarity between husband and wife that could provide the basis for companionship and affection.

Of course, these representations mask a great deal of variation in people's experience. Some Victorian wives had very close relationships with their husbands, and equally some interwar husbands made sure of their wives' thorough subordination. Nevertheless, the period did see a marked change in the representations and discourses about marriage. The use of contraception came to accompany expectations of the "sensuous wife" and mutually fulfilling sexual experience within marriage. These views gained publicity and greater acceptance through the writings of such Social Darwinists as Marie Stopes.[82]

The increasing availability of consumer goods not only changed household labour, it also enhanced domesticity through family-based leisure activities. A piano in the parlour, and later a radio, formed the centrepiece of family evenings at home. Cheaper rail travel, the development of holiday resorts and the mass production of the bicycles also broadened the scope of commercially provided leisure opportunities. By 1940, England had 4,800 cinemas. Shorter working hours gave more opportunity for leisure. Although people shared outings with friends, neighbours, workmates or fellow club, chapel or church members, families also spent increasing amounts of leisure time together. Smaller families made trips and seaside holidays together a more practical proposition. Among more affluent families too, the increased attention to parenting and companionship in marriage encouraged family leisure activities.[83]

Changing housing patterns and improved transportation led to the development of new suburbs. By the early twentieth century many middle-class suburbs sheltered acutely gendered patterns of daily life. Speaking of the affluent suburban village of Alderley Edge, south of Manchester, in the late nineteenth century, Katherine Chorley recalled that:

> After the 9.18 train had pulled out of the station the Edge became exclusively female. You never saw a man on the hill roads unless it were the doctor or the plumber, and you never saw a man in anyone's house except the gardener or the coachman.[84]

By the interwar period, working-class housing estates were being built outside the old urban centres from which men commuted daily to their work, and less affluent women were also experiencing the effect of comparative isolation in day-time. Economic change and depression had stimulated migration to larger urban areas and to the South and East of Britain. Housing estates provided better accommodation, but dimished the community life and employment opportunities available to women. State decisions, such as the size and design of council houses, encouraged smaller family size and reinforced privacy by spatial organization of the estate. The working-class or lower middle-class families on housing estates provide an apparent contrast to the more crowded communities in urban neighbourhoods, where domestic life perforce spilled on to the streets. Nevertheless, cultures of working-class respectability towards the end of the nineteenth century tended to move towards more domestic privacy as rising incomes allowed. The private household that "kept itself to itself" behind net curtains was earlier, perhaps, more typical of the lower middle class.[85]

The eventual widespread acceptance of a more companionate view of marriage can be seen in the legal changes enacted between the 1850s and the 1940s which gave married women control over their own property and enabled divorce on the same grounds for wives as for husbands. A number of significant Acts of Parliament were passed. The Matrimonial Causes Act of 1857 allowed divorce without the need for a separate Act of Parliament, but on unequal grounds. The Married Women's Property Acts in 1870 and 1882 eroded the legal doctrine of *couverture*, which stated that a married woman's property was owned by her husband. These Acts gave married women the right to control their own earnings and property. The Matrimonial Causes Act of 1923 stipulated the same grounds for divorce for men and women. Grounds for divorce were extended in 1937 to include cruelty, insanity and desertion.[86] However, the extent of the parliamentary and public resistance to this legislation and the fact that it took a century to achieve these changes indicates that companionate marriage did not necessarily mean an overturning of women's subordination within the family. As Finch and Summerfield have argued, even the new emphasis on companionate marriage during the period of social reconstruction following the Second World War did not envisage marriage as being egalitarian. True, there was to be "teamwork", but within an essentially unequal team: wives and mothers were now also allocated the responsibility of the family's emotional and psychological, as well as its material, well-being.[87]

Even apparently positive legislation had differential effects, particularly across class. For example, although the Married Woman's Property Acts gave property owning women rights to control their assets, working-class wives became comparatively even more disadvantaged. Though the legislation allowed them to control their own earnings, overall policy and legislation on marriage and a patriarchally-structured labour market still barred many women from earning a living wage. Differences by region, by occupational group and other factors also affected the ways in which social and ideological change had an impact on the experience of women and their families, and must qualify any assumption of a broad, progressive improvement in women's lives since the mid-nineteenth century.

Conclusion

Throughout the century after 1850 the private sphere was very much on the public mind. The Victorian middle-class had developed a culture with a role for women which, although subordinating them as individuals, gave great importance to domestic life and the role of the "angel in the house". The religious basis of these ideas gave way around the turn of the twentieth century to scientific and social Darwinist explanations which re-emphasised the importance of the maternal role. Whatever the professional, public service or academic challenges met by the "new woman", these gains remained in tension with heightened expectations of women as mothers. Family-centred social policy was not intended to improve the lot of women *as women*. An improved standard of living for most sections of society was eventually achieved through economic growth and industrial development, but very often women's subordination of their own interests to those of their families meant that they were the last to benefit. Marginal increments of household income were often spent on the material accoutrements of a new, more private domesticity, based on fewer children and a longer life span.[88] Even the development of more apparently companionate family relationships, because they were linked to higher standards of childcare and housecraft, did not necessarily mean any radical alteration to the power balance of gender relations in the family. With the concomitant diminution of women's neighbourhood solidarities and the critical importance of their skills as household managers, the improvement to their health and material comfort seems to have been bought at the loss of some autonomy. Many middle-class women, too, were further committed to housecraft and domesticity. Consequently, the family remained an important site of women's subordination into the mid-twentieth century.

Notes

1. Two particularly opinionated studies are, L. Stone, *The family, sex and marriage in England from 1500 to 1800* (London: Weidenfeld & Nicolson, 1977); E. Shorter, *The making of the modern family* (London: Fontana, 1977).
2. M. Llewelyn-Davies (ed.), *Maternity, letters from working-class women* (London: Virago, 1978; first published 1913), p. 60.

3. E. Slater & M. Woodside, *Patterns of marriage* (London: Cassell, 1951), p. 198.

4. M. V. Hughes, *A London family, 1870-1900* (London: Oxford University Press, 1946), p. 33.

5. C. Dyhouse, *Girls growing up in Victorian and Edwardian England* (London: Routledge & Kegan Paul, 1981), p. 35; C. Dyhouse, *Feminism and the family in England, 1880-1939* (Oxford, Blackwell, 1989), pp. 45-6.

6. H. Mitchell, *The hard way up; the autobiography of Hannah Mitchell suffragette and rebel* (London: Faber & Faber, 1968; London, Virago, 1977); D. Chew (ed.), *Ada Nield Chew, the life and writing of a working woman* (London: Virago, 1982); Llewelyn Davies, *Maternity*, p. 41; C. Chinn, *They worked all their lives; women of the urban poor in England 1880-1939* (Manchester, Manchester University Press, 1988).

7. H. I. Dutton & J. E. King, *Ten per cent and no surrender* (Cambridge: Cambridge University Press, 1981), p. 52; J. Lewis, *Women in England 1870-1950: sexual divisions and social change*, (Brighton: Wheatsheaf, 1984), p. 34.

8. J. F. C. Harrison, *The early Victorians, 1831-1851* (London: Weidenfeld & Nicolson, 1971).

9. R. J. Morris, "The middle-class and the property cycle during the Industrial Revolution", in *The search for wealth and stability*, T. C. Smout (ed.) (London: Macmillan, 1979), pp. 91-113; L. Davidoff & C. Hall, *Family fortunes, men and women of the English middle-class 1780-1850* (London: Hutchinson, 1987), Ch. 1, 6; C. Hall, *White, male and middle-class; explorations in feminism and history* (Oxford: Polity, 1992).

10. D. Gorham, *The Victorian girl and the feminine ideal*, (London: Croom Helm, 1982), pp. 3-4, 8.

11. J. Purvis, *Hard lessons, the lives and education of working-class women in nineteenth-century England* (Oxford: Polity Press, 1989), p. 53; Davidoff & Hall, *Family fortunes*; A. Levy, *Other women; the writing of class, race and gender, 1832-1898* (Princeton, NJ.: Princeton University Press, 1991), pp. 20-47; J. N. Burstyn, *Victorian education and the ideal of womanhood*, (London: Croom Helm, 1980), Ch. 1; A. Digby, "Victorian values and women in public and private", in T. C. Smout (ed.) *Victorian values*, Proceedings of the British Academy **78**, pp. 195-217, 1992.

12. P. Branca, *Silent sisterhood; middle-class women in the Victorian home* (London: Croom Helm, 1975), pp. 40-45; T. McBride, *The domestic revolution; the modernisation of household service in England and France, 1820-1920* (London: Croom Helm, 1976), pp. 19-20; Gorham, *The Victorian girl*, p. 9.

13. McBride, *Domestic revolution*, p. 29; Mrs I. Beeton, *The book of household management* (London: S. O. Beeton, 1861); L. Davidoff, *The best circles; society etiquette and the season* (London: Cresset, 1986), Ch. 3.

14. E. Gaskell, *Cranford* (Oxford: Oxford University Press, 1972), p. 3. *Cranford* was first serialised in *Household Words* in 1851-2; the first edition in book form was published in 1853. J. Uglow, *Elizabeth Gaskell; a habit of stories* (London: Faber & Faber, 1993), p. 618; Gorham, *The Victorian girl*, p. 11.

15. S. O. Rose, *Limited livelihoods, gender and class in nineteenth-century England* (Berkeley & Los Angeles, California, 1992); P. Levine, "Consistent contradictions; prostitution and protective labour legislation in nineteenth-century England", *Social History* **19** (1), pp. 17-35, 1988. For the Langham Place group, see C. Lacey (ed.), *Barbara Leigh Smith Bodichon and the Langham Place Group* (London: Routledge & Kegan Paul, 1987).

16. F. M. L. Thompson, *The rise of respectable society* (London: Fontana, 1988), pp. 52-3; D. Gittins, *The fair sex* (London: Hutchinson, 1982), p. 33.

17. Lewis, *Women in England*, pp. 4-5; Gittins, *The fair sex*, pp. 33-5.

18. P. Hollis, *Women in public, 1850-1900* (London: Allen & Unwin, 1979).

19. *Ibid.*, M. Vicinus, *Independent women: work and community for single women 1850-1920* (London: Virago, 1985); V. Brittain, *Testament of experience* (London: Gollancz, 1957).

20. Thompson, *The rise*, pp. 57-70.

21. *Ibid.*, pp. 66, 70, 81; Gittins, *The fair sex*, p. 185.

22. Thompson, *The rise*, pp. 95-8, 100.

23. Lewis, *Women in England*, pp. 4, 6.

24. *Ibid.*, pp. 17-18; Gittins, *The fair sex*, p. 33; Thompson, *The rise*, p. 77; A. McLaren, *Birth control in nineteenth-century England* (London: Croom Helm, 1978), pp. 182-90. For an argument of the more extensive, earlier use of barrier contraception, see M. Mason, *The making of Victorian sexuality* (Oxford: Oxford University Press, 1994).

25. Lewis, *Women in England*, pp. 25-6; P. Thane, *The foundations of the welfare state* (London: Longman, 1982), p. 85; Gittins, *The fair sex*, p. 42; M. Llewelyn Davies (ed.), *Maternity*.

26. Thompson, *The rise*, p. 115; Gittins, *The fair sex*, pp. 34, 62; McLaren, *Birth control*, p. 232.

27. Chinn, *They worked all their lives*, p. 135.

28. Thompson, *The rise,* p. 119.

29. *Ibid.*, pp. 120-2; A. Martin, *The married working woman; a study* (London: National Union of Women's Suffrage Societies, 1911); J. Burnett, *Plenty and want; a social history of diet in England from 1815 to the present day* (London: Scolar Press, 1972), p. 272.

30. T. Vigne, Parents and children, 1890-1918; distance and dependence, *Oral History* **3** (2), pp. 6-7, 1975.

31. Lady Bell, *At the works* (London: Edward Arnold, 1907; New York, Augustus Kelly, 1969), p. 194.

32. M. S. Pember Reeves, *Round about a pound a week* (London: Garland Publishing, 1980; first published 1913).

33. E. Roberts, *A woman's place, an oral history of working-class women 1890-1940* (Oxford: Blackwell, 1984); S. Pennington & B. Westover, *A hidden workforce, home-workers in England 1850-1985*, (London: Macmillan, 1989); D. Gittins, Marital status, work and kinship, 1850-1930", in *Labour and love, women's experience of home and family, 1850-1940*, J. Lewis (ed.) (Oxford: Blackwell, 1986), pp. 249-67; T. Thompson, *Edwardian childhoods* (London: Routledge & Kegan Paul, 1981), pp. 71-2.

34. P. Ayres, "The hidden economy of dockland families, Liverpool in the 1930s", in *Women's work and the family economy in historical perspective*, P. Hudson & W. R. Lee (eds) (Manchester: Manchester University Press, 1990), p. 280.

35. Lewis, *Women in England*, pp. 62-4, E. Ross, "Lady philanthropists and London housewives before the First World War" in, *Lady Bountiful revisited. Women, philanthropy and power* (New Brunswick, 1990), pp. 174-98; F. Prochaska, *Women and philanthropy in nineteenth-century England* (Oxford: Clarendon, 1980).

36. T. Thompson, *Edwardian childhoods*, pp. 10-11, 59.

37. N. Tomes, "A torrent of abuse; crimes of violence between working-class men and women in London, 1840-1875", *Journal of Social History* **11** (3), pp. 328-45, 1978; E. Ross, "Fierce questions and taunts', married life in working-class London, 1870-1914", *Feminist Studies* **8** (3), pp. 575-602, 1982; P. Ayers & J. Lambertz, "Marriage

relations, money and domestic violence in working-class Liverpool, 1919-39", in *Labour and love*, J. Lewis (ed.), pp. 195-222; A. James Hammerton, *Cruelty and companionship, conflict in nineteenth-century married life* (London: Routledge, 1992); M. Pember Reeves, *Round about a pound a week*, pp. 97, 103; C. Booth, *Life and labour of the people of London* (London: Macmillan, 1902); S.B. Rowntree, *Poverty, a study of town life* (London: Macmillan, 1903).

38. Chinn, *They worked all their lives*, pp. 62; J. Benson, *The working-class in Britain, 1850-1939*, (London: Longman, 1989), pp. 96-7; J. Burnett, *Plenty and want.*

39. J. Barlow Brooks, *Lancashire bred; an autobiography* (Cowley, Oxford, Church Army Press, 1950), p. 16; Pember Reeves, *Round about a pound a week*, p. 172-4; Chinn, *They worked all their lives*, p. 55; L. Oren, "The welfare of women in labouring families, England 1860-1950", *Feminist Studies* **1**, pp. 107-25, 1973; M. Spring Rice, *Working class wives, their health and conditions* (Harmondsworth: Penguin, 1939).

40. Roberts, *A woman's place*, pp. 82, 117-8; Lewis, *Women in England*, p. 6; M.E. Loane, *From their point of view* (London: Edward Arnold,1908), see Ch. 6, on the working-class father.

41. R. Crooks, "Tidy women; women in the Rhondda between the wars", *Oral History* **10** (2), p. 44, 1982.

42. Chinn, *They worked all their lives*, p. 66.

43. E. Ross, "Survival networks: women's neighbourhood sharing in London before World War 1", *History Workshop Journal* **15**, pp. 4-27, 1983; E. Roberts, *A woman's place*, Ch. 5.

44. B. Leach, "Grandma Page's workshop; outwork in Birmingham 1911-1914", *Oral History* **22** (1), pp. 35-42, (1994).

45. M. Tebbutt, *Making ends meet. Pawnbroking and working-class credit* (Leicester: Leicester University Press, 1983).

46. Chinn, *They worked all their lives*, pp. 35-6; P. Thane, *The foundations*, pp. 84-7; *Lancaster Gazette* (3 April 1875), p. 8; M. Pember Reeves, *Round about a pound a week*, p. 72.

47. E. Ross, *Love and toil, motherhood in outcast London, 1780-1918* (Oxford: Oxford University Press, 1993).

48. Thompson, *The rise*, p. 152.

49. Ibid., p. 157.

50. Roberts, *A woman's place*, p. 129.

51. E. Ross, *Love and toil*; T. Vigne, "Parents and children", p. 8.

52. C. Davidson, *A woman's work is never done: a history of housework in the British Isles 1650-1950* (London: Chatto & Windus, 1982), pp. 36, 38.

53. *Ibid.*, p. 125; B. Hill, *Women, work and sexual politics in eighteenth-century England* (Oxford: Blackwell, 1989), Ch. 7; S. Jackson, "Towards a historical sociology of housework, a materialist feminist analysis", *Women's Studies International Forum* **15** (2), pp. 153-72, 1992.

54. T. McBride, *The domestic revolution*, pp. 68-9; *The diaries of Hannah Cullwick*, L. Stanley (ed.) (New Brunswick: New Jersey, Rutgers University Press, 1984).

55. T. McBride, *The Domestic Revolution*, p. 55.

56. Ibid., pp. 67, 74.

57. Chinn, *They worked all their lives*, p. 122.

58. L. Wright, *Home fires burning; the history of domestic heating and cooking* (London: 1964), p. 121.

59. M. Powell, *Below Stairs* (New York: Dodd Mead, 1970).

60. C. Davidson, *A woman's work*, p. 16; M. Pember Reeves, *Round about a pound a week*, pp. 55-6; C. Zmroczek, "Dirty linen; women, class, and washing machines, 1920s-1960s", *Women's Studies International Forum* **15** (2), pp. 173-85, 1992; C. Zmroczek, "The weekly wash", in S. Oldfield (ed.), *This working day world: women's lives and culture(s) in Britain 1914-1945* (London: Taylor & Francis, 1994), pp. 7-17.

61. Davidson, *A woman's work*, pp. 31-2.

62. Roberts, *A woman's place*, p. 132.

63. *Ibid.*, p. 131.

64. *Ibid.*, pp. 133-8.

65. *Lancaster Gazette* (27 March 1875), p. 6; (26 June 1875), p. 8; (29 May 1875), p. 6.

66. Roberts, *A woman's place,* p. 127.

67. Glucksmann, *Women assemble* (London: Routledge, 1990).

68. *The marriage book for husbands and wives - and all who love children* (London: Amalgamated Press, c. 1930), pp. 334, 338, 339, 343.

69. Dyhouse, *Feminism and the family*, pp. 141-4; Gorham, *The Victorian girl*, p. 120.

70. *Ibid.*, pp. 28-9, 118-19.

71. Lewis, *Women in England*, pp. x, 79; J. Lown, *Women and industrialization, gender at work in nineteenth-century England* (Cambridge: Polity, 1990).

72. P. Hollis, *Ladies elect; women in English local government, 1865-1914* (Oxford: Clarendon Press, 1987).

73. The "new woman" of the late-nineteenth century had benefited from secondary education, took to philanthropic work or earned her own living, often professed "advanced ideas" and was generally more independent and less homebound than earlier generations. Vicinus, *Independent women*, Ch. 1; J. Walkowitz, *City of dreadful delights* (London: Virago, 1992), pp. 61-5. For a fictional account, see G. Gissing, *The odd women* (Harmondsworth: Penguin, 1993; first published 1893).

74. J. Lewis, *Women and social action in Victorian and Edwardian England* (Aldershot: Edward Elgar, 1991), pp. 93, 95, 121-5; Walkowitz, *City of dreadful delights*, Ch. 5.

75. Lewis, *Women in England*, pp. 83-4.

76. A. Davin, "Imperialism and motherhood", *History Workshop Journal* **5**, pp. 9-65, 1978.

77. J. Lewis, "Welfare states: gender, the family and women", *Social History* **19** (1), p. 50, 1994; Lewis, *Women and social action.*

78. Lewis, *Women in England*, p. x.

79. *Ibid.*, pp. 98, 100.

80. *Ibid.*, pp. 101-4. From the mid-1920s "new" feminists sought to shift the emphasis of the women's movement away from the achievement of equality and instead emphasized women's distinctive needs and distinctive contribution to society. Eleanor Rathbone, the campaigner for family allowances, was a leading exponent of these ideas. For an informative discussion, see J. Alberti, *Beyond suffrage; feminists in war and peace, 1914-28* (London: Macmillan, 1989), Ch. 7, also O. Banks, *Faces of feminism* (Oxford: Martin Robertson, 1981), Ch. 9; A. Holdsworth, *Out of the dolls house, the story of women in the twentieth century* (London: BBC, 1988), pp. 116-25.

81. Gittins, *The fair sex*, p. 45.

82. McLaren, *Birth Control*, pp. 220, 221.

83. Gittins, *The fair sex*, pp. 54, 55, 58.

84. K. Chorley, *Manchester made them* (London: Faber & Faber, 1950), p. 149.

85. Gittins, *The fair sex*, pp. 40, 48; Roberts, *A woman's place*, pp. 198-9; Thompson, *The rise*, pp. 176, 193.
86. Lewis, *Women in England*, p. 78; J. Perkin, *Women and marriage in nineteenth-century England* (London: Routledge, 1989), pp. 304-5; A. James Hammerton, *Cruelty and companionship*, p. x; Holdsworth, *Out of the dolls house*, pp. 12-14.
87. P. Summerfield & J. Finch, "Social reconstruction and the emergence of companionate marriage", in *Marriage, domestic life and social change; writings for Jacqueline Burgoyne (1944-1988)*, D. Clark (ed.), (London: Routledge, 1991), pp. 7-32.
88. J. Scott & L. Tilly, *Women, work and family* (London: Routledge, 1987), p. 176.

Suggestions for further reading

There is a great deal of excellent modern work available on this topic. The best collection of articles remains J. Lewis (ed.), *Labour and love, women's experience of home and family 1850-1940* (Oxford: Blackwell, 1986); and a great deal of relevant material is included in Jane Lewis's authoritative study, *Women in England 1870-1950: sexual divisions and social change* (Brighton: Wheatsheaf, 1984). A useful new collection is S. Oldfield (ed.), *This working day world: women's lives and culture(s) in Britain 1914-1945* (London: Taylor & Francis, 1994). On women in the middle-class family, two studies that address the issues from the perspective of daughters are Carol Dyhouse, *Girls growing up in late Victorian and Edwardian England* (London: Routledge & Kegan Paul, 1981); and Deborah Gorham's *The Victorian girl and the feminine ideal* (London: Croom Helm, 1982). Patricia Branca, *Silent sisterhood; middle class women in the Victorian home* (London: Croom Helm, 1975) is still useful. Carol Dyhouse, *Feminism and the family in England, 1880-1939* (Oxford: Basil Blackwell, 1989) gives a useful overview of contemporary feminist critiques of the family. Numerous autobiographies of middle-class women describe family life: for example, K. Chorley, *Manchester made them* (London: Faber & Faber, 1950). Excellent modern studies of women in the working-class family include Elizabeth Roberts, *A woman's place, an oral history of working class women 1890-1940* (Oxford: Basil Blackwell, 1984). On the household economy and the interface between work and home, see P. Hudson & W. R. Lee (eds), *Women's work and the family economy in historical perspective* (Manchester: Manchester University Press, 1990). The work of Ellen Ross is important, particularly *Love and toil, motherhood in outcast London, 1870-1918* (Oxford: Oxford University Press, 1993); "Fierce questions and taunts', married life in working-class London, 1870-1914", *Feminist Studies* **8** (1982); and "Survival networks: women's neighbourhood sharing in London before World War 1", *History Workshop Journal* **15**, 1983. Social investigations of the first half of the twentieth century provide a wealth of material, and several are available in modern reprints, for example the volumes of letters and accounts produced by the Women's Co-operative Guild: M. Llewelyn Davies (ed.), *Life as we have known it* (London: Hogarth Press, 1931; London: Virago, 1982); and *Maternity: letters from working women* (London: G. Bell, 1913; London: Virago, 1978). See also, M. S. Pember Reeves, *Round about a pound a week* (London: G. Bell, 1913; London, Garland, 1980), M. S. Rice, *Working class wives* (Harmondsworth: Penguin, 1939; London, Virago, 1981). Of working-class autobiographies, Hannah Mitchell, *The hard way up; the autobiography of Hannah Mitchell suffragette and rebel* (London: Faber & Faber, 1968; London: Virago, 1977); or D. Chew (ed.), *Ada Nield Chew, the life and writing of a working woman* (London: Virago, 1982) are a good introduction.

Chapter Four

ఆక్గ.

Women and paid work

Jane Humphries

Introduction

Women have always worked. What has changed historically has been the form that their work has taken. In 1842, when times were hard, a miner's wife reported that she "[got] a little to make up the rent by making colliers' flannel shirts at 7d apiece", paid for black lead and mustard "by any little job" she could get, obtained salt in exchange for the bones left from their meat, and took in a lodger![1] This woman's efforts illustrate the problems involved in writing a history of women's "paid work". Historically, women made money and obtained things of value in many ways other than working for wages. They often did more than one thing at a time, they did different things at different times of year and at different phases of the business cycle, and they adapted their efforts to the structure and circumstances of their families.[2] For example, at times and in places when work was organized on the basis of putting-out using family labour, women worked not for individual wages but for a collective wage determined by how much the whole family could produce and the prevailing piece rate. Their efforts and their pay were buried in the family economy. Such energetic and flexible exploitation of local opportunities to get a living is difficult to trace historically let alone measure, and so resists capture in modern terms of activity rates and occupational designations.[3]

On the other hand, an overall picture of trends in women's paid work is of enormous value to economic historians, facilitating, albeit cautious, comparisons with more recent experience, and putting into perspective the regional and occupational case studies that have proliferated since the 1970s. The census is the only historical record that offers the possibility of developing a coherent historical picture of this kind. But census data illustrate the conceptual and measurement problems noted above. Nineteenth-century censuses recorded women's paid work only imperfectly, and their degree of misreporting was not uniform. Worse still, the 1841 Census was particularly problematic and the earlier censuses useless as far as records of women's work are concerned. Baldly put, there are no census totals of the numbers of women active economically in Britain before 1841.

One response to these problems is to use the census to document trends from 1851 onwards, abandoning the attempt to develop an aggregate quantitative evaluation of women's work before that date and relying instead on case studies containing fragmentary quantitative data and extensive but particularized qualitative evidence for the earlier period. To some extent this has happened, with the historiography of women's work compartmentalized awkwardly and broken methodologically around mid-century.

The inability to construct aggregate indices of women's activity and relative concentration before 1851 is particularly unfortunate because this period is of crucial importance, representing the archetypical industrialization experience and setting up the subsequent trends. Women's experience of the Industrial Revolution is widely regarded as being of deep significance, producing institutions and culture which moulded subsequent developments.

This chapter attempts to bridge the break in the historiography and provide a more continuous view of the extent of women's paid work. The first section looks in more detail at the debate about women's experience of industrialization and introduces the problems encountered with census data. Late-nineteenth-century trends, and developments in the twentieth century, are less contested, perhaps because a clearer aggregate narrative comes through from the more reliable data. Nonetheless there are some interesting themes in the literature and some areas of uncertainty as the second section suggests. The third section puts together an overall picture of women's activity rates in the nineteenth and twentieth centuries, using raw census data, amendments to that data and supplementary estimates. Conclusions for the analysis of women's paid work are then drawn, in the final section.

Debate and drama: the Industrial Revolution

The classic texts on the Industrial Revolution simply assumed that it created new jobs for women and children, especially in manufacturing.[4] It was left to others to infer that industrialization promoted women's independence and emancipated them from the patriarchy of the pre-capitalist household.[5] More recently, mainstream economic historians have attempted to develop this theme. Lindert and Williamson, for example, in their study of workers' living standards during industrialization, add some limited quantitative data on women's work and wages.[6] Although their evidence seems to be inconclusive, Lindert and Williamson conclude that women's activity rates declined during industrialization, but that this was voluntary, a result of women weighing up rationally the gains from their activities in the home in comparison with market wages.[7]

The view that the Industrial Revolution increased women's and children's employment is not always associated with an optimistic reading of the effects of industrialization on the standard of living. So-called pessimists, historians who have doubted that industrialization improved conditions of life for working people for at least a generation, have made much of the negative effects of women's and children's employment in mines and mills.[8] More recently, Berg and Hudson, in restating the case for the Industrial Revolution as a major discontinuity, have cited the employment of women and children as one of its novel features, implying that in aggregate their employment increased.[9]

Meanwhile, a separate but parallel debate on the implications of industrialization for women's well-being has been rumbling along in the pages of specialist journals and monographs focused explicitly on gender issues.[10] Authors have searched for ways of conceptualizing the links between changes in the economy and changes in women's work and family lives. In this context, feminist pessimists have argued that in the eighteenth and nineteenth centuries women's access to resources was unequal. Market, state and familial processes of allocation discriminated against them. Debate here has revolved around whether women's inequality spanned economic eras, equally characteristic of unevenly capitalist early modern England as of the late Victorian economy, or was created within capitalist industrialization.[11] The latter view has been highlighted in English historiography, which includes many detailed studies of women's exclusion from occupations as industrialization developed.[12] But the responsibility for the narrowing of women's opportunities was assigned in general terms to capitalism or industrialization. Such analyses remained unsatisfactory, both because they failed to understand the continuities as well as the changes in women's position, and because they failed to identify the specific institutions that produced and reproduced women's inequality within the economy. The influential "dual systems" theoretical description of capitalist-patriarchy as the "cause" of women's inequality broke away from the empirical tradition of English historiography, but in other ways complemented the traditional approach. By emphasizing that patriarchy was a thriving and vibrant aspect of capitalism and not a vestigial remnant from an earlier time, the dual systems approach provided a way of seeing continuities within the changes. Moreover, the approach has highlighted the role of specific institutions in the deteriorating position of women, institutions which were associated with the development of capitalism in the English case, but which need not be so associated, and which also empowered patriarchal impulses.

The most compelling historically specific version of the capitalist patriarchy model associates it with protective labour legislation, the growing influence of chauvinist trade unions, and campaigns for "a family wage".[13] These institutions are depicted as excluding women from jobs which were sufficiently well paid that they were able to support themselves and their children. Women were crowded into badly paid and insecure sectors of the labour market, thereby promoting their dependence on husbands and fathers.

Is it possible to reconcile these seemingly disparate views? One source of compromise is *timing*. Perhaps the process of industrialization first increased female opportunities, only to shut them down subsequently. Some authors have hinted at such a scenario.[14] Reconciliation can also be pursued by distinguishing between *proto-industrial activities* and *factory production*. For some authors it is the expansion of the former that was associated with the growth of female employment, while others have emphasized factory production.[15] More generally, if outcomes for women were occupationally or regionally specific, it might help to explain how authors can see opportunities waxing and waning simultaneously. Also, occupationally specific stories seem essential to tighten the links between outcomes and the proximate institutional causes cited in the capitalist-patriarchy model.

It might be possible to square the claim that industrialization increased women's work with the evidence of a strong female involvement in domestic industry by shifting the emphasis to the *terms and conditions* of the work. Thus Berg and Hudson write that what was new about women's employment "in the period of the classic industrial revolution was the extent of its incorporation into rapidly expanding factory and workshop manufacturing and its association with low wages, increased intensification of work and labour discipline".[16] But as it stands, as one recent survey concludes: "Histories of women on the grand scale, whether optimistic or pessimistic, are amazingly premature when the available documentation is so sketchy".[17] Whatever strategy is pursued to make sense of the variety of competing claims, empirical evidence appears to be vital.

Consensus and quietude: the late-nineteenth century, the Edwardian period, and the years between the wars

In comparison with the enormous interest in the Industrial Revolution period, historians of women's work have paid scant attention to developments in the later nineteenth century, the Edwardian period and the years between the two world wars. More reliable data has left less room for dispute, and the evidence that exists is not indicative of dramatic shifts in women's involvement in the economy. Significantly, feminist historians interested in these periods have followed contemporary commentators and been more concerned with women's family lives, their struggles with poverty, and their pursuit of political emancipation, than with their involvement in paid work.[18] There are exceptions to the lack of interest in women workers, however.

The late Victorian and Edwardian periods saw significant activity by women in the labour movement. Women sought to play a role in established unions, and to form new unions by organizing women workers. There have been several important studies which have built on classic analyses of women's role within the labour movement.[19] These include Liddington and Norris's study of working-class support for women's suffrage. Liddington and Norris redress the imbalance in orthodox treatments of women's struggle for the vote, focused as they are on the middle-class leadership, by highlighting the campaigns by working women and linking these to experiences of working for wages in the Edwardian economy.[20] But much women's labour history of these periods is a story of retreat and containment. Bornat, for example, shows that behind their formal support for women's rights, union leaders were paternalistic, and their paternalism was locked into an employer-sanctioned organization of work that reflected wider social assumptions about the place of women. Women's blocked progress in the labour movement reflected their segregation in the workplace, and both were embedded in the social perception of women's role as being primarily domestic.[21]

These studies continue the theme of chauvinist trade unions and their oppressive use of the family wage slogan as institutions which excluded and marginalized women. They help to create an overwhelming sense of continuity in the history of women's work. The later nineteenth century simply sees the working out of those mechanisms of exclusion and marginalization established during industrialization.

The conflation of the experience of industrialization and its aftermath is also evident in monographs which concern the later period. Thus Sonya Rose's *Limited livelihoods: gender and class in nineteenth-century England*, though focused on the second half of the nineteenth century, claims to discuss the experience of industrialization: "the massive reorganization of lives and livelihoods that accompanied the economic, social, political, and cultural revolutions of industrial capitalism in England".[22]

The First World War constitutes another exception, as it was subject to intense scrutiny by contemporary investigators and has been of interest to later historians as a dramatic interruption of women's retreat into domesticity. Yet the involvement of women in paid work during the First World War appears to have had little long-term impact on their activity rates or the institutional constraints that surrounded them. Indeed, the wartime experience itself has been interpreted as institutionalizing a sense of women's unequal capacities by integrating into the structure of work processes of dilution and substitution that acknowledged women as emergency workers and constructed war work as women's work.[23] The war of 1914–18 strengthened, not weakened, the social and cultural construction of women as wives and mothers primarily, and barely disturbed the continuity of the late-nineteenth and early-twentieth centuries retreat from paid work.

The feminist historian of the interwar years has also been less interested in how women fared in the shifting fortunes of paid work than with their struggles with the poverty associated with the long-term unemployment of the male head of household. Again, there is an exception, because women have emerged as an important component in the growing labour forces of the new industries. Located in London and the South, the new industries recruited women and juveniles, perhaps because employers preferred not to hire the long-term unemployed males put out of work by the decline of the staple industries because they had acquired inflexible attitudes about work pace and organization.[24] For the first time, women are seen to inherit a sector of the employment structure because of their flexibility, a theme that would be echoed in much later analyses. With this theme too came studies of the organization of work in these new assembly industries.[25] But how this exceptional experience related to the long-term trends, and indeed whether the institutions governing the deep inertia in women's activity rates remained constant over the period, remain unexplored. Can a second look at trends in activity rates over the whole period cast light on the conventional interpretation of a long nineteenth century of slow retreat? Can it help to see the late Victorian period, the Edwardian period and the interwar years as anything other than a footnote to the drama of the Industrial Revolution: the slow working out of women's earlier defeat? These are the questions taken up in the last section of this chapter. But first we turn to the background data.

Introducing the census data

The census has to be the starting point for an analysis of this kind, but as no census enumeration of women workers took place before 1841, this leaves the crucial period of the Industrial Revolution, usually dated between 1780 and 1850, essentially undocumented. As far as activity rates and the concentration of women workers is concerned, on a national scale the period of industrialization has to be labelled "the great unknown".

The censuses did count women workers from 1841 on, and these numbers have been used to argue that the nineteenth century saw a slow retreat of women from the paid labour force, accompanied by increasing employment segregation.[26] But there are many reasons to look carefully at the early census totals and activity rates based upon them.[27]

In 1841, householders were advised that "the profession etc. of wives, or sons or daughters living with and assisting their parents but not apprenticed or receiving wages need not be inserted" on the census return. The many wives and daughters whom studies of domestically organized industries have documented as "assisting" would go uncounted according to this instruc-tion.[28] As a result, the 1841 Census probably displays a gross level of underenumeration of women workers.[29] In 1851, householders were instructed that "the occupations of women who are regularly employed from home, or at home, *in any but domestic duties*, [are] to be distinctly recorded".[30] But the guidelines did not refer explicitly to the work of women in the family economy, and the directive probably served to restrict the census to work done in a market setting. Moreover, no guidance was given to the treatment of part time, casual or seasonal work except that to be recorded it had to be "regular". The result appears to have been considerable variation in the extent to which householders and enumerators recorded women's work.

Whether or not women were married appears to have prejudiced enumerators' judgements about their employment status. Married women were assumed to have no occupation other than the care of their husbands and families.[31] The injunctions about domestic duties had particularly negative implications for women who worked by taking in lodgers, a common income earning strategy of married women. Davidoff has demonstrated the ambiguous treatment of lodging-house-keepers in nine-teenth- and twentieth-century censuses.[32] Walton and McGloin also note that for Keswick, for example, the published census recorded no landladies, whereas the local directory recorded 69.[33] On the other hand, Higgs has pointed to another error commonly made by the enumerators which led to the overestimation of women working in domestic service. Higgs points out that the confusion between domestic service and the work of women in the family home sometimes led the census clerks to count everyone described as having a servant occupation as being in domestic service. But many recorded thus as "servants" were not servants in relation to the head of the household in which they lived, and a large number of the remainder were related by kinship to the household head. To illustrate the importance of this point, Higgs works out that if it is assumed that all the women in servant occupations whose relationship to the household head was one of kinship were working at home for their relatives, and were not domestic servants in the sense of being employed for wages, then the census figures for domestic service in Rochdale in 1851 would have to be reduced by a third.[34]

But the problems are not confined to the enumeration of domestic workers. Checks provided by other local and national evidence such as wage books and oral histories suggest considerable underreporting of women's work in the agricultural sector, in manufacturing and in other service occupations.[35] Lown's study of women's employment at Courtaulds' silk mill in Halstead, Essex suggests that many women workers do not appear in the enumerator's books. Specifically, enumerators omitted any occupational designation to married women.[36] Oral histories suggest that part time work was also underrecorded systematically, again with particularly severe implications for an accurate view of married women's work.[37]

If the census is likely to be misleading in several important ways, and too late to cover the main drama of industrialization, how can we proceed? One approach is to provide and compare a range of figures based on the census totals, but making different assumptions about the errors made by the enumerators and corrections based on these assumptions. This is the strategy pursued in the next section. But to reach back into the great unknown of the period before 1851 we need to put together a picture of trends from piecemeal data on employment and occupation. Creative researchers have mined other sources to try to establish trends in the pre-census period. Earle has searched depositions of female witnesses before the London church courts in the late-seventeenth and eighteenth centuries for detail on women's employment, on which basis he has argued that a high proportion of women of the period were wholly or partly dependent on their own earnings; that the structure of occupations was close to that revealed by the 1851 Census, as was the degree of gender concentration; and that a high proportion of women's occupations were casual, intermittent and seasonal.[38] Snell has used settlement examinations of applicants for Poor Relief to establish the seasonal distribution of employment by gender, and inferred from this that the division of labour by sex in agriculture tightened after 1750, bringing with it a decline in women's participation in the agricultural labour force. Horrell and Humphries have used records of household accounts to construct estimates of married women's participation rates defined according to both whether an occupational designation was accorded a woman, or whether a women contributed to household income.[39] These studies, along with even more fragmentary evidence, can be used to estimate pre-1841 trends which can then be linked to the census figures. A first such attempt is tried in Table 4.1.

Table 4.1 provides several census-based estimates of women's participation rates for the nineteenth and early-twentieth centuries. Column 1 shows raw census estimates of the female population recorded as occupied according to the various census definitions and the interpretations of enumerators and householders. Column 2 reports a recomputation of the census figures by Joshi et al. intended to make them more consistent with modern definitions.[40] Joshi et al. limit their attention to the population aged 20-64. Not surprisingly, cutting out women under 20 and women over 64 from the numerator and denominator of the activity rate increases the measure of activity compared with the figures in column 1. Younger and older women had lower activity rates, as we would expect. But Joshi et al. also estimate the rates for 1851-71 to make them consistent with later estimates. The censuses of 1851, 1861 and 1871 used a different concept of the occupied population from the censuses of 1881 and after. But a consistent series of the occupied population aged 20-64 spanning the two eras has been estimated by the Department of Employment and Productivity.[41] On this basis, Joshi et al. compute total activity rates for 1851, 1861, 1871 and 1881 (the Department of Employment and Productivity's consistent series of the occupied

Table 4.1 Female activity rates (per cent) from census data.

Year	(1)	(2)	Periodization	(3)	(4)	Periodization
1801	n.a.	n.a.	The great	n.a.	n.a	The great
1831	n.a.	n.a.	unknown	n.a.	n.a.	unknown
1841	18.6	n.a.		23	n.a	
1851	26.3	34.5	The slow	42	n.a.	The nineteenth
1861	27.2	35.2	retreat	43	n.a.	century plateau
1871	27.5	34.5		42	n.a.	
1881	25.5	33.1		32	n.a.	Retreat
1891	25.5	33.5		32	n.a	
1901		33.9		32	38	Stagnation
1911		32.5		32	38	
1921		30.6		32	38	
1931		31.6		34	38	
1941		n.a.		n.a.	n.a.	
1951		36.3	The social	35	43	The social
1961		41.0	revolution	38	47	revolution
1971		51.5	of our time	44	55	of our time
1981		57.7		48	64	

(1) Percentage of female population occupied. Raw census data from England and Wales, C. H. Lee, *British regional employment statistics, 1841-1971* (Cambridge: Cambridge University Press, 1979).

(2) Percentage of female population aged 20-64 occupied. Estimated from *Population census reports for England and Wales*; and Department of Employment and Productivity, *British labour statistics: historical abstracts 1886-1968*, (London: HMSO, 1971); table 102 in H. E. Joshi, R. Layard and S. J. Owen, "Why are more women working in Britain?", *Journal of Labour Economics* **3**, p. 5151, 1985.

(3) Percentage of female population aged 20 and over occupied. Estimated from "Population census reports for England and Wales" in C. Hakim, "A century of change in occupational segregation 1891-1991", *Journal of Historical Sociology* **7** (4), December 1994.

(4) Percentage of female population aged 10 and over, 1901-11; aged 12 and over, 1921; aged 14 and over, 1931; aged 15 and over, 1951; estimated as above in Hakim, "A Century of Change".

population divided by total population aged 20-64). They also compute the ratio of the actual activity rate for women aged 20-64 to the total activity rate in 1881. On the basis of this ratio and the total activity rates of the earlier years, they predict female activity rates in 1851, 1861 and 1871. In other words, they are not computing female activity rates from 1851 to 1871 independently, but predicting them on the basis of the total activity rates and the relationship between the total activity rate and the female activity rate that obtained in 1881. Changes in female activity rates are reduced to changes in total activity rates. As we suspect that female activity rates may have shifted relative to male and total activity rates, this method, although it produces a consistent series, is not appropriate.

Moreover, although the Joshi et al. series does show a trend decline in female activity rates, it is very mild and should perhaps be dated from the late- rather than the mid-nineteenth century. We are on much more stable ground in extending the decline into the twentieth century, with activity rates falling consistently during the first three decades and turning up slightly only in 1931. We have to wait until after the Second World War for female activity rates to reverse their decline. Significant increases are delayed until the 1960s. By the 1980s, increasing female activity rates have become, as the *Wall Street Journal* has trumpeted, "the social revolution of our time".

The third and fourth columns provide alternative estimates also based on census totals, but calculated by Catherine Hakim.[42] Hakim's column 3 estimates are for women aged 20 and over and she explicitly excludes unpaid household work, which she notes was listed as an occupation from 1851-71 although perhaps only patchily recorded. Not surprisingly, her estimate for 1881 is close to Joshi et al.'s, but slightly lower because of the inclusion of women aged over 64, who would have low participation rates. But Hakim's independent estimates for 1851, 1861 and 1871 suggest a much sharper retreat from the labour force compared with the 1881 and 1891 figures. The problem is to gauge the extent to which this is a result of a genuine decline in female activity rates and the extent to which it reflects the change in 1881 in the definition of the occupied population. The concept of the occupied population used before 1881 was more inclusive. For example, the average activity rate of men aged 20 and older for 1851, 1861 and 1871 from census figures was 99 per cent, which compares with 94.5 per cent for the average of the last two censuses of the decade. But this represents a decline of 4.6 per cent, whereas the average female activity rate fell 24.4 per cent from 1851-71 to 1881-91, suggesting that the switch to a less inclusive definition of "occupied" cannot account for the whole change.

For 1901 onwards, Hakim's figures are based on varying age-related definitions of the population and so are not comparable with the figures for the nineteenth century.[43] As these figures include some varying proportion of the population under 20, they would be expected to be in lower than Joshi et al.'s, which were based uniformly on the population aged 20-64. For example, the inclusion of girls aged 10-20 in the 1901-11 estimates would reduce this figure relative to an activity rate based on the population aged 20 and over. For the twentieth century, Hakim's figures are similar to Joshi et al.'s, and any differences are readily explained by minor changes in the age limits on the population considered.

Column 4, also taken from Hakim, is a series of activity rates for women aged 15-59. These figures throw into relief the way in which the inclusion of women over 59 reduces the activity rate. For this core group of adult women, the picture is one of stagnation through the first four decades of the twentieth century, and growth gathering momentum after the Second World War.

To summarize then, there was no significant increase in women's activity rates until after the Second World War. Activity rates have stagnated over the long run, hovering around one-third from 1881 to 1931. But it is a mistake to conflate the nineteenth century with the early-twentieth century as marking a slow retreat by women from paid work. The retreat appears to have been quite sharp from 1861-71 to 1881-91, after which stagnation set in. Although the shift in the concept of the occupied population contributed to the apparent decline over this period, it appears that some part of it was real. So attempts to link trends in women's activity rates to economic and political institutions have to look for some significant negative influence in the late-nineteenth century and a holding of the line thereafter. Superficially at least, this does not fit with the grand theorizations mentioned earlier which cite capitalism or industrialization as explanations. Theorizations which look to specific intermediate institutions such as chauvinist trade unions, campaigns for family wages, and protective labour legislation, are less damaged because these institutions have always seemed more relevant to the later nineteenth century than to the period of the Industrial Revolution.[44]

But 1841 does not fit within this periodization. Whether reference is to the raw census data or Hakim's estimate re-based on the population aged over 20, the activity rate for women in 1841 appears to be only three-quarters to half of its level in 1851-71, and affords a dramatic interruption to the story of decline from a mid-nineteenth-century plateau. The census figures for 1841 suggest that the trend for the nineteenth century was not linear: there was an increase in female activity rates from 1841 to 1851 before the sharp decline of the late-nineteenth century. This has significant implications for theories which seek to link trends in women's activity rates to the progress of industrialization. A periodization which postulates first a rise to a mid-nineteenth-century plateau of activity, followed by a fairly sharp retreat and subsequent stagnation, is more cumbersome to relate to economic development than the standard story which has ignored evidence before 1850 and interpreted a rather vaguely dated retreat as the result of capitalism or industrialization in new partnership with patriarchy.

But can the figure for 1841 be taken at face value? The 1841 figure may be low for cyclical rather than secular reasons, as 1841 marked the bottom of possibly the worst recession in the century. Activity rates, particularly female activity rates, move pro-cyclically; they rise in booms and fall in slumps. Significantly, the proportion of men aged over 20 recorded as being occupied in 1841, as reported by Hakim, is also substantially below rates recorded earlier and later.[45] But in addition to any cyclical decline in activity, Higgs, on the basis of a detailed analysis of trends in the numbers of women reported as being occupied in various sectors, argues that the 1841 Census exhibits a gross level of underenumeration.[46] Table 4.2 shows the census activity rates for the population as a whole, and figures adjusted upwards by Higgs. The

Table 4.2 Female activity rates (per cent), corrected census figures and other estimates.

Year	(1)	(2)	(3)	(4)	
			29.4	46.4	1787–1815
			28.3	36.6	1816–20
			21.1	44.0	1821–40
			36.2	41.5	1841–45
			19.2	34.2	1846–65
1841	18.6	21.2			
1851	26.3	28.5			
1861	27.2	28.3			
1871	27.5	28.2			
1881	25.5	25.6			
1891	25.5	25.4			

(1) Census data, see Table 4.1.
(2) Higgs, "Women's occupations and work" (see Note 27).
(3) Constructed from Horrell and Humphries, "Women's labour force participation" (see Note 28).
(4) Constructed from Horrell and Humphries, "Women's labour force participation".

latter are based on upward revisions of the numbers of women employed in agriculture and retailing. The adjustments are based on crude assumptions, that *all* the wives and female relatives of farmers and retailers were *always fully employed* in the market economy, and that *all* servants living with farmers or retailers were *always fully employed* as agricultural workers or shop assistants. Both the total activity rates and the relative importance of different occupational categories are shifted as a result of the recomputation.

The Higgs adjustments suggest that the 1841 total for occupied women was underestimated relative to later censuses, but significant upward revisions are also in order for 1851, 1861 and 1871, whereas the 1881 and 1891 totals (and so activity rates) are unaffected. This goes some way to pull 1841 into line with subsequent enumeration, but without eliminating all evidence for a dip in the occupied female population. More important perhaps, the Higgs adjustments exaggerate the decline in activity from 1851-71 to 1881-91 which was partly disguised by the systematic underrecording of women workers in the censuses of 1851. Finally, the figures confirm that female activity rates in 1851-71 were almost certainly higher than any that were recorded again until after the Second World War, and perhaps even until the 1960s.

Horrell and Humphries constructed female activity rates from accounts of the sources of income of working-class families in the pre-census period.[47] While their data is, inevitably, limited and not directly comparable with the census estimates, it is possible to make some tentative comparisons. Horrell and Humphries work with three definitions of participation: whether a women was accorded an occupational designation; whether she made any contribution to family income; or whether she either had a recorded occupation or made a contribution.[48] Part of the interest of their analysis is in comparing the different measures of activity across occupations and over time. Not surprisingly, the occupational definition yields lower estimates of activity and appears to be a decreasingly accurate barometer of whether women earned anything. However, it is closest to the census definition and so is pursued here first.

Horrell's and Humphries' data is not representative of the population of households. Specifically, they found that women's activity rates varied according to the occupation of the head of household. To aggregate, they weighted the activity rates recorded by occupational sub-groups of households in their sample by the proportion that each male occupation represented in the actual population. This strategy is pursued here also.[49]

Horrell's and Humphries' data is for married women in working-class families, but by making some simple assumptions it can be generalized to the population as a whole. It is assumed that: one-third of the population is middle class and upper class, and that women in this class do not do paid work; and, of the remaining two-thirds, 10 per cent are single or widowed and have 100 per cent activity rates, while 90 per cent have the participation rates obtained by reweighting the Horrell–Humphries occupational activity rates as described above. The resulting estimates for the period of industrialization are provided in column 3 of Table 4.2. Small numbers in certain occupational cells of the underlying data mean that the figure for 1841-5 is likely to be an overestimate.[50] The figures fit surprisingly well with the census data. They suggest that activity rates during industrialization were high by historical standards, similar to those recorded in the 1851-71 censuses. They also suggest, but less clearly, that there was a dip in activity rates before mid-century.

However, it is important to counterpoise these trends in activity rates defined by the award of an occupational title with the alternative hybrid definition preferred by Horrell and Humphries, which defines participation according to either an occupational title or a contribution to family income. The more inclusive definition provides the basis of the aggregate activity rates shown in column 4 of Table 4.2. They suggest activity rates of over 40 per cent for some stretches of the Industrial Revolution. They illustrate the point underlined by Horrell and Humphries, that earnings definitions of activity produce higher measured activity rates than occupational definitions. Again, so long as women's activity was couched in the economy of makeshift, and concerned more with adding something to the family pot than with practising an occupation, it was probably underestimated by the nineteenth-century censuses. Nonetheless, although it is not possible to compare these activity rates with estimates for later in the nineteenth century, which also focus on whether or not women did contribute something rather than whether they were perceived as being occupied, it seems unlikely that the censuses produced such underenumeration as to wipe out the secular decline in activity suggested. Finally, the earnings-based data do not exhibit the dip around mid-century, diverging most dramatically from the occupation-based rates during these years. Perhaps this was a period when there was a marked gap between perceptions of women's activities and their actual behaviour. But perhaps also women's activity rates moved down in two stages from the peaks experienced during industrialization, first towards the middle of the nineteenth century, and then again from 1871. As it stands, the data cannot rule this out.[51]

Women's paid work in historical perspective

Do these findings clarify the history of women's paid work? They make several contributions. First, the evidence supports the view that women were active economically in the period of the Industrial Revolution, more active than they were to become by the end of the nineteenth century, and more active than they were to be in the first three decades of the twentieth. Unfortunately, we have no way of comparing this period with earlier in the eighteenth century and so cannot comment on whether early industrialization elevated women's activity rates. But far from destroying women's jobs and driving them out of paid work, industrialization seems to have sustained relatively high activity rates. There is little evidence that the period of industrialization proper saw any significant decline in activity rates overall, the evidence for 1841 being more than likely a cyclical and statistical phenomenon.

Industrialization undoubtedly eliminated some women's work. Hand spinning is the obvious, but not only, example. Overwhelming evidence also exists to suggest that women's jobs in agriculture were also reduced. But industrialization also *created* jobs for women. Factory production of textiles is again an obvious example, but others could be cited. What the aggregate data suggest is that perhaps, on average, job creation matched job destruction for the first 60 or so years of the Industrial Revolution. This does not mean that there was no unemployment or dislocation caused by the restructuring of the industrializing economy. Far from it. For the jobs destroyed were often ones widely available in many locations, and ones which could be done for a few hours at a time and combined with other activities, while the jobs created were often only available in specific locations and were more likely to involve long hours and presence at a centralized workplace.

Perhaps by mid-century the ongoing processes of job creation and destruction had begun to work against women's jobs. Lace making and straw plaiting, the domestic industries that had partly taken the place of handspinning, had never mopped up the labour of the wives and daughters of agricultural labourers, trapped by their husbands' work and settlement in rural locations, and had begun to fade badly. These developments may have contributed to that first decline in the aggregate activity rates around mid-century.

But why be concerned only with work traditionally done by women; what stopped women pursuing some of the new and better paid jobs appearing in the industrializing economy? There are many strands to this story. Women, then (as now), were less geographically mobile than men. Married women could only move with their families, while young women moving on their own were very vulnerable. Significantly, the most rapidly growing job for women, domestic service, was one that eased the strain of moving to a strange place and acquiring a new home. But Higgs' exposure of the frequency with which kinship ties existed between "servants" and their household's head casts doubt on interpreting all this relocation as market mediated. Domestic service may have mopped up and disguised significant amounts of unemployment in the mid-Victorian economy, and it may have achieved this through a finely balanced mix of social responsibility, kinship ties and increasing domestic standards. Another neglected point is the extent to which the better paid jobs and the jobs that had prospects attached to them in the mid-Victorian economy were still jobs which required physical strength. Women's relative weakness, and perhaps exaggerated perceptions of that weakness, segmented the labour market.

But what of the standard themes of the feminist literature: that protective labour legislation, chauvinist trade unions and the campaign for a family wage barred women's access to paid work and so depressed activity rates? If the retreat from paid work occurred during industrialization, this argument lacks conviction because the institutions were too weak to have played the parts assigned. Early unions did not have the influence that this thesis implies.[52] Unskilled workers remained unorganized until the 1880s. Early protective labour legislation was not effective. Evasion was widespread until modifications to the 1847 Factory Act, legislated in 1850, for the first time established a legal working day. Remember too that this legislation only applied to textile factories. Extension to other kinds of factories and to workshops proceeded slowly and unevenly during the next 50 years. For much of the nineteenth century most women's jobs remained outside the legislative purview. Redating the decline in women's activity rates to the late-nineteenth century, as has been done here, makes it more plausible that unions and labour laws played a role.

But although chauvinist trade unions, protective labour legislation and campaigns for a family wage make more sense as institutional constraints on activity in the late-nineteenth century, reconfiguring the argument in this way leaves these intermediate institutions hanging; they are detached from their socio-economic context. They no longer boil out of the bitter crucible of industrialization. But here the long view comes into its own. For what cries out for explanation in these data is not dramatic change over the period of the Industrial Revolution, but a retreat much later in the nineteenth century that is then maintained through the first 30 years of the twentieth century. This reperiodisation implicates the slack labour market of the British economy in the late-Victorian, Edwardian and interwar years in the emergence of institutions that inhibited women's activity rates. Chauvinist trade unions, protective labour legislation and campaigns for a family wage played their part, but other institutions also acted as obstacles to women working. For example, the marriage bar, introduced in the last quarter of the nineteenth century, became increasingly important in the depressed 1920s and 1930s when unemployment rates averaged 10 per cent. Most important of all were the cultural productions of the late-nineteenth century which inhibited women's activity rates from within by moulding self-perception and identity. Gender itself, defined in terms of the role of the housewife and mother, and its mirror image, the breadwinner male, appear culturally constructed within the tissues of an underemployed and patriarchal capitalism.[53] What historians need to do now is to look in detail at the operation of specific institutions which presented obstacles to women's work, and to chart their influence over time and space. A move away from general and amorphous explanations, such as capitalism and patriarchy, to implicate specific institutions in specific ways, is useful not only to convince the sceptical but also to understand the accumulation of disadvantages that women have inherited within labour markets that appear to offer equal opportunities.

Reasonable conjectures about the history of women's paid work suggest that historians should revise their periodization and their priorities. The historical keys to women's inequality in the labour market lie not only in the Industrial Revolution but also in its aftermath: in sluggish growth, relative industrial decline and persistently slack labour markets. It was in this context that capitalist patriarchy flowed through institutions such as the labour movement and protective labour legislation, brought employers and unions to agreement on marriage bars, and convinced women themselves that their identities were founded in being housewives and dependents.

Notes

1. Midland Mining Commission, Parliamentary Papers, 1843, xxiii, p. 116, quoted in S. Horrell & J. Humphries, "Women's labour force participation and the transition to the male-breadwinner family, 1790–1865", *Economic History Review*, forthcoming.
2. The fragmented and opportunistic character of women's work has long been recognized by historians. See S. Alexander, *Women's work in nineteenth century London* (London: Journeyman Press, 1976) for an early emphasis on these

characteristics; and D. Bythell, "Women in the workforce", in *The Industrial Revolution and British society*, P. O'Brien and R. Quinault (eds) (Cambridge: Cambridge University Press, 1993).

3. The proportion of women working is only one measure of women's work. It is also important to know something about where women work, in particular the degree of employment segregation, the terms and conditions of women's work, and how these compare with men's. But establishing trends in activity rates is prior to looking at these other dimensions of paid work. Certainly, some of the conceptual problems that dog the history of women's paid work recur in the context of tracing employment segregation and tracking relative pay. Some of the strategies pursued here to uncover trends may also be relevant in the context of employment segregation and relative pay.

4. See P. Deane and W. A. Cole, *British economic growth* (Cambridge: Cambridge University Press, 1962), pp. 139-40; P. Deane, *First Industrial Revolution* (Cambridge: Cambridge University Press, 1967), p. 147; P. Mathias, *First industrial nation* (London: Methuen, 1983), pp. 175-6. For useful further discussion relevant to this chapter see Chapter 2 by Pat Hudson in this volume.

5. Thus among the beneficial long-term consequences of the Industrial Revolution is listed its contribution to "the emancipation of women". See R. M. Hartwell, "The rising standard of living in England, 1800-1850", *Economic History Review*, 2nd series, xiii (1961), pp. 397-416. For the importance of this theme in historical sociology, see J. Thomas, "Women and capitalism: oppression or emancipation", *Comparative Studies in Society and History* 30, pp. 534-49, 1988.

6. P. H. Lindert & J. G. Williamson, "English workers' living standards during the Industrial Revolution: a new look", *Economic History Review*, 2nd series, xxvi, pp. 1-25, 1983.

7. Lindert & Williamson, "English workers' living standards", p. 19: "the shadow price of women's time rose faster than the observed wage rate". The conceptualization of the allocation of women's time as the outcome of such a rational maximization exercise is the standard neoclassical approach to female labour supply. Of course, the shadow price of women's time is not observable directly. Moreover, Lindert and Williamson's claim that women's wages rose is based on thin empirical evidence.

8. See, K. Marx, *Capital* (New York: International Publishers, 1967 originally published 1867-95); B. Hammond & J. Hammond, *The town labourer* (London: Longman, 1917).

9. M. Berg & P. Hudson, "Rehabilitating the Industrial Revolution", *Economic History Review*, 2nd series, xlv, pp. 25-50, 1992.

10. For useful summaries and bibliographies, see Thomas, "Women and capitalism", and P. Hudson & W. R. Lee, *Women's work and the family economy in historical perspective* (Manchester: Manchester University Press, 1990), Ch. 1.

11. J. Bennett, "Women's history: a study in continuity and change", *Women's History Review* 2, pp. 173-84, 1993; and B. Hill, "Women's history: a study in change, continuity, or standing still?", *Women's History Review* 2, pp. 5-22, 1993.

12. Classic examples of this genre are I. Pinchbeck, *Women workers and the Industrial Revolution, 1750-1850* (New York: Augustus Kelley, 1969; originally published 1930); and A. Clarke, *Working life of women in the seventeenth century* (London: Frank Cass, 1968; originally published 1919).

13. H. I. Hartmann, "The unhappy marriage of Marxism and feminism: towards a more progressive union", *Capital and Class* 8, pp. 1-33, 1979; M. Barratt, *Women's oppression today* (London: Verso, 1980); S. Walby, *Patriarchy at work* (Cambridge:

Polity Press, 1986). Later contributions to this literature have developed in detail the institutional mechanisms that were only sketched in the original work; see H. Benenson, "The 'family wage' and working women's consciousness in Britain", *Politics and Society* **19**, pp. 71-108, 1991; S. Rose, *Limited livelihoods: gender and class in nineteenth-century England* (London: Routledge, 1992).

14. Berg & Hudson, "Rehabilitating", p. 37.

15. D. Levine, *Reproducing families* (Cambridge: Cambridge University Press, 1987).

16. Berg & Hudson, "Rehabilitating", p. 37.

17. Thomas, "Women and capitalism", p. 547.

18. The classic texts on women in industrialization, Pinchbeck and Clark, are mainly concerned with women's work, how it was embedded in the family economy and how it was affected consequently by the increasing importance of markets and waged labour. In contrast, the classic work on the late-Victorian and Edwardian periods involves social anthropological studies of the working class that bring women's domestic roles to the fore: housework, the management of the wage, maternity and motherhood. References here include: Lady Bell, *At the works: a study of a manufacturing town* (London: Virago, 1984; first published 1907); M. S. Pember Reeves, *Round about a pound a week* (London: Bell, 1913); M. Spring Rice, *Working-class wives: their health and conditions* (London: Virago, 1981; first published 1939); R. Roberts, *The classic slum: Salford, life in the first quarter of the century* (Manchester: Manchester University Press, 1971). The same is true of Elizabeth Roberts' oral history of working-class women, *A woman's place* (Oxford, Basil Blackwell, 1984). The issues of the day had shifted.

19. The best single source for women's trade unionism is Barbara Drake, *Women in trade unions* (London: Virago, 1984; originally published 1920). Other classics include B. L. Hutchins & B. Harrison, *A history of factory legislation* (London: P. S. King and Son, 1903).

20. J. Liddington & J. Norris, *One hand tied behind us: the rise of the women's suffrage movement* (London: Virago, 1978).

21. J. Bornat, "Lost leaders: women, trade unionism and the case of the General Union of Textile Workers, 1875-1914", in *Unequal opportunities: women's employment in England, 1800-1918*, A. V. John (ed.) (Oxford: Basil Blackwell, 1986). See also the essays by D. Thom and E. Mappen in the same volume.

22. S. Rose, *Limited livelihoods*.

23. D. Thom, *The ideology of women's work, 1914-1924, with special reference to NFWW and other trade unions*, Phd thesis, Thames Polytechnic, 1982.

24. C. Heim, "Structural transformation and the demand for new labour in advanced economies: interwar Britain", *Journal of Economic History* **44**, pp. 585-95, 1984.

25. M. Glucksmann, *Women assemble: women workers and the new industries in inter-war Britain* (London: Routledge, 1990).

26. E. Richards, "Women in the British economy since about 1700: an interpretation", *History* **59**, pp. 337-47, 1974; Humphries, "'The most free from objection' . . . the sexual division of labour and women's work in nineteenth-century England", *Journal of Economic History* **47**, pp. 929-50, 1987; E. Jordan, "The exclusion of women from industry in nineteenth-century Britain", *Comparative Studies in Society and History* **31**, pp. 309-26, 1989; D. C. Betts, "Women and work: industrial segregation in England and Wales, 1851-1901", Department of Economics, Southern Methodist University Working Paper (1991); H. E. Joshi, R. Layard, and S. J. Owen, "Why are more women working in Britain?" *Journal of Labor Economics* **3**, pp. S147-S176, 1985.

27. E. Higgs, "Women's occupations and work in the nineteenth century censuses", *History Workshop* **23**, pp. 59-80, 1987.

28. Studies that have highlighted the role of women in domestic industries in the early/ mid-nineteenth century include: N. G. Osterud, "Gender divisions and the organization of work in the Leicestershire hosiery industry", in *Unequal opportunities: women's employment in England, 1800-1918*, A. V. John (ed.) (Oxford: Basil Blackwell, 1986), pp. 45-70; S. O. Rose, "Proto-industry, women's work and the household economy in the transition to industrial capitalism", *Journal of Family History* **13**, pp. 181-93, 1988; D. Levine, *Family formation in an age of nascent capitalism* (London: Academic, 1977); J. Lyons, "Family response to economic decline: handloom weavers in early nineteenth century Lancashire", *Resources in Economic History* **12**, pp. 45-91, 1989; J. Lown, *Women and industrialization: gender at work in nineteenth-century England* (Cambridge: Polity Press, 1990). Classic studies of domestic industry include: A. Clark, *Working life of women in the seventeenth century* (London: Frank Cass, 1968); L. A. Tilly & J. W. Scott, *Women, work and family* (New York: 1978); I. Pinchbeck, *Women workers and the Industrial Revolution* (New York: Augustus M. Kelley, 1969). Horrell and Humphries find relatively high rates of participation of married women in paid work as measured by contributions to family income in households where the husband/father is in a domestically organized industry; see Horrell & Humphries, "Women's labour force participation and the transition to the male-breadwinner family, 1790-1865", *Economic History Review* XLVIII (forthcoming), 1995.

29. Higgs also suggests that this is the case, see "Women's occupations and work".

30. Higgs, "Women's occupations and work", p. 63.

31. An assumption which continues to contaminate data even today, see H. E. Joshi & S. J. Owen, "How long is a piece of elastic", *Cambridge Journal of Economics* **11**, pp. 55-74, 1986.

32. L. Davidoff, "The separation of home and work? Landladies and lodgers in nineteenth- and twentieth-century England", in *Fit work for women*, S. Burman (ed.) (London: 1979).

33. J. K. Walton & P. McGloin, "Holiday resorts and their visitors: some sources for the local historian", *The Local Historian* **13**, pp. 323-31, 1979.

34. E. Higgs, "Domestic service and household production", in *Unequal opportunities: women's employment in England, 1800-1918*, A. V. John (ed.) (Oxford: Basil Blackwell, 1986) pp. 125-52.

35. E. Higgs, "Women workers in agriculture", paper presented at a conference on "Gender and History" in honour of Leonore Davidoff, February 1992.

36. J. Lown, *Women and industrialization*.

37. E. Roberts, "Working wives and their families", in *Population and society in Britain*, T. Barker & M. Drake (eds) (London: 1982). The invisibility of married women's work may well have distorted not just views of the gender composition of the labour force but also where women worked. For example, the view that factory work was confined to the young and single may be a statistical artefact. For the classic presentation of the latter view, see B. L. Hutchins & A. Harrison, *A history of factory legislation* (London: G. Bell and Sons, 1903); see also P. Branca, "A new perspective on women's work: a comparative typology", *Journal of Social History* **9**, pp. 129-53, 1975.

38. P. Earle, "The female labour market in London in the late seventeenth and early eighteenth centuries", *Economic History Review*, 2nd series, XLII, pp. 328-54, 1989.

39. Horrell & Humphries, "Women's labour force participation".

40. H. E. Joshi, R. Layard, S. J. Owens, "Why are more women working in Britain?", *Journal of Labor Economics* 3, p. S151, 1985.
41. UK Department of Employment and Productivity, *British labour statistics: historical abstract 1886-1968* (London: HMSO, 1971) table 102.
42. C. Hakim, "A century of change in occupational segregation 1891-1991", *Journal of Historical Sociology* 7 (4), December 1994.
43. The figures for 1901-11 are based on people aged 10 and over; for 1921 on people aged 12 and over; 1931 on people aged 14 and over; 1951-71 on people aged 15 and over, and 1981 on people aged 16 and over.
44. For evidence of this see the recent careful research tracing the development and power of such institutions, in S. O. Rose, *Limited livelihoods: gender and class in nineteenth-century England* (London: Routledge, 1992).
45. Hakim reports a male activity rate of 94 per cent for 1831; 89 per cent for 1841; 98 per cent for 1851; and 99 per cent for 1861: Hakim, "A century of change", table 1.
46. Higgs, "Women's occupations".
47. For a description of the data, see S. Horrell & J. Humphries, "Old questions, new data, and alternative perspectives: families' living standards in the Industrial Revolution", *Journal of Economic History* 52, pp. 849-80, 1992.
48. Horrell & Humphries, "Women's labour force participation".
49. See Horrell & Humphries, "Old questions", n. 40 for the construction of these weights.
50. The records for only a single trademan's family were located for this period, which means that the occupational designation of the wife in this family via the implied 100 per cent activity rate for such wives boosts the aggregated figure. See Horrell & Humphries, table 1.
51. Taking into account variations in the relative size of women's contributions to family income as well as participation, Horrell and Humphries conclude that the independence afforded to women by the economic opportunities associated with industrialization were fading by mid-century.
52. A. C. Musson, *Trade union and social history* (London: Frank Cass, 1974).
53. See S. O. Rose, *Limited livelihoods*; J. Humphries, "Industrialization and the making of gender", in *History and Development*, E. Rothschild & G. Stedman Jones (eds) (Oxford: Oxford University Press, forthcoming).

Suggestions for further reading

The classic studies of women's work during industrialization, Ivy Pinchbeck, *Women workers in the Industrial Revolution* (New York: Augustus M. Kelley, 1969, first published in 1930) and Alice Clark, *Working life of women in the seventeenth century* (London: Frank Cass, 1968, first published in 1919) have much to say about women's paid work, its embeddedness in the family economy and its complicated connections to the process of economic change. Joan W. Scott & Louise A. Tilly, *Women, work and family* (New York: Holt, Rinehart and Winston, 1978) provided an influential conceptual framework through which to understand the history of women's work. Scott's subsequent work, *Gender and the politics of history* (New York: Columbia University Press, 1988) has, through gender analysis, developed a powerful criticism of history's positivism. On another level, many authors, most of whom are cited in this chapter, have demonstrated the social construction of evidence, including the census recordings of women's paid work (but see also Nancy Folbre and Marjorie Abel, "Women's work and women's households: gender bias in the US census", *Social Research* **56**, pp. 545–69). Sara Horrell and Jane Humphries, "Women's labour force participation and the transition to the male-breadwinner family, 1790–1865," *Economic History Review*, XLVIII (forthcoming), provides quantitative evidence on women's paid work for the pre-census era. Miriam Glucksmann's work, *Women assemble: women workers and the new industries in interwar Britain* (London: Routledge, 1990) on the new industries of the interwar years is rich theoretically as well as empirically. Sonya O. Rose's *Limited livelihoods: gender and class in nineteenth-century England* (London: Routledge, 1992) is interesting for its cultural approach to gender and its insistence that gender is basic to all social processes. My own views on the cultural production of gender are outlined in "Industrialisation and the making of gender", in *History and development*, E. Rothschild & G. Stedman Jones (eds) (Oxford: Oxford University Press, forthcoming). A good overview of the history of women's work, which draws on economists' approaches as well as those of historians is provided by Alice Amsden (ed.), *The economics of women and work* (Harmondsworth: Penguin, 1980).

Chapter Five

ৠ

Women and education

Jane McDermid

Introduction

At least until the First World War, the majority of girls in Britain received a crucial part of their education in the home. Carol Dyhouse argues that there was a strongly held notion of schooling as encouraging academic aspirations in girls, undermining their attachment to home and to the domestic duties.[1] All women were expected to conform to the ideology of domesticity, which disapproved of working women and which located feminine virtue in a domestic and familial setting. Domesticity, however, differed according to class, which had implications for female education. Middle-class women were ladies, for whom waged work was demeaning, indeed a slur on middle-class manhood. Middle-class girls' education, therefore, had to correspond to their status: it should inculcate the domestic ideal; and it should also polish the young lady through a training in the social graces, which would render her competitive on the marriage market. There was no need for a grammar school or university education, whose function was to prepare middle-class boys for service to Church or state.

For working-class girls, however, who were expected to serve their betters, educational opportunity in the nineteenth century meant at most elementary schooling, and then only for a minority. The majority attended dame schools (small, private schools run by working-class women in their own homes), Sunday schools (often a combination of the two), and charity schools. The interaction of class and gender was seen at its starkest in the education of working-class girls. Besides the basic curriculum of reading, writing and arithmetic, which they shared with boys, and whose content reinforced gender divisions, working-class girls were additionally taught domestic skills, especially sewing. Historians see a variety of motives behind this stress on domestic tasks for the female lower orders: to imbue them with middle-class notions of femininity; to ensure that working-class wives acted as agents of social control in the home, influencing husband and children to accept their station in life; to prepare working-class women for the role of domestic servant; and to raise the moral standards of working-class women.

From the time of charity and dame schools, needlework had been seen as an integral part of working-class girls' education. After the Elementary Education Act of 1870, however, there were increasing arguments that domestic training for girls was essential. In the state aided schools established by the School Boards set up by the Act, domestic economy became a Specific Subject, for which a grant was available in 1874. It became compulsory in Board schools in 1878. Four years later, cookery became a Specific Subject for which a grant was available; similarly laundry in 1889. The report of the Cross Commission (1888) led to an increase in the time spent on domestic subjects, and after 1893 domestic economy became a class subject for girls, rather than as formerly a Specific Subject that they could choose not to take. In the late-nineteenth century, this stress on domestic education was related to fears of social disintegration caused by industrialization and urbanization, and from Social Darwinist fears for the race in an age of aggressive imperialism, reinforced by the revelations of the unhealthy and unfit condition of working-class men during the Boer War. Female education, it was felt, should be geared towards women as mothers; but while it was necessary to make women fit mothers, it was believed that too much education could result in infertility through overstraining the delicate female constitution. By the early twentieth century, fears about social welfare led to pressure to introduce lessons in childcare and infant management into the curriculum offered to working-class girls. Housewifery, introduced in 1897, became a grant-earning subject in 1900.

The pioneers of academic secondary education for middle-class girls resisted the introduction of domestic training for their pupils; such a subject, they believed, undermined a serious, that is male education, and was more appropriate for lower-class women. This move to include domestic science in the elementary school curriculum, however, provided a new subject of expertise for middle-class women teacher-trainees and schoolteachers, a case of increased educational opportunities shaped by conservative arguments which reinforced the separate spheres of the sexes and social divisions among women. Turnbull, however, has pointed to the contradictory position of the domestic subjects teacher, who struggled to achieve equal professional status with the elementary class teacher, even as she reinforced outmoded ideals of separate spheres for the sexes.[2]

Educational reform began in the 1840s, stimulated by a variety of factors, including the rising wealth and expectations of the middle-class; the belief that the mother, as first educator of her children, needed a sound education;

an effective increase in the number of unmarried middle-class women by 1850, when the census revealed that adult women outnumbered men in the population; the need for better education and training if such women were to get respectable employment; and the stress on equal educational opportunity in the developing feminist movement. In the first half of the nineteenth century, the only respectable occupation open to unmarried middle-class women was the position of governess. However, not only was their education inadequate to prepare them for such a post, the work was poorly paid and often brought penury in old age. In 1843, the Governesses' Benevolent Institution was founded to help any such women who found themselves in financial straits. It was soon realized, however, that financial assistance was a mere palliative. The middle-class women who needed work also needed a serious education to fit them for the post of governess. Hence the foundation in London in 1848 of both Queen's College and Bedford College to train women as teachers.

Queen's College was founded by Christian socialists, and Bedford College by a Unitarian, Mrs Elizabeth Reid. However, generally, according to Joan Burstyn, clergymen were ardent supporters of the traditional ideal of middle-class womanhood.[3] True, by the 1830s they were dissatisfied with the shallow education women received, and like the lay public were divided over how best to improve it to make women fit housewives and mothers; but generally they opposed higher education for women, basing their arguments on biblical authority and conventional wisdom. Although they failed to stop the development of higher education for women, they certainly influenced it. Moreover, educational reformers may have redefined the Victorian concept of femininity, but they did not in the main reject it. Even Emily Davies (1830–1921) of Girton College, who wanted equal education with men, was trapped between the conventions of femininity and the standards of the male academic establishment.

Education of middle-class girls and women before 1900

England led the way in reforms of middle-class girls' education. Two major parliamentary investigations, the Taunton Commission of the 1860s and the Endowed Schools' Commission of the 1870s, led to improvements for middle-class girls' schooling in both England and Wales. The Taunton Commission noted evidence which showed that the mental capacity of the sexes was virtually the same, though the education of middle-class girls before the mid-nineteenth century was, at best, frivolous, with an emphasis on the social graces. In her study of the development of girls' education in the nineteenth century, Fletcher points out that the success of two or three pioneer academic establishments was no guarantee that girls generally would be given serious secondary education.[4] Such establishments, which at least served as models for girls' academic education, included the North London Collegiate School founded by Miss Frances Buss (1827–94) and her mother in 1850, and the Cheltenham Ladies' College opened in 1854, of which Miss Dorothea Beale (1831–1906) was the celebrated second Lady Principal.

An important step towards improving the standard of education of middle-class girls and women came when Maria Grey set up in 1871 the National Union for Improving the Education of Women, and in 1872 the Girls' Public Day School Company (GPDSC). The schools established by the GPDSC were pre-eminently fee-paying, boarding establishments which sought to provide a sound liberal education, rather than professional or technical instruction. Fletcher, however, questions the progress made by the GPDSC, which by 1900 had established over 30 schools. In contrast, the Endowed Schools Act (1869) founded over 90. Yet even in 1895, girls numbered less than a quarter of the total number of pupils in endowed schools.[5] Nevertheless, it was pioneer headmistresses such as Buss and Beale in England, frustrated by the fact that the education of girls was terminated at secondary level, who pushed forward the campaign for higher education for women.

The London-based GPDSC soon extended its activities to Wales. Evans claims that the ethos of middle-class schools in nineteenth-century Wales was English.[6] Indeed, in the 1850s, those middle-class families who could afford to would send their daughters to boarding schools in England. The Association for Promoting the Education of Girls in Wales (1886–1901) sought to improve on an education which lagged behind other parts of Great Britain. Some members wanted to regard Wales as a distinct national entity. This viewpoint reflected opposition to the domination of Welsh female secondary schools by the Church of England. Evans argues that the struggle for improvement in female education was part of the Liberal–Nonconformist struggle for equality in Wales. The pioneers of female education in Wales saw themselves as starting from a different standpoint than their English counterparts. Whereas in England the campaign was to enable women to share in the educational advantages of men, in Wales the struggle was to create a higher education system for both sexes.

In Scotland, there was a general belief by the mid-nineteenth century that middle-class girls' schools were sound, so that reform was not such a pressing issue. There seems to have been no Scottish equivalent of Miss Beale. Indeed, the most prestigious private girls' schools were run by men who were interested in educational reform. The tradition in Scotland since the Reformation, which had led to the development of a parish school system, was co-educational, but by the 1850s, under the influence of the English preference for single-sex schools, private, middle-class, mixed-sex schools often split into two.[7] The growing middle-class in Scotland from the late-eighteenth century had been critical of the mixing of social classes as well as of the sexes in Scottish parochial schools. As Paterson and Fewell show, beliefs about domesticity were implicated in the gendering of education in Scotland, just as in England, as reformers sought education for girls and boys appropriate to their separate spheres and social station.[8] In contrast to England, however, middle-class girls' schools tended to be day schools. Staying at home or with a substitute family was seen as being preferable to the English tradition of boarding. In addition, many girls attended more than one school at a time. Since fees were expensive, fewer middle-class girls, generally from the upper middle-class, attended private schools in Scotland.

In the campaign for the entry of women into higher education on the same basis as men, England again led the way. Still, as June Purvis notes, it was a painfully slow process.[9] In both England and Wales, the stress on high academic standards for female middle-class education was accompanied by the continued insistence on ladylike behaviour. The new reforming head-mistresses of the late-nineteenth century felt it necessary to disprove the charge that serious education would "unsex" women. At the same time, they changed the focus of middle-class female education from the social accomplishments and the domestic ideal, to academic excellence, at least for a minority.

There were tremendous obstacles, particularly social and cultural, in the way of higher education for women, which might explain the focus in studies of women's education in the nineteenth century on a few pioneers, such as Emily Davies and Elizabeth Garrett, who were close friends. In her biography of Emily Davies, Bennett records that Davies sought educational reform step by step, by persistence and moderation. With the improvements in girls' education begun by Frances Buss and Dorothea Beale, Emily Davies soon turned her attention, in the early 1860s, to getting girls to sit Cambridge University Local Examinations on the same basis as boys. She met constant resistance. Even when the Cambridge Local Examination for girls became permanent in 1865, no names of female candidates were published.[10]

Recognizing the generally still deplorable condition of middle-class girls' education, Davies pushed, successfully, for it to be investigated by the Royal Commission into boys' schools, whose 1868 Report upheld her judgement. In her study of nineteenth-century developments in women's and girls' education, Bryant argues that the campaign for improved female education was an aspect of the reform of secondary and higher education for boys and men in the same period. Indeed, she claims that Emily Davies's insistence on her Hitchen (1869) and then Girton (1873) College students taking the same examinations as the men, and her refusal of special concessions was invaluable in raising the standards of the girls' secondary schools and colleges.[11]

Others such as Anne Jemima Clough (1820–92), were willing to compromise. In Leeds in 1867, she helped establish the North of England Council for Promoting the Higher Education of Women, whose president was Josephine Butler. The Council developed the system which came to be known as "university extension" – that is, a lecture programme for women and special university-based examinations that would give an entry into teaching. In contrast to Emily Davies, Anne Jemima Clough, the first principal of Newnham College (1871), was prepared to accept such special provisions for women.[12] On the one hand, she realized that women were not yet adequately prepared, compared to men, for university entrance, and on the other hand, she believed that the improvements in girls' secondary education would soon make any special concessions unnecessary. Emily Davies, however, felt that concessions undermined both her work at Girton and the cause of higher education for women generally. In her view, university extension classes were "ladies' lectures", not serious, systematic study.

The resistance to higher education for women came from a number of groups of people, including those who considered women would be a disruptive influence at university; doctors who insisted that female students' health would suffer from serious study; and parents who feared that their daughters would be radically transformed, believing that a girl's proper university was her home. In view of the widespread opposition to women's entry into higher education, Davies felt it was essential that Girton students observe the proprieties. She feared any loss of decorum would undermine the cause.

It was virtually impossible to refute the medical and religious arguments against higher education for women in the late-nineteenth century. There were in addition economic arguments against it, including the fear of introducing competition between the sexes for the professions, and the claim that higher education for women was an unsound investment, since they would stop work on marriage - women's supreme profession. Higher education for women nevertheless expanded. London University was the first to award women degrees on the same terms as men, in 1878. Yet in 1881 women at Cambridge University were allowed only to sit the degree examinations on the same terms as men, but not be awarded a degree if successful; it was not until 1947 that women were finally awarded degrees on the same terms as men. Indeed, by the late 1870s, small but growing numbers of women were studying scientific subjects, though they were restricted to the supposedly "feminine" ones of biology, physiology and botany. Moreover, women also faced a tremendous struggle to enter medicine. In an article written in 1873, Sophia Jex-Blake (1840–1912) recorded the struggle Elizabeth Garrett had to achieve a medical education (she ultimately had to take her MD degree in Paris):

> When in 1860 Miss Garrett desired to enter the profession, she applied for admission to one college and school after another, but with no success, until at length she discovered that the Company of Apothecaries were unable to refuse to examine any candidate who complied with their conditions. She accordingly went through a five years' apprenticeship, attended all the needful lectures, and passed all the prescribed examinations, and at length received the licence to practise, in virtue

of which she was admitted to the register. In order, however, to observe the regulations of Apothecaries' Hall, she was obliged to attend the lectures of certain specified teachers; in some cases she was admitted to the ordinary classes, but in others she was compelled to pay very heavy fees for separate and private tuition. Not content, however, with indirectly imposing this heavy pecuniary tax on women, the authorities now bethought them to pass a rule forbidding students to receive any part of their education privately – this course being publicly advised by one of the medical journals as affording a safe way of evading their legal obligations, and thus shutting out the chance left to women![13]

Developments in female higher education lagged behind in Wales. However, from 1884, women were admitted to all three of the University Colleges of Wales (Aberystwyth, Cardiff and Bangor), and from its establishment in 1894, to the University of Wales. In Scotland, a few references can be found to girls or women attending university from the late-eighteenth century, but the admission of women to Scottish universities followed the opening up, a century later, of London and Manchester Universities to women. Queen Margaret College, Glasgow, founded in 1893 and opened in 1894, was seen by many as the Scottish Girton. Indeed, in 1901, Emily Davies was awarded an honorary degree from Glasgow University.

By the last decade of the nineteenth century, a university education for women was by no means a passport to a profession. Thus, the history of higher education for women was one of struggle; and the reforms in the second half of the nineteenth century resulted in two female roles, according to Delamont: the celibate careerist, and the cultured, well-educated wife who was an intelligent partner to her husband.[14] Neither was new; and both were in keeping with the sexual division of labour.

Still, as June Purvis shows, while the female educated elite gained in self-confidence, the institutions in which they were taught remained conservative and patriarchal. In addition, higher education widened the gap between women of the middle and working-classes. The leading profession for women was teaching. Purvis maintains that college-educated women in England avoided teaching in the state-financed elementary sector which catered exclusively for the working-class. The teachers of the working-class came from the pupil-teacher system, introduced into England and Wales in 1846, and from the development of teacher-training colleges which pupil teachers could enter on a Queen's Scholarship.[15] Bergen has argued that in England, with the exception of university level, teaching was not highly regarded by the middle-class, and teaching in elementary schools was the lowest rung of the ladder.[16] Copelman's study of women teachers in London between 1870 and 1930 shows that elementary education was not thought to be respectable enough for ladies, and that elementary teachers tended to come from the labour aristocracy and the lower middle class.[17]

In her study of women at Aberdeen University between 1860 and 1920, Moore has shown a similar pattern. Most of the first female graduates went into teaching. She found social differences among these graduates: women from middle-class commercial and manufacturing families were least likely to teach in Board schools, and women from farming families were least likely to go into secondary education; most female secondary teachers came from lower middle-class backgrounds and from the daughters of labourers; and women from professional families looked for positions in the higher grade public schools for girls.[18]

Corr argues that the feminization of the teaching profession in Scotland paralleled the English experience, though at a later stage.[19] There were differences, however. Whereas women already outnumbered men in English elementary schools by the mid-nineteenth century, until then the Scottish parish schools were almost entirely run by men. The Scottish tradition was that only a graduate could aspire to be a parish schoolteacher, which precluded women, since they were excluded from the universities until the 1890s.

It was with the development of teacher training in Scotland from the 1830s that women found an entry into what had been an exclusively male profession. The moving force behind that was David Stow, who believed that infant schools should resemble a family. Given the general belief in the mother as first educator, infant teaching immediately became a female preserve. With the introduction of the pupil-teacher system, women schoolteachers became more common in Scotland. The pupil-teacher system was greatly resented, being seen as an alien English imposition, undermining the traditional link between Scottish universities and schools. Nevertheless, schools increasingly depended on pupil-teachers, the majority of whom were girls, not surprisingly given the limited number of relatively well paid occupations open to females.

Still, the Scottish educational tradition, with its stress on university education for teachers persisted, and differentiated the profession from the English situation, even as it entrenched gender divisions. Whereas in England, teachers struggled in the nineteenth century to achieve recognition as a profession, in Scotland teachers fought to prevent what was already recognised as a profession from being diluted through the admission of teachers, especially women, with no experience of university. In Glasgow especially, which was the largest School Board in Scotland, every encouragement was given to teachers to improve their educational standard, by supplementing their training with university courses. Of course, until women were admitted to universities they could not avail themselves of this opportunity for advancement, although a few took the certificate of Lady Literate in Arts (LLA). By 1895, however, training college women were admitted to university classes, and women with LLA were being appointed to training colleges.[20]

Welsh students had to go to England until 1872, when Swansea College was established (partly in response to a scarcity of Welsh-speaking elementary teachers). Welsh women continued to attend colleges in England. In colleges throughout Britain, the teaching of domestic subjects consolidated existing patterns of the sexual division of labour, and gave special responsibility to middle-class women for the inculcation of feminine qualities into their working-class counterparts. As the teaching profession in Britain was being feminized, the relationship between schooling, femininity and domesticity was strengthened, with middle-class women as key agents in the process.

Indeed, feminists in the late-nineteenth century championed gender differences in education as a means of providing middle-class, single women with career opportunities that men could not claim, and which would bring the woman teacher both status and influence in public life, as domestic science teachers. The first school of cookery in Britain was opened in London in November 1873. Two years later, two schools were opened in Scotland, one in Edinburgh and one in Glasgow. Once it became clear that working-class women were not being attracted to these schools in sufficient numbers, it was decided to reach the working-class through its daughters rather than its mothers, by training middle-class domestic science teachers. Working-class women resented what they saw as the patronizing attitude of these middle-class professionals, but the few women on School Boards tended to champion the cause of the latter. Indeed, in Scotland, they campaigned under the slogan "Home Rule for Women", with the aim of raising the status of domestic economy as a subject, and so of the domestic economy teacher, by renaming it domestic science. As Corr points out, however, even many certificated women teachers regarded the cookery teacher as having inferior status and qualifications.[21]

Widdowson has shown that whereas in England in the 1850s, elementary teaching had been an essentially working-class occupation, from the 1870s, it came to be dominated by lower middle-class women. Indeed, the increasing numbers of lower middle-class girls in training colleges in the 1860s had, she maintains, a crucial part to play in changing and liberalizing these institutions. By 1899, the examinations taken by middle-class girls at secondary schools made them eligible for training colleges. Widdowson notes that by the late nineteenth century, some lower middle-class parents were using elementary schools as a means of helping their children win scholarships to secondary schools, so that the way was open for more lower middle-class girls to become elementary teachers.[22]

However, elementary teaching did not become a generally accepted occupation for the high school educated middle-class girl before 1914, while those who entered it found the elementary system, with its stress on basic literacy, numeracy and needlework, limiting and frustrating. Thus lower-middle-class girls in particular benefited from the advances in women's education, especially from 1870, while working-class girls lost out to some extent since by the 1880s they were already being edged out of training colleges by the lower middle class.

Education of working-class girls and women before 1900

Before the 1870 Education Act, there was little formal educational provision for working-class children, boys or girls, in England and Wales.[23] Yet in what there was, the curriculum was sex-specific, in that only the girls did sewing. The main institutions attended by working-class girls before 1870 included dame schools, Sunday schools, the Church of England's National Schools (from 1811) and the Dissenters' British (and Foreign) Schools (from 1808). The influence of religion is especially clear for the last three.

Dame schools, which developed from the eighteenth century, were generally small, private ventures run by working-class women, and occasionally men, in their own homes. They were generally heavily criticised by government inspectors, and yet continued to flourish in England into the 1880s, revealing that universal education was not achieved by the 1870 Education Act. It was the School Attendance Act of 1899 which dealt the death blow to such private schools, although some survived until well into the twentieth century. By then, Britain was very much an industrial society. The dame schools had been a social, rather than an educational, response to the needs of a rural community.

Following contemporary condemnation, historians generally viewed dame schools as a cheap form of childminding. However, there has been a revisionist interpretation, notably by Phil Gardner in *The lost elementary schools of Victorian England* (1984), who argues that they were a genuine approach to infant education, and reflected a working-class rejection of middle-class prescriptions. The label "dame's school" was a middle-class one, pejorative and patronizing. Girls and boys appear to have acquired a minimum of education in dame schools, with domestic responsibilities expected especially of the former. Nevertheless, as Purvis points out, dame schools, especially when combined with attendance at Sunday school, were important to working-class girls, who were less likely than boys to attend day school. Both reinforced gender differences.[24] For those girls who attended the charity day schools of the National and British Societies, the lessons, both explicit and implicit, were in the duties of class and gender, from good servant to perfect wife and mother.

Perhaps to reflect the needs of both, the emphasis was on plain sewing for girls. Indeed, in the second half of the nineteenth century, various educational inquiries, reports and Acts advocated the expansion of domestic training for working-class girls. Thus from 1878, domestic economy was made a compulsory subject for girls; from 1882 grants were made available for the teaching of cookery; and from 1890 for laundry work. Writers on female education in the later nineteenth century generally point to two reasons for this concern: a belief in the need to inculcate middle-class standards of morality and behaviour in working-class girls, without giving them ideas above their station; and eugenicist fears for the decline of the British race and empire.[25]

In his work on female education in nineteenth-century Wales, Evans has identified a specifically Welsh dimension. The Reports of the Commissioners of Inquiry into the State of Education in Wales, published in 1847, drew a connection between the prevalence of Nonconformity in Wales and what the inspectors claimed was the especially low moral standard of the women of the lower orders. This was a charge angrily refuted by Welsh patriots. Yet they too sought improvements in female education to raise moral standards because they saw the mother's role as being crucial for the Welsh nation.[26]

Thus in the Welsh case there was the added element of nationality to the interaction of class and gender in the development of female education. Ultimately, however, throughout the nineteenth century Britain generally clung to a conservative cult of home and female domesticity, whether for class or national reasons, a cult which intensified in the late-nineteenth century as the opportunities for female education widened and seemed to threaten that ideal of domesticity.

The Scottish system of education differed, in both social and religious respects, which had an influence on female education. Whereas the Church of England was extremely wary of education for the poor, fearing a potential threat to the social order, the Protestant Reformation in Scotland had stressed the need for universal education, regardless of class or sex. By the later eighteenth century, most of the population in the Scottish Lowlands was literate. The parish school (from an Act 1696) was believed to develop a common culture for the whole nation. It taught a wide range of subjects, in sharp contrast to the narrow curriculum, and social and sexual segregation of English elementary education. Of course, affluent children could attend the parish school with regularity for several years, whereas poor children could not; but what set Scottish education apart from the English was that it represented a complete structure: a national system of education for all classes and both sexes.

Defenders of the Scottish tradition in education in the nineteenth century contrasted its democratic base – each parish had a school open to all social classes and both sexes – and its meritocratic standards – the brightest male pupil could reach university directly from the parish school, no matter how poor – with the socially divisive nature and structure of English education. There was an element of truth to the ideal of universality. A comparison of Scottish and English marriage registers for 1855 shows that in Scotland, 88.6 per cent of the new husbands and 77.2 per cent of their wives signed their names, while the corresponding figures in England were 70.5 per cent and 58.8 per cent.[27]

Yet even as education was seen as being integral to Scottish distinctiveness, as a key agent in preserving Scottish identity, that identity was essentially masculine. Girls were less likely than boys to be sent to school; girls attended schools for a shorter time than boys; and girls were taught a more restricted curriculum. Moreover, Scottish education was influenced by, and had to respond to, English practices, while English concerns of the later nineteenth century – the middle-class stress on domesticity, the eugenicist fears for the health of the future population – helped shape the experience of working-class children, especially girls.[28]

In practice, beliefs about female domesticity were reflected in the gendering of Scottish education, as in England and Wales. Yet it seems from school log books and inspectors' reports that parental resistance among the Scottish poor to their daughters being taught domestic subjects was strong, and stronger than in England and Wales. Scottish parents did not refute the notion of separate spheres for the sexes; rather, they believed that domesticity should be learned in the home, with the daughters as their mothers' apprentices. The school was for booklearning, for girls as well as for boys. Parents, it seemed, seldom differentiated between courses intended to train girls as servants, and those intended to train them as housewives. They resisted such courses, because they were not strictly educational. In her essay on educating for the "women's sphere", Moore points to a number of reasons for the opposition to the teaching of sewing, on which girls spent four hours each week, and domestic economy in Scotland, including a belief that intellectual discipline was the best means of developing an intelligent, moral and cultured individual; the tradition of mixed schooling and higher subjects; the opposition of teachers, and the initial lack of female teachers; and the attendance of a proportion of middle-class girls.[29]

Ironically, it was women, including feminists, who criticized the male educational establishment in Scotland for its opposition to domestic training. It was the upper and middle-classes who were in favour of such training, which they believed would improve working-class living standards. Whereas the stress was on sewing in the mid-nineteenth century, it shifted to cookery and laundry in the later decades. The number of girls studying domestic economy increased in the later nineteenth century, with government grants. Specific Subjects had been introduced into elementary schools to broaden the education of working-class children who stayed on to the later standards. Schools generally offered two subjects, but girls had to take domestic economy as one, while those who wanted to take cookery had to do so at the expense of more "academic" subjects. A year's cookery course consisted of forty hours, twenty of them practical. Given the cost of cookery, the onus was on the teacher to economize, so that rather than learning basic cooking of cheap produce, girls baked items for sale.

Those who championed the teaching of cooking argued that the great aim was to help working men's wives provide thoroughly good and nutritious food for their families at the smallest possible cost. Thus in a cookery book for working men's wives, published in 1889, Martha Gordon insisted that, although some of the ingredients were not commonly used, the mother of a family should grudge no trouble to gain skill and knowledge of how best to provide palatable as well as nourishing meals for her husband and children. Moreover, she claimed that "a working-man's wife who studies economy and tries by careful cooking to get all the nourishment possible out of food, will be able to feed her family on the tenth of what one, who is careless and ignorant, requires". In the introduction to Martha Gordon's recipes, Dr James Russell argued the case for a domestic education for women:

> It is as absurd for a woman to begin the business of house-keeping, without a previous apprenticeship, as it would be for a man to start right off as a journeyman, without having been an apprentice . . . Let her remember that she has not been endowed with instinct, as the lower animals are, but only with capacity, and that unless she fills up this capacity with the acquirements of education and study, she will fall far beneath the lower animals in the discharge of her duty to her husband and family.

The majority of children who left school at fourteen were pushed into "vocational" courses, including household management for girls. By the early twentieth century, the English tradition of a gendered curriculum, in which working-class girls devoted almost all the afternoons to practical domestic training, finally prevailed in Scottish schools.

Higher Grade schools were established throughout Britain in the later nineteenth century for the minority of pupils studying at least three years post-elementary. They offered girls, mainly from the lower middle and upper working classes, a wider curriculum geared to external examination, suitable for future employment in the expanding commercial sector. Nevertheless, domestic subjects retained an important place in the curriculum for girls, while the science studied by girls, with its emphasis on botany, physiology and hygiene, differed from the boys' curriculum.

It was primarily at endowed institutions and at Industrial Schools or Ragged Schools established as reformatories, or to provide for potential vagrants, that girls were to be found being prepared specifically for domestic service. In the late Victorian period, there was a sentimentalization of childhood which was linked to the dual notion of girls and women as being simultaneously sexually innocent and threatening. Industrial Schools and corrective institutions were discussed in the context of a perceived need to protect "at risk" girls and young women. Again, the social difference in virtue was stressed: the latter were of the working-class, their saviours the ladies.[30]

Lady child-savers believed that a girl's place was in the family, yet working-class girls as well as boys were expected by their parents to work outside the home. The ladies were shocked by the sexual precocity of independent working-class girls. Mahood argues that female delinquents were treated more harshly than males, because girls were seen as being especially vulnerable to the temptations of the street, thus leading to prostitution. Hence, girls were sent to reformatories and Industrial Schools to protect them from future offences. In these institutions, the stress was on discipline and domesticity to equip the girls for their future careers as domestic servants and mothers.[31]

Thus educational opportunities for working-class girls were limited in the later nineteenth and early-twentieth centuries. Moreover, the main educational efforts directed at adult women continued to emphasize their domestic role. Evening classes, for example, besides reinforcing the 3Rs, included dressmaking and cookery. Women had to struggle to be accepted into the Mechanics' Institutes (established from the early 1820s), and even then were not treated on an equal basis with men. Certainly, as Purvis has shown, despite a widening of the curriculum for working-class women to include commercial and clerical subjects, especially with the development of elementary education after 1870, it remained narrower than that offered to men.[32]

Moreover, those working-class women who sought further education were expected to do so not for reasons of self-improvement, but primarily as a benefit to others. Purvis discusses another significant adult education movement of the second half of the nineteenth century, the Working Men's College Movement. As with the Mechanics' Institutes, there was reluctance to admit women, and when they *were* admitted, women were not offered the same educational opportunities and facilities as men, though the better-off women of the Labour aristocracy and lower middle-classes could afford a wider curriculum than could poor women. Still, one result was a movement, based mainly in southern England, to establish separate working women's colleges, leading to the opening of the Working Women's College of London in 1864. Purvis sees this college as providing a different education for women, based on the pursuit of knowledge for its own sake. Nevertheless, the female students were still expected to behave with decorum, and while it was accepted that working-class women would be wage earners, at least before marriage, their main job in life was still assumed to be motherhood.[33]

Developments in the first half of the twentieth century

By the beginning of the twentieth century, then, the education of girls and women in Britain was heavily influenced by the expectations and assumptions of gender and class. In addition, there were national differences between England, Wales and Scotland, but with definite trends towards anglicization. The period up to 1945 was dominated by military involvements, economic difficulties, political crises and social conflict. The position of women was affected by all of these, and change was reflected in the growth of the feminist movement. However, the feminist movement had shifted emphasis from educational reform to suffrage, after some limited success in the former.[34]

There were Education Acts in 1902, 1918, 1936 and 1944. Yet the patterns of differentiation by gender and social class continued to shape the female experience of education. The Education Act of 1902 simplified the organization of education, doing away with the School Boards to which a few women at least had been elected, and replacing them with unelected local education authorities. The Act encouraged the development of second-ary education, but elementary education and its association with the working-classes continued.

Along with the School Boards, the Higher Grade Schools, which had provided opportunities of a cheap secondary-type education for upper working-class girls, either reverted to elementary status, or were elevated to grammar schools. The 1904 Regulations for Secondary Schools had included the idea of different curricula for girls and boys; the 1905 Regulations made housewifery a compulsory subject for girls in secondary schools; the 1907 Regulations allowed certain girls to take domestic science instead of science; by 1909, the Regulations stated that all girls were to receive training in domestic science and permitted certain girls to drop mathematics, except for arithmetic. This development might be considered to be a break with the nineteenth-century female reformers' ideal of a liberal education for middle-class girls on an equal basis to that which boys received. Domestic education, or domestic science, had been perceived not as an academic subject but as a practical, vocational subject, and as such was reserved for the lower-classes and the academically less able. Secondary schools remained very much middle-class institutions designed with university requirements in mind. Throughout the first half of the twentieth century, few working-class women entered university.

There were local differences, however. In her study of Aberdeen University, for example, Moore has found that the women who matriculated between 1894 and 1920 were overwhelmingly local, a quarter coming from professional families (especially daughters of rural ministers and teachers), and a fifth from farming families. There were working-class students (daughters of tradesmen and skilled manual workers), but they remained underrepresented. Moore suggests that, in contrast to other universities in Britain, there was at Aberdeen a belief that girls who were not ladies should still have an opportunity to study at university. The relative poverty and lower-social-class composition of female students at Aberdeen was, Moore explains, due to the relatively low cost of attendance and greater availability of financial assistance, and to the free or cheap secondary education.[35]

Certainly, facilities for women at the university were inadequate, and Aberdeen lacked the funds to follow the moves towards residential accommodation for women students which elsewhere, notably in England, was considered essential for the protection of female morality. Some saw residential accommodation as anglicizing, but the lack of it meant that almost no upper-class girls attended Aberdeen, and few upper middle-class girls did so unless they lived with families or relatives. The practice at Aberdeen was for students to stay in lodgings, separate for women and men. Possibly the cheapest in Britain, these lodgings were another factor that allowed lower-class girls to gain a university education.

Yet Moore's study shows that even at what was considered to be a "poor man's" university, the position of women students was peripheral. The Student Representative Council remained a male bastion. Most university societies and rituals were either exclusive to, or dominated by, male students; student magazines used ridicule and sarcasm to undermine women; and women were excluded from honours degrees. Not surprisingly, Moore contends, few female students challenged conventional notions of femininity.[36]

The 1918 Education Act, coming after the First World War, accepted in principle the extension of state responsibility into the area of nursery education, and raised the school leaving age to 14. After the war, however, came economic depression, with high and long-term unemployment throughout the interwar period, so that in practice nursery education was limited and most children left school at 14. Indeed, the system of half-time education, in which children worked for half the week, continued to be a feature of the British educational system into the 1920s, notably in farming and textile areas. The 1918 Act certainly indicated a shift from elementary schooling, with its stress on the 3Rs, to primary education, which was more child-centred. Yet secondary education remained the privilege of the middle-classes, while the stress in both was for an education appropriate to gender. Moreover, while the Education Act of 1936 raised the school leaving age to 15, this change was postponed by war.

Jamieson and Toynbee point out that for most rural children growing up in Scotland between 1900 and 1930, secondary education was not only culturally and socially an unlikely option, it was geographically remote, except for the offspring of wealthy farmers.[37] Elementary education was valued, despite having little relevance for the pupils' job prospects. It was more important for girls and boys to earn some money in the limited and gender-segregated labour market than to advance through the education system.

Indeed, until war broke out in 1939, most working-class children left school as soon as possible: an abrupt transition. While boys could see the move into paid employment as a rite of passage into adulthood, they still had time for leisure. Yet whether at school or in a job, girls were expected to help their mothers with housework. Traditionally, textiles had been a major employer of women, and heavy industry of men; but whereas there was this "choice" of jobs in Scotland and England, the Welsh economy was dominated by coalmining, seriously restricting employment opportunities for women. Up to

1939, there were lower rates of participation of women in the Welsh than in the English or Scottish paid labour force, and fewer job opportunities – even fewer in industrial South Wales than in the more rural West – with women concentrated in domestic service. As John remarks, images of Wales are of "a land of our fathers", in which education reinforced gender divisions. Williams suggests that the Welsh ideal of womanhood, with a strong emphasis on motherhood, was of importance to the growth of Welsh national consciousness, with its emphasis on the Welsh language and upholding the character of the nation, which were identified as female tasks.[38]

The Second World War, however, saw the 1944 Education Act, which seemed to be a radical departure from the nineteenth-century class-based system. It provided all children, to the age of 15, with the right to free secondary education. However, as Skelton points out, the decision as to the type of secondary education depended on pupils' performance in the 11-plus examination. When it was realized that girls performed better than boys in this examination, the educational authorities perceived this to be a problem. The solution, Skelton argues, was to weight girls' performances differentially from those of boys, so that the girls received fewer places than their results should have merited.[39] This solution reflected the continuing assumption that girls were to have an education in domesticity, that their future was motherhood. Moreover, although the 1944 Act was to encourage social mobility, there remained a class basis to domestic education for girls, which represented continuity with nineteenth-century ideas. Thus domestic subjects were targeted at the less able and the lower-classes, and so were relatively neglected in grammar schools, but were significant in the low status secondary modern sector.

Why was this so? Since the late nineteenth century there had been fears for the future of the race which had seemed validated by the physical examination of working-class men for first the Boer War and then the First World War. In 1907 the Eugenics Education Society was founded, which produced a journal, *Eugenics Review*, from 1908. The Society reflected the general unease over the international decline of Britain, the causes of which were believed to be domestic; hence the stress on teaching working-class women household management and infant care: to enhance national efficiency. Also from the late-nineteenth century, there was considerable emphasis placed on the physical education of girls as well as boys. Here again, there were differences, with the stress for the latter on drill and team games, and for the former on hygiene and gymnastics.

In addition, the aftermath of the Second World War had brought growing anxieties about the stability of the family. In particular, there were worries about the social behaviour of young people, and the changing role of women. Once again, education was to achieve moral improvement; once again, for girls this meant a stress on domesticity; and once again, women were to be educated, not for self-improvement, but to promote social cohesion.

The reforming Labour administration under Clement Attlee promoted welfare legislation, with the focus on the mother and the family. It viewed any demands for equal pay and educational and career opportunities as the preoccupation of a minority of middle-class, childless spinsters. Education was still not seen as the basis of a career for women; rather it was to make them more interesting companions. After the war there was a labour shortage, yet there were renewed calls for the education of girls in mothercraft. Ellen Wilkinson, as Minister of Education, saw the mother's place as being in the home.[40]

Indeed, in 1948, John Newsom advocated a separate curriculum for girls, firmly grounded in domestic subjects. He criticized grammar schools for girls because they placed too much stress on public examinations and success in obtaining professional careers. He lamented that the "clever" girl was being encouraged to give up domestic subjects in favour of academic ones. Newsom did not deny that girls should get equal opportunities in education with boys; instead, he insisted that girls had different needs, to prepare them for homemaking and motherhood.[41]

Skelton argues that the intentions laid down in the 1944 Education Act to address equal opportunities in fact did nothing to further educational chances of the girls'.[42] The Act established the right to free secondary education for all children, to encourage social mobility. Based on the 11-plus examination, it was a meritocratric structure which ideally would reward the talented child, irrespective of sex, class or ethnic origin. However, the Act also recognized that there were different aptitudes, as well as abilities, and implicitly those of girls were seen as being domestic. Even though it was recognized that education influenced employment opportunities, and that married women might want to return to the labour force once their children were no longer infants, it was still expected that women combined their primary career, the home, with their supplementary one, the job.

Moreover, Newsom believed that the unmarried career schoolmistress was a poor role model. He advised that female teachers should be attractive, to give their girl charges the impression that they were not spurning marriage, so that any with "strong homosexual impulses" should be excluded. He recommended a mixture of unmarried and happily married teachers. (The 1944 Act had removed the marriage bar for teachers.) Modern society, he felt, was undermining the woman's role of nurturer to both sexes, whether as wife, mother or teacher.[43] He had the support of middle-class women. "Problem" families were seen as being, above all, working-class, and the stress was on the need to educate future mothers. Indeed, few female academics or educationalists seemed to question the notion of marriage and motherhood as a career. Whatever Newsom's fears, the unmarried female teacher presented her pupils with traditional images of women's expectations in life.

In any case, the choice of professional careers for women remained restricted, and dominated by primary teaching. Few primary teachers had a university education; most had been to teacher training colleges. Even for those few women who entered medicine, there were limits to what they might aspire to. For example, in her study of early Glasgow women medical graduates, Alexander found that only one of the city's three large voluntary teaching hospitals accepted women residents.[44] Women were accepted to residencies in only two out of a total of over ten specialist hospitals, and both of them dealt exclusively with gynaecology, indicating a "ghettoization" of women into the "female" sectors of medical practice. Indeed, Glasgow's foremost teaching hospital (the "Western") did not admit women to clinical instruction until 1920, and did not appoint women residents until forced to do so during the Second World War. Women were pushed into less prestigious posts, such as in the Poor Law Infirmaries, or into general practice.

Alexander believes that while there was public hostility to female graduates, it was the medical profession and male boards of management that offered the greatest resistance, perhaps because they felt threatened more directly. Indeed, generally female university students were outnumbered three to one, and women had less chance of admission to the more prestigious universities and professions.

Conclusion

When looking at the history of women's education in Britain, England has generally been taken as the model. It is clear from this overview that however strong the trends of anglicization, there were still differences of nationality between Wales, Scotland and England which interacted with social class and gender differentiation. Moreover, within each country there were regional differences – for example, between rural and urban, and textiles and heavy industry – which influenced education.

In addition, the religious influences, and differences, that have been alluded to here (Nonconformity in Wales, Anglicanism in England, Presbyterianism in Scotland) reflect the dominant Churches. Thus, for example, the Roman Catholic Church had to respond to the mass Irish immigration of the nineteenth century, as well as the host nations' anti-Catholicism. The reaction was to establish separate schools for Catholic children. The Catholic Poor Schools Committee was set up by the bishops of England and Wales in 1847, and joined later by the Scots. It faced problems of generalized poverty, so that it might be argued that Catholic girls and boys, the majority of whom were working-class, had a common experience of school: the emphasis was on elementary education, very few having the opportunity to take Specific Subjects, and most went on to unskilled work. Yet Catholic education too was influenced by gender. For girls, the stress was on sewing and, if possible, domestic economy. Indeed, there was an implicit fear in school log books and inspectors' reports that the low level of female education would continue into the next generation because of the mothers' ignorance: hence the need for improvements in the education of Catholic girls, not for themselves but for the good of their families, and indeed of the standing of the Catholic community within the national community.

Thus over the century from 1850, female education was influenced by gender, class, religion and nationality, while local studies would reveal the impact of regional as well as national economic factors. There was also the influence of feminist campaigners for reform in female education, especially at secondary and higher level, of eugenicist ideas and of the Victorian ideology of domesticity. Ideas of femininity were imparted not only through the formal educational structure, but also through reading material directed at girls and women. Thus both Gorham and Tinkler highlight the importance of fiction for girls. Again, there was a class dimension. Gorham, who examines the period 1850 to 1914, points out that the schoolgirl fiction of the turn of the century reflected upper-class and middle-class girls' experience. Tinkler argues for the later period (1920 to 1950), that, while girls' magazines varied according to age and social class, all offered common images of femininity and prescriptions of female behaviour.[45] Certainly, girls were to be socialized for their station in life, and discouraged from ambitions of rising up the social scale; but they were also all encouraged to look for job satisfaction, not in a career of paid employment, but in marriage and motherhood. Wherever they lived in Britain in the century from 1850 to 1950, they were not born a woman, they became one.

Notes

1. C. Dyhouse, *Girls growing up in late Victorian and Edwardian England* (London: Routledge, 1981), p. 103.
2. A. Turnbull, "An isolated missionary: the domestic subjects teacher in England 1870–1914", *Women's History Review* 3 (1), pp. 81–100; 95–6, 1994.
3. J. Burstyn, *Victorian education and the ideal of womanhood* (London, 1980) p. 38.
4. S. Fletcher, *Feminists and bureaucrats: a study in the development of girls' education in the nineteenth century* (Cambridge: Cambridge University Press, 1980), p. 13.
5. *Ibid.*
6. W. G. Evans, *education and female emancipation: the Welsh experience* (Cardiff: University of Wales Press, 1990), p. 60.
7. For the Scottish tradition in education, see, for example, *Scottish Culture and Education, 1800-1980*, M. Walter, Humes & Hamish, M. Paterson (eds) (Edinburgh, 1983). For female education and the Scottish tradition, see F. Paterson & J. Fewell (eds) *Girls in their prime: Scottish education revisited*, (Edinburgh: Scottish Academic Press, 1990), especially Ch. 1 by the editors; Helen Corr, "An Exploration into Scottish Education", Ch. 10 in *People and Society in Scotland*, vol. 2: *1830-1914*, W. H. Fraser and R. J. Morris (eds) (Edinburgh, 1989).

8. Paterson & Fewell, *Girls in their Prime*, p. 6.

9. J. Purvis, *A history of women's education in England* (Milton Keynes: Open University Press, 1991), p. 116.

10. D. Bennett, *Emily Davies and the liberation of women* (London: Andre Deutsch, 1990). See also S. Fletcher, *Feminists and Bureaucrats*, pp. 13–27; J. Purvis, *A history of women's education in England*, Chs. 4, 5.

11. M. Bryant, *The unexpected revolution: a study in the history of the education of women and girls in the nineteenth century* (London: London University Institute of Education, 1979), pp. 64–87. Hitchen moved to the Girton site, nearer Cambridge, in 1873: see Bennett, *Emily Davies*, pp. 141-8.

12. For a discussion of the Davies–Clough disagreement over part-time university classes, see Purvis, *A history of women's education*, pp. 109–15; and see Bennett, *Emily Davies*, pp. 200-2 on strained relations between the two women's colleges of Girton and Newnham.

13. S. Jex-Blake, "The medical education of women (1873)", in *The education papers: women's quest for equality in Britain 1850-1912*, Dale Spender (eds) (London: Routledge & Kegan Paul, 1987), pp. 268-76; 273.

14. S. Delamont & L. Duffin (eds), *The nineteenth-century woman: her cultural and physical world* (London, 1978), pp. 182, 184.

15. J. Purvis, "Women and teaching in the nineteenth century", in *Education and the State*, vol. 2: *Politics, patriarchy and practice*, R. Dale, G. Esland, R. Ferguson, M. MacDonald (eds) (Falmer: Taylor and Francis, 1981), pp. 359-75; 365.

16. B. H. Bergen, "Only a schoolmaster: gender, class, and the effort to professionalize elementary education in England, 1870-1910", *History of Education Quarterly* 22 (1) pp. 1-21, (Spring 1982); 10, 14. See also C. Heward, "Men and women and the rise of a professional society: the intriguing history of teacher educators", *History of Education* 22 (1), pp. 11-32, 1993.

17. D. Copelman, *Gender, class and feminism: women teachers in London, 1870-1930* (London: Routledge, 1995).

18. L. Moore, *Bajanellas and semilinas: Aberdeen University and the education of women 1860-1920* (Aberdeen: Aberdeen University Press, 1991).

19. H. Corr, " 'Home-rule' in Scotland: the teaching of housework in schools, 1872-1914", Ch. 3 in Paterson & Fewell, *Girls in their prime*.

20. See H. Corr, "The sexual division of labour in the Scottish teaching profession", Ch. 7 in Humes & Paterson, *Scottish culture and education*.

21. H. Corr, " 'Home-Rule' in Scotland". For England, see Turnbull, "An isolated missionary".

22. F. Widdowson, *Going up into the next class: women and elementary teacher training 1840-1914* (London: Women's Research and Resources Centre Publications, 1980), p. 46.

23. Purvis, *A history of women's education*, Ch. 2.

24. *Ibid.*, p. 15.

25. See for example, C. Dyhouse, "Social Darwinist ideas and the development of girls' education in England, 1800-1920", *History of Education* 5 (1), pp. 41-58, 1976.

26. W. G. Evans, *Education and female emancipation: the Welsh experience 1847-1914* (Cardiff: Cardiff University of Wales Press, 1990), pp. 46-9. See also Angela V. John (ed.), *Our mothers' land, chapters in Welsh women's history 1830-1939*, (Cardiff: University of Wales Press, 1991), pp. 69-70, 141-2, 148.

27. J. Scotland, *The history of Scottish education*, vol. 1, (London, 1969), p. 359; R. A. Anderson, *Education and opportunity in Victorian Scotland*, (Oxford, 1983), p. 8.

28. L. Moore, "Invisible scholars: girls learning Latin and mathematics in the elementary public schools of Scotland before 1872", *History of Education*, **13** (2), pp. 121-37, 1984; Robert Anderson, "Secondary schools and Scottish society in the nineteenth century", *Past & Present* **109**, pp. 176-203, November 1985.

29. L. Moore, "Educating for the 'woman's sphere': domestic training versus intellectual discipline", Ch. 2 in *Out of bounds: women in Scottish society, 1800-1945*, Eleanor Gordon and Esther Breitenbach (eds) (Edinburgh: Edinburgh University Press, 1992), pp. 31-2.

30. See, for example L. Mahood, "Family ties: lady child-savers and girls of the street, 1850-1925", Ch. 3 in Breitenbach & Gordon, *Out of Bounds*.

31. *Ibid.*, p. 46.

32. J. Purvis, *Hard lessons: the lives and education of working-class women in nineteenth-century England* (Cambridge: Polity Press, 1989): Ch. 5, for women and the Mechanics' Institute movement; p. 141, for evening class curriculums for working-class women.

33. *Ibid.*, Chs 7 and 8.

34. See, for example, O. Banks, *Faces of feminism: a study of feminism as a social movement* (Oxford: Martin Robertson, 1981); P. Hollis, *Women in public: the women's movement* (London: George Allen and Unwin, 1979); L. Leneman, *A guid cause: the women's suffrage movement in Scotland* (Aberdeen: Aberdeen University Press, 1991).

35. L. Moore, *Bajanellas and Semilinas*, pp. 120; 122; 134.

36. *Ibid.*, pp. 105; 111; 135.

37. L. Jamieson & C. Toynbee, *Country bairns: growing up 1900-1930* (Edinburgh: Edinburgh University Press, 1992), pp. 9-10.

38. A. John, *Our mothers' land*, p. 1; and S. R. Williams, "The true 'Cymroes': images of women in women's nineteenth-century Welsh periodicals", Ch. 3 in John, *Our mothers' land*.

39. C. Skelton, "Women and education", Ch. 4 in *Introducing women's studies*, D. Richardson & V. Robinson (eds) (London: Macmillan, 1993), p. 329.

40. J. Lewis, *Women in Britain since 1945* (Oxford: Blackwell, 1992), p. 23; R. Lowe, *Education in post-war years: a social history* (London, 1988), introduction; B. Vernon, *Ellen Wilkinson 1891-1947* (London: Croom Helm, 1982), Ch. 10, esp. pp. 222-4.

41. J. Newsom, *The education of girls* (London, 1948), p. 108.

42. Skelton, *Women and education*, p. 329.

43. Newsom, *The education of girls*, p. 149.

44. W. Alexander, "Early Glasgow women medical graduates", Ch. 4 in *The world is ill divided: women's work in Scotland in the nineteenth and early twentieth centuries*, E. Gordon & E. Breitenbach (eds) (Edinburgh: Edinburgh University Press, 1990), see pp. 76-7 (career patterns) and 81-6 (areas of speciality).

45. D. Gorham, "The ideology of femininity and reading for girls 1850-1914", Ch. 3; and P. Tinkler, "Learning through leisure: feminine ideology in girls' magazines 1920-50", Ch. 4 in *Lessons for life: the schooling of girls and women 1850-1950*, Felicity Hunt (ed.) (Oxford: Basil Blackwell, 1987).

Suggestions for further reading

You will find a variety of sources in the footnotes, which cover girls' and women's education at all levels, both formal and informal, consider issues of class and gender, and discuss the feminization of elementary teaching in the nineteenth century. For an accessible introduction to the themes in, and sources (both primary and secondary) for, female educational history, see Deirdre Beddoe, "The education of girls", in her book *Discovering women's history: a practical manual*, (London: Pandora, 1983). You will find a concise overview of the history in Christine Skelton, "Women and education", in *Introducing women's studies*, Diane Richardson & Victoria Robinson (eds) (London: Macmillan, 1993). A valuable selection of documents, articles and papers on women's education is Dale Spender (ed.) *The education papers: women's quest for equality in Britain 1850–1912* (London: Routledge & Kegan Paul, 1987).

The history of female education in Britain developed first in England, with what would now be considered classic texts such as Dorothy Gardiner, *English girlhood at school: a study of women's education through twelve centuries* (London: Oxford University Press, 1929) and Josephine Kamm, *Hope deferred: girls' education in English history* (London: Methuen, 1965). These, along with Margaret Bryan, *The unexpected revolution: a study in the history of the education of women and girls in the nineteenth century* (London: University of London Institute of Education, 1979), might be considered the optimistic school of female educational history, with a tendency to focus on the achievements in reforming middle-class girls' education and women's entry into higher education. A useful survey of this early literature, which takes into account the developments in feminist approaches to women's history of the early 1970s, is Joan Burstyn, "Women's education in England during the nineteenth century: a review of the literature", in *History of Education* **6** (1), 1977.

More recent studies, which reflect historiographical developments (such as gender and history, and history from below) include Carol Dyhouse, *Girls growing up in late Victorian and Edwardian England* (London: Routledge, 1981) and the work of June Purvis, both her general survey, *A history of women's education in England* (Milton Keynes: Open University Press, 1991) and her special study *Hard lessons: the lives and education of working-class women in nineteenth-century England* (Cambridge: Polity, 1993). A book which covers the century we have been dealing with, looking not only at what girls and women were taught, but also at what they read, is Felicity Hunt (ed.), *Lessons for life: the schooling of girls and women 1850–1950*, (Oxford: Basil Blackwell, 1987).

In Scotland and Wales, there has been some recent work on female education which has both learned from the pioneering English studies, and revealed differences (notably national and religious), as well as points in common, in female education in Britain. For Scotland, see Lindy Moore, "Education for the 'woman's sphere': domestic training versus intellectual discipline", in *Out of bounds: women in Scottish society 1800-1945*, Eleanor Gordon and Esther Breitenbach (eds) (Edinburgh: Edinburgh University Press, 1992) and the interesting collection of essays by Fiona Paterson and Judith Fewell (eds), *Girls in their prime: Scottish education revisited* (Edinburgh: Scottish Academic Press, 1990). For Wales see W. Gareth Evans *Education and female emancipation: the Welsh experience* (Cardiff: University of Wales Press, 1990).

Finally, if you want to pursue the themes of national difference within the UK, and the interaction of nationality with gender, class and religion, you should turn to Mary Cullen (ed.), *Girls don't do honours: Irish women in education in the nineteenth and twentieth centuries* (Dublin: Women's Education Bureau, 1987).

Chapter Six

ꙮ

Women and popular literature

Penny Tinkler

The period 1850-1945 was, as we saw in Chapter 5, significant for the development of schooling for girls. This education was differentiated by both social class and, importantly, gender. The education of girls and young women was not solely the province of formal institutions. Gendered lessons, infracted by social class and also by age, were conveyed informally through the organization of everyday life; the structuring of home, workplace and community; relationships; appearance; and leisure.[1] Historical research has begun to unravel the ways in which gender was embodied in, and transmitted through, historically specific cultural practices, including reading.[2] It also addresses representations of girls and women and the construction of femininities, especially in popular literature.[3] This interest in popular literature stems from two main sources. First, the recognition that throughout the period, popular novels and magazines attracted a large and wide-ranging female audience.[4] Also, that the print media was important in the cultural reproduction and construction of gender. Secondly, the period after 1850 is seen as being particularly significant for the advent and proliferation of popular literature targeted specifically at women and girls. Indeed, by the turn of the twentieth century, girls and women were constituted as a gender-specific market for the expanding publishing industries. Somewhat more ambiguously, this market was also differentiated by social class and age.

This chapter examines the significance which historians of women have placed on the study of popular literature, in terms of its realism, for example, and its contribution to the cultural construction of gender. Focusing on a particular form of literature, namely the girls' magazine, this chapter will examine some of the strategies that magazines used to communicate with their readers. While magazine form and content was throughout the period

1850-1945 characterized by gender-specificity, magazines and their representations of femininity have also been characterized by variation and change. Using examples from popular magazines produced for young women between 1900 and 1945, this chapter will examine the ways in which magazines constructed and managed difference along gender, class and age lines, and how they addressed change through their representation of the modern girl.

Popular literature and women's history[5]

The study of popular literature, in particular novels and periodicals, has contributed important dimensions to the history of girls and women in England during the nineteenth and twentieth centuries. The segmentation of publishing along gender, class and age lines has been the subject of particularly fruitful enquiry. This research has traced the creation of a gendered juvenile literature which contributed to the construction and institutionalization of youth and adolescence.[6] Editorial processes and policies, and the role of women *in* cultural production has, however, been a somewhat neglected topic of research. Women novelists have received attention, but very little is known about women's contribution to the production of periodicals.[7] Research into the content of popular literature is, in contrast, more extensive. Historians have, for instance, focused on realism in literature as a source for researching the conditions of women and girls. Beauman, for example, examines novels written by women in the 1920s and 1930s for an audience of mainly middle-class women. These novels, she argues, were permeated with the "certainty of the like speaking for the like"; subsequently, she extracts from this fiction details about the daily lives and concerns of middle-class women during the interwar period.[8] In a study of didactic literature written for middle-class Victorian girls, Judith Rowbotham similarly looks for information about the experiences of readers. She argues that authors utilized an illusion of reality in order to give credibility to an otherwise unconvincing narrative. They also incorporated a wide picture of society into their novels to convey the pivotal nature of the female role. Subsequently, "it is possible to learn almost as much from these books as those for boys about military matters, to say nothing of ideals of masculinity and expectations of male stereotypes".[9] Bratton similarly utilizes the mimetic strategy of popular literature for these purposes.[10]

Historians have also mined popular novels and periodicals for the insights they offer into the cultural construction of femininity and the ways in which it has varied by age and social class and changed over time. Gorham, for example, explores the construction of girlhood and femininity in Victorian "prescriptive and imaginative literature", showing how this literature responded to the "widening sphere" of middle-class women's employment and fears concerning the women's movement.[11] The ways in which popular magazines for girls and young women constructed femininity in the period between 1920 and 1945 will be looked at later in the chapter.

Popular literature has also been studied for its representation of contemporary value systems. Bratton's conclusions regarding this dimension of Victorian juvenile literature are more widely applicable to prescriptive literature:

> In the case of so didactic, so intention-ridden a creation as the Victorian moral tale for children, the author's avowed desire to teach is an unavoidable starting point. The story may have several other layers worth exploring, but its surface is more or less entirely covered by the author's intentions – fully conscious didactic aims and transmission of other values which are part of any literary production.[12]

Even those forms of literature that eschewed didactic aims can be used in this way. Auchmuty, for example, draws upon her study of schoolgirl stories for insights into attitudes towards friendships between girls. More broadly, she argues:

> popular fiction is both evidence of, and propaganda for, a particular world view. It posits certain institutions, ideals and moral values as the unquestioned and unquestionable norm. These institutions (for instance, marriage and the family), ideals (romantic love, chivalry), and values (respect for authority, the team spirit) help to ensure a docile, submissive population.[13]

The popularity of certain forms of literature with different groups of female readers has also been addressed by historians. Drotner, for instance, attributes the success of the juvenile periodical to its ability to organize the contradictory experiences of childhood and youth in pleasurable ways. In relation to school stories of the 1920s, she argues that they had a wide appeal because "they captured and successfully harmonised, for working-class and lower-middle-class girls in particular, the real-life dilemmas caused by innovations within the school system".[14] This resolution of conflict is also a central feature of Reynold's analysis of the attractions of juvenile popular literature between 1880 and 1910.[15] Auchmuty is similarly concerned with appeal. Focusing on the novels of Elsie Oxenham, Elinor Brent-Dyer, Dorita Fairlea Bruce and Enid Blyton, Auchmuty considers why these schoolgirl stories have remained popular with girls for nearly a century. She concludes that in reading these fictions "girls and women escape temporarily into a world dominated by women – where patriarchal values, while rarely actually absent, may be softened by feminine influence, avoided as far as possible, or transformed at the hands of women into something positive for themselves."[16]

A further approach, and one that overlaps with the others, concerns the contribution of representations of women to the historical construction of gender identity. This has been a key concern of research on contemporary women's and girls' literature; it has also been a preoccupation of feminist historians and a primary motivation behind much historical research in this area.[17]

Putting the message across

Since the beginnings of mass literature there has been both optimism and anxiety about its possible influence, and attention has been directed at how to utilize or restrict this power. Certain forms of popular literature have been promoted as a means to guide and educate mass audiences. Flint details some of the ways in which the reading matter of Victorian girls and women was promoted as a form of social education.[18] Many popular girls' and women's magazines were quite explicit about their intention to influence or advise their readers. The *Girl's Own Paper*, for example, was blatantly missionary in intent, while the aptly named women's "service magazines" such as *Woman's Own* (1932) aimed to provide young wives and mothers with detailed information on home management. During the Second World War these magazines were mobilized by the government for the purposes of propaganda and information dissemination.[19] While some magazines admitted freely their education objectives, most twentieth-century fiction papers denied any attempt at instruction.[20] Irrespective of their intentions or claims, however, these magazines did convey messages about gender, class, and also age.

Popular literature has also been attacked by critics for exerting a harmful influence on the working-classes, especially on young women and men.[21] Describing the "informal education" of a group of girls aged 14 to 18 years in the early 1940s, Jephcott pointed to the unhealthy influence that magazines had on elementary schoolgirls and young working-class workers, particularly in the absence of alternative reading.[22] Middle-class girls, she suggests, were generally immune to such influence because they received an extended formal education and a more supervised informal one. Although motivated by different concerns, feminist historians have also been concerned with the influence of popular literature, particularly in relation to the construction of gender, and the implications of representations of femininity for the ways in which female readers come to understand themselves, and how they are perceived by others.

According to socialization theory, girls' experiences of the family, schooling and the media have an important role to play in the acquisition of gender identity. More specifically, socialization refers to the ways in which girls and boys learn the appropriate behaviour for their gender, class, ethnicity and "race".[23] While the family has been identified as crucial to early gender socialization, providing "the first lessons in femininity",[24] historians

134

have also perceived the media, especially its representations of femininity, to be an important source of feminine socialization.

Initial assumptions about the effect of representations have been hard to prove. As Bratton points out, historians encounter problems in attempting to assess the impact of reading.[25] Aside from the methodological difficulty of researching effect, however, the theory of socialization has, in recent years, also been subject to extensive criticism on a number of grounds. Walby, for example, criticizes socialization theory for placing too much emphasis on the cultural as opposed to the structural. Women's activities, she argues, have been attributed too readily to internalized ideas rather than being seen as responses to limited options. She also points out that socialization theory fails to address the contradictory nature of many of the messages that women are exposed to. Moreover, it assumes that girls and women are merely passive consumers of culture, a model that leaves little space for resistance and difference.[26] As Dyhouse demonstrates in *Feminism and the family*, women did not meekly accept prevailing ideas about the family and femininity: there was much discontent and, importantly, resistance.[27] It is now widely recognized that texts can be read in different ways, and that the audience – "girls" or "women" – are neither homogenous nor passive in their reading of popular cultural forms.[28] In other words, we cannot assume effect because meaning is neither singular nor transparent, and does not reside solely in the text. This development has had methodological implications in that it problematizes the historian's reading and interpretation of the text.

Historians of culture have not, however, been deterred by these developments; they have become more alert to the ways in which texts frame "preferred readings", and they have become more sensitive to the diversity of audiences and the possible ways in which readers construct meaning.[29] Drotner, for instance, uses reader reception theory to explore the varied ways in which children from different gender and class groups read and enjoyed magazines, and how this may have changed over time. She looks for congruence between the historically-specific conditions and experiences of childhood for different groups, and the content of magazines.[30] Flint similarly focuses on the practice of reading, comparing different perceptions of the "woman reader" between 1837 and 1914 with accounts of the actual reading practices of Victorian and Edwardian girls and women.[31] Reynolds examines the ways in which popular authors inscribed their definition of femininity as right and natural, using language, structure and content. She also employs psychoanalytic, feminist and structuralist approaches to understand the possible consequences of reading for gender development.[32]

Despite the challenge of recent theoretical developments, historians continue to view popular literature as a powerful source of messages. Drotner concludes that: "Popular reading, then, held a strong emotional appeal to the generation of interwar children who had lost traditional areas of independence and who had not yet witnessed the deluge of the welfare state".[33] Reynolds similarly views juvenile literature as being influential, in that it created readers who could be relied upon to read – and probably to select – safely: "By drawing readers into ideological and discursive positions which encouraged them to accept as right and natural the existing social structure . . . these books together became a lens through which all other fictions were likely to be perceived and filtered . . . Furthermore, because such works give the impression of resolving conflict and offer fantasy-alternatives to difficult or uncongenial realities, they may set up a kind of dependency in the reader who wishes to regain the pleasurable sensation of harmony, resolution and emotional gratification they offer".[34]

Before moving on to examine magazine publishing and content, I want to look in more detail at some of the ways in which magazines produced for adolescent schoolgirls and young working women conveyed their messages. I shall focus here, for purposes of illustration, on the period 1920–50. An initial consideration in magazine production was to ensure that the presentation was appropriate to the intended reader: this often involved "sugaring the pill". Fiction magazines conveying information employed different means from those papers that had explicit advisory or instructional intentions. *The Girl's Own Paper*, for example, presented occupational advice regularly throughout the 1940s in a feature entitled "Carol's Career Corner", which provided detailed description of a range of careers. In contrast, *Girls' Favourite*, a paper for working-class readers, presented advice about work and careers through the fictional dialogue of a group of friends, each in a different occupation.[35] *Girls' Weekly* similarly fictionalized its careers advice. In one series entitled "From Kitchen To Cinema Star",, the reader is invited to follow the account of a movie star's rise to fame through a number of different jobs:

> A well known movie favourite has written her experiences and told how, by her own determination to succeed, she rose from the humble post of kitchen-maid to the one she now occupies. From kitchen-maid she became a waitress in a tea-room, then a clerkess, and from this to receiving 'sitters' in a photographers. After serving for a short time in a hat shop she became a musical comedy actress. Next came her big opportunity – the chance to work for the films.[36]

The use of a "famous actress" was a particularly clever ploy, given the popularity of cinema and acting ambitions at this time.[37] This autobiography, which was probably fictional, provided direct information about the range of jobs open to the magazine's intended readers. At each stage of her reminiscences, the "famous actress" describes the pros and cons of her work, its duties, and how and why she moved on to something different. It also communicated persuasively the ethos of individual betterment.

While on the one hand magazines adjusted their presentation to maintain their readers' attention, on the other they incorporated strategies to frame the "preferred meaning".[38] Narrative structure and conventions were important and, more directly, editorials, feature titles, illustrations, and other techniques of repetition and reinforcement. Other strategies included the marginalization or exclusion of certain themes and issues. In many respects, the messages conveyed through magazines were reinforced by other sets of messages and practices, both material and ideological.

Mechanisms of persuasion were also employed. At one end of the scale, editors attempted to befriend their readers by using forms of personal identification. The "editress" of *Girls' Friend* in her promotion of *Poppy's Paper*, declared, "You will find in 'Poppy' a friend whom you may safely take into your confidence"; Peg, of *Peg's Paper*, referred to her readers as "my girls" and in her introductory editorial of 1919 she set about establishing a rapport based on similarity of interests: "let's be pals" – not so long ago I was a millgirl, too, and my clogs clattered with yours down the cobbled street . . . Because I've been a worker like you I know what girls like, and I'm going to give you a paper you'll enjoy".[39] Other techniques, such as the use of illustrations and warnings invoked fear, and amounted to emotional black-mail. This advertisement from *Poppy's Paper* in 1930, which presents female body hair as unnatural and unfeminine, provides a typical example of this process: "There is nothing more repellant to a man than a masculine growth of hair on the limbs and arms – it robs a woman of every vestige of daintiness and charm. Remove this disfigurement which breaks romance and spoils your happiness and joy".[40]

Perhaps most importantly, popular magazines were influential because they were widely disseminated and read.[41] More specifically, their potential influence derived from the fact that they were one of the few media to address young female readers specifically, and ostensibly from a feminine vantage point. Linked to this, they offered advice and information on issues of concern to many girls and women which were rarely addressed elsewhere, particularly concerning the private sphere, relationships and emotions and, by the 1940s, the female body. Particular guidance was offered on the construction of a feminine appearance, which included tips on posture, makeup, dress, skin and general health care. This information, readers were assured, was essential for every girl who sought to be successful in courtship and marriage. Alongside articles, the letter pages were particularly important for addressing readers' concerns. Although doubts have sometimes been expressed about the authenticity of letters printed in correspondence features, my interviews with those who worked on girls' and women's magazines suggests that most letters were genuine, but that censorship was strict, thereby ensuring that certain issues never achieved public exposure.[42] References to the physical changes associated with puberty, (hetero)sexual relations and, importantly, actual or desired sexual relations with women, were most certainly taboo. Readers' requests for information usually concerned courtship, appearance and, importantly, relationships with parents, in particular mothers. In reply to a letter from a girl who complained that her mother never let her out of her sight, the correspondence editor advised;

> if you are not too young, there is no earthly reason why you should be tied to your mother's apron-strings in this way, and she is exceedingly selfish to expect you to put up with it. Mothers so often forget that they were once young themselves and although I am not advising you to defy your mother or to be rude to her, I think you should point out to her that you have your own life to live and tell her you're not content to be treated as a child.[43]

Not only did magazines respond to readers' perceived interests, they also solicited their views and in doing so contributed to a longstanding tradition in the women's periodical press. "Our Girls' Parliament", which regularly appeared in *Girls' Reader* in 1915, and various letter competitions in the *Girl's Own Paper* and *Miss Modern* during the 1930s offer a few examples of attempts to engage the female reader seriously as contributor.

Given the possible influence of these papers, the ways in which they constructed female readers, and the representations they offered to girls, would seem to be important concerns for historians of women. In what follows, I will look at how publishers constructed a specifically female market for periodicals, and how they also sought to establish sub-groups of readers by class and age.

Magazines for "girls"

Periodicals for children proliferated during the nineteenth century, although it was not until the 1860s that gender-specific literature emerged, targeted at the middle-class girl and her brother. Magazines launched included the *Girl of the Period Miscellany* (1869); *Every Girl's Magazine* (1878); *Girl's Own Paper* (1880); and the *Girl's Realm* (1898). Drotner attributes this attention to the late-nineteenth-century rise and prosperity of the middle-classes, and the recognition by publishers of the commercial possibilities of upper-class and middle-class girls and boys. The discovery of this audience was particularly important, Drotner argues, as mass circulation publishers competed fiercely for new customers, profits and security.[44] Reflecting and reinforcing the gender demarcations of middle-class education provision, girls and boys were catered for by separate books and magazines.

The passing of the Education Act in 1870 and the introduction of compulsory education in 1880 served to construct, institutionalize and universalize childhood as a period distinct from adulthood. Curriculum differentiation in elementary schooling extended and formalized existing gender differences in the treatment of working-class children, as boys and girls were expected to pursue sex-specific types of education in line with their assumed different capacities and adult roles. These developments in education provision prompted in publishing circles a heightened sensitivity to both gender and age. This is apparent in the production of novels, and also periodicals, for children and young people during the late-nineteenth century, including the release of a range of books for "the school girl". These early school stories, such as L. T. Meade's *A world of girls* (1886) and Angela Brazil's *The naughtiest girl in the school* (1910) marked a significant departure from previous literature in that the characters portrayed were considerably younger than those appearing in earlier domestic or romantic fiction. The extension of formal education also alerted publishers to the commercial possibilities of a large audience of working-class girls and boys. Although novels were often aimed at girls and boys from all social groups, it was the periodical which was to exploit, and indeed construct, the young working-class reader most fruitfully.

It was Alfred Harmsworth (later Lord Northcliffe), founder of the *Daily Mail* (1896) and *Daily Mirror* (1903), who first targeted working-class working girls as a distinct consumer group catered for by a number of halfpenny and penny weekly magazines, including *Girls' Friend* (1899–1931), *Girls' Reader* (1908–1915) and *Girls' Home* (1910–15). Interestingly, no working-class male equivalents were published. Harmsworth and other publishers then turned their attention to schoolchildren. Interestingly, it was schoolboys who first caught the attention of periodical publishers, but it was probably when girls were discovered to be avid readers of schoolboys' papers that publishers recognized schoolgirls as a specific group that they then proceeded to cater for in a separate range of magazines. In 1919, D. C. Thomson launched *School Friend*, declaring that it is a "paper of an entirely new type, and cannot be compared with papers published in past years. Essentially the *School Friend* will appeal chiefly to the girl at school – the girl whose tastes have not previously been catered for".[45] This marked the first of a stream of schoolgirl papers which included *School Days, Schoolgirls' Own* and *Girls' Crystal*. By 1920, commercial publishing for adolescent girls included all social class groups, catered for in gender-specific publications, a stratification which reflected the divisions within the education system.[46]

The twentieth century marked the acknowledgement of young people as consumers, but also recognition, and construction, of difference along the lines of social class and age. But, while during the nineteenth century, gender and social differences were more important than differences of age, during the twentieth century gender and age differentiation acquired increased significance: exactly how important, relative to class, is a matter of debate. Drotner argues that the juvenile press of the twentieth century cut across social class, but not across gender or age differences.[47] It is the case that interwar publishers did aim at a mass audience, and that class divisions were less clear than in prewar days. Nevertheless, social class differences remained

139

significant for girls and women throughout the twentieth century in terms of their education, employment, health, housing, family, sexuality, leisure and reading.[48] Social class differences were also evident in the tone and content of popular magazines. Papers aimed at young women were differentiated according to the types of employment their readers were assumed to be in or aspire to; schoolgirl papers differed according to whether they catered principally for a mass audience of elementary schoolgirls, or mainly middle-class secondary schoolgirls.

Age, as we have seen, was an important consideration in publishing circles after 1880. The ways in which publishers segmented the female market by age are revealing about the social construction of age by gender. Magazines devoted considerable energy to marking out the boundaries of their readers' concerns in terms of the activities and interests considered appropriate to each age group. Publishers of weekly and monthly papers catered for different groups of readers according to whether they were at school or in paid employment. Magazines also defined and demarcated their female readers according to ideas about the sort of relationships with boys they could or should be engaged in – friendship, courtship or marriage. However, the intended audience and actual readership were often quite different. What girls of a certain age were supposed to want was not always sufficiently satisfying – girls had other interests, and often those ascribed to older females. Of particular note, schoolgirl readers looked to magazines aimed at older girls for coverage of romance and marriage.[49] This suggests a tension between magazine attempts to regulate heterosexual interest, and pressures which stressed the urgency of finding a man, for economic reasons as well as social status and worth.

It is particularly noticeable that magazines for working girls, such as *Girls' Favourite* and *Peg's Paper*, and the middle-class *Girl's Own Paper*, saw their readers as occupying a sort of twilight zone between childhood and womanhood – "neither fish nor fowl". This notion of their readership clearly owed much to the increased acceptance and institutionalization of adolescence as a specific stage between childhood and adulthood character-ized by physical, psychological and social changes.[50] Unmarried adolescent girls required a distinctive approach that recognized the specificities of their position in society. *Girls' Favourite*, for example, clearly articulated the distance between its readers and married life in this interwar editorial:

> there was once a terribly efficient, brogued and horn-rimmed-spectacled person who paid me daily visits for a week armed with "A hundred steps towards home-making". It took me about ten thousand words . . . to convince her that *Girls' Favourite* readers did not, as a general rule, want to know about how to make homes, not yet awhile, at any rate.[51]

Miss Modern similarly presented itself as in touch with the unmarried working girl:

I may be a woman in years, but I am still a girl at heart. Girlhood interests me intensely. I am only one step away from it, and that pleases me, for if I were older I might be too far removed from you to sympathise with you and, if I were younger, I could sympathise but I couldn't advise, not having the necessary experience.[52]

The periodical press did have problems in maintaining the boundaries between different age groups especially when it addressed readers who had left full-time schooling. In relation to schoolgirl magazines, the institutional organizer of schooling was particularly important. But the differentiation possible between adolescent working girls and married women was more difficult to draw and maintain.[53] Employment was the key differential, but both adolescent girls and older women were perceived to share an interest in romance and marriage. During the 1930s most of the papers for single working "girls" disappeared; they either merged with papers which addressed "women", or they folded. At this time there emerged a new range of magazines produced and even edited by the same teams that had worked on magazines for working girls. Nell Kennedy and her team moved from producing *Peg's Paper* to *Glamour*, *Silver Star* and *Lucky Star*. In fact a number of the working girls' papers were amalgamated into the new fiction magazines: *Girls Weekly* into *My Weekly* (1922), *Poppy's Paper* became *Fortune* before being amalgamated with *Oracle* (1937), *Peg's Paper* amalgamated with *Glamour*, then *Lucky Star* (1940). The new fiction magazines were clearly intended to absorb the readership previously attracted to these younger magazines. For example, in the last issue of *Girls' Weekly* the editress claimed that "All the charm of *Girls' Weekly* will be retained in the new paper, and added to it will be the splendid attractions of *My Weekly*".[54] These magazines which addressed "women" were dominated by fiction; they also featured a few articles and problem pages dealing with the concerns of mainly older and married women. While in some respects these changes resulted from rationalization of the women's press, it is nevertheless clear that the interests of young working women were not regarded as being sufficiently specific to warrant a separate type of magazine.

The way in which working-class magazines of the interwar period addressed the issue of age demarcation is in marked contrast to how this was managed in the middle-class women's press. Whereas the postwar working-class magazines found it difficult to differentiate between readers because they were seen to share an interest in heterosexual romance, middle-class papers found it difficult to distinguish between girls and women because of their perceived common interest in the home and domesticity. The *Girl's Own Paper*, for example, was linked with *Woman's Magazine*, a domestic paper for mothers, between 1908 and 1931. When the *Girl's Own Paper* became a monthly in 1908, its title was changed to the *Girl's Own Paper and Woman's Magazine*; in 1928 it again changed its name, to

Woman's Magazine and Girls' Own Paper, and it was not until 1931 that the *Girls' Own Paper* was finally liberated from *Woman's Magazine* as a paper which targeted mainly middle-class adolescent schoolgirls.

The changing contours of girls' and women's lives contributed to the production of new potential groups of readers and purchasers. Central to the ways in which the periodical press constructed and demarcated its readers were various age markers – whether readers were at school or in full-time paid work, and whether they had "chums", boyfriends or husbands. However, as other chapters illustrate, experiences of education, paid work and relationships, both within and outside the family, were not static. The periodical press was confronted by readers with different, and also changing, experiences and opportunities. What implications did this have for representations of girls and women? In what ways can an examination of popular magazines contribute to our understanding of the changing conditions of girls and women during the twentieth century? The next section moves on to look at the representational management of change.

The "modern girl"

In the interwar period, popular literature addressed "the girl of the period", the "modern girl", "Miss Modern". These titles suggest the specificity of the present: they also hint at generational specificity, contrasting the girl of today with her sister of the past; not *all* girls, but *today's* girls. The term "modern" was also linked to progress; according to Graves and Hodge, during the twentieth century, modernism threw off its eighteenth- and nineteenth-century connotation of something to be disparaged because it was new; instead, it became synonymous with lively progress.[55] In what ways did girls and girlhood change over time? What constituted the modernity of readers?

One of the most notable characteristics of girls' modernity was that "today's" girls had wider opportunities than had their predecessors. Magazines referred constantly to progress, drawing on a unilinear evolutionary model of social change which contrasted the modern with the traditional. Central to the depiction of the *modern* girl were her employment prospects. By the 1920s, the term *Miss Modern* referred almost exclusively to the working girl. "Stay- at-home-girls" were acknowledged, but they were not a staple of these magazines;[56] they were not consumers in the way their working sisters were and, deprived of economic independence, were not seen to share in the freedom and modernity which access to paid work conferred on young women.

The equation of modernity with employment for women was not specific to the postwar period. The Victorian *Girl's Own Paper*, which essentially was addressed to middle-class readers, acknowledged and positively embraced a "widening sphere" of employment opportunities in the public sphere for young women although, at the same time, it promoted Victorian norms of femininity.[57] The new magazines for young working women that emerged after 1880 similarly equated modernity with women's access to paid work. The "new woman" of the 1890s was also a working woman. According to Gardner, she:

> was seen typically as young, middle-class and single on principle. She eschewed the fripperies of fashion in favour of more masculine dress and severe coiffure. She had probably been educated to a standard unknown to previous generations of women . . . She was financially independent of father or husband . . . She affected emancipated habits, like smoking, riding a bicycle, using bold language and taking the omnibus or train unescorted. She belonged to all-female clubs . . . She sought freedom from, and equality with, men. In the process she was prepared to overturn all convention and all accepted notions of femininity.[58]

The modern girl of the 1920s was quite different from this "new woman", despite their shared engagement in the labour market. "Modern girls" were not confined to the middle-classes as the "new women" had been. Moreover, they were not presented as being politically motivated or informed. Most importantly, the "modern miss" was a "girl" and not a "woman", the assumption being that modern girls did eventually get married. In fact, one of the problems with the 1920s "girl" was seen to be the containment and management of her newly discovered sexuality and sexual freedom. This marks a significant contrast from the earlier "new woman", who was portrayed as rejecting marriage and heterosexual relations for feminist reasons. It is noticeable, however, that when magazines confront the modern woman who rejects marriage, they are extremely critical.

Throughout the interwar period, magazines expressed concern about the need for their readers to be prepared to support themselves; this issue emerged both in articles and in fiction. One of the reasons for this was that it was increasingly likely that a large minority of women would not marry, because of the surplus of women. Spinsterhood was a very real prospect during this period. In 1921, 36.5 per cent of all women over the age of 15 had never been married; by 1951 this figure had risen to 40 per cent of women.[59] Women who did not get married had to remain financially independent: in 1931 single women comprised 51 per cent of the female workforce aged over 35 years.[60] Many of these women had elderly dependent relatives, a fact that was pointed out in the campaign for equal pay and the abolition of the male "family wage".[61] It was for these reasons that women needed to secure long-term careers with good prospects and pay; it was also important that girls should find work that both interested and satisfied them. The handicap of inadequate training was addressed in articles as well as fiction and was seen to be particularly acute because of high unemployment; *Girls' World*, for example, stressed the necessity of occupational training for girls.[62] It was not, however, only single women who had to work. Married women were often compelled to return to paid work to supplement or replace their husband's earnings. Financial hardship was also a common problem for engaged or newlywed women, who were attempting to set up home before starting a family; this problem was often raised in the letters printed in the correspondence pages. According to Mary Pratt, a headmistress, "if and when a girl marries the chances are, on a conservative estimate, one in ten that she will some day, by reason of widowhood or hard times of some sort or other, find it convenient, if not necessary, to earn for herself".[63]

In the case of middle-class and upper-class girls, preparing for a career was not solely a matter of necessity or prudence. Editors of magazines for middle-class girls believed that their readers should pursue an education, training and professional work for its intrinsic value and because they should utilize their skills in the service of society. Female editors such as Nell Kennedy, Biddy Johnson and Mary Grieve had themselves forged careers in a male dominated profession, and they all believed in the importance of middle-class women's contribution to the public sector. Nell Kennedy, for instance, was insistent that intelligent, middle-class girls should equip themselves for a career; however, in spite of this, she did not think it appropriate for her working-class readers to aspire to careers, although work prior to marriage was necessary and desirable.[64]

While working-class magazines promoted women's work, they also expressed concern about the independent modern girl. Career opportunities were presented as the crux of female independence; they had important consequences for contemporary girls in terms of how the young women related to marriage and men. Employment prospects enabled girls to develop new attitudes and ambitions that were less dependent on the traditional destinations of marriage and motherhood. The First World War was presented by magazines as having played a crucial role, clearly demarcating girls of the interwar period from their Edwardian and Victorian counterparts.

The ways in which magazines represented the First World War is, rather interestingly, reflected in mainstream history's interpretation of the economic and social implications of this period for women. Marwick, who exemplifies this perspective, claims that the First World War was significant for young women of all social classes, especially middle- and upper-class girls, in introducing social and economic independence and freedom. Such freedom he attributed to the conditions and demands of war work, the way in which young girls regularly travelled long distances from home, or, in many cases, left home to live in hostels or lodgings. Middle- and upper-class women, he argues:

> had been in pre-war times a depressed class, tied to the apron-strings of their mothers or chaperones, or to the purse strings of their fathers or husbands. Now they were earning money on their own account, they had economic independence; now they were working away from home,

they had social independence. Above all, in their awareness that they were performing arduous and worthwhile tasks, were living through experiences once confined only to the most adventurous males, they gained a new self-consciousness and a new sense of status.[65]

Lower-class women similarly gained access to work which offered economic status, and confidence in the performance of tasks that had once been the preserve of skilled men. Marwick also distinguishes changing morals. He interprets these from the rise in illegitimacy rates, the increase of venereal disease, and the higher incidence of divorce. He also points to a change in manners: "The unabashed ordering of restaurant meals, the public smoking of cigarettes, the much publicised invasion of the public houses."[66] Short hair and short skirts were seen as the most striking outward signs of "freedom".[67] Feminist historians have challenged these claims about freedom, although recognizing the significance of the war for many women.[68] What is perhaps interesting is that Marwick offers an interpretation of the war's effects, which is also evident in young women's magazines of the time.

Magazines conveyed anxiety about what they saw as the independence and freedom of the modern girl. In this respect, they were part of a wider popular concern in the postwar years that women would reject marriage, motherhood and domesticity and expect more egalitarian relations between the sexes.[69] Can magazine responses to the "modern girl" in the immediate postwar years be understood as part of the back-to-the-home movement, so evident in pressures on women to return to traditional areas of work and, in particular, domestic employment?[70] Did young women's magazines contribute to a cultural backlash? According to Beddoe, the "single most arresting feature of the inter-war years was the strength of the notion that woman's place is in the home".[71] Women's magazines, as White observes, made a "substantial effort to curb restlessness on the part of wives, and to popularise the career of housewife and mother".[72] It would be misleading, however, to extrapolate from the evidence of *women's* magazines to *all* magazines, including those aimed at young women and schoolgirls. Beddoe makes this mistake when she claims that in "the inter-war years only one desirable image was held up to women by all the mainstream media agencies – that of housewife and mother. This single role model was presented to women to follow and all other alternative roles were presented as wholly undesirable."[73] This marginalizes the extensive range of magazines aimed at young working readers and those still at school. Moreover, it glosses over the ways in which change was managed in the periodical press. A study of magazines for young women reveals a more complex response and more diverse images of both girlhood and womanhood. Representations of the modern girl were shaped and constrained by prevalent concerns and domestic pressures, but magazines were also motivated by a commercial imperative and, linked to this, a commitment to their young female readers, and their interests.

Magazines addressed these perceived changes in interesting ways. It was not a case of outright praise, acceptance or criticism, but a more subtle reworking of the modern girl to draw out her links with traditional feminine ideals. *Girls' Favourite* asked "Is the Modern Girl Different?", and concluded that although she went out to work, the modern girl was surprisingly traditional in many ways - "Oh grandmamma, we're not so different after all!"[74] *Girls' Weekly* conveyed a similar approach in a poem it printed in 1920, entitled "The Modern Girl", which closed with the line: "she's just like girls before her for 20,000 years".[75] "The modern girl is alright" said Jane Blunt in *Pam's Paper* (1927). Blunt looks at the myth of the modern girl and argued that while she was more independent, less obsessed with men, and more concerned to have fun than her predecessor, she nevertheless coped with domestic crises admirably.[76]

In relation to popular literature for girls from 1880 to 1914, Reynolds argues that rebel heroines did not pose a significant challenge to the status quo: "In spite of these superficial features, which seem to be embracing a new image of womanhood and a revised notion of femininity, these 'naughty' girls exist as part of a convention which is as reactionary as its adult counterpart was radical." She continues:

> in girls' fiction, the tenacity of the traditional representation of acceptable womanhood is clear: the old ideal is perpetuated, not eradicated. Indeed, one of the most interesting features of this new literature is the way it takes details from contemporary debate about the behaviour associated with the new imagining of women, and contrasts them with the internal values identified with old notions of femininity. The result is an essentially conservative attack on the "girl of the period".[77]

Inter-war management of modernity was somewhat different. Rather than an outright rejection or castigation of the new and modern, there was an attempt to redefine change to be consistent with traditional ideals.

There seem to be two important aspects of traditional femininity which magazines worked to incorporate into contemporary representations of the modern girl. First, they attempted to establish continuity regarding the young woman's heterosexuality, which would find expression in marriage and motherhood. Secondly, they were at pains to stress the continued, if somewhat latent, domesticity. This seems in part to be a response to press complaints about girls' lack of domesticity and more general pressures on women in the1920s to return to the home and embrace domesticity, either as wives or as domestic servants working in other people's homes.

While on the one hand magazines attempted to redefine perceptions of the modern girl, on the other they published cautionary tales warning of the misery that awaited the overly independent young woman and, in particular, the woman who professed to despise marriage. While single women had, in the nineteenth century, been scorned as having failed in the marriage market, after the First World War, this contempt was fuelled by the influence of sexology and the new psychology which pathologized the spinster.[78]

The *Girl's Own Paper*, however, was more definitely on the side of the single working woman. Vicinus describes the nineteenth-century tradition of single women, living and working together in the service of the community. She notes that, in the twentieth century, "amid a wholesale effort to revive marriage and delicate womanhood, single women and their communities were covertly and overtly attacked."[79] But, as Oram illustrates, interwar spinster feminists did contest and resist the negative psychological views of spinsters on which these hostilities were based and rationalized.[80] Certainly the team of women who worked on the middle-class *Girl's Own Paper* continued to praise the single professional woman, adhering to a nineteenth-century notion of the social value of the spinster; indeed, many of the heroines they featured, such as Florence Nightingale, were avowed professional spinsters.[81] Marriage was, nevertheless, always presented as a fitting feminine ambition.

Discussions of the "modern girl" in working-class magazines were often characterized by tension and inconsistencies. Magazines were motivated largely by commercial concerns, which dictated that they entertain and sell. This meant catering to their readers' interests and needs, and also their fantasies, in order to maintain or increase sales and profits. Victorian didacticism was, in this context, firmly rejected by publishers. However, attempts to engage with readers' lifestyles, which were shaped in part by the vicissitudes of the labour market, were complicated by the fact that magazines also acknowledged the prevalent view that girls' work posed a threat to heterosexual relations and, more specifically, to the institution of marriage. Moreover, the work realities of adolescent girls were often sharply inconsistent with prevalent notions of femininity, which did not accommodate the feared implications of female work experience readily, especially financial independence. Editors attempted to resolve these contradictions by redefining girls' careers and re-establishing the dependence of girls on men and marriage, thereby removing any threat to the status quo. In redefining girls' work to be compatible with patriarchal interests, magazines updated notions of femininity to accommodate female work experience.

"As the river runs to the sea"

The papers of the 1920s and 1930s, even those aimed at a working-class readership, did not expect their readers to be totally absorbed by the prospect of marriage. However, papers for working-class readers presented marriage as a latent need. It is interesting that single readers and heroines were referred to as "bachelor girls", suggesting that the single status was specific to girlhood and not to mature womanhood. Indeed, there were no positive representations of "bachelor *women*", or spinsters. These magazines hinted at an anti-marriage fashion in the 1920s. Editors' insistence that girls did desire marriage thus acquired a defensive note:

> But is there a single modern girl for all her modernity and, perhaps, her occasional scoffs at romance who doesn't deep down in her, look forward to a time when she will make a little home for herself and the boy she loves? Even though she may affect to despise and detest housework, and threatens to expire at the mention of darning a manly sock, doesn't she in her inmost thoughts rather love the idea of doing these same despised things for the one who can endow them with major charm?[82]

This editorial is interesting for its expression of a shift from Victorian expectations that girls should be naturally drawn towards the domestic sphere throughout their lives,[83] to a biographical model, in which domesticity surfaces fully when young women discover their potential heterosexual partner. In other words, heterosexual love was presented as the catalyst for the emergence of a domestic inclination. This account of domestic development seems to have been informed by the ideas of the sexologists, which essentially established the blossoming of heterosexual interest and love as the key to female development.[84] While editors gave the impression that modern girls were being sidetracked by fashion and a desire for independence, readers were still persuaded that they would, inevitably, seek a husband: "It's all right to talk about marriage going out of fashion, and to declare that business and public life prove more fascinating than houses and husbands to the modern bachelor girl, but that is all nonsense. Jack still seeks Jill, and Jill, if she is a sensible girl, will go half-way to meet him, so long as the river runs down to the sea".[85]

Negotiation was one of the key strategies by which magazines managed change. As *Miss Modern* illustrates:

> Do you realise, Miss Modern, the wonderful opportunity within your grasp? You are one hundred times luckier and more fortunate than all the girls who have gone before you. Life for them was circumscribed, but every door is opened to women to-day. You have your careers, your charm, your games and, best of all, your wonderful sense of companion-ship with both men and women. Yet you inherit a precious legacy – Eve's problems are still your problems for all your modernity – you have not lost that romance and womanliness which is ever your most precious heritage.[86]

It is interesting that woman's legacy of "womanhood" and "romance" is here described as a "problem". Presumably this represents an attempt by the magazine to justify its existence in terms of its self-appointed role of heterosexual problem-solver. Woman's precious heritage of heterosexuality, is clearly presented as innate and unchanging. In 1930, *Miss Modern* presented HRH the Duchess of York as "the ideal modern girl"; she was also, rather tellingly, "the model for every wife and mother throughout the world".[87] The modern girl was presented as a combination of both the new and the traditional, although there was an age dimension to this in that school-age girls were temporarily permitted a broader scope for non-traditional behaviour.

Relaxed relations between the sexes were just one of the developments that modern schoolgirls could look forward to, according to contemporary magazines. Ironically, it was around this time that the depiction of relationships between schoolgirls, and women generally, become more constrained.[88] The liberalization of heterosexual relationships was seen to be a legacy of the First World War and women's perceived new-found economic independence. As *Pam's Paper* explained in 1924: "Gone are the days when girls had to be virtually engaged before they could enjoy a man's companionship".[89] In postwar society, fidelity and complete loyalty were only expected once a girl got engaged. Flirtation was dealt with as a fashion but, echoing the cautionary note of various contemporary popular songs, girls were warned not to take flirtation too far.[90] Pre-engagement friendships were fine as long as the girl did not encourage a male friend who was starting to fall in love. In this case she was expected gently to discourage his affections. Men, however, did not have the same responsibilities towards their female "friends". This apparently more comradely trend in male–female relations did nothing to challenge the sexual double standard whereby women were held to be responsible for the management of heterosexual relationships. The flipside to the newly emancipated male–female relations was that women were increasingly available to men, and yet were denied the right to make demands of males; to top it all, they were held to be almost totally responsible for contact between the sexes.[91] *Pam's Paper* applauded the more comradely relations between the sexes, but warned that:

> the pity is that sometimes girls begin to hope that the nice boy in question is a lover before the idea has entered his own head, or heart. It doesn't do to assume that because he thinks you pretty or has kissed you once or twice that he is making up his mind to devote his life to you. Therefore be kind and friendly, but don't take his compliments lightly, make no demands on him, leave him free as the wind, and whatever you do, don't ask him when he is coming round to call for you again.[92]

According to contemporary magazines, the question of whether wives should work was a further issue on the modern girl's agenda. During the 1920s, the issue of married women's work was rarely aired, although, as we saw in Chapter 4, poorly paid work in both the formal and informal economies was an experience of many wives and mothers.[93] Working girls' magazines of the 1920s assumed that once a girl married she was situated centrally in the home and family; her chief roles of wife and mother were inextricably linked to this responsibility for the home. During the 1930s, these papers maintained a strong commitment to the home-based ideal, but they also confronted the issue of wives working. In one sense, magazines can be seen to be responding to the increased need of many married women to secure paid work. However, magazine acknowledgement of working wives and the way in which they accommodated this development depended on their ability to interpret this issue within their distinct philosophies. For example, romance magazines, aimed primarily at young working-class women, argued that it was necessary to accept working wives because families depended on them. According to the correspondence editor of *Oracle* (1933): "Many women are breadwinners now, and in many cases I have seen it makes for happiness and not for discontent".[94] The effect of the Depression and pockets of high unemployment, coupled with rising standards of living, meant that many newlyweds found it financially difficult to start a family. Where a wife worked, however, she could contribute financially to the setting up of a home in preparation for the arrival of the couple's first child. In contrast, middle-class magazines promoted married women's work because of their liberal notion of equality and their ideal of service: professional women had a duty to themselves, to God and the community to utilize their skills fully in paid and unpaid work. By the 1940s, the *Girl's Own Paper* was positively in favour of wives, and even mothers, continuing with their careers:

> I would like to see almost every girl married. Even more fervently I would like to see her equipped for a career. Both offer different ways of enriching and fulfilling her individuality. Marriage and motherhood can, of course, be a whole-time job, and the most selfless career in the world. But motherhood should be regarded as a temporary one, for the sake of the children as well as the parents.[95]

Conclusion

Burke argues that the concept of "cultural reproduction" is useful in "drawing attention to the effort involved in running on the spot, in other words keeping a society more or less as it is".[96] Magazines, as we have seen, were involved actively in the cultural reproduction of gender in the years between 1920 and 1945. However, as Sahlin puts it, "every reproduction of culture is an alteration", in that the social world and the context of cultural production is not static.[97] In the case of popular magazines, we have seen some of the ways in which they addressed, constructed and managed social change. These processes varied between magazines by social class and also by age; while the middle-class *Girl's Own Paper* embraced certain types of change, working-class magazines attempted to redefine them. Magazines were, in other words, actively involved in both the cultural *reproduction* and *production* of gender. They were also concerned with the modernization of gender, the production of updated ideals and norms which engaged with the perceived socio-economic changes relevant to contemporary young women. The representation of "Miss Modern" is illustration of how femininity was modernized in magazines for young working women in the period 1920 to 1945. This modernity, however, was not always in a girl's best interests. In many cases, magazine responses to change can be seen as an exercise in "defensive modernization";[98] the recognition but also the containment of change in ways which maintained reader support without undermining the crux of femininity: namely domesticity and heterosexuality, and the patriarchal interests these served.

Notes

1. On informal education, see the chapters on education, the family and ethnicity, "race" and empire in this volume.
2. "Culture" is here understood quite broadly as the shared meanings which inform and underlie the practices of everyday life. For a discussion of the concept of culture, see P. Burke *History and social theory* (Oxford: Polity, 1992) pp. 118-26. Two recent studies of gender and culture in the twentieth century are J. Bourke, *Working-class cultures in Britain 1890-1960: gender, ethnicity and class* (London: Routledge, 1994); and A. Davies, *Leisure, gender and poverty: working class culture in Salford and Manchester 1900-1939* (Buckingham: Open University Press, 1992). For studies that address reading as a cultural practice see Note 3 below.
3. On reading and popular literature, see D. Gorham, *The Victorian girl and the feminine ideal* (London: Croom Helm, 1982); K. Drotner, *English children and their magazines 1751-1945* (New Haven, Connecticut: Yale University Press, 1988); K. Reynolds, *Girls only? Gender and popular children's fiction in Britain 1880-1910* (Brighton: Harvester Wheatsheaf, 1990); C. White, *Women's magazines 1693-1968* (London: Michael Joseph, 1970), C. Craig & M. Cadogan, *You're a brick, Angela! The girls' story 1839-1985;* J. Rowbotham, *Good girls make good wives. Guidance for girls in Victorian fiction* (Oxford: Basil Blackwell, 1989); J. S. Bratton, *The Impact of Victorian children's fiction,* (London: Croom Helm, 1981); R. Auchmuty, *A world of girls,* (London: The Women's Press, 1992); P. Tinkler, "Learning through leisure: feminine ideology in girls' magazines, 1920-50", in F. Hunt (ed.) *Lessons for life: the schooling of girls and women 1850-1950* (Oxford: Basil Blackwell, 1987); D. Gorham, "The ideology of femininity and reading for girls, 1850-1914", in Hunt (ed.) *Lessons for life*; D. Beddoe, *Back to home and duty. Women between the wars 1918-1939* (London: Pandora, 1989). On representations of women in theatre, also on film and the cultural practice of viewing, see V. Gardner & S. Rutherford (eds) *The new woman and her sisters. Feminism and theatre 1850-1914* (Brighton: Harvester Wheatsheaf, 1992); M. Haskell, *From reverence to rape: the treatment of women in the movies* (New York: Holt, Reinhart and Winston, 1973); J. Thurmin, *Celluloid sisters: women and popular cinema* (London: Macmillan, 1991); J. Stacey, *Star gazing: Hollywood cinema and female spectatorship* (London: Routledge, 1994).

4. For discussion of this point see for example, K. Flint, *The woman reader 1837-1914* (Oxford: Oxford University Press, 1993); White, *Women's Magazines*; and Tinkler, "Learning through leisure", pp. 61-3.

5. Although historical interest in popular literature has, in recent years, been increasingly concerned with "gender", as opposed to women and femininity, this chapter is solely concerned with the significance of popular culture for *women's* history. June Purvis comments on this trend towards gender in "Doing feminist women's history: researching the lives of women in the suffrage movement in Edwardian England", p. 167 in *Researching Women's Lives From A Feminist Perspective* M. Maynard & J. Purvis (eds) (London: Taylor and Francis, 1994).

6. For example, Drotner, *English children and their magazines*.

7. On women novel writers, see, for example, N. Beauman, *A very great profession. The woman's novel 1914-1939* (London: Virago, 1983). The place of women in the production of girls' magazines during the twentieth century is discussed in P. Tinkler, *Constructing girlhood: magazine representations of adolescent girlhood and femininity, 1920-50* (Taylor and Francis, forthcoming).

8. Beauman, *A very great profession*, p. 3.

9. Rowbotham, *Good girls make good wives*, p. 8.

10. Bratton, *The impact of Victorian children's fiction*.

11. Gorham, *The Victorian girl*, Ch. 3. On Victorian literature, see Rowbotham, *Good girls make good wives;* on magazines, see Tinkler, "Learning through Leisure"; and Tinkler, *Constructing girlhood*.

12. Bratton, *The impact of Victorian children's fiction*, p. 24.

13. R. Auchmuty "You're a dyke, Angela!"; Elsie J. Oxenham and the rise and fall of the schoolgirl story in Lesbian History Group, *Not a passing phase. Reclaiming lesbians in history 1840-1985* (London: The Women's Press, 1989), p. 123. See also Auchmuty, *A world of girls*.

14. Drotner, *English children*, p. 212: for her argument, see p. 4.

15. Reynolds, *Girls Only?*, pp. 100-101.

16. Auchmuty, *A world of girls*, p. 25.

17. Contemporary research includes: J. Winship, *Inside women's magazines* (Pandora, 1987); A. McRobbie, "Working-class Girls and the culture of femininity", in *Women take issue: aspects of women's Subordination*, Women's Studies Group, CCCS Birmingham (London: Hutchinson, 1978); M. Ferguson, *Forever feminine. women's magazines and the cult of femininity* (London: Heinemann, 1983); R. Ballaster et al., *Women's worlds: ideology, femininity and the woman's magazine* (London: Macmillan, 1991). Examples of historical work are noted in Note 3 above.

18. Flint, *The woman reader*.

19. White, *Women's magazines*, p. 96 uses the phrase "service magazines" to convey the aim of these papers, which was to serve women in their domestic and wifely duties. White, p. 123, refers to these magazines being utilized in the war effort. The enrolment of the *Girl's Own Paper* in the war effort is mentioned in Craig & Cadogan, *You're a brick, Angela!*, p. 273.

20. G. Trease, *Tales out of school*, (Surrey: Windmill Press, 1948), p. 83.

21. Flint, *The woman reader*, looks at why the "woman reader" was the subject of attention in the nineteenth century. She also addresses the same issue for the eighteenth century (Ch. 1).

22. P. Jephcott, *Girls growing up*, (London: Faber, 1943), Ch. 5.

23. For a summary of Socialisation Theory, see S. Walby, *Theorising patriarchy* (Oxford: Basil Blackwell, 1990), pp. 91-4.

24. C. Dyhouse, *Girls growing up in late Victorian and Edwardian England* (Oxford: Basil Blackwell, 1981), esp. Ch. 1; E. Roberts, *A woman's place. An oral history of working class women 1890-1940* (Oxford: Basil Blackwell, 1984).

25. Bratton, *The impact of Victorian children's fiction*, Ch. 1.

26. S. Walby, *Theorising patriarchy* (Oxford: Oxford University Press, 1993), pp. 91-4.

27. C. Dyhouse, *Feminism and the family in England 1880-1939* (Oxford: Basil Blackwell, 1989); Dyhouse, *Girls growing up*, pp. 31-9.

28. K. Flint, *The woman reader 1837-1914* (Oxford: Oxford University Press, 1993). For an introduction to recent theoretical developments, see F. Bonner et al. (eds), *Imagining women: cultural representations and gender* (Oxford: Polity, 1992).

29. It should be noted, however, that much of the recent historical work on women and popular culture has been produced by scholars who have backgrounds in cultural and literary studies rather than history.

30. Drotner, *English children*.

31. Flint, *The woman reader*.

32. Reynolds, *Girls only?*, Ch. 1.

33. Drotner, *English children*, p. 200.

34. Reynolds, *Girls only?*, pp. 100-101.

35. *Girls' Favourite*, 16 September 1922, p. 151.

36. *Girls' Weekly*, 7 August 1920, p. 99.

37. Magazines received many letters from readers concerning stage careers, e.g. *Poppy's Paper* 9 February 1924, p. 27. The popularity of film is also evident in the proliferation of film magazines during the interwar period.

38. For a discussion of the concept of "preferred meaning", see S. Hall, "Encoding/decoding" in *Culture, Media, Language*, S. Hall et al. (eds) (London: Hutchinson, 1980).

39. *Girls' Friend*, 31 January 1931; *Peg's Paper*, 5 May 1919, p. 1.

40. *Poppy's Paper*, 25 January 1930. For further examples of this, see Tinkler, "Learning through leisure", pp. 68-70,.

41. For further discussion of readership, see P. Tinkler, *Constructing girlhood* (London: Taylor and Francis, forthcoming)

42. Stacey addresses a similar point in her consideration of fan mail printed in film magazines, *Star gazing*, p. 55.

43. *Oracle*, 4 March 1933, p. 14.

44. Drotner, *English children*, p. 119.

45. *School Friend*, May 1919.

46. Reynolds, *Girls only?*, p. 27.

47. Drotner, *English children*, p. 201.

48. "Class was still important in interwar Britain, even though its precise economic boundaries were becoming harder to define"; quoted from G. Braybon & P. Summerfield, *Out of the cage, women's experiences in two world wars* (London: Pandora, 1987) p. 137. The authors also detail the persistence of class difference throughout the First and Second World Wars. For evidence of the significance of class for women in the family and employment, see J. Lewis, *Women in England 1870-1950. Sexual divisions and social change* (Brighton: Harvester Wheatsheaf, 1984). See also chapters in this collection. On magazine reading and social class, see Tinkler, "Learning through leisure".

49. This is revealed in P. Jephcott, *Girls growing up*, p. 101; A. J. Jenkinson, *What do boys and girls read?* (London: Methuen, 1940), p. 218 refers to "erotic bloods" (romance magazines) being popular with schoolgirls of 12 years and over.

50. See Dyhouse, *Girls growing up*, Ch. 4.
51. *Girls' Favourite*, 26 March 1927, p. 192.
52. *Miss Modern*, October 1930.
53. For a discussion of gender and adolescence, see Dyhouse, *Girls growing up*, Ch. 4.
54. *Girls' Weekly*, 4 March 1922.
55. R. Graves & A. Hodge, *The long weekend. A social history of Great Britain 1918-1939* (London: Cardinal, 1991; first published 1940), p. 114.
56. The phrase "Stay-At-Home-Girls' was used in *Girls' Favourite*.
57. D. Gorham, "The ideology of femininity and reading for girls", pp. 50-1. See also Gorham, *The Victorian girl*.
58. V. Gardner, "Introduction", pp. 4-6 in *The New woman and Her Sisters, Feminism and Theatre 1850-1914*, V. Gardner & S. Rutherford (eds) (Hemel Hempstead: Harvester Wheatsheaf, 1992).
59. OPCS, *Census England and Wales*, Occupational Tables, 1921 & 1951 (London: HMSO).
60. OPCS, *Census England and Wales*, Occupational Tables 1931 (London: HMSO).
61. E. Rathbone, *The case for family allowances*, (Harmondsworth: Penguin, 1940).
62. *Girls' World*, 14 March 1927, p. 2; see also *Miss Modern*, "Ice Drome", November 1935, p. 24.
63. M. Pratt, "Reflections of a headmistress on vocational guidance" *Journal of occupational psychology* **xiii** (4), p. 285, 1934.
64. Interviews with Pat Lamburn and Mrs Jean Lee. Correspondence with Mary Grieve. See also M. Grieve, *Millions made my story* (London: Victor Gollanz, 1964).
65. A. Marwick, *The deluge. British society and the First World War* (London: Macmillan, 2nd edn, 1991), p. 134.
66. Marwick, *The deluge*, p. 151.
67. Marwick, *The deluge*, p. 151; Graves and Hodge, *The long weekend*, p. 39.
68. Braybon & Summerfield, *Out of the cage*.
69. Braybon & Summerfield, *Out of the cage*, Ch. 7; P. Summerfield, *Women workers in the Second World War* (London: Croom Helm, 1984); D. Beddoe, *Back to home and duty, Women between the Wars 1918-1939* (London: Pandora, 1989) Ch. 3.
70. Beddoe, *Back to home and duty*, p. 3; G. Braybon, *Women workers in the First World War* (London: Routledge, 1981), p. 220.
71. Beddoe, *Back to home and duty*, p. 3.
72. White, *Women's magazines*, p. 101.
73. Beddoe, *Back to home and duty*, p. 8.
74. *Girls' Favourite*, 12 March 1927, p. 122.
75. *Girls' Weekly*, 24 Jan 1920.
76. *Pam's Paper*, 7 May 1927.
77. Reynolds, *Girls only?*, p. 98.
78. See S. Jeffreys, *The spinster and her enemies, feminism and sexuality* (London: Pandora, 1985); J. Weeks, *Sex, politics and society. The regulation of sexuality since 1800* (London: Longman, 1981).
79. M. Vicinus, *Independent women. Work and community for single women, 1850-1920* (London: Virago, 1985), p. 285; A. Oram, "Embittered, sexless or homosexual": attacks on spinster teachers 1918-1939" in *Current issues in women's history*, A. Angerman et al. (London: Routledge, 1989).
80. A. Oram, "Repressed and thwarted, or bearers of the new world? The spinster and inter-war feminist discourse", *Women's History Review* **1** (3), 1992.

81. See Dyhouse, *Feminism and the family*, p. 10 for comments about the ways in which some women saw marriage as being incompatible with a life of self-respect and service.

82. *Girls' favourite*, 5 March 1927, p. 122.

83. For details about Victorian female domesticity, see Gorham, *The Victorian girl*; Dyhouse, *Girls growing up*; also other chapters in this collection.

84. Jeffreys, *The spinster and her enemies*, Ch. 9 regarding twentieth-century ideas about female sexuality; see Dyhouse, *Girls growing up*, Ch. 4 for a discussion of adolescent female sexuality.

85. *Girls' Weekly*, 21 January 1922, p. 67.

86. *Miss Modern*, "Editorial", October 1930.

87. *Miss Modern*, December 1930, p. 11.

88. Auchmuty, "You're a dyke, Angela!", pp. 136-7; see also Jeffreys, *The spinster and her enemies*, Ch. 6.

89. *Pam's paper*, 1 March 1924.

90. Summerfield and Braybon, *Out of the cage*, p. 148.

91. Jeffreys, *The spinster and her enemies*, similarly criticizes the double standards of heterosexual liberalism in the 1920s.

92. *Pam's paper*, 1 March 1924.

93. See Chapter 4 on women's work; Lewis, *Women in England*.

94. *Oracle*, 9 December, 1933.

95. *Girls' Own Paper*, November 1945, pp. 6-7.

96. Burke, *History and social theory*, p. 25.

97. M. Sahlin, *Islands of History*, (Chicago: Chicago University Press, 1985) cited in Burke, *History and social theory*, p. 126.

98. The concept of "defensive modernization" is usually employed to refer to the introduction of reforms by a dominant class out of fear and as a means to avoid revolution. For references, see Burke, *History and social theory*, p. 135.

Suggestions for further reading

The cultural construction and management of both social differences and change are themes which are dealt with more fully in my book, P. Tinkler, *Constructing girlhood: magazine representations of adolescent girlhood and femininity, 1920-50* (London: Taylor and Francis, forthcoming). This explores the content and production of magazines for girls and young women, addressing the significance of social class, age and social change. It also addresses girls and women as both readers of, and contributors to, the "girls' magazine". Deborah Gorham, *The Victorian girl and the feminine ideal* (London: Croom Helm, 1982) explores the cultural construction of femininity and the informal education of girls in an earlier period. She examines Victorian novels and periodicals as well as advice manuals and other prescriptive literature. Carol Dyhouse, *Girls growing up in late Victorian and Edwardian England* (Oxford: Basil Blackwell, 1981) focuses on different media of informal education, namely the family and school experiences of working-class and middle-class girls. Cynthia White, *Women's magazines, 1693-1969* (London: Michael Joseph, 1970) remains the most comprehensive overview of magazines produced for women. The history of girls' magazines is best documented by Kirsten Drotner, *English children and their magazines, 1751-1945* (New Haven, Connecticut: Yale University Press, 1988). This study also presents an interesting consideration of the changing appeal of juvenile magazines to girl, and also boy, readers. The issue of reading practices is further explored in Kate Flint, *The woman reader, 1837-1914* (Oxford: Oxford University Press, 1993).

Oral history and autobiography are particularly fruitful sources for exploring the cultural dimensions of girls' and women's lives. See, for example, E. Roberts, *A woman's place. An oral history of working-class women 1890-1940* (Oxford: Basil Blackwell, 1984). Pearl Jephcott, *Girls growing up* (London: Faber, 1943) and Jephcott, *Rising twenty* (London: Faber, 1948), provide fascinating insights into the cultural dimensions of adolescent girlhood in the 1940s.

Chapter Seven

᪥

Women and health

Barbara Harrison

In the nineteenth century, physicians contributed to a wider discourse about women's nature, capabilities and their place in society, the constitution of women, and gender relations tied to women's unique biological character-istics and functioning. Entrenched in medical theories about both physical and mental illness was that the reproductive organs (the ovaries and uterus), and the periodicity of reproductive biology as exhibited in the menstrual cycle, caused women's weakness, nervous debility, sickness and disease. Women's life cycles were equivalent to the events of their reproductive years.[1] The biologically determined phases of the life cycle, from puberty to the menopause, also became part of women's self identity. Significantly, interest in women's health other than this reproductive cycle was largely absent, and continued to be so until the mid-twentieth century, although the particular focus on reproduction changed.

A major event in the lives of all women – menstruation – was regarded as being pathological, but despite the dominant role of reproductive biology in the construction of women's disease, physicians understood neither it nor women's sexuality. Generally in this period, interest in sexuality was on its containment within definitions of reproduction. Any deviations from that definition were viewed as a failure to maintain appropriate standards of feminine behaviour, and, therefore, as illness. In this way sexuality, repro-duction and sickness became as one: women would by nature have a poten-tial for sickness, since all women shared the same biological attributes. The disordered nature of women's bodies thus became a powerful metaphor in the social and cultural construction of gender roles. Medical arguments mediated gender relations by confirming the threat of feminine disorder on the social and moral order.

In this chapter I have chosen to focus on four areas: physical ill health, mental illness, reproduction and maternity, and intervention, practice and services. I will address both representations of women's health and, as far as possible, its actuality. Inevitably, there is a difficulty with such an approach, since the discourse, including medical theories and subjective perceptions and experiences, are mutually constitutive of one another. It is thus possible to find elements of a shared discourse between medical men and women themselves within surviving records. There were areas of women's health and well-being that were experienced, but excluded from discussion, debate and intervention, and this also has consequences for the contemporary feminist historian working in this field, and for those aspects of women's health that are studied.[2] Finally, despite some omissions in both topic and depth, the chapter aims to demonstrate the pervasiveness of a constitution of women as reproductive beings in the service of others, and the oppressive consequences this had for women's health and social status. This renders a focus on discourse as important as empirical data about women's health status and health experiences.

Physical ill health

In examining medical theorizing and the representation of women's health in the second half of the nineteenth century, it is evident that despite an emphasis on a commonality rooted in biology there were obvious class differences between women. Thus different material circumstances and styles of life, as well as health "needs", had to be accommodated while keeping intact the underlying characterization of women's biological destiny as wives and mothers, as well as their socially gendered roles in the public and private domain. In some cases the theories could accommodate this diversity; in others, theory and/or practice reflected the class divide and then tended to focus only on one class of women. It is also important to consider the dynamic nature of class- and gender-based characterizations of women's health in response to changing economic and social conditions.[3]

The tying of women's physical frailty to their reproductive organs and thence to the nervous system resulted in a set of "feminine" attributes that were part biology and part idealized social characteristics. Thus a frail and delicate physiology was ideally suited to nurturance, emotionality and sensitivity – a basis for domesticity. Simultaneously, however, these characteristics were pathological, emphasizing women's propensity to invalidism.[4] This pathological weakness required that women be "protected", sheltered from the stresses of participation in the public domain. It was both a form of self-fulfilling prophecy, and a "double bind". Women were restricted to a sedentary and often socially isolated existence and then pilloried for the failure of their wills, the neglect of household and childcare duties, and their idleness. Duffin[5] has described this pervasive cultural construction as one of the "conspicuous consumptive", and Ehrenreich and English[6] as the "cult of hypochondria". These metaphorical descriptions suggest that the useless days and dissipated nights that typified medical descriptions of invalidism were not "real" illness. However, it seems just as likely that a social role which resulted in a passive, idle and confined life style did indeed lead to female maladies. The sickness of idleness was the idleness of sickness. There were certainly aspects of middle-class family existence that mothers and daughters found constraining, but an enforced idleness also belied the constant claims made on women, and the physically demanding nature of household duties.[7] Branca describes the middle-class woman's day as one that involved a great deal of physical labour: "Her new concern for cleanliness drove her up and down stairs constantly, along with dusting and lifting quite heavy furnishings, preparing meals, shopping and caring for children."[8] They were also indoors all day in dark, fume-filled, poorly ventilated rooms. Florence Nightingale's writings have been used as evidence for middle-class women's predicaments, and the extent to which such women may also have feigned or used illness as means of dealing with the lack of time and space, as the often quoted passage from *Cassandra* illustrates: "A married woman was heard to wish that she could break a limb that she might have a little time to herself. Many take advantage of the fear of infection to do the same."[9] I discuss the thesis of illness as a form of rebellion more fully in the next section.

In the case of working-class women, characteristics of frailty and physical weakness were problematical. Middle-class men, including doctors, would have been aware of the physical labour of those working-class women they employed as servants, and in many instances in other forms of employment also. The ideal[10] of an "idle" life style was not appropriate here. This did not prevent issues of "protecting" women against the effects of physical labour, or questioning their physical capacity for it, from arising, although rarely in the case of domestic servants.[11] By the end of the nineteenth century, agitation and official concern about the effects of working conditions on working-class women's health was evident, as were further examples of contradictions in Victorian thinking. Proposals generally favoured restrictions on married women's work, ignoring the fact that poor conditions do not discriminate between single and married, or that pre-natal health would be implicated in the future health of mothers and children.[12] Arguably, the attention to married women was because it was this group that contravened their primary responsibility for their families. It has also been seen as an important dimension of male trade unionists' exclusionary strategies to maintain men's economic or labour market dominance: a confluence of male opinion about mothers at work occurred.[13] However, politicians, doctors, activists and reformers also recognized that the income from paid work for many women was a means of taking such responsibility for their own as well as their family's survival.[14]

In the event, factory legislation did circumscribe some areas of women's industrial work by gender-specific regulations, particularly in the "dangerous trades", where women were often considered to be more susceptible to the effects of industrial poisons. In the case of lead, for example, poisoning rates were observed to be higher for women than men working in lead industries, and in 1898 women were excluded from certain processes in white lead manufacture and from the weighing and mixing of glazes in the potteries in 1903. In the former there is evidence that male rates in that industry then reached those of women prior to exclusion, suggesting that it was the dangerous work and not susceptibility that was responsible, but ideas of gendered susceptibility remained.[15] In the case of phosphorous, the issue was again debated, although it was concluded that any greater susceptibility among women was due to the fact that their dental health was worse.[16] The idea of inherent weakness in women's bodies based on reproductive biology was thus significant in the campaigns and rationale for the regulation of women's work. The idea of susceptibility re-emerged in a similar way in relation to women ammunition workers in the First World War over trinitrotoluene (TNT).[17] It is also significant that the many other damaging aspects of working conditions received relatively little attention, consistent with preventive strategies that targeted individuals rather than social factors.

Working-class women did not escape the attribution of inherent sickness, even if invalidism was not appropriate. Their sickness was different: it was a danger to others, encompassing ideas of contagion and pollution. This was particularly evident in the early twentieth century, when concern about the falling birthrate, initially among the middle classes, was perceived as a threat to the "health of the race", a concern fostered by the continuing high infant death rates, the poor health of young men who sought recruitment into the Boer War, and encouraged by eugenic ideas that gained in popularity at the turn of the twentieth century.[18] I return to issues of fertility, and maternal and infant health later in this chapter. The idea of working-class women as "sickening" lay both in ideas about their failure as mothers, and also in perceived dangers from "deviant" female sexuality.[19] A view of working-class women as weak and sick in this way was an important component in the increasing maternalism of twentieth-century social policy, and it served to preserve both class and gender relations.

There were medical theories that were concerned with specific complaints or "diseases" in women. One such "disease" – chlorosis, or "green sickness" – which had characteristics similar to anaemia, and often commenced at puberty, has attracted historical investigation. As with some mental disorders, which are discussed in the next section, this is because it had a class, gender and age dimension, and because it exemplified a biomedical condition that also represented a social conception of adolescence and women.[20] As a diagnosis, the condition of chlorosis came and went, giving weight to the argument that it was a historically specific, socially and culturally needed category: a "disease" with its own life and time.[21] Figlio[22] suggests chlorosis mediated social relations, and these social relations constructed the "disease". It exemplified how a theoretical system transmitted forms of domination that were both symbolic and real. In his analysis, class domination is central, chlorosis being an example of medical ideology that functioned to obscure the exploitation and work related illness of late-nineteenth-century industrial capitalism.

From 1898 to 1900 chlorosis represented 18 per cent of all hospital admissions in several large British hospitals, dropping to about 8 per cent by 1913–15.[23] Since hospital patients were at this time predominantly working-class, these figures demonstrate there were working-class sufferers of a condition usually considered to be of the middle classes.[24] How, then, could working-class sufferers of a disease associated by physicians with refinement be explained? Chlorosis was associated with puberty and adolescence, and marked by asexuality, which encompassed the unmarried; and as a disease it reinforced ideas of innocence and sexual respectability. Treatment regimes were "wholesomely childlike". In both Britain and America, explanations contrasted urban with rural living, failings in personal behaviour, and the association with menstrual disorders, and these provided for a coincidence of medical and household perceptions of chlorosis that could encompass all women. Brumberg also suggests that it was common for girls to use the label to describe debility, and that mothers and daughters were bonded together by their ill-health, implying that the role of a "chlorotic" could be learned.[25] Finally, as with other aspects of women's sickness, Figlio argues that the emergence of chlorosis as a disease of refinement was related to the class marginality of physicians, and an expressed ambivalence about the habits and tastes of a class which doctors generally aspired to join, and not the deliberate misapplication of knowledge to oppress women.[26] The tenacity of the idea that it was idle and well-to-do girls who were at risk in the face of contradictory evidence, Figlio argues, served to conceal the relationship of illness to work, and the exploitative nature of employer/servant relations. In this way, medicine "naturalized" existing inequalities by throwing into sharper relief the image of asexual, non-working, delicate femininity. Such a conception was inappropriate to working-class girls and maintained their social distance. In America, it seems, doctors dealt with the class issue by utilising class-specific causes: environment and work for working-class girls, excessive study and lack of exercise for college girls, and American physicians concentrated more on the pathology of menstruation itself, which made all women potentially chlorotic.[27]

A further instance of the perceived sickening and weakening potential of menstruation, and how biology would of necessity confirm existing gender roles and women's social inferiority was revealed in the debates about women and higher education in Britain and the USA.[28] Doctors argued that menstruation rendered women vulnerable and unstable, and therefore unsuitable for the rigours of education. If women were educated, the excitement and strain would result in increased pathological menstruation, or damage their childbearing capacities.[29] (It was noted that some educated and occupationally employed women were often ill and childless.) The idea that the reproductive cycle could exhaust mental capabilities was extended to justify different curriculum content when education provision was extended to young women. Such arguments increased towards the end of the nineteenth century and into the early twentieth, feeding into theories about the innate inferiority of different people in terms of gender, class and race, and when maternalism and its possible link with degeneracy was raised. Maudsley's views were typical: "it would be a ill thing, if it should so happen that we got the advantages of a quantity of female intellectual work at the price of a puny, enfeebled and sickly race".[30] This claim was prefaced by references to the need "for difference in the method of education of the two sexes answering to differences in [the] physical and mental natures" of men and women.[31] Despite criticisms of Maudsley's argument, including those of the woman physician, Elisabeth Garrett Anderson, views about women's vulnerability and pathology persisted well into the twentieth century, alongside demands for opportunities by, and for, women. As with mental illness, menstruation and other "disordered" aspects of women's nature entered into the discourse on modernity, and the threats posed by women's demands for a greater stake in it.[32]

What differential patterns of health status were visible? I have already alluded to the difficulty in the availability of empirical sources outside the medical constitution of illness. However, there is some statistical evidence that warrants discussion in this context. In contemporary studies of gender and health, investigators readily point to women's advantage in mortality and life expectancy, although it is argued that these indicators obscure considerable amounts of female morbidity.[33] There is evidence of class based inequalities in health between women,[34] and continuing work on the links between paid work, gender roles and health. The evidence and interpretation of both class and gender differences also remains a complex one in the historical context.

Johansson[35] argues that the contemporary pattern of greater longevity for women has not always been the case. Mid-nineteenth-century patterns show that while life expectancy was marginally higher (by 1.9 years) for women, in several age groups women were still more likely to die than men. From the 1870s, the trend toward greater female life expectancy continued, but mortality decline was still retrogressive in some groups. Only by the end of the century had females begun to outlive males at all ages. Shorter[36] suggests that the evidence leads to the conclusion that whether or not women or men were more likely to die at certain ages depended on the harshness of their lives and thence their resistance to infection. It was advantages at birth and after middle age that contributed to women's better life expectancy, and this more than compensated for the mortality disadvantage of girls between 5 and 20 years, and among married women in their thirties.[37] These groups were the last to show signs of a decline in mortality rates, which suggests that parturition-related dangers were not responsible for any female excess in deaths, but that the most likely cause was tuberculosis, the primary cause of women's mortality. As Shorter argues, women had a special "predilection" to this disease:

> For teenage English girls the story is also clear: half of the deaths among fourteen to twenty-four year olds were from pulmonary tuberculosis, a further eleven percent from typhus and typhoid fever . . . For women in childbearing years respiratory TB was again the number one killer, causing forty percent of all deaths among twenty-five to forty-four year olds.[38]

The dominant cultural metaphor of this largest single killer of women associated it with effeteness, emotionality and feminine beauty, when in reality it was a disease of poverty.[39] The difficulty of dealing with the most probable causes of the high incidence of TB in women – that is, poverty and environment – led instead to explanations that focused on sedentary lifestyles, and the habit of corseting or tight lacing – both middle-class factors that laid the blame on women for this and other illnesses. The popularity of a lifestyle factor such as corseting indicates its ideological significance. In fact corseting was a minority practice and mainly in the lower middle class.[40]

Gender differences in death rates posed particular problems, since they contradicted the belief that women were necessarily physically delicate and sickly. Those who might be most vulnerable (girls and older women) fared best, and interest in the anomaly was dropped. Johansson further stresses that women lived and worked in diverse conditions, and that class alone could not explain differential death rates. Geographical location, rural or urban living, work, wage levels and available diet were all possible explanations. She noted that where daughters were valued for their productivity, they received better care and had less tuberculosis, despite poor sanitary conditions.[41] Stearns[42] has suggested also that girls who became independent of parental care, usually by working, took better care of themselves. Although it is difficult to analyse the impact of paid work on mortality because of the lack of data before 1907, there is some indication that women in industrial work and domestic service had lower death rates than women overall, and charwomen had the highest.[43] Despite continuing attempts to argue that industrial labour affected the health of women and children adversely, there continued to be little evidence to support it.[44]

During the nineteenth century there were few differences in the health status of working-class and middle-class women. In any case, the majority of the population were working class, with no more than 5 to 15 per cent in the middle and upper strata, according to Johansson.[45] Branca[46] has argued there were improvements in the health of middle-class women by the end of the century, although the relative rates of mortality remained much the same. This, she suggests, was the result of a number of factors: a less willing acceptance of pain and disability – which in turn led to increased interaction with medical practitioners, whose own knowledge and practice had improved – and greater use of patent medicines. At the same time, she points to a number of limitations to the efficacy of medical practitioners in matters of women's health. On the one hand, while women were an increasingly important client group for doctors, and more successful surgical and non-surgical treatments were available, on the other there were limits to consultation, given the financial resources available and the need for chaperonage, and many advances were in the doctors' interests, not women's. Despite advances in medical knowledge and technology, the etiology and treatment of much disease and ill health remained speculative, untried and certainly unevenly distributed among practitioners.[47] Remedies offered by medical professionals often relied on tradition rather than new knowledge, as illustrated by the use of purgatives for nearly every complaint, and the persistence of bleeding well into the twentieth century. From my own work on industrial disease in women, it is evident that there was little consensus about cause or remedy, and that doctors' judgements often reflected prevailing social attitudes rather than clinically based knowledge.[48] While some small advantage might have accrued to middle-class women from access to medical practitioners, there is little direct evidence for any inferences that morbidity improved. Many common conditions, such as vaginal complaints, in both working- and middle-class women, still went unacknowledged and untreated,[49] and Branca concludes that the use of doctors probably exceeded their usefulness to women.[50]

It seems likely that any reduction in mortality and morbidity in middle-class women lay outside the role of the medical profession, and that health improvements were mainly brought about by the decline in fertility and the rise in population, accounted for largely through public health reforms, higher incomes and dietary improvement.[51] Harrison[52] suggests that feminism also eroded the doctor's role, and encouraged healthier life styles and preventive medicine. Finally, as we shall see later in the chapter, middle-class women's fertility did begin to decline at the end of the nineteenth century and preceded, as well as exceeded, a decline in working-class families. As a major factor in women's morbidity, limiting the number of pregnancies probably began to bring some benefit. For working-class women, however, frequent pregnancies and births continued to be the norm until the end of the Second World War.

But improved circumstances for middle-class women in the twentieth century, mainly as a consequence of changing lifestyle, were limited. The stresses and strains of running households in the earlier period, and artificial, cramped and dependent lives, may have been replaced by equally debilitating constraints. Higher standards of "housewifery" and childcare were required, with less assistance than in earlier times, and Lewis[53] suggests that:

> in the interwar years mainly middle-class mothers followed complicated feeding routines devised by (male) infant care experts . . . and both working-class and middle-class women strove to maintain elaborate household routines.

The growth of suburban living has also been attributed with increasing social isolation and anxiety for women – a new kind of confinement.[54]

Outside of issues to do with reproduction, some categories of disease and observed mortality patterns, historical scholarship has largely ignored questions of middle-class women's physical health in the first half of the twentieth-century. This is in marked contrast to the amount of material and analyses about working-class women. This invisibility is probably due to a number of factors. First, in the early decades of the twentieth century it was infant mortality and welfare that were perceived to be the problem. As working-class infants were most at risk, working-class mothers were a logical target for health policy.[55] Secondly, historians of middle-class women's health in this period have focused on sexuality, reproduction and the family, and particularly on birth control, and we may be guilty here of not extending our interests beyond the dominant discourse of the time. Finally, there had developed within many middle-class and working-class women's organizations an investigative tradition which concentrated on working-class women, and feminists campaigns such those around venereal diseases were about the "double standard" of morality rather than about health.[56] Interestingly, the Women's Health Enquiry (WHE)[57] in 1933 attempted to recruit middle-class respondents but received no response. This source provides detailed testimony of working-class women's material circumstances, resources, daily lives and health status, which remained largely unchanged until the Second World War.

In the WHE *Report* in answer to the question about whether they usually felt "fit and well", only 31 per cent gave a positive response. For the remainder, there were degrees of "wellness" alongside chronic ailments, and the 31.3 per cent who replied "no" or "never" to the question gave a record of serious chronic conditions. Given the propensity among working-class people to have lower expectations for their health, and to consider some ailments as being "expected", the report rightly claimed these self reports were likely to be an underestimation. Those categories of illness most commonly specified were anaemia (by 558 women), headaches, constipation, rheumatism, gynaecological troubles, toothache, varicose veins, ulcerated legs, and numerous references to gastric and respiratory problems.[58] Some of these complaints would be related to repeated births, exhausting domestic labour, and the double burden of paid and unpaid work. Headaches emerged in women's accounts only when more serious conditions were not present, which may indicate a hierarchy of "seriousness" that depended on the circumstances of their lives.[59] The *Report* suggests that for many women "good health" is any interval between illnesses, or at best the absence of any incapacitating ailment. Women consider themselves "fortunate but well as long as they can keep going and can get through the work that must be done".[60] Women's perception, and possibly a lack of knowledge, led to a plethora of untreated conditions. A legacy of enforced suffering combined with little or no access to health care, made such resignation an understandable response to symptoms and the circumstances of working-class lives.

Mental illness

In the nineteenth century, the discourse of causality in reproductive biology applied equally to physical or mental symptomology. Mental illness could be included within reproductive explanations because there was perceived to be a connection between the uterus and the brain mediated by the nervous system. If the uterus and the bodily system were subjected to interruptions and cyclical "shocks" or strains this would render women highly susceptible to disorders that were emotional, nervous or mental in kind.[61] The theory of reflex insanity, encapsulated this mental/mind soma/body link, and were also consistent with the development of general somatic theories in late-nineteenth-century psychiatry.[62]

In the nineteenth century the idea of womanhood as being coincident with sickness and weakness, it is argued, encompassed the culturally pervasive idea of women as being mad.[63] Showalter, for example, demonstrates the visibility of this equation in the literature and imagery of the time. This is not the same argument that is implied by Busfield's[64] recent critique, that madness was female. It was, as she argues, gendered, although her article is important for raising questions about the evidence of support from available statistical data for a conception of women's predisposition to madness.[65] Women asylum patients were mainly working class and poor, and those with disabilities who had no other means of support; middle-class and upper-class women were cared for at home, in private homes or were boarded out. A detailed examination of asylum records in the nineteenth century has revealed some examples of mainly single, middle class women patients, at least in Scottish asylums.[66] The visible numbers of women in the public institutions represented a partial picture.

A major source of derangement, according to nineteenth century psychiatric theory, was sexuality. Early in the Victorian period it was common to find labels of perceived sexual deviations, such as masturbation and nymphomania, becoming synonymous with categories of madness. Victorian ideas of the need for sexual restraint and, in women, an absence of passion, were in marked contrast to earlier times, when restraint was thought to be "unnatural".[67] Ideas of sexual pleasure for women were not countenanced in Victorian times, and "normal" sexuality was defined within reproduction, indicating not only "idealized" womanhood but also male fears of women and their sexuality.[68] The representation and treatment of women's insanity certainly suggests a deep-rooted misogyny, which adjusted to the changing circumstances of women and the social roles of men and women over time.[69]

The organic antecedents to mental instability allowed the rising professional specialisms of gynaecology and obstetrics to be as visible in therapeutics as neurologists and alienists (psychiatrists), particularly in the 1850s and 1860s. It was they who advanced the theoretical basis for interventions aimed at the regulation of periodicity and sexuality: essentially a "reprogramming" so that women could overcome their weakness, conform to "proper" feminine behaviour, manifest ladylike values and virtue, and accept their gender role. For women in asylums there was considerable emphasis on "domestic" tasks and duties such as laundry work, and the display of appropriate manners and dress.[70]

Some middle-class women found themselves subject to the therapies of individual physicians, including surgical intervention and other brutal treatments such as rectal irrigation and the administration of leeches on the labia and cervix.[71] The form of surgery that achieved most notoriety was clitoridectomy.[72] Sexual surgery, including ovariectomy, continued to be practiced in the USA until the early twentieth century,[73] and its use linked to the reproductive organs and "deviant" sexuality as causes of female disorder (including a desire for independence). A leading British proponent was Isaac Baker-Brown, a gynaecologist who had built up a reputation for his surgery around the mid-nineteenth century. He argued that the hysteria and nervous complaints of his female patients were due to "excitement of the pubic nerve", i.e. masturbation, and thence exhaustion of the whole bodily system. Baker-Brown was later involved in a "cause célèbre", and lost his career and status, but not because the brutality or efficacy of his surgical treatments were in question. The medical press of the time indicates that his fall in 1866 was not only because he broke the gentlemanly code of medical ethics, seeking neither the consent of the patients nor of their husbands for his treatment; his thinly veiled commercialism and illegal use of asylum patients were also contributing factors. Thus it was professional, social and economic interest in the potential damage to the credibility of gynaecology and medicine that led to his downfall.[74] Finally, although sexuality and ideas of moral respectability would remain important to psychiatric theory into the twentieth century, masturbation as a cause for mental illness fell out of favour. Furthermore psychiatrists sought increasingly to distance themselves from other medical practitioners in order to claim insanity as their specialist expertise.

Towards the end of the nineteenth century and into the early twentieth the link between women's social roles and mental illness was continued through psychiatry's increasing interest in "nerves".[75] For my purpose, two of the principal categories – hysteria and neurasthenia – are interesting, for two reasons. First, neurasthenia was also found among men, and the explanations for sufferers of each gender were rooted in the relative roles of men and women within middle-class, urban existence. Neither disease had any proven organic origin, and encompassed an almost limitless array of symptoms. Such categories therefore provide further examples of how issues of modernity as well as gender and class relations had to be accommodated within medical theorizing.[76] Because neurasthenic men and women were usually found among the "more sensitive", literate urban middle classes, the discourse on the condition emphasized the link between modern life and nervous debility. Uterine or hereditary deficiencies remained as explanations for women, but two new causes: the "stresses of brain work" and the "trauma of war", were utilized for men.[77] There were examples also of neurasthenic women who had indulged in excessive "brain work".[78] While it was probable that some working-class men and women shared the typical symptomology and experiences of middle-class neurasthenics, they were not countenanced as sufferers. Cayless suggests that they were probably incarcerated as insane.[79] Nervous disorders essentially became middle-class complaints within the context of perceived middle-class problems, and the discourse on neurasthenia, as with hysteria, did not differ from representations around other women's complaints.

A second reason for my interest in hysteria and neurasthenia arises in relation to a long-running debate between feminist scholars about the extent to which the symptoms, and their "disease" labels, were forms of female rebellion and protest. In the case of hysteria, Smith-Rosenberg[80] has posited that hysteria might have been a behaviourial option for women – a mode of expressing discontent, anger and pain. She is not claiming that this was a consciously chosen option, rather it was a role that was available within the boundaries of socialization, prescribed social roles and experience. The "hysterical" role did confer certain advantages, which was necessary for it to be a genuine option. The "sick role", legitimately conferred by diagnosis and medical intervention, could enable a woman to dominate her family and to be released from familial obligations. In some cases it would remove her altogether. Some argue that rest cures in relation to "nervous debility" might have been therapeutic,[81] although others suggest they served to enforce a childlike dependency and female subservience to male will.[82] Smith-Rosenberg suggests that the hostility of doctors to "hysterics" was not another instance of misogyny, but a consequence of enforced collusion with women and a role as mediators of familial conflicts, when the organic and/or clinical basis for sick role legitimation was far from clear. However, many doctors did think that women were "shamming", or behaved like "petty tyrants", and this may explain the vindictive and often physically abusive treatments offered.[83] Both explanations might have validity, and, as I argue later in this chapter, it is important to understand the relationship of doctors to women, not just as an exercise in male power, but as part of their own problematic professional and class position.[84]

It seems that there were few categories of "illness" which did not attract gender-based explanations that linked disorder to social conditions. There were very similar analyses made in relation to a third important "nervous disorder": anorexia nervosa, in that medical and cultural constructions of the "fading away" of women and girls has been viewed as a psychosomatic response to female dilemmas, and as an expression of powerlessness and anger.[85] Consistent with the ideology of female roles and responsibilities in modern urban life, lower suicide rates in women were explained by the protection that family values and the private domain gave them against the threats of the modern urban world. Equally, the higher suicide rate of women who took an active part "in the business of life was a caution in terms of politics".[86] Kushner and Anderson[87] have both argued that official statistics on suicide simply provided illustrations or confirmation of these ideas.

In the aftermath of the First World War, men and the wrongs of men occupied a central place in the history of madness. "Shell shock" indicated the possibility that nervous disorders might have a functional basis, and that emotional incapacity was not restricted to women. However, even in men, the disorder was associated with feminine qualities (among susceptible males) and emasculating consequences.[88] The minor inroads made by women into psychiatric and psychoanalytic practice did not result in any substantial challenge to the established view of gender roles. In the 1920s and 1930s, when debate focused on Freud's theoretical links between femininity and female sexuality, women psychoanalysts (for example, Karen Horney and Melanie Klein), despite departures from Sigmund Freud himself, remained preoccupied with the importance of marriage and mother–child relations which in essence accepted a prewar view of woman's place within the family.[89]

For women incarcerated in male-dominated asylums in the interwar period, harsh treatments remained commonplace, and asylums continued to be used as places for women who did not conform to social roles. There was also a new disorder, schizophrenia, and Showalter has argued that this became the central constituting category of twentieth-century female madness.[90] Available treatments for schizophrenia were used overwhelmingly on female patients. Insulin therapies, electroshock and lobotomy all resulted in submission and infantilization, and perpetuated dependence and subservience. It is in this period that we begin to witness in women's writing the inmate's view of powerlessness, the disembodied female self, and institutionalization as punishment (see, for example, Antonia White's *Beyond the glass*).[91]

What of women themselves? Did women experience mental incapacity and distress, as opposed to being constituted as mad? The answer is undoubtedly "yes", although it is difficult to gauge the nature or extent. The privacy of health matters, particularly where the illness was stigmatizing, means that we have to infer that experience from a limited number of sources, such as literary ones. In a recent paper based on American case records, Theriot[92] has been able to show that women patients were themselves part of the social constitution of their illness and active in the process of being "medicalized". Women were not simply "victims" of labels imposed by male practitioners, but sought out practitioners themselves. At the same time, Theriot's evidence does suggest that the initial definition of a woman or her behaviour as being "out of order", was often made by relatives such as mothers and husbands. Women's involvement may not always have been of their own volition.[93]

What is interesting about Theriot's data is that many women saw their problems as being related to childbirth. British evidence we have at this time and up to the Second World War suggests that childbirth was a real source of fear and distress, accompanied by feelings of anxiety and depression, and that such feelings were common across the classes.[94] Puerperal insanity accounted for 7–10 per cent of all asylum admissions,[95] and although viewed by some psychiatrists as a failure of mothering, it may equally have been an unrecognized response to the meaning of childbirth. Ironically, for both middle-class and working-class women, medical ideas that reproduction represented bodily and mental trauma may have been women's experience. The orthodoxy of privacy around sexuality and women's bodies resulted in women being ill-prepared for either menstruation or childbirth, and there were the practical problems of continuing with domestic duties and childcare resulting in feelings of exhaustion and sometimes despair.[96]

However, it is important to remember that those working-class women most likely to be incarcerated were domestic servants, whose lives were often a combination of hard physical labour, long hours and a solitary existence.[97] For middle-class women it would seem that it was the constrictions of their everyday lives, with few opportunities and a lack of power to alter things that sapped their physical and mental strength. Women's writing confirms a view of the middle-class women's mental distress as arising from the restraints of Victorian family life. There is also some support for the idea that madness was a means of experiencing anger, hostility and discontent, lending weight to Smith-Rosenberg's view of illness as rebellion.[98] While nervous or mental crises and distress might have been "options" for women, there is a danger of "romanticizing" such heroic resistance, to the exclusion of forms of madness as real suffering of desperate women. Equally, this may confirm women's sickness without considering other forms of resistance to oppression including redefinitions of gender roles.[99]

In summary, despite some commonality in the causes and experience of women's mental distress across the classes, this was not the case when it came to diagnostic categories or treatment. For middle-class women there were more options. Working-class women either had to bear their mental distress while continuing to manage their households, or when they could not look after themselves they were incarcerated in the asylums and poor law institutions. Incarceration was to remain the principal "treatment" for working-class women's distress beyond the 1950s and widespread drug therapy. To my knowledge, there were few alternative forms of care. One example of a community-based institution providing "preventative" short-stay and outpatient care by women physicians for working-class women and their children, was the Lady Chichester Hospital in Brighton. Set up by a leading woman member of the mental hygiene movement, Dr Helen Boyle, it functioned in this capacity from 1899 to 1948.[100] As with physical ill-health, the real sources of mental distress went unacknowledged and untreated.

Reproduction: fertility control, childbirth and maternity

At the outset I argued that a history of women's health and health care in this period was dominated by a discourse that defined women's health as being tied to reproductive biology and function. In this section I focus on aspects of reproduction itself, and especially on maternity. Although it is important to address the many other facets of women's health and life cycle, and not exclude those women who did not become mothers, equally the topic must be addressed. For many women, maternity was an important personal experience and, whatever their marital or childbearing status, its personal and social significance impinged on most of their lives. It was pregnancy and childbirth that were most likely to bring women into contact with medical and health services, and within the developing professions and institutions of surveillance of maternal care and infant health, under the auspices of the British state.[101] Reproduction in relation to childbearing adds to a comprehension of the way in which the social constitution of womanhood in terms of women's biological functioning was fundamental to the ideological mapping of gender roles at the macro and micro levels of social life.

Despite the idea that childbirth was a natural process, and was viewed by women themselves as being "normal", the consequences were often otherwise. Childbirth was probably the most important cause of ill-health, chronic debility and disability in women, and an important cause of death in women of childbearing age. In 1870, 3,875 women in England and Wales died either of childbirth or puerperal fever, and numbers reached 4,400 in the last year of the Victorian era.[102] Although other areas of health improved, maternal mortality remained stubbornly immune to all the measures that social policy and professional health care aimed at it.[103] Despite better obstetric knowledge, improved midwifery training and technological developments such as asepsis, as well as improved environments for births occurring in hospital and at home, the fear, rigours and disability associated with childbirth and repeated pregnancy continued to be documented.[104]

Maternity thus engendered a great deal of ambivalence for all women. Their health was put at risk, but they feared also for the health of their baby, and the consequences of births on family resources. High rates of infant mortality also placed burdens on women. Despite their fears,[105] women gained an important sense of "self" through motherhood. It was an achievement of a role not just expected but desired, and mothers loved their children so that their frequent loss was painful and distressing.[106]

In the context of maternity, the idea of women's sickness as the conspicuous display of invalidism seems a pernicious one. Indeed, levels of morbidity warranted a more "idle" existence, but in reality most ailments were left untreated and had to be accommodated in women's lives.[107] Furthermore, despite some real differences in the ways in which middle-class and working-class women would have experienced childbirth and its aftermath, it is unlikely that even middle-class women got the rest they probably required, or that medical or midwifery assistance always ensured safe births for mother or baby. Into the twentieth century, however, some differences in experience became apparent. Two things in particular seem important in this change.

First, there was already evidence by the turn of the twentieth century of a decline in the fertility rate, and this was much more marked among the middle classes. This impinged directly on to increasing class differences in women's health. In the 1870s, the fertility rate (births per thousand women in the 15–44 year age group) was 295, and by the 1930s this had fallen to 111, with an accompanying decrease in family size.[108] This overall decline obscures the fact that working-class women had more conceptions and live births than had middle-class women, and this differential widened, so that by the 1920s the number of births to wives of manual workers represented an excess of 42 per cent.[109]

Methods of controlling births have existed for centuries, so the decline in fertility over the period examined here was not only because of the availability of new methods to limit births. What did change was the context for such practices. Within wider society there was increasing public interest in birth control and population issues, and within couples/families, social and economic circumstances became material in their decision making.[110] These factors had different impacts on working-class and middle-class couples, and family limitation practices adopted also varied.[111]

Abortion had a long tradition within working-class families as a means of limitation,[112] and in the late-nineteenth century it was concern with preventing the use of abortion by working-class working women that fuelled reformers' and campaigners' condemnation of the immorality of factory work.[113] Preventive means more consistent with the middle-class ideal of family life, particularly coitus interruptus, were advocated. Gittins argues that these two methods of contraception reflected differences in gendered responsibility and power, and that opposition to abortion might need to be seen in this context also. Abortion was essentially a woman's decision, and it contravened the idea of the private nature of fertility decisions by involving others (usually women) outside the family unit. The decision to limit births in middle-class families, she argues, involved the exercise of male power, often for financial or economic motives. Although women might have desired small families also, limitation in middle-class families reflected men's greater influence in the private sphere. In working-class households, the responsibility for home and children more clearly lay with women.[114]

By the turn of the twentieth century mechanical methods of birth control became available, and there was a growth in advertisements for such products. Although all classes availed themselves of these, there was still differential use. Throughout the first half of the twentieth century, working-class women continued to make extensive use of abortion, and the burden of frequent births and large families failed to have any impact on working-class men's attitudes towards sexual practices. The "maternity letters" collected by the Women's Co-operative Guild[115] testify to both. Despite working-class women's own desire to limit fertility, they had difficulty in persuading their husbands to change their behaviour: "she is at the prey of a man just the same as though she was not pregnant. Practically within a few days of the birth, and as soon as the birth is over, she is tortured again".[116] It was men, many of them asserted, that needed to learn to "control themselves". The letters also indicate that women used both implements and drugs actively to abort their foetuses. Margreat Llewelyn Davies, general secretary of the Women's Co-operative Guild from 1889–1921, pointed out:

> Where maternity is only followed by an addition to the daily life of suffering, want, overwork, and poverty, people will continue to adopt the most dangerous, uncertain and disastrous means of avoiding it.[117]

It is difficult to estimate what the incidence of abortion was, and figures are likely to be an underestimate. Brookes[118] cites birth control clinic data, where between a third and a half of pregnancy losses were from natural or induced miscarriage. Prosecutions doubled between 1900 and 1910, and doubled again in the following two decades.[119] The state's encouragement of motherhood meant that legal access to birth control and abortion was difficult, and the 1939 Interdepartmental Committee on Abortion reflected this view. It recommended only therapeutic abortion on health grounds.[120]

For other forms of birth control, Gittins' data based on clinic records in Salford and Manchester during 1928–33, shows that class differences remained in both the utilization of clinics, and in methods favoured. The unskilled sector sought advice later in marriage and after more pregnancies, while the skilled working class and non-manual groups visited earlier. In addition, there is some indication that female methods of contraception such as pessaries, douches, sponges, pills, the cap or use of the "safe period", were increasing among these groups, which might indicate more joint decision making.[121] However, conditions in many working-class homes, such as the lack of running water and privacy, as well as the cost, would have restricted the use of such methods.[122]

Finally, despite the fact that the twentieth century witnessed a gradual recognition of women as being sexually active, with some middle-class showing an interest in deriving sexual pleasure, as witnessed by the sales of Marie Stopes' book *Married love*,[123] birth control remained entrenched in patriarchal visions of women's needs and the biological potential for motherhood. While new manuals and birth control literature gave support to both partners' "needs" and more companionate relationships, it is difficult to ascertain how far these were realized in practice.[124] Dyhouse has also suggested that because birth control was not openly discussed, historians may have underestimated the enthusiasm for new techniques of contraception.[125]

Class differentials in fertility and family size meant that for working-class women the vicious cycle of childbirth in relation to their own health continued. Their low standard of health, which I discussed earlier in this chapter, and a legacy of lifetime deprivation had an impact on pregnancies and births, and on the likelihood of survival and health of their infants. Shorter,[126] for example, points to the problems caused by rickets:

> it seems to be likely that before the 1920s when Vitamin D was finally isolated and the mechanism of rickets understood, one lower class urban woman in four was likely to have had pelvic bones sufficiently misshapen to cause delay in labour.

Childbirth itself effected further problems, often leading to chronic morbidity, which, when left untreated, impinged on later pregnancies and births. It was not just lack of access to medical care that was important here, but material and environmental circumstances and the burdens of exhausting domestic labour which had to continue immediately following birth.[127] The scale of miscarriages and stillbirths was considerable, and the pain and misery of many women in the face of what was a constant life of pregnancy was vividly reported in the "maternity letters".[128] The neglect of morbidity was in marked contrast to both infant and maternal mortality.

On balance, throughout the period, it was infant deaths and child welfare that received most attention. Interest in mothers was essentially to consider what degree of responsibility the mothers had for those deaths, and there was little change in this approach.[129] When the state did assume some responsibility for what was seen as the "social problem"[130] of the nation's health from the turn of the century, maternal ignorance, lack of domestic skills and women's failure to perform their duty were targeted. There had been some recognition prior to the early twentieth century of the dangers to women of childbirth. Robert Farr, the Registrar-General, in his *Vital Statistics of 1887* referred to the 106,565 maternal deaths during 1847–76 as "a deep, dark, and continuous stream of mortality",[131] but there was a noticeable lack of response to, or interest in it. By contrast, in the 1930s when, unlike the improvement in infant mortality figures, there was little visible change in maternal mortality, the latter assumed a higher profile. The resources that had been provided for improved antenatal and maternal care had evidently not achieved the expected effect. A decline in death rates occurred from 1937, which Loudon[132] argues was primarily brought about by the use of sulphonomides drugs, which effected a reduction in puerperal fever, the major single cause of mortality.

As with infant mortality, there was constant debate and investigation into causal factors. Over time there was a switch from environmental to personal or individual causes, then a revival of poverty and unemployment, and then a combination of these alongside maternity and obstetric care.[133] Loudon, for example, concludes that the high rates of infact mortality in areas of conspicuous poverty were not caused by the direct effects of poverty, but by factors associated with it, such as access to care, and the quality of that care.[134] Thus a further factor in the increasing difference in maternity experience in the twentieth century was the inequality in access to both economic and health care resources for maternity. The letters sent to the Women's Co-operative Guild also reveal that there were differences within the working class itself.[135] I shall examine issues of health care provision in the next section.

Intervention in and services for women's health: a century of missed opportunity

Having already discussed forms of treatment in relation to mental ill-health, this section concentrates on intervention and the development of services that might have had an impact on women's physical health status. It is important to stress at the outset that I am not arguing that access to medical men, or later to other health professionals, was necessary to achieve improvements in health. On the contrary, as I implied earlier, much medical practice was ineffective in eliminating ill-health, and many improvements were the result of better social and economic conditions. Furthermore, even when there were the beginnings of state and local-government sponsored health services, these largely failed women themselves. Thus, as described above, despite increasing provision of maternal care, levels of maternal mortality across the class divide were constant until the late 1930s.

In the nineteenth century there was a growth in the number of medical practitioners, with an increasing middle-class and urban clientele to which some middle-class women had access as private patients. In addition, the growth of voluntary hospitals to which many medical practitioners were attached meant that some working-class women also had access to medical care. Such access did not, however, guarantee any relief from symptoms, nor remedies for those serious illnesses which might result in death. Within medical practice, traditional remedies or treatments persisted – even when new knowledge or techniques were available. Doctors essentially used prevailing cultural ideas about women as a basis for their treatment. An understanding of doctors' theories about women's health and treatments offered requires a consideration of doctors' own professional insecurity. This was a consequence of competition for clients in the private health market, and doctors' own class marginality in that their aspirations to gentlemanly status did not necessarily coincide with the status of their practice having an associations with trade.[136] In addition, there were fears that "intruders of every kind" desired to enter the profession, and it was primarily against women that exclusionary tactics were employed.[137] A combination of the increasing prestige attached to "science", and their own lack of knowledge about specific clinical conditions, resulted in doctors pronouncing on a wide range of social issues, thus increasing their social power.[138] This in turn gave them an opportunity to reinforce the biological basis for women's oppression.

The position of male doctors with respect to their female "invalid" patients, for example, was problematical. Because of their professional interests, doctors were on the one hand having to develop a "sensitivity" in their dealing with women, and yet they also expressed dislike of the habits and lifestyles of their female clients. A potential conflict of male and class interests was present. Peterson[139] has demonstrated, however, that we have to be cautious about contributing to a stereotypical view of doctors. In her view, this has been the case when single sources are taken as being typical, and are then used to accuse doctors of upholding a male repressive view of women's sexuality. While we have a considerable amount of evidence about these aspects of late-nineteenth-century medical practice, we know very little about women's real relationships with their doctors, or their experiences as hospital patients.

At that time there was little medical interest in pregnancy and childbirth, and antenatal care was an unknown concept, although some doctors may have treated pregnant women if they presented themselves.[140] Medical treatment and advice provided in manuals, was for "troublesome" symptoms which arose from a "natural" process. Given physicians' poor knowledge of the biology of reproduction, on the basis of experience most women knew more than doctors about what was going on! Midwives were mainly used for deliveries, but in working-class households this was often in the form of an untrained person who would also offer domestic help. Shorter estimates that in 1892 midwives were present at fewer than half of all births in England.[141]

The provision of lying-in hospitals for married and poor women of a parish was important in the development of a specialisation of obstetrics, giving doctors control over clients and restricting competition from midwives.[142] These hospitals paved the way for a later "medicalization" of pregnancy and childbirth as pathological. Overall, maternity provision was a rarity in nineteenth-century Britain.

The Women's Health Enquiry initiated in 1933, which documented the extent of married working class women's morbidity, noted that 60 per cent had paid to see a doctor. Despite this level of consultation there was a disinclination to do so, both because there were genuine constraints of domestic economy and workloads, and also a judgement that the complaints were "safe" to ignore or to leave untreated.[143] Of course it is difficult to discern whether such perceptions might have been necessitated by the realities of the domestic constraints. Other studies have confirmed that there was a considerable pool of untreated problems, although these were not restricted to women alone. A study by doctors at the pioneering Peckham Clinic in South London revealed that 83 per cent of their caseload had something wrong and had done nothing about it,[144] and evidence from the birth control clinics set up by Marie Stopes confirmed a large residue of untreated illness.[145] Not seeking treatment was also because of fear, with one respondent in the WHE *Report* testifying to her "horror of hospitals".[145] Fear was also a problem in relation to dental health.

A further obstacle to seeking advice or treatment lay in women's own ignorance of, and alienation from, their bodies, which women frequently acknowledged to investigators. As one woman told the Co-operative Guild; "I might say I was very ignorant when I was married, my mother did not consider it at all proper to talk about such things",[147] and another describes how she had to ask an aunt a month before her baby was born "where the baby would come from".[148] If such knowledge was not passed from mother to daughter it is hardly surprising that women should be shy of talking to male doctors about their bodies. Also, there was little consideration given to privacy, either in general practice or in hospitals. In the WHE survey, 32.3 per cent said they had received no health teaching whatsoever.[149]

Even if working class women did have access to medical practitioners this did not necessarily guarantee any relief. Their experience in the twentieth century was similar to that Branca had described for middle class women in earlier times.[150] Frequently they were given little advice at all, especially on problems to which doctors were unsympathetic, such as menstrual problems; or the advice was inappropriate. Women were told to space or limit their births but not how to do this, or to "take things easy", eat more nourishing food and get more fresh air. In one case cited in the WHE *Report*, a 43 year old woman who had 10 children and had had 5 miscarriages suffered nine years of haemorrhaging and was advised that it was due "to a certain age" and she should rest in bed![151]

A second and different strand of health intervention occurred at the macro level of local and state government policy. In the nineteenth century the most important of these was what can broadly be termed public health. Public health measures were directed mainly at conditions in towns and cities that affected everyone. However, a legacy of poverty and related conditions continued to have an impact on working-class health. The agitation and reform around public health from the 1830s onwards did effect improvements in water supply, excrement removal, street cleaning, food quality and personal hygiene, but problems still persisted.[152] In the 1880s, the Royal Commission on Housing revealed that working-class families, with regular employment, and who, contrary to some middle-class views, did not spend their wages on gambling and drink, still could not afford adequate and healthy housing, and that their diet remained poor in terms of quantity and quality.[153] It is likely that women bore the brunt of these conditions, and it was not until the interwar years that any major reforms were targeted at improvements in housing. Both low wages and insecure employment continued to leave the working classes vulnerable to the diseases of poverty.

Within working-class and poor families it was also evident that available resources were not distributed equally, and this would have consequences for women's health. This was especially so with food. Women received the least, and studies show that working-class women and girls were smaller in stature until the 1950s.[154] Working-class women testified to a lack of food even while pregnant. In one of the letters to the Women's Co-operative Guild a woman whose husband earned 28 shillings a week, and who had had seven children (four of whom were stillborn) and four miscarriages wrote: "I looked after my husband and children well, but I often went short of food myself, though my husband did not know it".[155] Another described her practice of going without food and "saying she had dinner before her husband came home". There was an acceptance that "if father takes his food it must be as good as can be got, then the children come next and mother last".[156]

It was only at the end of the nineteenth century that there began to be some acceptance that municipal and state authorities should intervene in areas that had been seen traditionally as a matter for the family. Adherence to *laissez-faire* economic and social principles made it difficult to consider intervention at all, let alone into the private domain of family life.[157] As one factory inspector addressing a public meeting in 1874 put it: "I would rather see even a higher rate of infant mortality . . . than intrude one iota farther on the domestic hearth and the decent seclusion of private life."[158] Despite the continuing strength of this ideological position there were state, local authority and volunteer-directed attempts to "interfere" with the working-class family, particularly after the "shocking" revelations of the health of Boer War (1907–10) recruits.[159]

In the 1890s there were proposals to protect the health of mothers and children, mainly through factory legislation which covered only selected industrial employments. In 1891, legislation prohibited the "knowing" employment of women within four weeks of giving birth. This proved to be largely ineffective because of lack of enforcement and because it ignored the realities of both employers' and working women's own priorities, which led to contravention. In general, regulation to improve the working conditions of women did not measure up to what was being demanded by both protagonists and antagonists of working women, or to the scale of the problems being faced.[160] Measures aimed at working women were concerned with the evident contradiction of "separate spheres ideology" rather than with the health of women or their children.[161] As the Women's Co-operative Guild was later to point out the evils of factory labour received attention "but what of the evils of domestic labour?"[162]

The first national provision for health care came into effect in 1911 with the National Insurance Act. Under this Act, only those women who worked and paid National Health Insurance could have access to a panel doctor and receive free medicine. This applied to less than 10 per cent of women.[163] Lewis points out that women were also subject to a considerable amount of surveillance with respect to insurance claims because of assumptions about their greater risk.[164] In addition, the wives of male insurees were entitled to a maternity grant of £30, which was initially paid to husbands, then from 1913 to wives, after a vigorous campaign. There is evidence from both the "maternity letters" and the WHE *Report*,[165] that this £30 did enable some working-class women to pay for a midwife, or doctor's assistance, during childbirth. The early decades of the twentieth century also saw the development of health clubs, and those working-class families in receipt of the higher wages necessary for the contributions were able to draw on these for some health care at this time. For non-insured working-class women the only other free health care available was from the poor law infirmary, and from 1918 onwards at maternity and child welfare clinics.

Just prior to the First World War, there was a shift toward national medical intervention in childbirth, with a Local Government Board Circular (1914) emphasizing the provision of antenatal care, supervision of midwives, skilled assistance at birth, and postnatal care of mothers. Oakley argues that this circular was important because it laid down two overlapping principles: that the state's interest in motherhood should continue from conception until the child enters full-time schooling, and the continuous and systematic provision of antenatal care.[166] In the event, the 1918 Maternity and Child Welfare Act enabled, but did not require, a local authority to fund and support maternity and child welfare work. The 120 clinics that came into existence in 1918 were intended for working-class women. Although clinics were to increase in number as the century progressed, the major emphasis of this provision was on infant health. These were not services for women, only for those who were pregnant or who had produced a child. It is also likely that infant mortality was already substantially in decline by the time of this initiative, although, as I indicated earlier, maternal mortality was not. Yet very few local authorities provided any postnatal clinics. Official concern around maternity and the services provided served to confirm the view that "the woman comes onto the map of the public conscience only when she is performing the bodily function of producing a child".[167]

In the 1920s within the Ministry of Health, Dr Janet Campbell mounted a concerted campaign to eliminate the 50 per cent of maternal deaths she regarded as "avoidable". This, she concluded, required improved standards of obstetric practice and better provision of antenatal care. A Departmental Committee on Maternal Mortality set up in 1928 demonstrated a polarization of opinion as to whether it was clinical standards or the service user that were at fault. Despite reports which suggested that Campbell was largely correct as to the causes of "avoidable" mortality, the message that emerged from the committee report was that while services were important, attendance at them was more so.[168] From this time, non-attendance was to assume a high profile in official and medical perceptions of the health problems associated with pregnancy and birth.

The 1930s also saw a return to a consideration of the impact of social conditions on infant and maternal health, given the high levels of unemployment consequent on economic recession. It had been noted that while aggregate health indicators showed improvement there were considerable disparities regionally.[169] As Mitchell argues, the strength of evidence in favour of environmental or social conditions was not favoured in official circles.[170] Nor did they accept a growing body of expert nutritional knowledge since diet was related to income, and this would involve acknowledging a link between income and unemployment. It was more likely that these same indicators would be used as evidence of poor "housewifery".[171] There was government intransigence in the face of the evidence: particularly the success of a scheme in the Rhondda Valley which achieved a sharp fall in maternal mortality.[172] Nor was the case against obstetric practice pursued with any vigour outside of an initiative to set standards for antenatal care by the Ministry of Health in 1929, and Janet Campbell's success in twice increasing the period of training for midwives in the 1920s. The evacuation and care of pregnant women in a network of maternity hospitals during the Second World War, despite an excess of supply over demand, paved the way for postwar hospitalized birth. The attention to diet and vitamin supplements also probably contributed to eventual improvements in rates of infant and maternal mortality.[173]

In the pursuit of improved standards of motherhood, considerable attention was paid to forms of surveillance and education targeting working-class and poor women. An earlier voluntary tradition of "petticoated" (as they were called) inspectors or visitors, became professional and salaried health workers from the early twentieth century.[174] There was still a role for women's organizations and other voluntary societies to continue the work they had begun earlier, and these were probably the most important sources of preventive work. While these women may have been an important source of health advice and support for women, their work essentially confirmed that it was women's inadequate performance of their domestic role that threatened the nation's health constantly.

There was also feminist activism around issues of birth control, working conditions, state support for maternity, and welfare provision.[175] But here, as when they challenged doctors, their right to medical education, or medical practice (such as the Contagious Diseases Acts) they did so within a moral framework and a definition of welfare which left the gender roles of marriage and motherhood unquestioned.[176] Harrison concludes that health was only a minor theme in British feminist periodicals both before and after 1914.[177] Neither did women doctors specialize in problems of women's health. However, it is also understandable that health, as an intensely private and personal concern, might have difficulty in making it to the centre stage of the political agenda in this period. It is also important to consider the extent to which feminist activists, in seeking opportunities for women, in fostering female autonomy, and in challenging male and medical definitions of their sexuality, bodies, aptitudes and treatment received, did contribute to improved health status for women without an explicit health campaign.

Conclusion

An understanding of women's health in this period requires an analysis that recognizes not only the similarity in the construction of women's health problems and their experience of their bodies in health and sickness, but also the importance of the class dimension. Since health and well-being have a material basis, then at this fundamental level life-chances and degrees of ill-health will not be shared by women equally. One of the most striking features of women's health status for the Victorian period at least is the relative absence of such inequalities, but these became increasingly evident as the twentieth century advanced. The "progress" that improvements in diet, living conditions and income achieved in health status overall did not benefit women equally, nor was the impact as dramatic for women as for other groups in the population, especially children.

In the discourse about women's health, late-nineteenth-century medical theory was dominated by conditions which it encountered largely through middle-class clients. Although doctors increasingly had access to working-class women through the expanding voluntary hospitals or lying-in hospitals, this was rarely reflected in theories advanced for mental or physical complaints. Even in chlorosis, which had both middle- and working-class sufferers, a middle-class conception of the disease was maintained. Medical views of women's health were able to confirm gender roles that were class-specific, and a condemnation of women's ways of life: they were idle, they worked (outside the home), they pandered to fashion, neglected personal care – constant dualities that ensured women's actions were always responsible for their health.

This chapter has argued that interest in the health of women centred around a single issue manifested in two principal strands of debate. This single issue was reproduction in all its aspects. First, it was the health of the physical body of the nation that was of concern. Secondly another concern was the social body, and the extent to which women's health could be used as a political strategy to maintain a rigid sexual division of labour in the public domains of work and education, and the private domains of the family. Blame for the various crises over the health of the nation could be laid at women's physical capacity and social role, and these were inseparable from one another. It was in this way that medical and "official" interests in women's health, limited though they were, further failed to deal with the real health problems which many women experienced. Throughout the period women continued to be denied access to health care for substantial amounts of physical and mental morbidity. Disordered women provided a rationale for the maintenance of existing gender relations and male power over women's lives, and thereby devalued women's own needs, including health needs.

Notes

1. This had both physiological and social dimensions. There was little medical interest in women's health outside their reproductive years, and older women had little social status either, despite a life expectancy that extended beyond the menopause. See P. Jalland & J. Hooper (eds), *Women from birth to death; the female life cycle in Britain from 1830-1914* (Brighton: Harvester, 1986), pp. 281-302.

2. Brian Harrison pointed out that the lack of survival of primary documents, and the focus of secondary sources, has made it difficult to assess many medical dimensions of " 'first wave' feminism; the subject of his work, Women's health and the women's movement in Britain 1840-1940", in *Biology, medicine and society 1840-1940*, C. Webster (ed.) (Cambridge: Cambridge University Press, 1981). There is certainly an absence of empirical sources on health experience, although I believe there are sources as yet untapped that may prove fruitful.

3. See, for example, the critique of some feminist writing which characterized late-nineteenth-century and early-twentieth-century ideology in terms of middle-class women as sick, and working-class women as sickening, as being too simplistic. M. Verbrugge, "Historical complaints and political disorders: a review of Ehrenreich and English's study of medical ideas about women", *International Journal of Health Services* **5** (2), pp. 323-33, 1975.

4. A number of writers provide an overview of this construction, including J. Ussher, *The psychology of women's bodies* (London: Routledge, 1991), Ch. 1; J. Lewis, *Women in England 1870-1950. Sexual divisions and social change* (Brighton:

Wheatsheaf, 1984), pp. 83-5; and its transatlantic commonality is exhibited in B. Ehrenreich and D. English, *Complaints and disorders: the sexual politics of sickness* (San Francisco: Readers and Writers, 1974); and A. Douglas Wood, "The fashionable diseases: women's diseases and their treatment in nineteenth century America", in *Clio's consciousness raised*, M. Hartman & L Banner (eds) (New York: Harper & Row, 1974). Jalland and Hooper, *Women from birth to death,* provides some examples of documents that support such a definition.

5. L. Duffin, "The conspicuous consumptive: woman as invalid", in *The nineteenth century woman* S. Delamont & L. Duffin (eds) (London: Croom Helm, 1979), pp. 26-56.

6. B. Ehrenreich & D. English, *Complaints and disorders: the sexual politics of sickness* (London: Writers and Readers Publishing Co-operative, 1976).

7. A number of writers have argued that middle-class women's lives were not lives of idleness. See, for example, P. Branca, *Silent sisterhood: middle class women in Victorian England* (London: Croom Helm, 1975); and C. Dyhouse, *Feminism and the family in England 1880-1939* (Oxford: Basil Blackwell, 1989).

8. Branca, *Silent sisterhood*, p. 70.

9. F. Nightingale, *Cassandra*, (1852; revised in 1859), reprinted in R. Strachey *"The Cause": a short history of the women's movement in Great Britain* (London: Bell, 1928) p. 402. For a further discussion of Florence Nightingale's views on women's experiences of family life see C. Dyhouse, *Feminism and the family in England 1880-1939*, pp. 7-39.

10. The notion of ideal here refers to the possibility that for middle-class men, "invalidism" or women idle at home was a "conspicuous display" of their economic standing. See L. Duffin, "The conspicuous consumptive", pp. 30-1.

11. This was so despite being the largest single group of women workers. Interestingly, however, Dr Thomas Oliver, a physician who specialised in occupational disease, included a chapter on domestic servants in his edited collection, *Dangerous trades: the history, social and legal aspects of industrial occupations as affecting health by a number of experts* (London: John Murray, 1902).

12. It should be pointed out that this argument was made by feminist activists at the time in the context of committees of inquiry and campaigns too numerous to mention. I have elaborated on examples in B. Harrison, "'Some of them gets lead poisoned': occupational lead exposure in women, 1880-1914", *Social History of Medicine* 2 (2) (1989), pp. 171-93; B. Harrison, "Women's health or social control?: the role of the medical profession in relation to factory legislation in nineteenth century Britain", *Sociology of Health and Illness* 13 (4), pp. 469-91, 1991; B. Harrison, "Feminism and the health consequences of women's work in late nineteenth and early twentieth century Britain", in *Locating health: historical and social perspectives*, S. Platt, H. Thomas, S. Scott, G. Williams, (eds) (Andover: Avebury, 1993) pp. 75-96, See also the importance of the confusion between motherhood as ideology and the health of mothers in A. Davin, "Imperialism and motherhood", *History Workshop Journal* 5, pp. 10-65, 1978.

13. See M. Hewitt, *Wives and mothers in Victorian industry: a study of the effects of employment of mothers in Victorian industry* (London: Rockliffe, 1958), esp. Ch. 8. B. Harrison & H. Mockett, "Women in the factory: the state and factory legislation in nineteenth century Britain", in *State, private life and political change*, L. Jamieson & H. Corr (eds) (London: Macmillan, 1990), pp. 137-62; and on male trade unionists' exclusionary strategies, in relation to "protective" legislation generally,

S. Walby, *Patriarchy at work*, (Cambridge: Polity Press, 1986); S. O. Rose, "Gender antagonism and class conflict: exclusionary strategies of male trade unionists in nineteenth century Britain", *Social History* **13** (2), pp. 191-208, 1988. J. Lewis & C. Davies, "Protective legislation in Britain, 1870-1990: equality, difference and their implications for women", *Policy and Politics* **19** (1), pp. 13-25, 1991; and in relation to the politics of the "family wage", H. Benenson, "The 'family wage' and working women's consciousness in Britain, 1880-1914", *Politics and Society* **19** (1), pp. 71-108, 1991.

14. This view was expressed in numerous quarters: in the evidence and recommendations of many committees of inquiry at this time, and there was considerable evidence of unsupported women, and low wages paid to men that necessitated women working. This may have mitigated against legislation to prohibit married women's work. See, for example, Harrison, "Women's health or social control?"; and Harrison & Mockett, "Women in the factory", p. 150.

15. For more detail on the nature of the evidence for female susceptibility, and the debates about exclusion, see Harrison, "'Some of them gets lead poisoned': women and occupational lead exposure 1880-1914".

16. B. Harrison, "The politics of occupational health: the case of the match-making industry in late nineteenth century Britain", *Sociology of Health and Illness* **17** (1), 1995.

17. A. Ineson & D. Thom, "TNT poisoning and the employment of women in the First World War, in *The social history of occupational health*, P. Weindling (ed.) (London: Croom Helm, 1987).

18. A. Davin,, "Imperialism and motherhood", esp. pp. 10-22.

19. L. Bland, "'Guardians of the race' or 'vampires upon the nations health'? Female sexuality and its regulation in early twentieth century Britain", in *The changing experience of women*, E. Whitelegge et al. (eds) (Oxford: Martin Robertson, 1982) pp. 373-88.

20. J. J. Brumberg, "Chlorosis and chlorotic girls, 1870-1920: a historical perspective on female adolescence", in *Women and health in America: historical readings*, J. Leavitt (ed.) (Madison, Wisconsin: University of Wisconsin Press, 1984) pp. 186-95.

21. *Ibid.*, pp. 186-7.

22. K. Figlio, "Chlorosis and chronic disease in nineteenth century Britain: the social constitution of a somatic illness in a capitalist society", in *Women and health: the politics of sex and medicine* E. Fee (ed.) (Amityville, New Jersey: Baywood, 1983), pp. 213-41.

23. E. Shorter, *A history of women's bodies* (London: Allen Lane, 1983), p. 252. See also K. Figlio, "Chlorosis and Chronic disease", pp. 224-5 for other references to working class sufferers.

24. See F. B. Smith, *The people's health* (London: Croom Helm, 1979); and K. Figlio, "Chlorosis and chronic disease", p. 222 cites one study which found hospital inpatients with chlorosis to include servants, dressmakers, boot sewers and machinists.

25. J. J. Brumberg, "Chlorosis and chlorotic girls 1870-1920", p. 193.

26. Figlio, "Chlorosis and chronic disease", pp. 234-5. I return to the position of doctors *vis-à-vis* women patients in the final section, but Figlio finds backing for his argument in R. Morantz, "The lady and her physician", in *Clio's consciousness raised* M. Hartman & L Banner (eds) (New York: Harper & Row, 1974), pp. 38-53.

27. Brumberg, "Chlorosis and chlorotic girls 1870-1920", p. 188. Indeed, one American doctor is cited here as claiming that chlorosis was "no respecter of rank or fortune".

The difference between America and Britain in this respect may reflect less rigid class ideologies.

28. See, for example, V. Bullogh & M. Vogt, "Women, menstruation and nineteenth century medicine", *Bulletin for the History of Medicine* 7 (1), pp. 66-82, 1973; V. Skultans, "Femininity and illness", in Skultans, *English madness: ideas on insanity* (London: Routledge & Kegan Paul, 1979); J. Burstyn, *Victorian education and the ideal of womanhood* (London: Croom Helm, 1980) Chs 4 & 5; J. Purvis, *A history of women's education in England* (Milton Keynes, Open University Press, 1991).

29. P. Jalland & J. Hooper (eds), *Women from birth to death*, pp. 53-8, provides an overview on views of menstruation, including its link with disease; and shows examples of documents on the problems of education in relation to menstruation, pp. 78-86.

30. H. Maudsley, "Sex, mind and education", *Fortnightly Review* 15, pp. 468-83, 1874.

31. *Ibid.*, p. 471.

32. In a number of the studies of "disease" categories, both physical and mental, issues of urban living, and the demands of women for education and work opportunities are construed as "dangers" to health. In addition, as Brian Harrison argues, although anti-feminism was not peculiar to doctors, they were prominent in their persons and arguments for the anti-feminist case. B. Harrison, "Women's health and the women's movement in Britain, 1840-1940", p. 28.

33. See, for example, S. Arber, "Gender and class inequalities in health: understanding the differentials", in *Inequalities in health in Europe* J. Fox (ed.) (Andover: Gower, 1987); S. Arber, "Class, paid employment and family roles: making sense of structural disadvantage, gender and health status", *Social Science and Medicine* 32, pp. 425-36; M. Verbrugge, "Gender and health: an update on hypotheses and evidence", *Journal of Health and Social Behaviour* 26, pp. 156-82.

34. In addition to the studies above, see M. Whitehead, *The health divide* (London Health Education Authority, 1986).

35. S. R. Johansson, "Sex and death in Victorian England: an examination of age-specific death rates 1840-1910", in *A widening sphere: changing roles of Victorian women*, M. Vincinus (ed.) (Bloomington, Indiana: Indiana University Press, 1978) pp. 163-81.

36. Shorter, *A history of women's bodies*, p. 228.

37. Shorter, *Ibid.*, p. 228, expresses this as "perhaps a twenty five percent greater risk of dying than their husbands", and notes that this is a world picture, and the actual percentage varied from country to country.

38. *Ibid.*, p. 231.

39. See S. Sontag, *Illness as metaphor* (New York: Farrar, Straus and Giroux, 1977) for an excellent exposition of the role of cultural metaphors in relation to illness, using tuberculosis and cancer as her main examples. As Wohl points out, although TB was associated with artists and poets, it was connected with nutritional standards and hit hardest those working-class families in poorly ventilated, overcrowded urban districts. A. S. Wohl, *Endangered lives: public health in Victorian Britain* (London: J. M. Dent, 1983) p. 130.

40. Duffin, "The conspicuous consumptive", pp. 39-40; Figlio, "Chlorosis and chronic disease", p. 223; and Shorter, *A history of women's bodies*, pp. 28-31; 252-3.

41. Johansson, "Sex and death in Victorian England", pp. 174-80.

42. P. Stearns, "Working class-women in Britain, 1890-1914", in *Suffer and be still*, M. Vicinus (ed.) (Bloomington, Indiana: Indiana University Press, 1973) pp. 100-20, esp. pp. 110-12.

43. Johansson, "Sex and death in Victorian England", p. 180.
44. These arguments were more often about the continuing high rate of infant mortality rather than women's mortality, and arguments about physical effects were conflated with social concerns. See *Report of the Inter-departmental Committee on Physical Deterioration, and Minutes of Evidence*, pp. XXXII (1904); and Harrison, "Women's health or social control?: the role of the medical profession in relation to factory legislation in nineteenth century Britain".
45. Johansson, "Sex and death in Victorian England", p. 174.
46. Branca, *Silent sisterhood*, Ch. 4.
47. *Ibid.*, pp. 67 & 70-1; J. M. Peterson, *The medical profession in mid-Victorian London* (Berkeley, California: University of California Press, 1978).
48. Harrison, "Women's health or social control? The role of the medical profession in relation to factory legislation in late nineteenth century Britain", p. 480.
49. Shorter, *A history of women's bodies*, pp. 255-63. Shorter notes that little relief of vaginal infections was available until the 1920s and 1930s.
50. Branca, *Silent sisterhood*, pp. 70-1.
51. This view has been posited by T. McKeown, "A historical appraisal of the medical task", in *Medical history and medical care*, D. McLachlan & T. McKeown (eds) (Oxford: Nuffield Provincial Hospitals Trust, 1971); and a lively debate continues as to the causes of mortality decline, see S. Szretser, "The importance of social intervention in Britain's mortality decline 1850-1914: a reinterpretation of the role of public health", *Social History of Medicine* 1, pp. 1-37, 1988.
52. Harrison, "Women's health and the women's movement 1840-1940", p. 38.
53. J. Lewis (ed.), *Labour and love: women's experience of home and family 1850-1940* (Oxford: Basil Blackwell, 1986), p. 4.
54. Lewis, *Women in England 1850-1950*, p. 116.
55. See, for example, A. Davin, "Imperialism and motherhood"; C. Dyhouse, "Working-class mothers and infant mortality in England 1895-1914", *Journal of Social History* 12, pp. 248-67.
56. F. Mort, "Purity, feminism and the state: sexuality and moral politics, 1880-1914", in *Crises in the British State, 1880-1914*, M. Langan and B. Schwartz (eds) (London: Hutchison, 1986), pp. 209-25; and Harrison, "Women's health and the women's movement", pp. 37-8.
57. M. Spring Rice, *Working class wives: their health and conditions* (Harmondsworth: Pelican, 1939; reprinted, London: Virago, 1981).
58. *Ibid.*, pp. 28-38.
59. It is interesting to note that this continues to be found in self-reports of working-class women's health. See, for example, M. Blaxter & E. Paterson, *Mothers and daughters: a three generational study of health attitudes and behaviour* (London: Heinemann, 1982).
60. Spring Rice, *Working class wives*, p. 72.
61. A. Scull & D. Favreau, "The clitoridectomy craze", *Social Research* 53 (2), 1986, pp. 243-60, esp. pp. 243-5. S. Cayless, "'Prisoners of their own feebleness': women, nerves and western medicine - a historical overview", *Social Science and Medicine* 26 (12), pp. 1199-208, esp. p. 1201.
62. See, for example, E. Showalter, *The female malady: women, madness and English culture 1830-1980* (London: Virago, 1987), see esp. Chs 4 & 5.
63. See, V. Skultans, *English madness: ideas on insanity*; E. Showalter, *The female malady*; J. Ussher, *The psychology of the female body*.

64. J. Busfield, "Men, women and madness in nineteenth century Britain", *Sociology* **28** (1), pp. 259-77, 1994.

65. *Ibid.*, pp. 263-9.

66. F. Rice, "Madness and industrial society: a study of the early growth and organization of insanity in mid nineteenth-century Scotland 1830-1870", unpublished Ph.D. thesis, Strathclyde University, 1981.

67. R. Porter, "Love, sex and madness in eighteenth century England", *Social Research* **53** (2), pp. 211-42, 1986.

68. Showalter, *The female malady*, Ch. 3; Lewis, *Women in England 1870-1950*, p. 84.

69. See S. Cayless, "'Prisoners of their nerves'"; E. Showalter, *The female malady* for such an overview.

70. Showalter, *The female malady*, pp. 79-84.

71. *Ibid.*, p. 75.

72. A. Scull & D. Favreau, "The clitoridectomy craze".

73. B. Barker-Benfield, *Horrors of a half known life* (New York: Harper Torch Books, 1972).

74. See Jalland & Hooper, *Women from birth to death*, pp. 250-65, which includes some excerpts from original documents on the case. It is also discussed in Showalter, *The female malady*, pp. 75-8; and Scull & Favreau, "The clitoridectomy craze", pp. 248-60.

75. S. Cayless, "Prisoners of their own feebleness".

76. A. Douglas Wood, "The fashionable diseases: women's complaints and their treatment in nineteenth-century America, in *Clio's consciousness raised*, M. Hartman and L. Banner (eds) (New York: Harper & Row, 1974), pp. 1-22; C. Smith-Rosenberg, "The hysterical woman: sex roles and role conflict in nineteenth century America", *Social Research* **39**, pp. 25-42, 1972; B. Sicherman, "The uses of diagnosis: doctors, patients and neurasthenia", *Journal of the History of Medicine* **32** (1), pp. 33-54, 1977; J. Haller, "Neurasthenia: the medical profession and the 'new woman' of late nineteenth century", *New York State Journal of Medicine* **71**, pp. 473-82, 1971; E. Showalter, *The female malady*, Chs 5 & 6.

77. S. Cayless, "Prisoners of their own feebleness", p. 1203; and see Showalter's discussion of "shell shock" as a form of male hysteria, *The female malady*.

78. J. Haller, "Neurasthenia", also notes that "mannish" attributes were often associated with both "new women" and neurasthenic women. See also, J. Ussher, *The psychology of the female body*, p. 5.

79. Cayless, "Prisoners of their own feebleness", p. 1204.

80. Smith-Rosenberg, "The hysterical woman: sex roles and role conflict in nineteenth century society".

81. Sicherman, "The uses of diagnosis: doctors, patients and neurasthenia", p. 50.

82. Douglas Wood, "The fashionable diseases", pp. 9-13.

83. See Ussher, *The psychology of the female body*, p. 5.

84. See also Peterson, *The medical profession in mid-Victorian London*; and Morantz, "The lady and her physician"; Figlio, "Chlorosis and chronic disease", pp. 234-5.

85. J.J. Brumberg, *Fasting girls: the emergence of anorexia nervosa as a modern disease* (Cambridge, Mass.: Harvard University Press, 1988); and Showalter, *The female malady*, pp. 127-9.

86. H. I. Kushner, "Suicide, gender and the fear of modernity in nineteenth century medical and social thought", *Journal of Social History* **26** (3), pp. 461-90, 1993, esp. p. 470.

87. *Ibid.*, pp. 464-5; and O. Anderson, *Suicide in Victorian and Edwardian England* (Oxford: Clarendon Press, 1987).

88. Showalter, *The female malady*, Ch. 7.

89. *Ibid.*, pp. 195-203. There has been a considerable amount of feminist scholarship covering Freudian and other psychoanalytic theories which cannot be considered here. See, for example, J. Sayers, *Sexual contradictions: psychology, psychoanalysis and feminism* (London: Tavistock, 1986).

90. Showalter, *The female malady*, pp. 203-4.

91. *Ibid.*, pp. 205-10. Antonia White was incarcerated in Bedlam in 1922; *Beyond the Glass* was published in 1954, and reprinted by Virago in 1979.

92. N. M. Theriot, "Women's voices in nineteenth century medical discourse: a step towards deconstructing science", *Signs: A Journal of Women, Culture and Society* **19** (1) (1993), pp. 1-32.

93. *Ibid.*, p. 17 refers to women who sought out doctors and "asked to be committed", while, p. 19 contains the data which suggests they often did not visit the doctor alone.

94. See, C. Huff, "Chronicles of confinement: reactions to childbirth in British women's diaries", *Women's Studies International Forum* **10** (1), pp. 63-8, 1987; M. Llewelyn Davies, *Maternity: letters from working women* (collected by The Women's Co-operative Guild, first published 1915; reprinted London: Virago, 1978). Further confirmation of Theriot's data on American women can be found in J. W. Leavitt, "Under the shadow of maternity: American women's responses to death and debility fears in nineteenth century childbirth", *Feminist Studies* **12** (1), pp. 130-53, 1986.

95. Showalter, *The female malady*, p. 57.

96. There are examples of such expressed emotions in Llewelyn Davies, *Maternity: letters from working women*.

97. See C. V. Butler, *Domestic service. An inquiry by the Women's Industrial Council* (London: Women's Industrial Council, 1916); and E. Higgs, "Domestic service and household production", in *Unequal opportunities: women's employment in England 1880-1918*, A. V. John (ed.) (Oxford: Basil Blackwell, 1986), pp. 128-50.

98. Dyhouse, *Feminism and the family*, Ch. 1; and Showalter, *The female malady*.

99. Harrison, "Women's health and the women's movement", suggests that political struggles were important for women's health, and that improvements in health might also have been important for women's struggles. Caution about the "illness as rebellion" thesis is expressed by Showalter in *The female malady*, Ch. 6; and by J. Oppenheim, *Doctors, nerves and depression in Victorian England* (New York: Oxford University Press, 1991).

100. V. O'Connor, "The Lady Chichester Hospital 1898-1988 and its founder Dr Helen Boyle: an historical appreciation", unpublished B.Sc. dissertation in Community Psychiatric Nursing, NESCOT, 1994.

101. See, for example, J. Lewis, *The politics of motherhood: maternal and child welfare in England 1900-1939* (London: Croom Helm, 1980); Davin, "Imperialism and motherhood", D. Armstrong, "The invention of infant mortality", *Sociology of Health and Illness* **8**, 1986.

102. Wohl, *Endangered lives*, p. 13; Smith, *The people's health*, p. 13.

103. See I. Loudon, "Maternal mortality 1880-1950: some regional and international comparisons", *Social History of Medicine* **1** (2) (1988), pp. 183-223; A. Oakley, *The*

captured womb: a history of the medical care of pregnant women (Oxford: Basil Blackwell, 1986) Chs 2 & 3.

104. See the letters elicited by the Women's Co-operative Guild in Llewelyn Davies, *Maternity*.

105. Huff, "Chronicles of confinement"; Llewelyn Davies, *Maternity*.

106. E. Ross, "Labour and love: rediscovering London's working class mothers, 1870-1918", in *Labour and love: women's experiences of home and family 1850-1940*, J. Lewis (ed.) (Oxford: Basil Blackwell, 1986), pp. 73-98, esp. pp. 80-83.

107. Shorter, *A history of women's bodies*, draws attention to the commonality of pelvic injuries caused by childbirth. Surgical techniques to deal with one example, prolapse of the uterus, did not develop until the 1920s, see pp. 268-75.

108. Lewis, *Women in England*, p. 5.

109. *Ibid.*, p. 6.

110. D. Gittins, *The fair sex: family size and structure 1900-1939* (London: Hutchison, 1982).

111. *Ibid.*, Ch. 6 & pp. 180-7; C. Dyhouse *Feminism and the family*, pp. 166-74.

112. P. Knight, "Women and abortion in Victorian and Edwardian England", *History Workshop Journal* 4, pp. 48-70, 1977.

113. A. McLaren, "Women's work and the regulation of family size: the question of abortion in the nineteenth century", *History Workshop Journal* 4, pp. 71-81, 1977.

114. Gittins, *The fair sex*, pp. 158-61.

115. Llewelyn Davies, *Maternity*.

116. *Ibid.*, letter 21, p. 49.

117. *Ibid.*, p. 18.

118. B. Brookes, "Women and reproduction c. 1860-1920", in *Labour and love: women's experiences of home and family*, J. Lewis (ed.) (Oxford: Basil Blackwell, 1986), pp. 149-71, p. 157.

119. Lewis, *Women in England*, p. 18.

120. *Ibid.*, pp. 32-3.

121. Gittins, *The fair sex*, pp. 165-80.

122. Brookes, "Women and reproduction c. 1860-1920", p. 158.

123. R. Hall, *Dear Dr Stopes: sex in the 1920s* (London: André Deutsch, 1978); and R. Hall, *Marie Stopes: a biography* (London: Virago, 1978), Ch. 8; L. Bland, "Marriage laid bare: middle class women and marital sex, 1880s-1914", in *Labour and Love*, J. Lewis (ed.), pp. 123-46; C. Dyhouse, *Feminism and the family*, Ch. 4.

124. Brookes, "Women and reproduction", p. 166.

125. Dyhouse, *Feminism and the family*, p. 171.

126. Shorter, *A history of women's bodies*, p. 25.

127. See Llewelyn Davies, *Maternity*; and Spring Rice, *Working-class wives*, for many examples of these circumstances.

128. Llewelyn Davies, *Maternity*.

129. See Davin, "Imperialism and motherhood"; Dyhouse, "Working class mothers and infant mortality", Lewis, *The politics of motherhood*; and D. Riley, "'The free mothers': pro-natalism and working women in industry at the end of the last war in Britain", *History Workshop Journal* 11, pp. 59-118, 1988.

130. George Newman, appointed Chief Medical Officer at the Board of Education in 1907, entitled his work on infant mortality *Infant mortality: a social problem*.

131. Cited in A. Oakley, *The captured womb*, p. 32.

132. Loudon, "Maternal mortality, 1880-1950".

133. J. Campbell, "Maternal mortality", Reports of public health and medical subjects, No. 25 (London: Ministry of Health, HMSO, 1924); Loudon, "Maternal mortality".
134. Loudon, *ibid.*, p. 222.
135. Llewelyn Davies, *Maternity.*
136. I. Waddington, "The development of medicine as a modern profession", in *The social history of the bio-medical sciences*, M. Piatelli-Palmarini (ed.) (Milan: Franco Maria Ricci, 1984).
137. See, for example, Harrison, "Women's Health and the Women's Movement", which suggests that feminism offered numerous threats to the role of doctors including their support for women doctors; and A. Witz, *Professions and patriarchy* (London: Routledge, 1990).
138. J. L'Esperance, "Doctors and women in nineteenth century society: sexuality and role", in *Health care and popular medicine* J.Woodward & D. Richards (eds) (London: Croom Helm, 1977), pp. 105-27. In my research I have also noted that doctors entered into the debates about women and factory work on social rather than clinical grounds. Harrison, "Women's health or social control?".
139. J. M. Peterson, "Dr Acton's enemy: medicine, sex and society in Victorian England", *Victorian Studies* **29**, pp. 469-590, 1986.
140. Oakley, *The captured womb*, Ch. 1.
141. Shorter, *A history of women's bodies*, p. 143.
142. M. Verslysen, "Midwives, medical men and poor women labouring of child", in *Women, health and reproduction*, H. Roberts (ed.) (London: Routledge & Kegan Paul, 1981); Oakley, *The captured womb*, Ch. 1.
143. Spring Rice, *Working-class wives*, pp. 38-9.
144. Cited in Spring Rice, *Working-class wives*, p. 30. Such estimates rest on assumptions of shared perceptions between doctors and patients which is highly problematic.
145. Hall, *Dear Dr Stopes.*
146. Spring Rice, *Working-class wives*, p. 42.
147. Llewelyn Davies, *Maternity*, letter 37, p. 61.
148. *Ibid.*, letter 11, p. 30.
149. Spring Rice, *Working-class wives*, p. 46.
150. Branca, *Silent sisterhood*, pp. 70-1.
151. Spring Rice, *Working-class wives*, p. 45.
152. Wohl, *Endangered lives* documents in depth the extent of improvements and persistent problems in this area.
153. *Ibid.*, Ch. 11; and the WHE *Report* is ample testimony to this. For Edwardian views of public health, see, D. Porter, "'Enemies of the Race': biologism, environmentalism and public health in Edwardian England", *Victorian Studies* **34** (2), pp. 159-77, 1991.
154. Wohl, *Endangered lives*, p. 13.
155. Llewelyn Davies, *Maternity*, letter 128, pp. 158-9.
156. *Ibid.*, letter 30, pp. 58-9.
157. See, for example, Langan & Schwartz, *Crises in the British state 1880-1914*; and J. Dale and P. Forster (eds) *Feminists and state welfare*, part 1. (London, Routledge & Kegan Paul, 1986).
158. Cited in Wohl, *Endangered lives*, p. 32.
159. *Ibid.*, Ch. 12; Davin, "Imperialism and motherhood"; and Lewis, "The working class wife and mother and state intervention 1870-1918", in her edited *Labour and Love*, pp. 99-120.

160. B. Harrison, "Suffer the working day: women in the 'dangerous trades' 1880-1914", *Women's Studies International Forum* **13** (1), pp. 79-91, 1990.
161. Harrison & Mockett, "Women in the factory: the state and factory legislation in nineteenth-century Britain", pp. 154-6.
162. Llewelyn Davies, *Maternity*, pp. 5-6.
163. Spring Rice, *Working-class wives*; C. Robertson's notes to the second edition on health services before the National Health Service.
164. Lewis, *Women in England*, pp. 48-9.
165. Llewelyn Davies, *Maternity*; and Spring Rice, *Working-class wives*.
166. Oakley, *The captured womb*, Ch. 2.
167. Spring Rice, *Working-class wives*, p. 18.
168. Oakley, *The captured womb*, Ch. 3.
169. See C. Webster, "Healthy or hungry thirties?", *History Workshop Journal* **13**, pp. 110-29, 1982; and M. Mitchell, "The effects of unemployment on the social condition of women and children in the 1930s", *History Workshop Journal* **19**, pp. 105-27, 1985.
170. Mitchell, "The effects of unemployment", pp. 114-15.
171. Webster, "Healthy or hungry thirties", pp. 118-21.
172. Mitchell, "The effects of unemployment", p. 115. The scheme was based on food provision through clinics.
173. Oakley, *The captured womb* Chs 3 & 4.
174. See, for example, C. Davies, "The health visitor as mother's friend: a woman's place in public health, 1900-14", *Social History of Medicine* **1** (1), pp. 39-59, 1988; R. Dingwall, A. M. Rafferty, C. Webster, *An introduction to the social history of nursing* (London: Routledge, 1988), Ch. 9.
175. Dale and Foster, *Feminists and state welfare*, Part I.
176. J L'Esperance, "Doctors and women in nineteenth century society".
177. Harrison, "Women's health and the women's movement", p. 40.

Suggestions for further reading

For an overview of gender differences in the Victorian period using mortality as a measure of health status, see S. R. Johanssen's chapter in Martha Vicinus (ed.), *A widening sphere* (Bloomington, Indiana: Indiana University Press, 1973). A number of more general works on women in this period cover some aspects of women's health and use the class dimension as a significant factor, in varying degrees of detail. The following are useful: Patricia Branca, *Silent sisterhood: middle class women in Victorian England* (London: Croom Helm, 1975); Jane Lewis, *Women in England 1870-1950* (Brighton: Wheatsheaf, 1984) and her edited collection *Labour and love: women's experience of home and family 1880-1940* (Oxford: Basil Blackwell, 1986); and Carol Dyhouse, *Feminism and the family 1880-1939* (Oxford: Basil Blackwell, 1989). There is more detail of life cycle aspects, both in the overview and the original documents in Pat Jalland & John Hooper (eds) *Women from birth to death: the female life cycle in Britain 1830-1914* (Brighton: Harvester Wheatsheaf, 1986). E Shorter's book, *A history of women's bodies* (London: Allen Lane, 1983) is international in scope, but includes some interesting material on Britain, including a considerable amount of detail about childbirth. The best account of working class women's health in the 1920s and 1930s is the classic study in Margery Spring Rice, *Working-class wives: their health and conditions* (London: Virago, 1981; First published 1939: Harmondsworth: Pelican); and an equally poignant presentation of women's own accounts of their lives and health around maternity slightly earlier in the century is found in Margaret Llewelyn Davies, *Maternity: letters from working women*, collected by The Women's Co-operative Guild (London: reprinted by Virago, 1978, first published 1915). A. Oakley, *The captured womb: a history of the medical care of pregnant women* (Oxford: Basil Blackwell, 1984) gives an overview of developing knowledge and practice in obstetrics as well as discussing issues of maternal and infant mortality, although for the latter, A. Davin, "Imperialism and motherhood", *History Workshop Journal* **5**, pp. 9–65, 1978, remains one of the most comprehensive. For an insight into issues of family limitation, see D. Gittins, *The fair sex: family size and structure 1900–1939* (London: Hutchinson, 1982). The most comprehensive overview of women and mental illness in this period is Elaine Showalter, *The female malady: women, madness and English culture 1830–1980* (London: Virago, 1986), although readers might want to refer to J. Busfield, "Men, women and madness in nineteenth-century Britain", *Sociology* **28** (1), pp. 259–77, 1994. Numerous areas of the history of women's health remain under- and unresearched, but there are works which address specific topics such as family planning, abortion, diagnostic categories and sufferers, including the author's own work on industrial ill health. For these the reader should refer to the end notes.

Chapter Eight

꽃

Women and sexuality

Sheila Jeffreys

Traditional male historians have tended to see the period of the late-nineteenth and early-twentieth centuries as one of progress in the history of sexuality.[1] They have represented science and liberal individualism as fighting back the forces of Victorianism, fundamentalist religion, and anti-sex prejudice, acting as the midwives to sex reform movements and sexual freedom. Feminist historians have seen this as a period of much greater complexity, in which a major struggle took place. Men's sexual prerogatives were under challenge from feminist campaigners who were concerned to end prostitution, sexual abuse of children and marital rape, and transform male sexual behaviour so that it constituted no threat to women. The scientists of sex, the sexologists, sought to revalidate and justify, in the name of science, traditional male-dominant, female-submissive sexuality. This chapter will look at the ideological struggle that was taking place between feminists and sexologists over the construction of male and female sexuality in this period. It will not cover women's experience in relation to such areas of their lives as anti-reproductive technologies, birth control and abortion.[2]

Sexology has been represented by many historians as the fount of sexual enlightenment, responsible for the creation of the modern way of looking at sexuality.[3] One historian described Henry Havelock Ellis's work as "one of the springs from which the broad stream of sexual liberalism has flowed with apparent effortless ease".[4] This was a period in which sexology took over from religion as the main regulator of correct sexual behaviour. But the effect of creating this "modern" model of sexuality has not necessarily been positive for women, and the work of the sexologists was often directed explicitly at overthrowing the new understandings of sexuality that feminists had been creating.

193

Feminist historians have argued that this was a period in which heterosexuality as a political institution had to be propagandized and enforced by that new regulatory mechanism of male supremacy, sexology.[5] Historians of women's passionate friendships and lesbianism have argued that this period ushered in a stigmatizing of women's love for other women which began a century in which there was to be an extreme fear and hatred of same-sex love.[6] The union of women with men in marriage, in which men gained ownership of women's bodies and all the resources of their free labour, could no longer be guaranteed in an era when women were acquiring more possibilities of independence. As a result, this period has been seen as one in which compulsory heterosexuality was enforced with particular vigour. But other feminist historians have disagreed with this analysis, seeing sexology as a positive influence in lesbian history and even seeing the sexological construction of sexuality in general as being in the interests of women. This chapter will seek to explain why such different perspectives have arisen.

The feminist campaigns

Feminist theorists, such as Margaret Jackson and myself, have generally seen the sexological construction of sexuality as a "sexual counter-revolution" developed to shore up men's power and privilege in response to feminist campaigns to transform male sexuality and end men's sexual abuse of women and children.[7] These campaigns were central to the women's movement. They were not given the attention they deserved until recently because historians were so steeped in the modern sensibility, the ideas of the "sexual revolution", that the views of women who were so critical of the construction of male sexuality could only be seen as being embarassingly retrogressive. It is from the understanding developed in contemporary feminist campaigns against male violence, and of the necessity to reconstruct male sexuality, that a reappraisal of these earlier feminist campaigns has come.

In the 1870s in Britain, a movement developed named by its proponents "social purity". Traditionally, this has been represented by historians as an anti-sex movement of prudes and puritans motivated by a moral panic about sex.[8] In fact, feminist concerns and ideas animated social purity at its inception. The primary aims were the elimination of prostitution and of the sexual abuse of girls. One of the currents which flowed into social purity was Christian revivalism, but the other was feminist concern about the Contagious Diseases Acts of the 1860s. The Ladies National Association (LNA), under the leadership of Josephine Butler, campaigned against these Acts, which allowed the police to force women supected of working as prostitutes in garrison ports and towns to be detained and tested for venereal disease. Feminist campaigners protested that the Acts contravened women's civil liberties and gave government approval to the notion that men had the right to use women in prostitution. The Social Purity Alliance was set up in 1873 by men involved in the campaign to unite those of their sex who wished to transform their conduct and that of other men. The object was the promotion of social control so that men's use of women in prostitution would cease.[9]

Feminists involved in Social Purity inveighed against the terrible injustice of the double standard of morality which justified men's sexual exploitation of women, while women were supposed to be "pure" and were punished if they "fell". Josephine Butler, in a speech to Cambridge undergraduates in 1879, stated that the result of the double standard was "that a large section of female society has to be told off – set aside, so to speak, to minister to the irregularities of the excusable man".[10] Her aim was the creation of a single standard by getting men to control themselves. Social Purity was a broad and complex movement. Some Social Purity Organizations, such as the Moral Reform Union, were explicitly feminist in intent. They, like the LNA, were determined to protect women in prostitution from unjust persecution. They saw men, not women, as being responsible for prostitution, although man-made laws had traditionally singled out women for punishment. Other Social Purity organizations, such as the National Vigilance Association, although also concerned to end prostitution, were not so scrupulous in avoiding any further disadvantaging of prostituted women, and suffered criticism by the feminist campaigners.[11]

The most influential female figure in Social Purity in this period, Jane Ellice Hopkins, shows an interesting fusion of feminist impulses within an old fashioned purity agenda. She was largely responsible for the foundation of the White Cross League which, resembling an Alcoholics Anonymous organization, aimed at supporting men in sexual self-control. Like the feminist campaigners, she indicted men for the abuse of women in prostitution:

> it is men who endow the degradation of women; it is men who, making the demand, create the supply. Stop the money of men and the whole thing would be starved out in three months' time.[12]

But her attitude to the relationship between men and women owed more to chivalry than to feminist principles, as she revealed in comments such as "the man is the head of the woman, and is therefore the servant of the woman".[13]

The feminist analysis of prostitution that developed through the campaigns against the Acts and through Social Purity differed very markedly from a traditional Christian one. The feminists saw prostitution as the sacrifice of women for men. They fought the assumption that prostitution was necessary because of men's biological urges, and stated that the male sexual urge was a social and not a biological phenomenon. They insisted that men were responsible for prostitution and that the way to end such abuse of women was to curb the demand for prostitutes by enjoining chastity upon men, rather than by punishing those who provided the supply. They employed similar arguments in their fight against other aspects of male sexual behaviour which they regarded as damaging to women, such as sexual abuse of children, incest, rape and street harassment.

An article entitled "How ladies are annoyed in London streets" in the *Pall Mall Gazette* in 1887 shows how women involved in Social Purity connected the issue of street harassment with the double moral standard. The article attacked the unjust laws that penalized women for street solicitation when there was no such concern for the issue of men's harassment of women. The details of the "commonest form of annoyance" are graphic:

> a man would stare, walk aggressively close, humming some tune, sometimes for a considerable distance, never attempting to speak, then suddenly wheel round with a suddenness almost to bring our faces together, and I would be obliged to jerk back; then, seeing it hopeless to expect encouragement he would walk quietly away. I never spoke, but always felt it hard to be subjected to such insolence.[14]

Laura Ormiston Chant, a prominent Social Purity campaigner active in the Gospel Purity Association and later editor of *The Vigilance Record*, journal of the National Vigilance Association, contributed to the article. She spoke of being harassed, even though she was middle aged, by a man on a train who changed carriages to follow her when she tried to avoid him. The article describes the harassment that could happen on horse-drawn buses too:

> The male pest secures a seat by the door, and, having persistently stared at you during the whole of your drive, officiously grasps your arm, under the pretence of assisting you to alight, and takes the opportunity of stepping out after you.[15]

On this occasion the harassed woman had to get a hansom cab to escape the attentions of the "pest". The writer asks whether these "hardships" are "any less severe than the molestation of which men complain so bitterly", though only women were prosecuted and fined.[16]

Bland describes Social Purity women such as Chant as "feminist vigilantes" engaged in "purifying" the public world in misguided activities for example, seeking to suppress the open use of music halls, such as the 'Empire' in London, for solicitation.[17] The repressive approach that Chant and some other Social Purity feminists took was condemned by other anti-prostitution campaigners such as Josephine Butler for being punitive towards women. But the issue of "male pests" was central to the new opportunities being demanded by women in this period. It came to the fore at this time because middle-class women were demanding their right to enter public spaces which had previously been closed to them. Judith Walkowitz describes how "shopping women", for whom the new department stores were vying in the late nineteenth century, were determined to challenge the harassment they experienced in the West End.[18] The streets were just one public space that women were demanding access to: they were also gaining access to local politics, to social work and to public entertainment, concerts, picture exhibitions and the British Museum Reading Room.

There was a keen understanding among the women in Social Purity and the feminist campaigners that women in marriage and in prostitution shared common concerns. Men's right to use women sexually in marriage irrespective of consent was seen as being similar to prostitution. As an American feminist, Mrs Lucinda B. Chandler, put it, at an international conference in 1888: "Women as well as men must eliminate from marriage the features of prostitution, for when prostitution ceases inside of marriage it will disappear outside".[19] One prominent member of the LNA, Elizabeth Wolstenholme Elmy, expressed the feminist perspective of the time well in writing of prostitution as the "profanation of the dignity and individuality of women".[20]

From women's campaigns against the state regulation of prostitution came campaigns against child sexual abuse as a result of revelations about men's sexual use of young girls. Feminist energies fuelled the movement to raise the age of consent to 16 for sexual intercourse (1885); and for indecent assault (1922). Alongside the legislative campaign, which was supported by a wide range of women's organizations, feminists monitored the courts to protest about the low sentences given to sexual abusers, and demanded women magistrates, women police and women doctors to deal with women and children who had been abused.[21]

Emerging from these activist campaigns there came a feminist analysis of male sexual behaviour and sexual intercourse (particularly from those who had rejected Christianity altogether), which aimed to protect women from men's sexual abuse. Writers such as Elizabeth Wolstenholme Elmy and Francis Swiney, among others, asserted that men's sexual behaviour was not biologically based. Men could control themselves and did not need to use women in prostitution, abuse their wives in unwanted sexual intercourse, or assault women and children. The criticism of marital rape was particularly significant as it challenged the very heart of male sexual privilege. Elmy challenged men's right to sexual intercourse with unwilling wives in language which well describes the injury and women's right to refuse:

> the conviction is every day growing that under no plea or promise can it be permissible to submit the individuality, either mental or physical, of the wife, to the will and coercion of the husband; the functions of wifehood and motherhood must remain solely and entirely within the wife's own option.[22]

It was a hundred years before a new burst of feminist activism in the late-twentieth century was effective in making marital rape a crime in some countries in the Western world, and the process of criminalizing it is by no means complete. Elmy and Swiney not only asserted that any non-mutual "embraces" were morally repugnant, they even questioned the necessity of sexual intercourse except for the purpose of creating children. This has been the most indigestible element of their philosophy for many contemporary feminist historians to approach. They stressed the dangers to women associated with that particular sexual practice, not only unwanted pregnancy or the technologizing of the female body to avoid it, but the transmission of venereal disease, as well as the potential for demonstrating and consolidating male dominance.[23] The sexologists responded throughout the twentieth century with the enforcement of compulsory sexual intercourse to such an extent that it has become difficult today even for many feminist theorists to contemplate the evacuation of the practice.

During the 1920s it was clear that the feminist analysis of prostitution was being challenged by the very different ideas of the new science of sexology. In 1926, one feminist sought to refute the sort of individualizing psychological explanations of male sexual violence that began in the 1920s to replace a feminist analysis, which focused on men's power over women. She expressed the connection between prostitution and other forms of the abuse of women succinctly when commenting on mass rapes carried out in the brothels of Strasbourg by youths at a youth conference:

> There is no need to imagine that people who criminally assault young persons and children are mentally abnormal, as what is right to buy is also right to have without buying, whether it is human beings or any other merchandise.[24]

Today's feminist campaigners against male violence might express a similar idea in slightly different language, by pointing out, for example, that the objectification of women lies behind both the stealing of women in rape and the buying of women in prostitution. Rape and prostitution were seen by the feminist campaigners against male violence as being inextricably linked. This contradicts sharply the traditional masculine sexual ideology which has taught that prostitution prevents rape by providing men with an outlet for their urges.

But the effect of sexological influence was such that feminists came to be labelled prudes and puritans for their views on men's sexual abuse of women and children. The feminist campaigns continued but were no longer of such influence and were constantly in competition with the revamped traditional masculine viewpoint of sexology. The main organization that expressed the feminist viewpoint, from its foundation in 1913 right through to the 1950s, was the Association for Moral and Social Hygiene (AMSH). It was a successor to the LNA. Right through to its demise after the passing of the Street Offences Act 1959, the organization strove to influence public opinion and legislation on prostitution. Its aim was to eliminate the punishment of women for what was seen as men's abuse. Throughout the 1920s and 1930s the AMSH devised Bills, sought sponsors and lobbied against all the injustices members saw in the legislation that punished prostitutes.

The AMSH also continued the work of the LNA against state regulation of prostitution. It networked internationally against state regulation, not just in the form of registration and examination of prostitutes for venereal disease but against the phenomenon of licensed brothels. The AMSH and its sister organizations worked through the League of Nations and the United Nations (UN) against regulation and against the international traffic in women and children. One effect of the "sexual revolutions" of the twentieth century has been to make it much more difficult to challenge the rights of men to buy women for sex. It is interesting that it was only in the 1980s that a new feminist organization, "The International Coalition Against the Trafficking in Women" drew up a Convention to submit to the UN stating that sexual exploitation, which included prostitution, was a violation of women's human rights.[25] The 1980s Coalition makes extensive reference, in support of the new Convention, to that of 1949, which was the result of the earlier feminist campaigns. In this way, feminists in the late-twentieth century are able to link up with the legacy of their predecessors which had been for so long forgotten. In the late-nineteenth century, when sexual liberalism was only just being invented, it was easier for women to be critical.

The impact of sexology

Sexology as it developed in the late-nineteenth century was to create a model of what sex was, based on scientific "truth", which was immensely hostile to the feminist analysis and to the success of the feminist concern to end sexual violence. The sexologists encoded traditional male sexual privilege, with just one variation. Whereas earlier in the nineteenth century there had not been so much concern, at least in the medical world, with women's pleasure, the new prescription was that women should respond sexually to men's sexual initiatives and their preferred practices.

The sexologists considered that men's sexual urges were ordained biologically and could not be controlled. In this way they countered that most important understanding of the feminist campaigns, that men were not subject to irresistible urges and did not need to use women in prostitution or in sexual abuse. The model of heterosexual sex which the sexologists promoted was one of missionary-position sexual intercourse, which clearly demonstrated male dominance, and to which women were expected to respond passively by finding their own subordination exciting.[26] The British sexologist Henry Havelock Ellis was particularly explicit about the forms that male and female sexual pleasure were to take. His scientific method was to gather his knowledge from studying the courtship patterns of non-human animals, and from anthropologists, letters from his friends, his own experience and studying his wife. His model of courtship, based on his interpretation of animal behaviour, was one of capture and rape:

the primary part of the female in courtship is the playful, yet serious, assumption of the role of a hunted animal who lures on the pursuer, not with the object of escaping, but with the object of being finally caught . . . [the male] will display his energy and skill to capture the female or to arouse in her an emotional condition which leads her to surrender herself to him, this process at the same time heightening his own excitement.[27]

Once she had surrendered, the scenario was one of violence and pain inflicted by the man and enjoyed by the woman:

While in men it is possible to trace a tendency to inflict pain, or the simulacrum of pain, on the women they love, it is still easier to trace in women a delight in experiencing physical pain when inflicted by a lover, and an eagerness to accept submission to his will. Such a tendency is certainly normal.[28]

This was a convenient enshrining in scientific truth of precisely the aspects of male sexual behaviour that feminists had been challenging. When women did write to him questioning this prescription he protested that he was telling the truth.[29]

It is not surprising, considering his ideas about sexuality, that Ellis was not sympathetic to feminist concerns about sexual violence. He reasserted the traditional notion that male sexuality was a biological force, not subject to social influences, and normalized rape and sexual assault by prescribing women's passivity and "modesty" and men's aggressive pursuit and initiative. He cheerfully dismissed the idea that children were sexually abused, and suggested that women only shouted rape if they had stayed out too late and got home after their parents had gone to bed. Rape would also be falsely alleged by women, he considered, when they felt ashamed about the sexual activity they had engaged in:

There can be little doubt that the plea of force is very frequently seized upon by women as the easiest available weapon of defence when her connection has been revealed. She has been so permeated by the current notion that no "respectable" woman can possibly have any sexual impulses of her own to gratify that, in order to screen what she feels to be regarded as an utterly shameful and wicked, as well as foolish, act, she declares it never took place by her own will at all.[30]

The male supremacist sexual ideology of men's uncontrollable urges which would always be enjoyed by the assaulted female in the end was legitimated and proof against the developing feminist assault. Ellis sought to establish that women enjoyed being battered too. But there were limits to the pain and insult women wanted to receive, he thought, and men should respect those limits:

"I like being knocked about and made to do things I don't want to do," a woman said, but she admitted, on being questioned, that she would not like to have *much* pain inflicted, and that she might not care to be made to do important things she did not want to do.[31]

Jackson has analysed the ways in which Ellis and other sexologists created a male sexual counter-revolution: "He thus provided a pseudo-scientific foundation for the construction of a form of heterosexuality and sexual pleasure through which women could be controlled and male power maintained."[32] His "art of love", which became the stuff of sex manuals throughout the twentieth century, was developed, she maintains, out of the importance of curing "frigidity", so that marriage could be maintained in the face of a rising divorce rate. The husband was given the task of arousing his wife to a point where she would not be averse to sexual intercourse because, as Ellis put it, the "real possession of a woman's soul and body" was a task "that requires the whole of a man's best skill and insight".[33] Ellis's concern for women's "erotic rights" is one of the main reasons why he has been hailed as progressive by pro-feminist scholars. When such concern is considered within the context of contemporary understanding of how women might be controlled through the orchestration of their sexual pleasure, then it can look decidedly less altruistic and enlightened.

Ellis asserted that the practices he named "erotic symbolism", such as fetishism and sadomasochism, were merely extensions of normal sexual behaviour. Jackson sees the inscription of this idea in sexual liberalism as one of his most important legacies. She comments that his argument that "the difference between normal and abnormal sexuality is merely one of degree, has become one of the basic assumptions of sexology right up to the present day".[34] His own sexual interests might have motivated his normalization of such perversions. His interests were wider than sexual intercourse; indeed, it is possible that he did not engage successfully in that practice. Like other famous twentieth-century sexologists, he used sexology to support a sexual liberalism about "erotic symbolism". His own "symbolism" entailed pleasure from listening to or watching women urinating. He even wrote poetry about his interest. His strength of feeling about the actual superiority of "erotic symbolism" is clear in his conclusion to his book on *Erotic symbolism*. Thus, after chapters devoted to foot fetishism, coprolagnia, urolagnia and bestiality, he notes:

Regarded as a whole, and notwithstanding the frequency with which they witness to congenital morbidity, the phenomena of erotic symbolism can scarcely fail to be profoundly impressive to the patient and the impartial student of the human soul. . . They constitute the supreme triumph of human idealism.[35]

The phenomena were also carried out almost entirely by men and appear, from his own description, to have entailed considerable inconvenience to, if not the abuse of, women.

But Ellis's unconventional tastes did not undermine his determination to promote male-dominant, female-subordinate sexual intercourse as the normal practice. He became known as the "prophet of love" and has had an immense influence on the writing of sex advice literature in the twentieth century. Even in Alex Comfort's (1973) *The joy of sex*, Ellis is referenced, appropriately for a theorist so determined to legitimate sadomasochism even in ordinary everday sexual intercourse, in the section on gagging and bondage.[36] In the late twentieth century his work seems to be having a revived popularity, as we shall see, particularly among a new generation of proponents of sadomasochism.

Ellis's opposition to feminism was not limited to his denial of women's concerns about sexual assault; he was also involved, as were other European sexologists, in opposing feminist attempts to challenge the notion of separate spheres. Ellis stated in the 1930s that the idea that women should do the same jobs or sports as men was "the source of all that was unbalanced, sometimes both a little pathetic and a little absurd, in the old women's movement".[37] It is surprising, then, that he has been seen by many as pro-feminist and "woman positive". The popular British sexologist Eustace Chesser put forward similar arguments supporting a separate sphere for women and bewailing the threats to motherhood caused by women's demand for equality after the Second World War. He protested:

> For the sexes are not alike. They never have been, and – let us hope – never will be alike. Recognising that men and women are equal is by no means the same as saying that they must be treated exactly alike in everything . . . Extreme feminism definitely has an element of childishness. The male has certain toys: the woman must have them.[38]

The role of sexologists in the twentieth century has centred overwhelmingly on creating traditional concepts of wifehood and motherhood, but with sexual enthusiasm thrown in as an extra requirement.

The orchestration of women's sexual pleasure has been a matter of urgent and central importance to sexologists throughout the twentieth century. The reasons behind the male doctors' enthusiasm do not seem to have been based upon altruism. Reading sexological literature from the 1920s to the 1950s makes it clear that there was a political purpose behind this concern. It was in the 1920s that anxiety about women's "frigidity" or lack of enthusiasm for sexual intercourse, peaked. I have suggested that this decade saw the invention of the frigid woman, a figure who has been the focus of the industry of sex therapy ever since. The sexologists, who tended to be more frank about their motives in the earlier part of the century, attacked frigidity as being responsible for the four terrible evils that they were concerned to conquer: feminism, manhating, spinsterhood and lesbianism. Walter Galli-chan, a popularizer of sexological ideas, wrote in his 1929 book *The poison of prudery* about the dangers of frigidity:

> The erotically impotent women have an enormous influence upon the young, the conventions and regulations of society, and even upon sex legislation. These degenerate women are a menace to civilisation. They provoke sex misunderstanding and antagonism; they wreck conjugal happiness, and pose as superior moral beings when they are really victims of disease.[39]

To say that women who were less than enthusiastic about sexual intercourse were a "menace to civilisation" suggests that Gallichan's alarm was about more than a concern for what women were missing; it was a concern about the maintenance of male power.

Women's sexual response would solve the problem of the "war" women were waging against men, because it would take the form of eroticizing their own subordination. Their resistance would be undermined. The Freudian psychoanalyst Willhelm Stekel demonstrated the political purpose well in his two volumes entitled *Frigidity in woman in relation to her love life*. He explained: "To be roused by a man means acknowledging oneself as conquered".[40] The sexologists approached their task with all the seriousness of a great crusade. The enemy was the "frigide", because she was not sufficiently conquered.

The sexological determination to achieve women's willing subjection to male authority through sexual pleasure has been an important theme of sex advice literature throughout the twentieth century. The writers were seldom as explicit as in the period after the supposed "sexual revolution" of the 1960s, but the message remained the same. In the late 1940s, when sexologists faced a problem similar to that of their colleagues after the First World War, namely women's increased opportunities for independence, the importance of women eroticizing their own subordination was again rein-forced. Eustace Chesser explained that a wife must really surrender in the sex act, not just submit. He wrote that a girl may:

> find it impossible to surrender herself completely in the sex act. And complete surrender is the only way in which she can bring the highest pleasure to both herself and her husband. Submission is not the same thing as surrender. Many a wife submits, but retains, deep within herself, an area which is not conquered, and which, indeed, is in fierce oppos-ition to submission.[41]

Sexual intercourse was meant to effect a total abandonment of any inde-pendence; it would root out the least resistance to her husband's authority.

"Modern" heterosexuality was born, taught and enforced through the science of sex. Sex was to be the new cement of marriage, which was seen as facing serious threats from women's new possibilities of independence. Marriage was to be based upon sexual attraction, and for this, women's active sexual enthusiasm was necessary. This was clearly a new picture. As far as we can tell from the anxious sexologists and from feminist writings, women had not previously entered marriage with the understanding that they would have to enjoy sexual intercourse. Heterosexuality as a "sexual orientation" was born in this period, at the same time as homosexuality was categorized as its opposite.

The spinster

Spinsterhood was seen as a worrying problem by early-twentieth-century sexologists. For men who believed that women's positive enthusiasm for their subordination could only be aroused through sexual intercourse, spinsters were a dangerous constituency. They escaped regulation through sex. Moreover, they were the backbone of the women's movement, particularly of its most radical elements. In the period immediately before the First World War, feminist spinsters spoke of their choice as being positively necessary to the achievement of women's freedom. Lucy Re-Bartlett, who was not herself a spinster, wrote positively in 1912 about celibate militant suffragettes who had chosen to stand "away from man until he understands" that:

> a period of this kind must needs be passed through before the old relations between men and women be set aside and the new and nobler ones established. Woman cannot truly struggle for the new order, until she hates the old.[42]

She was speaking of such "warrior maids" as Christabel Pankhurst, who stated that spinsterhood was a deliberate political choice made in response to the conditions of sex slavery: "There can be no mating between the spiritually developed women of this new day and men who in thought and conduct with regard to sex matters are their inferiors."[43]

A wonderful example of the spinster feminist theory of the period before the First World War on marriage and heterosexuality is the playwright Cicely Hamilton's *Marriage as a trade*.[44] Hamilton considered that spinsters were crucial to the improvement of the dire conditions in which women did the work of marriage. Only if marriage was voluntary and not forced, if there was a real alternative, which happy spinsters could exemplify, would men have to pay for the work they got for nothing; furthermore, men would have to exercise self-control instead of seeing "one half of the race as sent into the world to excite desire in the other half".[45]

Spinsterhood was now capable of being a form of resistance for women because social and economic changes had made it more likely that women could survive without marriage. Consequently, spinsters were viewed in much popular sexological literature as being destructive, warped and damaging to the social fabric. Walter Gallichan specifically attacked the spinster as an exemplar of dangerous feminism in a 1909 book, *Modern woman and how to manage her*:

> Among the great army of sex, the regiment of aggressively man-hating women is of full strength, and signs of the times show that it is being steadily recruited. On its banner is emblazoned, "Woe to Man"; and its call to arms is shrill and loud. These are the women who are "independent of men", a motley host, pathetic in their defiance of the first principle of Nature, but of no serious account in the biological or social sense.[46]

The lesbian

At the same time as the spinster was coming to be seen as a threat to male supremacy, sexologists were constructing the idea of the female invert as part of the categorization of homosexuality that took place in the late-nineteenth-century.[47] Lesbian historians have disagreed profoundly about the impact of sexology on the development of lesbian identity. Gay male historians have not found themselves embroiled in such controversy over the significance of sexology; the work of sexologists has generally been seen as being positive in forming a basis for the construction of identity in gay men.[48] This is, I suggest, because the historical situation of women was so different. The significance of the sexological construction of the lesbian must be seen in its historical context of the backlash against feminism, alarm at spinsters and celibacy, and of the importance of passionate friendships to women in this period.

Lesbian and feminist historians such as Faderman and Smith-Rosenberg have shown that before the late-nineteenth century, middle-class British and American women, married and single, would routinely engage in passionate, romantic, often very long-term friendships with each other.[49] These could include constant expressions of fulsome love, and sleeping in each other's arms and on the same pillow, even for a lifetime, without raising suspicion in their friends or those around them. This changed when the sexologists began, in the 1890s, to include these friendships within the category of the female invert. By the 1920s, spinster headmistresses and the writers of school stories were warning about the dangers of passions which had earlier been regarded as entirely healthy. Women's potential for loving one another, with passion and physical contact, seems to have been damaged profoundly by the stigmatizing of women's same-sex love. From the 1920s onwards women had to decide whether or not to enter the category "invert" when they loved each other. There was pressure for women to identify themselves as either heterosexual or homosexual.

Auchmuty's fascinating work on schoolgirl stories shows how the expression of love between women became circumscribed, and heterosexuality came to be enforced for the female characters. Before the very public outlawing of Radclyffe Hall's novel *The well of loneliness* in 1928 there was an innocence about passionate friendships in these stories. This book portrayed, in the hero, Stephen, a sexological stereotype of the lesbian. The novel was pilloried in the media and courts in such a way that few of the reading public could remain in ignorance about the sexological construction of love between women. Elsie Oxenham demonstrates the earlier innocence in her Abbey books: in the 1928 *The Abbey girls win through*, for instance, two women characters are introduced in a way which would be quite unacceptable later on:

> They were a recognised couple. Con, who sold gloves in a big West-End establishment, was the wife and home-maker; Norah, the typist, was the husband, who planned little pleasure trips and kept the accounts and took Con to the pictures.[50]

Auchmuty explains that this kind of writing did not reveal "unconscious perversion . . . but a very conscious love for women which in 1923 was fine and after 1928 became abnormal and unhealthy, representing a level of intimacy which was too threatening to be allowed to continue".[51]

The sexologists codified as "scientific" wisdom current myths about lesbian sexual practice, a stereotype of the lesbian and the "pseudohomosexual" woman. The sexological model of inversion was based upon congenitality. Ellis argued in 1897, in his *Sexual inversion*, that "any theory of the etiology of homosexuality which leaves out of account the hereditary factor in inversion cannot be admitted".[52] The congenital idea inspired male homosexual rights campaigners in the 1890s in Britain and Germany. It offered the possibility of asking for public sympathy and the repeal of hostile legislation, on the grounds that homosexuals were just a part of nature's creation rather than sinners, and so deserved sympathy. Radclyffe Hall, when she adopted sexological arguments in the 1920s, employed this strategy in *The well of loneliness* and had Ellis write a preface to the book so that her argument could be seen to be backed by science.

The original or congenital invert was seen as being masculine to some extent or another. This might manifest itself in appearance, or just in temperament. This is clear in a classic description from Ellis of the female invert:

> When they still retain female garments, these usually show some traits of masculine simplicity, and there is nearly always a disdain for the petty feminine artifices of the toilet. Even when this is not obvious, there are all

sorts of instinctive gestures and habits which may suggest to female acquaintances the remark that such a person "ought to have been a man".[53]

The masculine invert was seen as seeking a feminine counterpart to provide a homologue to the correct heterosexual relationship. Edward Carpenter, the British homosexual rights campaigner who made great use of sexological material to support his demands for acceptance, explained that the masculine invert would "generally" love the "rather soft and feminine specimens of her own sex".[54] This roleplaying idea was supported through the sexological division of lesbians into two types: the original or genuine invert, and the pseudohomosexual or pervert.

The original invert was deemed to be congenitally destined for homosexuality – this was the masculine type, while the pseudohomosexual, found commonly only among female homosexuals, was likely to resemble a feminine heterosexual woman. The pseudohomosexual was perverted by choice or accident rather than by biology, and was seen as being capable of reversion to heterosexuality. Feminism was held to be responsible for a wave of pseudohomosexuality. As Ellis explained it:

> These unquestionable influences of modern movements cannot directly cause sexual inversion, but they develop the germs of it, and they probably cause a spurious imitation. This spurious imitation is due to the fact that the congenital anomaly occurs with special frequency in women of high intelligence who, voluntarily or involuntarily, influence others.[55]

This idea of there being real and pseudo lesbians lingers into the roleplaying literature of the 1950s and 1960s, when the masculine lesbian was still seen as being the most original invert, and the femme as somehow inauthentic.[56] In the 1980s, roleplaying was revalidated by some lesbian theorists, novelists and sex therapists. In this new roleplaying literature, writers such as Nestle continue the tradition of seeing the masculine lesbian as somehow more "real", while giving the femme the role of supporting and celebrating the realness of the butch.[57]

The sexologists' anxieties about feminism caused them to classify those qualities which the independent "new women" of the 1890s sought to develop as being characteristic of inversion and therefore unnatural and perverse. The accusation of lesbianism was hurled then, as it still is today, at women who placed too great an emphasis on pursuing their freedom. After the First World War the anxiety of the sexological establishment and its popularisers about independent women reached crisis level because of the gains that such women had made through war work. Charlotte Haldane wrote in 1927 of the dangers of:

> the "warworking" type of "woman" – aping the cropped hair, the great booted feet, the grim jaw, the uniform, and if possible the medals, of the

military man. If this type had been transitory its usefulness might be accorded, but it is not doubtful, as I propose to show, that in a long run we shall have to regret its social and political influence, much as we may applaud its wartime works.[58]

Postwar, the women war heroes were expected to return to their rightful place in subordination. Radclyffe Hall's short story "Miss Ogilvie finds herself" demonstrates the confusion that independent women could experience when they found there was no social role for them.[59] In the story, a former ambulance driver returns to Britain to discover she is expected to accommodate herself once more to the role of the squire's eldest spinster daughter. This proves impossible to bear, but rather than transform her discontents into feminism she has a dream that reveals to her that she is a throwback to a Neanderthal man, and dies.

Oram has shown how the fear of spinsters and lesbians affected women teachers in Britain between the wars. A 1935 report in a newspaper of an educational conference expressed the threat in extreme terms: "The women who have the responsibility of teaching these girls are many of them themselves embittered, sexless or homosexual hoydens who try to mould the girls into their own pattern".[60]

Spinster teachers were a threat to men's dominance in the profession as well as to their economic interests through the demand for equal opportunities and equal pay. Male teachers, on the defensive, answered back using sexological ideas, attacking spinsterhood and the desire of feminists to be men.

The controversy about the impact of sexology on lesbians has focused upon the 1920s, and particularly on Radclyffe Hall's novel *The well of loneliness*. In the 1920s some women, like Radclyffe Hall, chose to adopt sexological language and concepts, partly because this was seen as a way of justifying homosexuality, and because it offered a definite identity. But others who saw themselves as spinsters or feminists, and many who were involved in passionate friendships with women, rejected a sexological lesbian identity.[61] Smith-Rosenberg, the historian who first drew attention to the phenomenon of passionate friendships, sees this division in the 1920s between women who identified themselves with the sexological notion of the invert, and those spinsters who would not, as damaging to the feminist project. A gap in communication developed and the two groups were unable to understand each other – they were speaking different languages.[62]

The American lesbian historian Newton sees the adoption of sexology by women who loved women as being positive.[63] Her perspective represents a puzzling tendency that emerged in lesbian scholarship in the 1980s. This was a return to sexology. Whereas lesbian feminists involved in lesbian theoretical and political work in the 1970s saw the rejection of the medical model as fundamental, some lesbians in the 1980s moved back to it with enthusiasm, as if it told the truth about their experience.

Radclyffe Hall employed the sexological idea of the lesbian in *The well of loneliness* deliberately to gain sympathy. Homosexuals are represented as "flawed in the making", or congenital accidents. The division between genuine inverts and pseudohomosexuals is clear in the book. Stephen is a masculine homosexual and Mary Llewellyn a pseudo who had to be rescued by the hero from the fate of being a homosexual. Stephen nobly sacrifices her to a male lover by pretending not to love her anymore. The book has drawn very different responses from lesbians over the last half century. When it was likely to be the only lesbian novel women were able to find, it was regarded as being very significant. Some lesbian readers loved it and felt validated, but some hated it and saw only a very negative representation of lesbianism.

Newton identifies with the masculine lesbian in the novel and says that, like Radclyffe Hall, she sees lesbianism as "sexual difference". Newton chooses to adopt the sexological idea of the lesbian because she personally finds it validating. She was involved in 1984 in founding the New York Butch Support Group.[64] However, Newton sees the practice of passionate friendships as being limiting for women because, she assumes, such relationships were not sexual. For this reason, she finds the sexological idea of the lesbian useful because it provided a model for specifically sexual love between women.

The return to sexology in the 1980s may be justified academically with reference to Foucault's idea of reverse discourse. Michel Foucault explained that although sexological categories may have been constructed as a form of social regulation of sexual behaviour, they could be employed positively by homosexuals and other sexual minorities. They could form the base of a homosexual identity and therefore of a movement for homosexual reform. As Dollimore explains it, Radclyffe Hall's *The well of loneliness* "helped initiate a reverse discourse in Foucault's sense: lesbians were able to identify themselves, often for the first time, albeit in the very language of their oppression".[65]

But the revival of enthusiasm for the medical model after such sturdy attempts to dismantle it in the 1970s by both lesbians and gay men remains puzzling. The revival has taken place in conservative times, a time of backlash against feminism and other progressive politics. But this model must offer some positive advantage to the lesbians who are drawn to it at the end of the twentieth century. For some of those who developed a sense of "outsiderhood" as a result of their lesbianism, it may be that the biological model of sexual difference offered by sexology seems to make sense. For those spinsters in the 1920s or lesbian feminists in the 1990s who see their choices as expressing their resistance to oppression as women and as a tactic to help end it, the sexological idea does not seem so attractive.

The significance of sexology: the controversy

The significance of sexology and of the ideas of the 1890s feminist campaigners is highly contested in the history and theory of sexuality. Feminists who start from a primary political concern in the present with the role of sexuality in the oppression of women, and men's sexual violence against women in particular, are likely to interpret the feminist campaigners of the late-nineteenth and early-twentieth centuries in a positive light. They are likely to have recognized a similarity of concerns even though the language used, and some of the strategies undertaken, might not sit well with late-twentieth-century feminist understanding. Those theorists who start from the perspective of defending or producing pornography, of seeing themselves as being in a persecuted sexual "minority" in a sexological sense, or being interested in the practice of "deviant" sexualities, sado-masochism, paedophilia and transvestism, are likely to view the feminist campaigners in a negative light as people who sought to constrain sexual freedom. They tend to see sexology as being very positive. It is because the battle over the political significance of sexual practice in the present is so heated that the period in question here has assumed such importance.

Rubin is an American lesbian theorist of sexuality and a proponent of sadomasochism who embraces sexological understandings of sexuality. In her paper "Thinking sex" she presents a stark opposition between feminist campaigners around sexuality and the sexologists and sex reformers who employed sexological insights. She identifies the feminists as the "anti-sex" tradition and the sexologists and their followers as the "pro-sex" tradition. Rubin sees feminist anti-pornography campaigners as having recreated a "very conservative sexual morality":

> For over a century, battles have been waged over just how much shame, distress and punishment should be incurred by sexual activity. The conservative tradition has promoted opposition to pornography, prostitution, homosexuality, all erotic variation, sex education, sex research, abortion and contraception. The opposing, pro-sex tradition has included individuals such as Havelock Ellis, Magnus Hirschfeld, Alfred Kinsey and Victoria Woodhull, as well as the sex education movement, organizations of militant prostitutes and homosexuals, the reproductive rights movement, and organizations such as the Sexual Reform League of the 1960s.[66]

Rubin sees the period in the history of sexuality that has been examined in this chapter as a positive one. She approves of and identifies with the modern sensibility created at this time:

> The legislative restructuring that took place at the end of the nineteenth century and the early decades of the twentieth was a refracted response

to the emergence of the modern erotic system. During that period, new erotic communities were formed. It became possible to be a male homosexual or a lesbian in a way it had not been previously. Mass-produced erotica became available, and the possibilities for sexual commerce expanded. The first homosexual rights movements were formed, and the first analyses of sexual oppression were articulated.[67]

Rubin was able to celebrate a "modern erotic system" in 1982, when the paper was written, in a way which should, perhaps, be more problematic after the impact of postmodern scepticism on the academy.[68]

Rubin was concerned to protect from feminist criticism the tradition of sexual liberalism derived from sexology and sex reform. Feminists in the late-twentieth century have attacked sexual liberalism for being a masculinist system of thought designed to protect male sexual privileges.[69] We have found it necessary to challenge the assumptions of sexual liberalism in order to confront pornography and sexual abuse. Rubin, on the other hand, asserts that feminists are simply too blinkered to look at many areas of sexuality. They should, she says, confine their passion for analysis only to certain limited areas of sexuality where gender is relevant. Sexuality, in her analysis, is a system of oppression separate from that of gender, in which the sexual minorities are the oppressed. Unlike most feminist theorists, she sees a feminist perspective as being quite inappropriate to phenomena such as "intergenerational" sex, sadomasochism and transsexualism. She states that as a matter of urgency "an autonomous theory and politics specific to sexuality must be developed".[70] This autonomous theory would protect these sexual minorities from an impolite feminist inspection.

In the decade since she wrote this piece, much work has gone into the construction of this autonomous theory of sexuality, free from feminist insights. This autonomous analysis has tended to come from lesbian and gay theorists, since the assertion of a feminism-free analysis of heterosexual sex would be harder to justify. It relies fairly heavily on sexological understanding of what sex is and how sexuality is organized. The politics of sexual minorities and now "queer" politics put practical political flesh on to sexological categories. A London Queer Power leaflet shows how these categories are being politicized:

> Queer means to fuck with gender. There are straight queers, bi-queers, tranny queers, lez queers, fag queers, SM queers, fisting queers in every street in this apathetic country of ours.[71]

The deviant sexualities, or erotic symbolists, have taken to the streets, with the praise of postmodern theorists, who one might have thought would have been more critical of science and of the "identities" that the sadomasochists and fetishists claim.

Conclusion

Those feminists, like myself, who are very critical of the sexological model, see the period 1870–1930 as one of backlash to feminist aspirations rather than one of progress. It saw a challenge to the traditional male supremacist understanding of sexuality through feminist campaigns and theorizing. Sexology enabled traditional views to be reinforced with the authority of science at a time when science was not regarded with the suspicion now directed at it by some contemporary feminist and poststructuralist thought. Sexology lent authority to the view that sexuality was determined biologically, that male sexuality was uncontrollable, that normal heterosexuality would take the form of aggressive, male dominant, and submissive, female-subordinate sexual intercourse, and that woman's place was in the home. These ideas undermined the feminist opposition to men's abuse of women in prostitution, in sexual abuse in childhood, and in rape within marriage.

By the 1930s, the way sex could be thought about had changed. The new medical authorities were regarded as speaking the absolute truth about sex, despite their regurgitation of traditional male myths of sexuality. Feminists who criticized male sexual behaviour were classified and derided as prudes and puritans, and as dangerous celibates, ignorant of science. Women had been reclassified in a way which ruled out the possibility of withdrawing from the male dominant sexual system. Spinsters and passionate friendships were under savage attack. Women were encouraged and propagandized into choosing one of only two categories: the wife who was really enthusiastic about sexual intercourse; or the lesbian who was sexually active in the form of butch/femme roleplaying. Both models constructed woman's identity around an ideal of eroticized masculine dominance and feminine subordination.

The contemporary controversy around the interpretation of this period in the history of sexuality is fierce because there is a division in feminist theorizing today between those who prioritize the ending of male violence and consider that male and female sexuality need to be radically reconstructed, and those who prioritize, as male historians traditionally have, "sexual freedom". The construction of "modern" sexuality took place in this period and is central to this debate. The fierceness of the disagreements would suggest the great importance of sexuality to feminist theory and practice. For students of women's history or politics, what have been termed the "feminist sexuality debates", as they apply to the period covered here, should be an exciting and challenging area to explore.

Notes

1. See, for example, E. Shorter, *The making of the modern family* (London: Collins, 1976).
2. For discussion of these issues, see Shani D'Cruze, "Women and the family", Ch. 3 and Barbara Harrison "Women and Health", Ch. 7 in this volume.
3. J. Weeks, *Sex, politics and society* (London: Longman, 1981); S. Rowbotham & J. Weeks, *Socialism and the new life* (London: Pluto, 1977).
4. J. Weeks "Havelock Ellis and the Politics of Sex Reform", in Rowbotham & Weeks, *Socialism and the new life*, p. 142.
5. See, for example, L. Faderman, *Surpassing the love of men. Romantic friendship and love between women from the Renaissance to the present* (New York: Morrow, 1981; and London: The Women's Press, 1985); and S. Jeffreys, *The spinster and her enemies. Feminism and sexuality 1880-1930* (London: Pandora, 1985).
6. See R. Auchmuty, "You're a dyke, Angela! Elsie J. Oxenham and the rise and fall of the schoolgirl story", in *Not a Passing Phase. Reclaiming Lesbians in History 1840-1985*, Lesbian History Group (eds) (London: The Women's Press, 1989); and C. Smith-Rosenberg, "The female world of love and ritual: relations between women in nineteenth-century America", in *A heritage of her own*, N. F. Cott and E. H. Pleck (eds) (New York: Touchstone Books Simon and Schuster, 1979).
7. See Jeffreys, *The spinster and her enemies*; and M. Jackson, *The "real" facts of life. Feminism and the politics of sexuality c1850-1940* (London: Taylor and Francis, 1994).
8. Weeks, *Sex, politics and society*; and E. Bristow, *Vice and vigilance* (Oxford: Oxford University Press, 1977).
9. J. Butler, *Social purity: an address* (London: Social Purity Alliance, 1879).
10. *Ibid.*, p. 8.
11. See L. Bland, "'Purifying' the public world: feminist vigilantes in late Victorian England", *Women's History Review* 1 (3), pp. 397-412, 1992.
12. J. E. Hopkins, *The ride of death* (London: White Cross League, n.d.), p. 5.
13. *Ibid.*
14. *Pall Mall Gazette* **6969** (xlvi), 19 July 1887.
15. *Ibid.* See also Bland, "'Purifying' the public world".
16. *Pall Mall Gazette*, as Note 14.
17. L. Bland, "'Purifying' the public world".
18. J. Walkowitz, *City of dreadful night. Narratives of sexual danger in late-Victorian London* (London: Virago, 1994), pp. 50-2.
19. *Report of the International Council for Women* (Washington, 1888), p. 289.
20. E. Wolstenholme Elmy, in *Shafts* (March 1897), p. 87.
21. Feminist campaigns against the sexual abuse of children are described in Chs 3 & 4 of Jeffreys, *The spinster and her enemies*.
22. E. Ethelmer, *The human flower* (Congleton: Women's Emancipation Union, 1892), p. 43. Ellis Ethelmer is one of the pseudonyms of Elizabeth Wolstenholme Elmy.
23. For the perspective that such late-nineteenth-century feminist campaigners were prudes and puritans, see L. Gordon & E. Dubois, "Seeking ecstasy on the battlefield: danger and pleasure in nineteenth century feminist thought", in *Pleasure and danger: exploring female sexuality*, C. Vance (ed.), (London: Routledge & Kegan Paul, 1984); and M. Hunt, "The de-eroticization of women's liberation: social purity movements and the revolutionary feminism of Sheila Jeffreys", in *Feminist review* **34**, pp. 23-46, Spring, 1990.

24. *The Woman's Leader* (22 January 1926).

25. UNESCO and the international coalition against trafficking in women, *The Penn State Report*, International Meeting of Experts on Sexual Exploitation, Violence and Prostitution, State College, Pennsylvania, USA (New York: United Nations, 1991).

26. For a discussion of the idea of women's sexual passivity in Victorian England, see M. Vicinus (ed.), *Suffer and be still* (Bloomington, Indiana: University of Indiana Press, 1972).

27. H. H. Ellis, *Studies in the psychology of sex, volume 3. Analysis of the sexual impulse, love and pain, the sexual impulse in women* (New York: F. A. Davis, 1923; first published 1903), p. 68.

28. *Ibid.*, p. 89.

29. *Ibid.*, p. 90.

30. *Ibid.*, p. 226.

31. *Ibid.*, p. 101.

32. M. Jackson, "Sexology and the social construction of male sexuality (Havelock Ellis)", in *The sexuality papers. male sexuality and the social control of women*, L. Coveney et al. (eds) (London: Hutchinson, 1984), p. 65. See also M. Jackson, *The "real" facts of life*.

33. Jackson, "Sexology and the social construction of male sexuality", p. 64.

34. *Ibid.*, p. 61.

35. H. H. Ellis, *Studies in the psychology of sex. Erotic symbolism, the mechanism of detumescence, the psychic state in pregnancy* (Philadelphia, Pennsylvania: F. A. Davis, 1926; first published 1906), p. 114.

36. A. Comfort (ed.), *The joy of sex* (London: Quartet, 1974), p. 123.

37. H. H. Ellis, *Sex in relation to society. Studies in the psychology of sex*, vol. 6 (London: Heinemann, 1946), p. 247.

38. E. Chesser, *Love and marriage* (London: Pan Books, 1957), pp. 88–9.

39. W. Gallichan, *The poison of prudery* (London: T. Werner Laurie, 1929), p. 184.

40. W. Stekel, *Frigidity in woman in relation to her love life*, 2 Vols (New York: Livewright, 1936; first published 1926), p. 1.

41. Chesser, *Love and marriage*, p. 66.

42. L. Re-Bartlett, *Sex and sanctity* (London: Longman, 1912), p. 32.

43. C. Pankhurst, *The great scourge and how to end it* (London: E. Pankhurst, 1913), p. 98.

44. C. Hamilton, *Marriage as a trade* (London: Chapman and Hall, 1909; republished London: The Women's Press, 1981); L. Whitelaw, *The life and rebellious times of Cicely Hamilton* (London: The Women's Press, 1990).

45. Hamilton, *Marriage as a trade* (1909 edn), p. 278.

46. W. Gallichan, *Modern woman and how to manage her* (London: T. Werner Laurie, 1909), p. 49.

47. S. Jeffreys, *The lesbian heresy. A feminist perspective on the lesbian sexual revolution* (Melbourne: Spinifex, 1993; London, The Women's Press, 1994; Munich: Frauenoffensive, 1994). See also M. Vicinus, "'They wonder to which sex I belong': the historical roots of the modern lesbian identity", in *The Lesbian and Gay Studies Reader*, H. Abelove et al. (eds) (New York: Routledge, 1993).

48. See J. Weeks, *Coming out. Homosexual politics in Britain from the nineteenth century to the present* (London: Quartet, 1977); and J. Dollimore, *Sexual dissidence. Augustine to Wilde, Freud to Foucault* (Oxford: Clarendon Press, 1991).

49. Faderman, *Surpassing the love of men*, Smith-Rosenberg, *The female world of love and ritual*.

50. Auchmuty, "You're a dyke, Angela!", p. 135.
51. *Ibid.*, p. 140.
52. H. H. Ellis, *Studies in the psychology of sex volume 2. Sexual inversion* (Philadelphia, Pennsylvania: F. A. Davis, 1927, first published 1901), p. 308.
53. *Ibid.*, p. 250.
54. E. Carpenter, *The intermediate sex* (London: George Allen & Unwin, 1921), p. 31.
55. Ellis, *Sexual inversion*, p. 262.
56. S. Jeffreys, "Butch and femme: now and then", in *Not a passing phase*, Lesbian History Group (ed.) (London: The Women's Press, 1989).
57. J. Nestle, *A restricted country* (London: Sheba, 1987).
58. C. Haldane, *Motherhood and its enemies* (London: Chatto and Windus, 1927), p. 94.
59. R. Hall, "Miss Ogilvy finds herself", in *The other persuasion*, S. Kleinberg (ed.) (New York: Vintage Books, 1977, first published 1926).
60. A. Oram, "'Embittered, sexless or homosexual': attacks on spinster teachers 1981–1939", in *Not a passing phase. Reclaiming lesbians in history 1840-1985*, Lesbian History Group (ed.) (London: The Women's Press, 1989), p. 105.
61. See V. Brittain, *Radclyffe Hall. A case of obscenity* (London: Feminia Books, 1968).
62. C. Smith-Rosenberg, "Discourses of subjectivity: the new woman 1870-1936", in *Hidden from history. Reclaiming the gay and lesbian past*, M. Duberman et al. (eds) (Harmondsworth: Penguin, 1991).
63. E. Newton, "The mythic mannish lesbian: Radclyffe Hall and the new woman", in *Hidden from history*, M. Duberman et al. (eds) (Harmondsworth: Penguin, 1991).
64. J. Loulan, *The lesbian erotic dance* (Spinsters, Aunt Lute, 1990).
65. Dollimore, *Sexual dissidence*, p. 15.
66. G. Rubin, "Thinking sex: notes for a radical theory of the politics of sexuality", in *Pleasure and danger*, C. Vance (ed.) (London: Routledge & Kegan Paul, 1984), p. 302.
67. *Ibid.*, p. 310.
68. Postmodern feminists have emphasized the existing suspicion of science in feminist theory and have been critical of ideas of progress, particularly scientific ones, but interestingly, sexology seems, up to now to have escaped their critical gaze. As an introduction to these ideas, see L. Nicholson (ed.), *Feminism/postmodernism* (New York: Routledge, 1990).
69. See D. Leidholdt & J. G. Raymond (eds), *The sexual liberals and the attack on feminism* (New York: Pergamon, 1990).
70. Rubin, "Thinking sex", p. 309.
71. C. Smyth, *Lesbians talk: queer notions* (London: Scarlet Press, 1992), p. 17.

Suggestions for further reading

Feminist campaigns around sexuality in the late-nineteenth and early-twentieth century are covered in S. Jeffreys, *The spinster and her enemies. Feminism and sexuality 1880-1930* (London: Pandora, 1985), and in M. Jackson, *The 'real' facts of life. Feminism and the politics of sexuality c1850-1940* (London: Taylor and Francis, 1994). For a rather less positive approach to the feminist campaigns, see J. Weeks, *Sex, politics and society* (London: Longman, 1981). The development and political impact of the science of sexology is described in Margaret Jackson's contributions to the collection: in L. Coveney et al. (eds), *The sexuality papers. Male sexuality and the social control of women* (London: Hutchinson, 1984), and in her book *The 'real' facts of life*. For the impact of sexology on lesbian identity, the most influential book from a feminist perspective has been: L. Faderman, *Surpassing the love of men. Romantic friendship and love between women from the Renaissance to the Present* (New York: Morrow, 1981; and London: The Women's Press, 1985). For lesbian history in Britain in this period, see Lesbian History Group (ed.), *Not a passing phase. Reclaiming lesbians in history 1840-1985* (London: The Women's Press, 1986). The collection by M. Duberman et al. (eds), *Hidden from history. Reclaiming the gay and lesbian past* (Harmondsworth: Penguin, 1991), also has useful contributions on the themes in lesbian history addressed here, but mostly from an American perspective. J. Weeks, *Coming out. Homosexual politics in Britain from the nineteenth century to the present* (London: Quartet, 1977) looks at the impact of sexology on lesbian and gay identity in a more positive light from the perspective of a gay male historian.

Primary sources which show the views of feminists involved in the campaigns are contained in S. Jeffreys (ed.), *The sexuality debates* (London: Routledge & Kegan Paul, 1987). This collection includes articles by Elizabeth Wolstenholme Elmy and Christabel Pankhurst. We are also lucky to have in print a fascinating book from a feminist spinster of the period, C. Hamilton, *Marriage as a trade* (London: Chapman and Hall, 1909; republished London: The Women's Press, 1981). This is a classic example of feminist theorizing on marriage and spinsterhood. There is a useful biography of Hamilton by L. Whitelaw, *The life and rebellious times of Cicely Hamilton* (London: The Women's Press, 1990). For unpublished primary sources the very best place to look is the Fawcett Library, part of the Guildhall University, in Old Castle St, Aldgate East, London, which has a wonderful collection of material on feminist campaigns around prostitution, venereal disease and sexual abuse.

Primary sources on sexology are easier to find. You might try the works of the sexologists who are regarded as the founding fathers of sexology in this period, notably Henry Havelock Ellis, Iwan Bloch and August Forel. For example, I. Bloch, *The sexual life of our time* (London: Heinemann, 1909); H. H. Ellis, *Studies in the psychology of sex, volume 2. Sexual inversion* (Philadelphia, Pennsylvania: F. A. Davis, 1927; first published 1901); H. H. Ellis, *Studies in the psychology of sex, volume 3. Analysis of the sexual impulse, love and pain, the sexual impulse in women* (New York: F. A. Davis, 1923, first published 1903); H. H. Ellis, *Sex in relation to society. Studies in the psychology of sex*, vol. 6 (London: Heinemann, 1946); A. Forel, *The sexual question* (New York: Medical Art Agency, 1922; first published 1908). Again, the Fawcett Library has a good collection of this material.

Chapter Nine

ᴥ

Women and politics

June Hannam

Introduction

Women's involvement in political activity from the early nineteenth century to the outbreak of the Second World War was extensive and varied. They engaged in general political and social reform campaigns as well as taking part in movements which focused on their own oppression as a sex and sought to challenge inequalities in all areas of their lives. No clear-cut distinction can be made between these two forms of political work. Campaigning on general questions often led women to take an interest in their own social position, while those already committed to a feminist perspective sought to influence the theory and practice of mainstream political parties and movements.[1]

This chapter seeks to explore the richness and diversity of women's political activity between the early-nineteenth century and the 1930s. It will examine the interrelationship between broader political campaigns and the women's movement, and will focus on the extent to which women's involvement in politics led them to question aspects of their own social position. In one chapter it would clearly be impossible to look at specific campaigns in any depth; the intention, therefore, is to examine a number of key issues raised in recent studies which have contributed to our understanding of women's political activity. These include the ideas which underlay women's political involvement, in particular the tensions between concepts of equality and difference; the debate over whether women should organize separately; the influence of other political ideologies, such as liberalism and Socialism, on feminist ideas and practice; and the extent to which feminism contributed to changing definitions of citizenship and democracy.

Social historians in particular have developed a broad definition of political activity which goes beyond the institutional politics of organized parties to encompass the "politics of everyday life". Savage and Miles suggest that the routines of people's daily existence involve "political choices, strategies and decisions. Personal relationships, between husbands and wives . . . can be political, as can the business of organising and participating in ostensibly non-political activities, such as religious worship, education or sport".[2] An understanding of the complex interrelationship between these different forms of politics helps to explain the process by which women became politicized and the choices that they make.

This chapter, however, will focus on more formal political activity. In the nineteenth century, women felt themselves to be restricted by the prevailing ideal that "the proper sphere of women is not politics or publicity, but private and domestic life". Harriet Taylor, demanding women's suffrage as early as 1851, denied "the right of any portion of the species to decide for another portion, or an individual for another individual, what is and what is not their proper sphere".[3] One of the main objectives of the Victorian women's movement, therefore, was to challenge the view that women should be excluded from fields of action which were deemed to be unfeminine. The formal political arena was seen as the main route to achieve a change in women's social position, and feminists claimed the right to enter all areas of public space. They called for "an armed movement, an invasion by women of the spheres which men have always forbidden us to enter".[4]

Nineteenth-century women's movement

Notwithstanding the Victorian ideal of domesticity, we know that, far from confining themselves to the home, a significant minority of women in the nineteenth century took an active role in public life. By doing so, they challenged Victorian ideas about a woman's place, both explicitly and implicitly. In the early-nineteenth century philanthropy provided middle-class women with an acceptable arena for public work. At the same time they took part in a range of political and social reform movements, including franchise reform unions, the Anti-Corn Law League, and anti-slavery societies.[5] Working-class women were also involved in a variety of political campaigns. They joined men of their class in the Owenite socialist movement, in industrial disputes, in franchise reform unions and in protests over food prices and the imposition of the New Poor Law.[6] They also played an extensive role in Chartism, which was "the first instance of a political movement initiated and sustained by working people relying on their own resources alone".[7]

Women tended to play a limited and subordinate role in these campaigns. They organized together in separate groups, although they rarely raised the specific needs of their own sex. Middle-class women in particular worked from behind the scenes; they met in each others' homes to organize fundraising events or to listen to speakers, but they were reluctant to attend public meetings and were excluded from policymaking positions. The working-class women's role, notably in Chartism, was far more visible and acknowledged publically. None the less, with the exception of Owenite Socialism, which was unique in addressing sexual oppression, working-class women justified their political activities with reference to their roles as the wives and mothers of working men, and to their need to protect the well-being of their families.[8] Thompson suggests that women's participation in popular politics was "related to their activities as workers and as members of radical families".[9] In manufacturing communities, for example, where whole families worked in the same industries and shared a common experience, women were drawn into political demonstrations and meetings in movements such as Chartism.

Working-class women did raise their own needs in the course of particular campaigns, such as the right to employment, but they were ambivalent in their attitudes. Their loyalties were primarily with men of their own class in their fight against exploitation and exclusion from political rights. With the failure of Chartism in the late 1840s and the increasing separation between work, family and community life, working-class women withdrew from political activism. As workbased, formal institutions such as trade unions became the main channel for working-class grievances, in particular those of the skilled male worker, women were left with no roles to play. It was only where older forms of protest, such as food riots, occurred in the late 1850s and 1860s that women could still be seen among the leaders.[10]

The ideology of Chartism itself contributed to this withdrawal of working-class women from more formal public activity. Leading male Chartists encouraged and valued women's support, but the aim of the movement was to restore the "traditional" division of labour and sexual power between men and women in the family which, it was argued, had been disrupted by industrialization. The ideal of a working-class family in which a male breadwinner supported his dependent wife and children, which subsequently became entrenched in the labour movement, was therefore encouraged by Chartism. Taylor suggests that this ideal of domesticity then hampered working-class women when new opportunities arose for them in the 1880s to take part in politics.[11]

While working-class women became less visible in the public arena, the opposite trend can be seen for middle-class women. Their involvement in early-nineteenth-century political campaigns, albeit from behind the scenes, had posed an implicit challenge to the view that it was inappropriate for them to take an interest in affairs beyond the home. From the mid-1850s, a more explicit challenge was mounted against the ideology of separate spheres, when a series of campaigns developed which sought to address the inequalities and disadvantages faced by women. The *English Woman's Journal*, founded in 1857, provided a focal point for this discontent and brought like-minded women in touch with each other.[12]

Although the struggle for the vote came to hold centre stage after 1900, this was not the case in the nineteenth century. The demand for parliamentary suffrage was only one of a range of campaigns. Some of these sought access to the public sphere, which was clearly defined as "the universities, the professions, central and local government".[13] Others aimed to improve women's legal and economic position within marriage, to challenge the double standard of morality, and to repeal the Contagious Diseases Acts which sought to regulate female sexuality. These varied campaigns were seen by contemporaries as forming a women's (or a women's rights) movement that was particularly active between the late 1850s and the 1880s.

The new women's movement encouraged some middle-class women to become involved in political campaigning for the first time. It was more usual, however, to find that women attracted to the movement had already gained experience in political reform campaigns of the early-nineteenth century. Many came from professional or business families where both sexes were encouraged to take an interest in political and social reform questions. Their friendship and family networks, based on shared religious or political beliefs, reinforced their commitment to social and political action. Quaker and Unitarian families, for example, such as the Brights, the Mclarens, the Clarks and the Davenport Hills, produced a large number of men and women committed to radical liberal causes and to women's rights campaigns.[15]

The links between women's experience of political reform campaigns, their philanthropic outlook, and the development of a commitment to women's rights were, however, by no means straightforward. After the World Anti-Slavery Convention of 1840, a small number of women did raise the issue of women's right to participate fully in the anti-slavery campaign. They compared their own position to that of slaves, and questioned aspects of separate spheres ideology. The majority of women, however, emphasized their duty to help others. In contrasting their more fortunate position with that of female slaves, they hoped that emancipation would enable the latter to give all their time to domestic duties and to the development of a stable family life.[16]

It was their "religious philanthropy" that had motivated female abolitionists in the first place to take an interest in anti-slavery work and they shared the aim of religious societies to expand evangelical Christianity. Rosamund and Louis Billington suggest, therefore, that in a context in which evangelicalism legitimized existing gender relations, it is little wonder that feminism surfaced only among a minority of radical women in the anti-slavery movement.[17]

In her comprehensive study, *Women against slavery*, Midgley also questions whether anti-slavery campaigning led directly to the development of a women's movement. She points out that many female abolitionists only put their energies into feminism once the anti-slavery societies had started to wind down. In the 1850s and 1860s, however, the links between the two campaigns did become stronger. The developing women's movement drew on anti-slavery for its ideological approach and "made use of the network of female abolitionists in creating its own network and leadership".[18] This overlapped with Quaker and Unitarian networks in towns such as London, Manchester, Bristol, Edinburgh and Leeds. Anti-slavery women brought experience in organizing women, "in canvassing, in fundraising, in propagandising and in petitioning Parliament" as well as contacts and friendship links which stretched beyond national boundaries.[19]

Similar points could be made about women's involvement in philanthropy, which is a problematic area when considering political activity. An increase in the number and scale of philanthropic societies in the nineteenth century expanded the opportunities for women to engage in activities outside the home. These could range from visiting the sick on behalf of a church group to pioneering new methods of dealing with social problems.[20] With its emphasis on individual voluntary work and suspicion of state intervention, however, philanthropy could be seen as a denial of the importance of political action. In practice, it is extremely difficult to disentangle philanthropic and political motivation and action in the nineteenth century. As Midgley has noted, women involved in anti-slavery societies were careful to stress that their activities were an extension of their domestic and religious duties, since they were concerned with the spiritual, moral and physical welfare of slaves. And yet these women were also "involved in a political movement, the leading reform movement of the period, one that pioneered methods of extra-Parliamentary agitation in order to bring about legislative change".[21] Women who played a leading role in philanthropic activities, such as Octavia Hill, Louisa Twyning and Mary Carpenter, also had to engage in a variety of "political" activities. They sought support from pressure groups, lobbied MPs, gave evidence to Royal Commissions and wrote policy papers on their ideas for reform.[22]

Both sexes justified women's philanthropic work with reference to their caring qualities, which had been developed in the home, and their duty to help the poor. It was thought that women's special mission was to work towards a moral transformation and regeneration of society – a view that was shared by feminists and non-feminists alike. This line of argument was based on, and helped to reinforce, existing gender divisions. On the other hand, it could also motivate women to become engaged in public life and provided them with a justification for their activities. In her study of women in local government, Hollis claims that it "encouraged women to come forward with the confidence that their domestic and family background was as useful and relevant to public service as men's commercial and business experience".[23] By this means, philanthropy could provide a route into feminist politics, in particular for those whose family background, religion, friendship networks and other political interests also proved conducive to that development.

As with anti-slavery work, there was no simple relationship between the two. Mary Carpenter, for example, the daughter of the Unitarian minister for Bristol, gained a national reputation for her work on behalf of juvenile delinquents. She took part in the anti-slavery campaign of the 1840s and 1850s and later agreed that her name could be used as a supporter of women's suffrage. She was ambivalent, however, about the demand for women's rights and preferred to devote her energies to establishing ragged schools and reformatories.[24] None the less, her work did become an inspiration for other women, such as Frances Power Cobbe, who later became active feminists. Frances Power Cobbe moved to Bristol specifically to work with Mary Carpenter and later claimed that:

> It was not until I was actively engaged in the work of Mary Carpenter at Bristol, and had begun to desire earnestly various changes of law relating to young criminals and paupers that I became an advocate of "Women's Rights". It was good old Samuel J. May of Syracuse, New York, who, when paying us a visit pressed on my attention the question "Why should you not have a vote?" Why should not women be enabled to influence the making of laws in which they have as great an interest as men?[25]

Involvement in a variety of philanthropic and political movements did help some women to develop political skills, which could then be taken into the women's movement. As their confidence grew, they were more willing to step out into the political limelight; they lobbied MPs, circulated petitions, organized large public meetings and debated topics such as prostitution, which would have been thought an impossibility only a decade before. Even so, in the 1860s and 1870s, female speakers on public platforms were still seen as being unusual. Lilias Ashworth Hallett, Secretary of the West of England Women's Suffrage Society, recalled that "the novelty of hearing women speakers brought crowds to the meetings . . . It was evident that the audience always came expecting to see curious masculine objects walking on to the platform, and when we appeared with our quiet black dresses, the whole expression of the faces of the audience would instantly change".[26]

While middle-class women broadened the scope of their political activities gradually, as already noted, the opposite was the case for working-class women. None the less, the interests of the two groups intersected throughout the nineteenth century. The work and family lives of working-class women continued to be the subject of concern for middle-class women, and provided another point of contact between philanthropists and women's rights campaigners. Attitudes towards the nature of the difficulties faced by working-class women and the best strategies to adopt to achieve change, revealed differences of approach between middle-class women that do not fall neatly into categories such as feminist or non-feminist.

The main concern of female philanthropists tended to be the problem of poverty rather than the specific needs of women. In their emphasis on the family as a key agent in social change, however, they focused on the pivotal role played by women. Good household management could make all the difference to meagre household budgets, while the mother's importance in socializing children meant that she could develop a sense of individual responsibility and the strong character that was so essential for the well-being of both families and the state. In seeking to change behaviour, philanthropists had a vision of a transformed working-class family life that mirrored their own middle-class norms and values, and could seem unsympathetic to the needs of working-class women themselves. On the other hand, Lewis suggests that the attitudes of many women involved in social reform work were complex and were modified through experience. Octavia Hill and Helen Bosanquet, for example, were convinced of the importance of voluntary action, and yet were willing to seek state intervention when this seemed necessary. They may have emphasized the mother's influence for good in the family, but could also display a real sympathy for the difficulties faced by poorer women and a respect for the autonomy of working-class family life.[27]

Feminist groups could also display complex attitudes towards working-class women. Members of the Ladies National Association (LNA) for the Repeal of the Contagious Diseases Acts, for instance, attacked the double standard of morality embodied by the Acts and deplored the control over women's bodies being given to men. They sought to understand the reasons why women turned to prostitution and attempted to defend their rights in the law courts. On the other hand, there was a tendency to portray women as victims of male lust and to seek to find prostitutes alternative employment, often as domestic servants. They called on males of the working class to protect their female relatives, which did little to empower working-class women themselves.[28]

Other members of the women's movement took an interest in work conditions, rather than in the moral and social questions arising from working women's family lives. Instead of rescue work they sought ways in which working-class women could take independent action, both politically and industrially, to improve their economic and social position. In 1874, Emma Paterson formed the Women's Protective and Provident League to encourage the development of trade union organization among women.[29] Feminists came forward at a local level to help in this work. In Bristol, for example, Mary Priestman, an LNA member and suffrage campaigner, was keen to involve working-class women in political activity and trade union work. She suggested to Josephine Butler that cards should be distributed to working women as a sign of their LNA membership, even if they could not pay the full subscription, and held numerous meetings in the working-class districts of Bristol. In 1874 she gave a paper at the Social Science Congress on the "Industrial Position of Women", which drew links between low wages, the restrictions placed on women's labour by factory legislation, and the need for women's suffrage. She urged the formation of trade unions and helped to organize relief for women on strike in Bristol in 1889, ensuring that the workers themselves organized the distribution of food tickets.[30]

There were many occasions on which feminists voiced the stated needs of working-class women, for example when they lobbied for the appointment of the first female factory inspectors, or demanded more technical education and training. Other issues were more controversial, in particular protective legislation. Until the 1880s, most feminists argued that protective legislation for women should be opposed. It was feared that women's ability to compete in the labour market would be hampered by restrictions placed on their labour. Feminists were also influenced by liberal arguments which saw protective legislation as an interference with individual liberty. Such a position might have seemed extreme when applied to the employment of women in white lead works, but there were many instances in which legislation was being used to expand male employment opportunities at the expense of women. The male trade union movement clashed with representatives of the women's movement on this issue, although neither group appeared to derive their arguments from the views of working women. Where women workers did express an opinion, their attitude to legislation was variable. It was more likely to be based on a pragmatic assessment of the potential impact on their work conditions or the availability of employment than on any ideological considerations.[31]

The different ways in which feminists approached questions relating to working-class women provides one example of the varied strands that went to make up feminism in the period, and the complexity of ideas within the women's movement. Embedded as they were in a particular political culture and set of assumptions about women's "nature" and capabilities, nineteenth-century feminists developed their own perspectives within a framework of beliefs that emphasized liberal individualism and biologically-based sex differences.[32] Feminist discourse throughout the nineteenth and early-twentieth centuries, therefore, was permeated by a tension between rights and duties, and between egalitarianism, sex difference and maternalism.[33]

Far from speaking with one voice, feminists disagreed about "the basis and nature of [women's] oppression and about how it should be reformed; about the nature of women and the extent to which the differences between men and women were innate or socially conditioned".[34] Such disagreements were not necessarily directly related to religious or party political differences. Josephine Butler, a Liberal, and the Conservative, Frances Power Cobbe, shared a common emphasis on the importance of sex differences between men and women, and based their demands for emancipation on a particular idea of woman's nature as being nurturant and compassionate. The Liberal, Millicent Garrett Fawcett, and the Conservative, Emily Davies, however, while agreeing that sex differences were innate, thought they had been exaggerated. They emphasized "the intellectual similarities between men and women rather than concentrating on their physical or moral differences".[35]

The organized women's movement emphasized women's shared interests as a sex which, it was assumed, would cut across and override other differences between them. On the other hand, whether they were feminists or not, women differed in their approach to specific political campaigns and issues. Divided by their politics, their religion and their class, women "occupied a place at the crossroads of several interlocking identities".[36] The tensions, in particular between women's common interests as a sex and their party political and class loyalties, became increasingly acute as women were drawn into work for mainstream political parties towards the end of the nineteenth century.

Women and party politics

Although they were denied access to the parliamentary franchise, women did have the opportunity to take part in political life at a local level through their election to a variety of public bodies. From the 1870s onwards women increasingly put themselves forward as candidates for school boards, boards of guardians, parish councils and later county councils. The relaxation of property qualifications for candidates to boards of guardians in the 1890s, coupled with the development of socialist groups, encouraged working-class women also to put themselves forward as candidates.[37] Their participation in local elected bodies enabled women from all social classes to "claim public space" and to exert some influence over the delivery of state welfare policies, in particular the Poor Law.[38]

Women stood as independent candidates and also as representatives of particular parties. None the less, Hollis claims that they shared a "cluster of common attitudes" which marked them off from their male counterparts. They were child and client centred, with an interest in community needs, public health, urban amenities and good-quality housing. Conscious of their role in "staking out women's citizen and suffrage rights" they were hardworking, conscientious and painstaking in their approach.[39] Hollis suggests that such women gained strength from the view that their home management skills and compassion would bring unique benefits to local elected bodies. Lewis, on the other hand, points to the differences between women on many issues, such as the payment of school fees, and suggests that their participation in local government was framed as much by party political allegiance as by any sense of solidarity with other women.[40] These issues, as to whether women shared a common outlook or whether party political differences predominated, were also increasingly mirrored at a national level.

During much of the nineteenth century, women's political activity tended to be the result of community or family involvement and took place outside mainstream party politics.[41] After the early 1880s, the extension of the franchise, coupled with legislation which prohibited the use of paid canvassers, led party managers to encourage women to work for the two main political parties. Women also joined the socialist groups which were established in the late nineteenth century and worked for the Labour Party after 1900. This immediately raised the issue of what women's role should be, and whether they should organize separately in order to create their own political identity.

These questions had already been raised in the early days of the women's movement and can be illustrated by arguments over the nature and purpose of the *English Woman's Journal* (EWJ). Bessie Rayner Parkes thought that the EWJ would show what women could do in association with each other, and would create a "new focus for political activity by women". Its reading room, club and associated societies would "offer women a rallying point for some form of action".[42] For Emily Davies, on the other hand, it was far more important for men and women to work together on equal terms, and she deplored any hint of antagonism between the sexes. Similar issues arose in the early organizations of the women's movement; suffrage societies were often formed with active male support and with many men listed among the officers, whereas the LNA chose to organize separately.

Underlying these varied tactics regarding political strategy were tensions between arguments rooted in equality and those based on difference. For Parkes, the EWJ was an opportunity to "carry private values into the public sphere" and to recognize the importance of ideas which came from the experience of domesticity and philanthropy rather than from employment. The journal also, however, expressed the liberal ideals of progressive, radical families which provided a particular model for political action and were rooted in a political economy that promoted the power of the middle classes. Jane Rendall suggests that such tensions, "representing the claims of class and gender", continued to pervade the women's movement later in the century.[43] They were also present as women took a greater role in the mainstream political parties.

The male-dominated political parties put forward contradictory messages in their attempts to attract women to their cause. As Hunt has shown in her study of the Social Democratic Federation, the process of politicization was highly gendered. Socialists assumed that women's position within the home posed a problem. Immersed in the details of family life, women could hold men back from political activism, while their lack of experience of collective industrial action made them less receptive to socialist propaganda. On the other hand, it was recognized that women's influence on other family members meant that it was important to gain their support and to tap what was considered to be their natural interest in social reform.[44]

The Conservative Party was also ambivalent in its attitude to women before they gained the vote. It hoped to mobilize women in support of "an exclusively male body", but they were largely ignored in the Party's magazines and propaganda literature. Where *women* were represented they were used as a "stimulus to male action in defence of honour and property".[45] Conservatives appealed to the popular vote with an emphasis on the male pursuits of "football, racing and beer" and it was not until the early 1900s that "domestically centred values articlulated by the Primrose League began to gain ground".[46]

In spite of this ambivalence towards their role as political activists, women were drawn in large numbers to work for political parties. Before 1918, women were unable to belong to the main party organizations and were "channelled into subsidiary organizations".[47] Tory women were admitted to the Primrose League in 1884, where they were organized in their own Ladies Grand Council, although in the local habitations they worked alongside men. They set themselves the limited brief of seeking to interest and educate women in politics and to develop their skills as canvassers, organizers and political propagandists. They emphasized that this in no way detracted from "womanliness", but rather was a natural extension of women's educative and moral role within the home. Women were to exercise indirect influence on politics and to co-operate with men rather than rival them. Although they did take an interest in issues of relevance to women, they did not seek to push these on to the political party agenda.

Walker suggests, therefore, that although the League did encourage a political awareness and sense of responsibility in women, "the argument that women had a special backroom role to play which was based on the traditional qualities of the old rather than the new woman, postponed the day of equality".[48] Nonetheless, both the Conservative and the Liberal auxiliaries did enable women to take part in "male" politics before they were enfranchised. They helped to undermine the view that women should be confined to the home, and played a part in politicizing women by familiarizing them with details of contemporary issues.[49]

Liberal Party women were particularly aggressive in pushing forward the claims of their sex. Local Women's Liberal Associations (WLA) were formed throughout the country during the 1880s, and joined together in the Women's Liberal Federation (WLF) in 1887. Some women saw the Associations as a way in which they could help their husbands by drawing women into political life to support Liberal policies. Others, who were usually already committed feminists, chose to organize separately in order to assert their autonomy. They may have wished to further the cause of liberalism, but they also saw women's participation in the Associations as a way to "validate their claims to full citizenship".[50] They aimed to "cultivate female political power" by urging women to shape policy and to stand for local elected bodies.[51]

The three main socialist groups established in the 1880s and 1890s – the Fabian Society, the Social Democratic Federation (SDF) and the Independent Labour Party (ILP) – were unusual in opening their membership to women on the same basis as men. In practice, only a small minority of office holders were women, but they did take a full part in the movement as speakers, organizers, writers and fundraisers. Socialist groups also provided an opportunity for working-class women to re-enter political life. Female socialists were convinced that the best way to achieve emancipation for women was to work alongside men in the socialist movement, and to seek change for both sexes. They did ensure, however, that the "woman question" was debated widely in the socialist movement. While sharing many of the aspirations of the women's movement, socialist women focused in particular on the needs of working women, and emphasized the material basis of women's oppression as well as their political inequalities.[52]

Some women in the labour movement, however, advocated the need for separate organizations to ensure that women's interests would not be neglected. They argued that women's experiences of work and family were different from those of men, and that they needed to be appealed to on this basis if they were to be mobilized. The Women's Co-operative Guild, established in 1884, was unusual in drawing its membership from among married working-class women. It reflected their concerns in its campaigns for improved maternity care, better housing and easier divorce, and took a strongly independent stand on these issues.[53] The WPPL was renamed the Women's Trade Union League in 1886 and, under the presidency of Lady Dilke, sought to encourage the organization of women into mixed-sex trade unions. Progress was slow, however, and the needs of women were often lost sight of in male-dominated unions. As late as 1906, therefore, a new general union, the National Federation of Women Workers, was formed by Mary MacArthur to make a specific appeal to women workers.[54]

In common with the other political parties, a women's auxiliary, the Women's Labour League, was formed in 1906 to support the Labour Party. Its main aim was to encourage women to become involved in labour politics and to help the Labour Party during elections. Its members also joined in numerous campaigns to improve the social, health and industrial lives of working-class women.[55]

Women's involvement in mainstream party politics increasingly raised issues of loyalty, in particular for feminists. Studies of the women's movement tend to emphasize the way in which British feminists derived their ideas and motivation from a common libertarian or reforming outlook, and disliked party politics.[56] Levine, for example, suggests that women distanced their feminism from the remainder of their politics and claimed for it "the status of a separately conceived and separately constructed entity".[57] The women's movement developed a feminist culture which bound women together regardless of political, religious or class differences and encouraged them to develop alternative values. Levine argues, therefore, that party politics was something apart from that all-encompassing feminism with which activist women ordered their lives and their choices.[58]

There is little doubt that women active in politics, including many non-feminists, were usually woman-centred in their approach and did share common values, including a belief in women's moral superiority and caring qualities, which they took into mainstream politics. On the other hand, for many women, their party political beliefs informed their feminism. The relationship between the two was complex and caused tension for those women who attempted to put their party politics and their feminism together. During the late 1880s the Women's Liberal Associations in particular faced internal conflicts about whether feminist causes should be put to the top of their agenda.

The Bristol WLA, for example, established in 1881 by Anna Maria Priestman, Emily Sturge and other members of the women's movement in the city, attempted to combine feminism and liberalism in ways which brought criticism from all sides. They hoped that one day men and women would work together on questions that affected them both, and took an interest in a wide range of topical issues. These included vivisection, Irish Home Rule, opium trafficking, taxation in relation to poor relief, and the needs of working women. In reply to complaints from some female members that too many subjects were being covered, Anna Maria Priestman argued that one of the principles of Liberalism was "enmity to privilege". Since privilege was likely to be usurped by any class of the community at any time, it was probable that they appeared to be taking up new subjects when they "were only working on behalf of one of the root causes of liberalism".[59]

When they were accused, on the other hand, of spending too much time on women's suffrage, Anna Maria Priestman responded with the argument that women could have no "security for their liberty as long as they had no control over the laws they had to obey". She was scathing about Joseph Chamberlain's suggestion that women should not be demanding the vote, while at the same time he set out a great deal of work for them to do. "The women of our Association do not choose to give up their individual responsibility and their consciences in order to become party drudges."[60] In the same spirit, the Bristol WLA were not content to leave women's needs until a distant future, and were one of the first groups to refuse to work for Liberal men who were not in favour of women's suffrage – a position taken up later by the WLF as a whole.

Differences between women who were overtly feminist and those who put other Liberal causes first came to a head in 1892, when Gladstone reaffirmed his opposition to women's suffrage. Many feminist members of the WLF wished to make women's suffrage an official part of the constitution, whereas those known as "neutrals" argued that suffrage was not a party political issue and therefore should not be included. After a lengthy campaign, the WLF committed itself to suffrage, but this caused a schism in the movement. A new group, the Women's National Liberal Association, was set up, taking 60 local Associations with it, to provide an alternative for those who found the feminism of the WLF too strong. The WLF, on the other hand, continued to take part in a whole range of campaigns affecting women's social position and was identified increasingly as a "women's lobby" as well as a Liberal Party auxiliary.[61]

Women active within the socialist and labour movement faced even greater difficulties in reconciling their feminism with their broader political beliefs. An emphasis on women's common interests as a sex, and a recognition that working women could be oppressed by male members of their own class at the workplace and in the home, sat uneasily beside a socialist focus on class exploitation and the need for class solidarity to achieve change. The Marxist-inspired SDF viewed "the woman question" as a diversion from the class struggle which could be resolved after a revolution had been achieved. It was assumed that feminist issues should be a matter of personal conviction rather than party policy.[62]

The ILP derived its Socialism from a wider range of sources, placed less emphasis on the class struggle, and showed a greater sympathy towards "sex equality". Nonetheless, in practice the ILP did not give a high profile in the 1890s to issues relating to sex disabilities. Instead, priority was given to economic questions such as unemployment and the need to build links with the trade unions in order to further the cause of independent labour politics. Women were most likely to be drawn into socialist politics at a local level during struggles over social issues such as housing, rents and education.[63]

Female activists did not necessarily see their feminism and their Socialism as being polarized, and attempted to accommodate both perspectives in their day-to-day activities. However, as in the case of the Liberal Party, the need to make decisions on specific issues where the interests of male and female workers conflicted posed dilemmas about whether to be loyal to the unity of the labour movement or to seek to redress women's specific grievances. These difficulties increased after 1900 with the formation of the Labour Representation Committee (renamed the Labour Party in 1906), an uneasy alliance between socialists and trade unionists. Issues which threatened this fragile alliance, such as a commitment to ending women's inequalities at the workplace, came to be seen as a test of party loyalty and made it more difficult to bring together a socialist and feminist perspective.[64]

Labour women differed widely in their attitudes towards party loyalty and issues raised by feminism. Many women, in particular members of the Women's Labour League, were active in seeking to improve the lives of working women but stopped short if this meant a real conflict with the mainstream party that might threaten the unity of the movement.[65] Others were more committed feminists and gave priority to redressing sex disabilities. They were women centred and looked at their Socialism "through the prism of gender".[66]

Committed feminists could still differ, however, in their approach to particular issues and political strategies. Enid Stacy, an ILP member and well-known speaker, was opposed to the suggestion made in the 1890s that the socialist movement should seek a close association with the women's movement, which she characterized as a "middle class fad". She was critical not only of the latter's neglect of the needs of working-class women, but also of the liberal, individualist philosophy upon which it was based. She thought that women's qualities, derived from their roles as wives and mothers, should be used for the good of all in the community and not for the achievement of individual rights.[67] Isabella Ford, on the other hand, an active member of both the ILP and the National Union of Women's Suffrage Societies (NUWSS), was convinced that both movements were inextricably linked, since women and workers suffered a common oppression. She thought that they brought different perspectives (the labour movement emphasized economics whereas women were concerned with the broad goal of moral regeneration) both of these were necessary for a socialist transformation of society.[68]

Suffrage and party political loyalty

When the Bristol WLA put forward the view that their aim should not be to keep the Liberal Party in office at all costs, but to keep it true to its principles of peace, retrenchment and reform, including women's suffrage, the group expressed a central dilemma of political activism that was not exclusive to women. It was highlighted increasingly by the activities of the women's movement, however, because of the obvious tensions between gender, class and general political ideology, and because of the growing importance of women's suffrage. The suffrage issue made it more and more difficult for women to balance their various loyalties in the face of the refusal of the mainstream parties to support their cause.

As has already been noted, disagreements over women's suffrage caused problems within women's Liberal groups, as well as between those groups and party leaders, as early as the 1890s. Nonetheless, it was the victory of the Liberal Party in the general election of 1905 which was to pose the greatest difficulty for members of the WLF. They were faced increasingly with a choice between party loyalty and their commitment to women's suffrage as the government repeatedly failed to give support to demands for the vote. Despite frequent clashes over women's suffrage, the executive of the Federation continued to give support to the Liberal Party. In a context in which the suffrage struggle had become central to feminist politics, however, the Federation began to lose members. Many women chose to work for their goal through women's suffrage groups, or drew closer to labour politics. Thus, when in 1918 the franchise ceased to be a source of conflict, it "came too late for the WLF which had been fatally fractured by years of internal strife", and the organization was left with little relevance in the 1920s.[69]

The demand for women's suffrage also polarized opinions and became a test case of political priorities in the labour movement. As the suffrage campaign revived after 1900, with the active participation of Lancashire working women, so its supporters within the labour movement argued that priority should be given to their demand for votes for women on the same terms as men, or a "limited franchise". When this was not forthcoming, in particular from the Labour Party, suffragists faced a dilemma. The leading members of the Women's Social and Political Union (WSPU), a militant suffrage group, severed their links with the Labour Party in 1907 and were actively hostile to Labour Party candidates during elections. Others, including the ILP members Isabella Ford, Selina Cooper and Ethel Snowden, refused to carry out propaganda against the Labour Party, but withdrew from active engagement in labour politics to give a full-time commitment to suffrage work. From their base in the NUWSS they continued to address trade union branches, trades councils and local socialist groups in order to achieve their aim of bringing both movements together.[70]

Some women in the Labour Movement were more wary of the demand for a "limited suffrage". They either refused to prioritize the franchise question, or called for adult suffrage, whereby all men and women over the age of 21 would be able to vote. Leaders of the Women's Labour League, for example, were unwilling to come into conflict with the Labour Party on this issue and refused to adopt a "limited suffrage" as official policy. Instead, individual branches were left free to make their own decisions.[71] Adult-suffragists, however, did not all have the same reasons for their opposition to votes for women on the same terms as men.

Ada Nield Chew, a trade union organizer and ILP member, critized the limited nature of many suffrage bills. She claimed that only well-to-do women would be enfranchised and that this would do nothing to benefit working-class women. When the NUWSS made an alliance with the Labour Party in 1912, however, she was engaged as an organizer for the Union and worked hard for women's suffrage.[72] Her essentially feminist views contrast with those of other adult-suffragists, such as Susan Lawrence and Marion Phillips, who were interested in particular reforms relating to working-class women's employment, housing or social welfare, but were reluctant to prioritize gender above class and labour unity.[73] Conflicts over the suffrage issue were reduced in 1912 when the Labour Party Conference finally passed a resolution which agreed that the Party would not support any further extensions of the franchise unless women were included. As a result of this decision, the NUWSS formed an alliance with the Labour Party and provided financial and practical support for its candidates in by-elections up to the outbreak of war.

Throughout the period up to 1914, women's involvement in political activity raised difficult issues concerning party loyalties, solidarity with their own sex and the basis on which they sought to enter public life. Feminists were more likely than others to emphasize the right of women to take part in the political arena on terms of equality with men, but they shared with non-feminists, and with those who gave priority to other questions, a belief in women's special qualities that stemmed from their maternal and domestic role. Caine contends, therefore, that despite their involvement in equal rights campaigns nineteenth-century feminists were keen to establish and maintain sex differences.[74]

The way in which women argued from a position of difference, however, was complex and varied over time in response to changes in the broader political context. Members of the women's movement before 1914 may have emphasized women's special qualities, but did not seek to confine them to the home. On the contrary, they argued that women should take their values into the public sphere, where they could offer positive benefits to the community. As Alberti suggests, they stressed women's rationality and were concerned to challenge any essentialist construction of difference.[75] This can be seen in campaigns around prostitution, when feminists argued that male sexuality was socially constructed and could be changed. They aimed "to create a society in which the positive qualities associated with each sex could be assumed by the other"; a society in which the "natural equality and freedom of both men and women could be achieved". [76]

Women involved in political life sought not just equal participation with men within an existing political framework, but also a transformation of political practice and values. In so doing they helped to shape twentieth-century concepts of democracy, citizenship and the role of the state. As members of elected public bodies, they infused their work with humanistic values and refused to accept a male version of what local government was all about.[77] Similarly, leading women philanthropists and social reformers developed new ideas about the relationship between the individual, the family and the state which were "forged both in relation to their gendered (and often contested) concepts of duty and citizenship and to their shared conviction that on the commitment to social action depended social progress".[78] Women's claim to take part in political life was based on liberal notions of equal rights and on the belief that women should have a say in laws that affected their lives. However, their sense of moral purpose, their work on behalf of poorer women, whether as philanthropists or in local government, and their development of a set of "female values", all served to modify liberal tenets of equality and individualism.

Before the First World War, therefore, women's engagement in political life was a varied one. The starting point was usually membership of one or more of the many women-only pressure groups which were established from the 1850s onwards. Some, such as the Women's Local Government Society, which aimed to extend women's representation and influence on local elected bodies, had a very specific set of objectives. Others, such as the Women's Labour League and the Women's Liberal Federation, tackled a wider range of issues and sought to influence the policies of the mixed-sex organizations to which they were affiliated. The analysis of the problems facing women, the strategies for change, and the extent to which gender questions were given priority also varied from group to group. Despite their differences, however, they did campaign together on numerous occasions and shared a common belief in the unique contribution that women could play in public life and the need for them to take a more active role as citizens.

By organizing together, women gained confidence, built strong friendships and developed a sense of identity that encouraged them to emphasize women's autonomy and to value their own needs and experiences, even within mixed-sex organizations. Their awareness of belonging to a "common cause", side-by-side with other women, reached its height in the struggle for the vote in the immediate prewar years. One suffrage worker claimed that the focus on the vote:

> compelled us to concentrate all our force, all our hope, all our enthusiasm, upon a single, narrow tenet. It immensely simplified the women's movement. And for those of us who grew up under the stimulus of that intense concentration, the ideals of the woman's movement seemed to be summed up in the three words of our battle cry, "Votes for Women".[79]

Interwar feminism

Once the vote was partially granted in 1918 (to women over 30 years of age who were householders, wives of householders, occupiers of property with an annual rent of £5 or more, or graduates of British universities) it became less easy to sustain a commitment to a common goal. Women who sought to be active in politics had a number of choices before them: whether to work within the existing political parties or to remain active in single-sex pressure groups; whether to concentrate on feminist goals or to engage in a broader range of issues; and, finally, whether their aim should be to seek equality with men or to emphasize women's special needs. These issues were not in themselves new, but they had to be worked out in a different context.

It was far more difficult for feminist politics to flourish in the interwar years. Sacrifices made by soldiers during the First World War a heightened awareness of class and the subsequent problems of unemployment, Fascism and the threat of another war could make sex-based demands seem "petty and uncharitable".[80] In this context, the feminist movement became more fragmented and failed to maintain a sense of identity and solidarity. Alberti and Kent both see the war as playing a crucial part in this process, because "by the time the war ended in 1918 masculinity and femininity had been construed in multiple and contradictory ways".[81] This led to a backlash against women, in which emphasis was placed on traditional femininity and motherhood. Kent suggests that a "psychologised version of separate spheres" resulted from the war, which limited women's scope as much as had the institutional barriers of the nineteenth century.[82]

Women who remained active as feminists and pursued their goals through separate women's organizations soon became divided in the 1920s about their aims and strategies. The declared aim of the National Union of Societies for Equal Citizenship (NUSEC), a new organization based on the former NUWSS, was to achieve equal suffrage and "all such other reforms, economic, legislative and social as are necessary to secure a real equality of liberties, status and opportunities between men and women".[83] This raised the question, however, of what was meant by "equality". Eleanor Rathbone, the president of NUSEC, argued that women could never attain equality unless their special needs as mothers and their economic dependence within the family were addressed. She advocated a range of welfare reforms, including an endowment of motherhood which, she hoped, would transform women's role within both the home and the workplace.[84] Rather than seeking equality with men, these "new feminists", as they became known, sought to use women's experience, which was seen as being different from that of men, to shape society to meet their own interests.

Rathbone's views predominated in NUSEC after 1926. They were not acceptable, however, to those feminists who continued to emphasize equal rights and who were active in the Six Point Group, founded by Lady Rhondda in 1922. The differences between "new" and "equality" feminists should not be exaggerated, however, since they frequently supported the same set of reforms. "New" feminists were in favour of equal opportunities in employment and education, while "equality" feminists such as Vera Brittain argued that "a better understanding of the needs of mothers was central to feminism".[85] There were differences, however, in the "assumptions underlying those reforms". "New" feminists referred to maternity as "the most important of women's occupations", and insisted that women's special needs as mothers should be recognized and valued. For "equality" feminists, this focus on motherhood and childrearing was a retrograde step since it would make it difficult for women to escape from "traditional roles". They preferred to emphasize the "common humanity of men and women" rather than highlight any differences between them.[86]

Recent studies of interwar feminism suggest that debates in the period cannot be categorised in simple terms of equality versus difference. In common with feminists before 1914, women used aspects of both arguments as they worked out their positions over specific reforms. There was also considerable continuity with the ideas of the prewar movement. During the first decade of the twentieth century, feminists were already showing their concern with the needs of mothers, while women's groups associated with the Labour Movement had always been critical of the preoccupation with the suffrage and had put economic and social welfare questions at the centre of their analysis.[87]

Nonetheless, there were differences of emphasis after the war, and a new context that reduced the impact of feminism. "New" feminism did have a radical potential, since it raised fundamental questions about the role of women in the family and made it possible to expand the feminist constituency by drawing in working-class women. This potential was, however, never realized. There was a failure to make analytical connections between the family and other social structures, such as unemployment and education, while the critical edge of "new" feminism was blunted by using women's needs as mothers, rather than their rights as women, on which to base demands for reform:[88] "When 'new feminists' made demands based upon women's traditional special needs and special functions, when they ceased to challenge the dominant discourses on sexuality, their ideology often became confused with anti-feminists".[89] By the 1930s, therefore, feminism was seen as being far less of a threat to traditional structures than it had been before.[90]

The winning of a limited vote in 1918 encouraged many women to pursue their political interests, either in more general reform campaigns or within the mainstream political parties, rather than through feminist groups. A younger generation of women who entered politics for the first time were not necessarily interested in issues relating to their sex. Bruley's study of women activists in the Communist Party, for example, found that they saw women's issues as being peripheral to the major questions of the day. They were reluctant to participate in women's sections, which were identified with the interests of housewives and therefore appeared to be devalued.[91]

Both the Labour Party and the Conservative Party sought to appeal to the new constituency of female voters after 1918. Conservatives were clearly nervous about the implications of female enfranchisement, but set out to attract women voters, which included producing a magazine for women members and supporters entitled *Home and Politics*. Jarvis suggests that the Conservative Party aimed deliberately to provide a strong sense of identity for Conservative women – they were to be "responsible, not feckless; hard-headed without being hardhearted; dedicated to Empire, not paralysed by misplaced guilt".[92] What it did not offer was any serious questioning of the traditional female role and the "comforting message that politics for the Conservative woman would never take precedence over domestic respon-sibilities was consistently stressed".[93] The Conservative Party also percep-tively pointed up the male culture of Labour and trade union politics in its attempts to appeal to the good sense of home-centred working-class women.

In an attempt to attract female voters, the Labour Party emphasized its commitment to welfare reforms, such as the provision of good food and good homes, rather than the ending of sex inequalities. Propaganda leaflets claimed that conditions for women needed to be improved so that they would not hold back their class from achieving political and social change: "The unsatisfactory condition of women in home and industry has degraded and impeded man as much as it has degraded woman herself. At every turn the toy woman, the slave woman, the ignorant woman has hindered the march towards progress and freedom. Man can only march to freedom with a comrade woman marching at his side."[94]

This rather ambivalent view of women's political potential did not appear to deter women from supporting Labour politics. When the new Constitution of 1918 enabled women to become individual members of the Party for the first time, they joined the newly-formed women's sections in large numbers. In 1929 there were 250,000 women in 1,867 sections and between the wars women comprised over half of all individual members.[95] Many prewar suffragists, encouraged by their alliance with the Labour Party and radicalised by the war, joined women who were already active in labour politics in seeking to pursue their feminist aims from within the Labour Party. The Party's class perspective, which had been strengthened by the war, and its domination by the predominantly male trade union movement made it difficult, however, for women to push their own issues to the top of the political agenda.

Women who wished to progress within the Party structure had to demonstrate their loyalty to Labour Party policy as a whole, and this tended to mean an emphasis on class issues. Margaret Bondfield, who was to become the first female Cabinet Minister, conducted her election campaign of 1920 around issues of capital and labour with virtually no mention of women's questions.[96] Ellen Wilkinson, a former member of the NUWSS, was elected as a Labour MP and gained a reputation for her strong support of industrial workers and the unemployed. She was more prepared to take up issues relating to women than was Margaret Bondfield, but did so from a class, as opposed to an overtly feminist, perspective. In 1929, for example, she sought support for a resolution on equal pay, with the argument that it would remove the threat to male wages from cheap labour, rather than that it would combat sex discrimination.[97]

Dorothy Jewson, on the other hand, MP for Norwich in 1923 and an active member of the ILP did keep sex disabilities at the forefront of her agenda. She championed economic support for mothers, the end of the marriage bar in employment and the right to birth control advice, arguing that family allowances would help to emancipate working-class women. In 1929 she signed an open letter with two other ILP members to urge the Labour Women's Conference to give a clear lead to the Labour Party on this issue.[98]

These differences of opinion ran throughout the Labour Party as a whole. The majority of women activists did pursue a whole range of women's issues; they sought improvements in working conditions, calling for equal pay and the right of married women to work for wages, and also campaigned for practical social reforms to improve women's health and their lives within the home. Disagreements surfaced, however, when decisions had to be made about how far to take more controversial questions, such as family allowances and access to birth control advice, when the party leadership, sensitive to the views of a socially conservative, male-dominated trade union movement, opposed them.[99]

For this reason, Alberti suggests that involvement in labour politics helped to strain feminist solidarity in the 1920s, and that there was a boundary between women in the labour movement and those in single-sex groups. She suggests that the solidarity of the suffrage movement came from women working together, and that once women left this environment they found it difficult to retain their confidence.[100] Issues such as protective legislation drove a wedge between labour women and feminists which, argues Harold Smith, was encouraged by a labour leadership hostile to feminism.[101]

Thane, on the other hand, is far more positive about the activities of Labour women and their feminist perspective.[102] She suggests that they encouraged women to use their civil rights and to get elected to local bodies where they could have an impact on policies. They wanted women to have real choices about paid employment, but also to value their home lives and to bring to society and politics all that was good in the characteristics acquired by both men and women. Thane argues that women put welfare on the Labour Party's agenda, brought more women into public life, and helped to improve local levels of health care. Nonetheless, she concedes that their gains were minimal compared to their ambitions, and that in any clash with male leaders they were likely to lose. Faced with the choice between the needs of their sex and class unity, Labour women tended to draw back from all out confrontation with the Party leadership.

The great variety of perspectives held by Labour women make it difficult to generalize about the nature of their feminism or their impact on policies. Even the most committed feminists disagreed, for example, about whether women should organize separately within mixed-sex groups. Dorothy Jewson supported the formation of a Women's Advisory Committee within the ILP, and edited its *Monthly Bulletin*. She thought this would help local groups to keep in touch and would enable ILP women to have a greater impact at the Labour Women's Conference.[103] Hannah Mitchell, on the other hand, disliked women's sections in the Labour Party and refused to be a member of "a permanent social committee, or official cake maker to the Labour Party".[104] Overall, it can be said that women did make many specific gains for their sex within the framework of the Labour Party, but class issues remained far more central than questions of women's emancipation, and hampered collaboration with single-sex feminist groups.

Joint campaigns did take place, however, over issues such as access to birth control information, which achieved some success by the early 1930s. Nonetheless, it was difficult for feminists to make gains in a period of economic difficulty when the Conservative Party predominated in politics, and class issues were more to the fore. Feminists themselves also recognized that gender inequalities were supported by "formidable social and economic forces" and it became clear that "the search for equality would not respond to a short, sharp campaign, but would need many more years of persistent work".[105]

Conclusion

Throughout the period under review women from all social classes played an increasingly active role in politics. For some, political or philanthropic work was not directed explicitly towards changing women's own social position. For others, political activity was based on a set of feminist beliefs which stressed the important contribution that women could make to public affairs, and which sought to challenge their inequalities and oppression. Working in separate women's organizations, they gained confidence, the pleasure of working with like-minded women, and a strong base from which to pursue specific campaigns. For many women, however, this was not enough and they sought change through broader, mixed-sex political parties. This brought tensions about conflicting political loyalties, and the danger that women's own needs could be lost.

When women did seek to make an impact in the political world they used arguments relating to their moral and caring qualities. In the nineteenth century, the emphasis was on women achieving their full humanity so that they could work alongside men rather than in antagonism to them. Their concern was with women's duty to preserve a moral order and create a social harmony, which was different from the preoccupations of the twentieth century. They used women's differences as a way to empower women in all areas of public life, and argued that their domestic experience should be a springboard to an interest in questions outside the home. After the First World War, although feminists still sought legislation to achieve equal rights for women, greater attention was paid to the health and welfare of working-class mothers within the home.

In the prewar years, single issue campaigns, such as the vote, transformed the lives of many who took part and engendered optimism that there would be steady progress towards improvement. The war, however, "dislocated women's lives and exaggerated the discontinuities between different generations".[106] Elizabeth Robins, a suffragist, claimed that before the war she had "seen the woman question clearly"; but after the war she found "that clearness breathed upon, till one lost sight for a while of what one had seen and learned".[107] In every period, feminists have to negotiate with and confront the preoccupations of the society in which they live and which affects their theories, their practical policies and their political strategies.[108] They have always fought, however, against the view that "women are mere appendages to men" and "that they own no duty to themselves as human beings".[109] They have sought, in particular, to claim a role for women in

239

political life and to insist that, far from being restricted to the domestic sphere, the whole world should be their concern.

Notes

1. The term "feminist" is used throughout to describe individuals or groups who recognized and challenged women's inequality and oppression explicitly.
2. M. Savage & A. Miles, *The re-making of the British working class 1840-1940* (London: Routledge, 1994), p. 19.
3. H. Taylor, "Enfranchisement of women", *Westminster Review* **55**, 1851, quoted in P. Hollis, *Women in public: the women's movement, 1850-1900* (London: Allen & Unwin, 1979), p. 293.
4. G. Gissing, *The odd women* (1893), quoted in A. Vickery, "Golden age to separate spheres? A review of the categories and chronology of English women's history", *The Historical Journal* **36**, pp. 383-414, 1993, esp. p. 401.
5. See, for example, J. Rendall, *The origins of modern feminism: women in Britain, France and the United States, 1780-1860* (London: Macmillan, 1985); C. Bolt, *The women's movements in the United States and Britain from the 1790s to the 1920s* (Hemel Hempstead: Harvester Wheatsheaf, 1993); C. Midgley, *Women against slavery: the British campaigns, 1780-1870* (London: Routledge, 1992).
6. D. Thompson, "Women, work and politics in nineteenth-century England: the problem of authority", in *Equal or different. Women's politics, 1800-1914*, J. Rendall (ed.) (Oxford: Basil Blackwell, 1987), pp. 57-81; M. I. Thomis & J. Grimmett, *Women in protest, 1800-1850* (London: Croom Helm, 1982); D. Thompson, "Women and nineteenth-century radical politics: a lost dimension", in *The rights and wrongs of women*, J. Mitchell & A. Oakley (eds) (Harmondsworth: Penguin, 1976), pp. 112-38; B. Taylor, *Eve and the new Jerusalem: Socialism and feminism in the nineteenth century* (London: Virago, 1983).
7. J. Schwarzkopf, *Women in the Chartist movement* (London: Macmillan, 1991), p. 1. See also D. Thompson, *The Chartists* (New York: Pantheon, 1984); D. Jones, "Women and Chartism", *History* **68**, pp. 1-21, 1983.
8. Schwartzkopf, *Women in the Chartist movement*.
9. Thompson, "Women, work and politics", p. 63.
10. Taylor, *Eve and the new Jerusalem*; Thompson, "Women, work and politics", p. 65.
11. Taylor, *Eve and the new Jerusalem*, pp. 273-5.
12. J. Rendall, "'A moral engine'? Feminism, liberalism and the *English Woman's Journal*", in *Equal or different*, Rendall, (ed.) pp. 112-38; R. Strachey, *The cause: a short history of the women's movement in Great Britain* (London: Virago, 1978 first published 1928); C. A. Lacey (ed.), *Barbara Leigh Smith Bodichon and the Langham Place Group* (London: Routledge & Kegan Paul, 1987).
13. Vickery, "Golden age to separate spheres?", p. 401. For a discussion of the varied concerns of the women's movement, see B. Caine, "Feminism, suffrage and the nineteenth-century English women's movement", *Women's Studies International Forum* **5**, pp. 537-50, 1982; S. K. Kent, *Sex and suffrage in Britain, 1860-1914* (Princeton: New Jersey: Princeton University Press, 1987).
14. J. Walkowitz, *Prostitution and Victorian society: women, class and the state* (Cambridge: Cambridge University Press, 1980); L. Holcombe, *Wives and property: reform of the Married Women's Property Law in nineteenth-century England*

(Toronto: University of Toronto Press, 1983); M. L. Shanley, *Feminism, marriage and the law in Victorian England*, 1850-1895 (Princeton, New Jersey: Princeton University Press, 1989).

15. P. Levine, *Feminist lives in Victorian England* (Oxford: Basil Blackwell, 1990); O. Banks, *Becoming a feminist: the social origins of "first wave" feminism* (Brighton: Harvester Wheatsheaf, 1986); Walkowitz, *Prostitution and Victorian society*, Ch. 6. For the importance of personal experience in explaining why women took up the women's cause, see Caine, *Victorian feminists*.

16. C. Midgley, "Anti-slavery and feminism in nineteenth-century Britain", *Gender and History* **5** (3), pp. 343-62, 1993.

17. R. & L. Billington, "'A burning zeal for righteousness': women in the British Anti-Slavery movement, 1820-1860, *Equal or different*, Rendall (ed.), pp. 82-111.

18. C. Midgley, *Women against slavery*, p. 174.

19. *Ibid.*, pp. 175-6.

20. For example, see F. Prochaska, *Women and philanthropy in nineteenth-century England* (Oxford: Clarendon Press, 1980); M. Vicinus, *Independent women: work and community for single women* (London: Virago, 1981); J. Parker, *Women and welfare: ten Victorian women in public social service* (London: Macmillan, 1989).

21. Midgley, *Women against slavery*, pp. 154-5. For the importance of moral reform, see B. Harrison, "State intervention and moral reform", in *Pressure from without*, P. Hollis (ed.) (London: Edward Arnold, 1974), pp. 289-322.

22. Parker, "Women and welfare"; H. W. Schupf, "Single women and social reform in mid-nineteenth-century England: the case of Mary Carpenter", *Victorian Studies* **17**, pp. 301-17, 1974; J. Manton, *Mary Carpenter and the children of the streets* (London: Heinemann, 1976); N. Boyd, *Three Victorian women who changed their world: Josephine Butler, Octavia Hill and Florence Nightingale* (Oxford: Oxford University Press, 1962); R. J. W. Selleck, "Mary Carpenter: a confident and contradictory reformer", *History of Education* **14** (2), pp. 101-16, 1985.

23. P. Hollis, "Women in council: separate spheres, public space", in *Equal or different*, Rendall (ed.), pp. 192-213, esp. p. 210. See also A. Summers, "A home from home - women's philanthropic work in the nineteenth century", in *Fit work for women*, S. Burman (ed.) (London: Croom Helm, 1979), pp. 33-63; P. Hollis, *Ladies elect: women in English local government*, 1865-1914 (Oxford: Clarendon Press, 1987).

24. J. E. Carpenter, *The life and work of Mary Carpenter* (London: Macmillan, 1879); Parker, *Women and welfare*.

25. F. P. Cobbe, *The life of Frances Power Cobbe*, 1894, p. 209, quoted in B. Caine, *Victorian feminists* (Oxford: Oxford University Press, 1992), p. 106.

26. H. Blackburn, *Women's Suffrage* (London: Williams & Norgate, 1902), pp. 110, 112.

27. J. Lewis, *Women and social action in Victorian and Edwardian England* (Aldershot: Edward Elgar, 1991), p. 13. The ideas for this paragraph are based on J. Lewis, "Gender, the family and women's agency in the building of 'welfare states': the British case", *Social History* **19** (1), pp. 37-55, 1994.

28. Walkowitz, "Prostitution and Victorian society".

29. S. Lewenhak, *Women and trade unions* (London: Ernest Benn, 1977); P. Levine, *Victorian feminism, 1850-1900* (London: Hutchinson, 1987).

30. M. Priestman, *The industrial position of women* (1874); *Annual report of the Ladies National Association* (1877); E. Malos, "Bristol women in action, 1839-1919", in *Bristol's other history*, I. Bild (ed.) (Bristol: Bristol Broadsides, 1983), p. 115; S. J. Tanner, *How the women's suffrage movement began in Bristol fifty years ago* (Bristol: Carlyle Press, 1918).

31. R. Feurer, "The meaning of 'sisterhood': the British women's movement and protective labour legislation, 1870-1900", *Victorian Studies* **31**, 1988; S. Boston, *Women workers and the trade unions* (London: Davis-Poynter, 1980); D. Rubinstein, *Before the suffragettes: women's emancipation in the 1890s* (Brighton: Harvester, 1986); J. Hannam, *Isabella Ford, 1855-1924* (Oxford: Basil Blackwell, 1989).

32. J. Lewis, *Women in England, 1870-1950* (Brighton: Harvester, 1984), p. 81; Caine, *Victorian feminists*, p. ix.

33. Midgley, "Anti-slavery and feminism", p. 357.

34. Caine, *Victorian feminists*, p. 7.

35. *Ibid.*, Ch. 1. For a discussion of the ideological tensions within suffragism, see S. S. Holton, *Feminism and democracy: women's suffrage and reform politics in Britain, 1900-1918* (Cambridge: Cambridge University Press, 1986).

36. A. Burton, "The feminist quest for identity: British Imperial suffragism and 'global sisterhood', 1900-15", *Journal of Women's History* **3** (2), p. 69, 1991, quoted in J. DeVries, "Gendering patriotism: Emmeline and Christabel Pankhurst and World War One", in *This working day world: women's lives and culture(s) in Britain, 1914-1945*, S. Oldfield (ed.) (London: Taylor & Francis, 1994), p. 76.

37. Hollis, *Ladies elect*.

38. Hollis, "Women in council", p. 210; P. Thane, "Labour and local politics: radicalism, democracy and social reform, 1880-1914", in *Currents of Radicalism*, E. Biagini & A. Reid (eds) (Cambridge: Cambridge University Press, 1991), pp. 244-70.

39. Hollis, "Women in council", p. 197.

40. *Ibid.*; Lewis, "Gender, the family and women's agency", p. 43.

41. L. Walker, "Party political women: a comparative study of Liberal women and the Primrose League, 1890-1914", in *Equal or different*, Rendall (ed.), pp. 165-91.

42. Rendall, "'A moral engine'?", p. 136.

43. *Ibid.*, p. 138.

44. K. Hunt, "Equivocal feminists: the Social Democractic Federation and the woman question, 1884-1911", unpublished Ph.D. thesis, Manchester University (1988).

45. D. Jarvis," Mrs Maggs and Betty. The Conservative appeal to women voters in the 1920s", *Twentieth-Century British History* **5** (2), pp. 129-52, 1994, esp. p. 135.

46. *Ibid.*, pp. 135-6.

47. Walker, "Party political women", p. 166.

48. *Ibid.*, p. 191. In 1912 there were nearly half a million Primrose Dames and 150,000 women in the two Liberal Party auxiliaries: C. Hirshfield, "Fractured faith: Liberal Party women and the suffrage issue in Britain, 1892-1914", *Gender and History* **2** (2), pp. 173-97, 1990, esp. p. 173.

49. Hirshfield, "Fractured faith", pp. 173-4.

50. *Ibid.*, p. 176.

51. Walker, "Party political women", p. 178.

52. Hunt, "Equivocal feminists"; J. Hannam, "Women and the ILP", in *The centennial history of the Independent Labour Party*, D. James et al., (eds) (Halifax: Ryburn, 1992), pp. 205-28.

53. J. Gaffin & D. Thoms, *Caring and sharing: the centenary history of the Co-operative Women's Guild* (Manchester: Co-operative Union, 1983); C. Rowan, "Mothers vote Labour!' The state, the labour movement and working-class mothers, 1900-1918", in *Feminism, culture and politics*, R. Brunt & C. Rowan (eds) (London: Lawrence & Wishart, 1982), pp. 59-84.

54. Boston, *Women workers and the trade unions*.

55. C. Rowan, "Women in the Labour Party, 1906-1920", *Feminist Review* **12**, 1982, pp. 74-91; C. Collette, *For Labour and for women: the Women's Labour League, 1906-1918* (Manchester: Manchester University Press, 1989).

56. Harrison, "State intervention and moral reform"; O. Banks, *Faces of feminism* (Oxford: Martin Robertson, 1980).

57. Levine, *Feminist Lives*, pp. 38-9.

58. *Ibid.*, Ch. 2.

59. Bristol Women's Liberal Association, *Annual report* (1892).

60. Bristol Women's Liveral Association, *Annual Report* (1891).

61. Walker, "Party political women"; Hirshfield, "Fractured faith".

62. K. Hunt, "Equivocal feminists"; see also M. J. Boxer & J. H. Quataert (eds) *Socialist women: European socialist feminism in the nineteenth and twentieth centuries* (New York: Elsevier, 1978).

63. Hannam, "Women and the ILP"; E. Gordon, *Women and the Labour Movement in Scotland, 1850-1914* (Oxford: Clarendon Press, 1991).

64. A. Phillips, *Divided loyalties: dilemmas of sex and class* (London: Virago, 1987); Rowan, "Women and the Labour Party"; J. Liddington & J. Norris, *One hand tied behind us: the rise of the women's suffrage movement* (London: Virago, 1978).

65. Rowan, "Women and the Labour Party"; Collette, *For Labour and for women*.

66. Hunt, "Equivocal feminists".

67. *Justice*, (13 October 1894); E. Stacy, "A century of women's rights", in *Forecasts of the coming century*, E. Carpenter (ed.) (Manchester: The Labour Press, 1897).

68. I. O. Ford, *Women and Socialism* (London: Independent Labour Party, 1906).

69. Hirshfield, "Fractured faith", p. 188.

70. Holton, *Feminism and democracy*; J. Liddington, *The life and times of a respectable rebel: Selina Cooper, 1864-1946* (London: Virago, 1984); Hannam, *Isabella Ford*.

71. Rowan, "Women and the Labour Party"; Collette, *For Labour and for women*.

72. D. N. Chew, *Ada Nield Chew: the life and writings of a working woman* (London: Virago, 1982).

73. Hollis, "Women in council", p. 211. For a more positive view of Marion Phillips" commitment to feminism, see Collette, *For Labour and for women*.

74. Caine, *Victorian feminists*, p. 16.

75. J. Alberti, "British feminists and anti-Fascism in the 1930s", in *This working-day world*, Oldfield (ed.), pp. 111-22, esp. p. 114.

76. S. K. Kent, *Making peace: the reconstruction of gender in interwar Britain* (Princeton, New Jersey: Princeton University Press, 1993), p. 5.

77. Hollis, "Women in council", p. 209. See also P. Levine, "Love, friendship and feminism in later nineteenth-century England", *Women's Studies International Forum* **13** (1/2), pp. 63-78, 1990.

78. Lewis, *Women and social action*, p. 1; Levine, *Victorian feminism*.

79. *The Woman's Leader*, 12 March 1920, quoted in J. Alberti, *Beyond suffrage: feminists in war and peace, 1914-28* (London: Macmillan, 1989), p. 2.

80. Kent, *Making peace*, p. 114. For general accounts of feminism between the wars, see Alberti, *Beyond suffrage*; M. Pugh, *Women and the women's movement in Britain, 1914-1959* (London: Macmillan, 1992); O. Banks, *The politics of British feminism, 1918-1970* (Aldershot: Edward Elgar, 1993).

81. Kent, *Making peace*, p. 115.

82. *Ibid.*; Alberti, *Beyond suffrage*.

83. Kent, *Making peace*, p. 116.

84. H. Smith, "Introduction", in *British feminism in the twentieth century*, H. Smith (ed.) (Aldershot: Edward Elgar, 1990), pp. 1–4; H. Land, "Eleanor Rathbone and the economy of the family", in *British feminism*, Smith (ed.), pp. 104–23.

85. D. Gorham, "Have we really rounded Seraglio Point?: Vera Brittain and inter-war feminism, in *British feminism*, Smith (ed.), pp. 84–103, esp. p. 85.

86. H. Smith, "British feminism in the 1920s", in *British feminism*, Smith (ed.), pp. 47–65.

87. For a discussion of the complex relationship between ideas of equality and difference, see J. W. Scott, "Deconstructing equality-versus-difference: or, the uses of poststructuralist theory for feminism", *Feminist Studies* **14** (1), pp. 33–50, 1988; Alberti, *Beyond suffrage*; Smith (ed.) *British feminism*. In *Making peace*, Kent, however, argues that new feminists were fundamentally different from prewar feminists. For the importance of the ideology of motherhood after 1900, see A. Davin, "Imperialism and motherhood", *History Workshop Journal* **5**, pp. 9–65, 1978.

88. J. Lewis, "Feminism and welfare", in *What is feminism?*, J. Mitchell & A. Oakley (eds) (Oxford: Basil Blackwell, 1986), pp. 88, 94 quoted in Kent, *Making peace*, p. 4.

89. Kent, *Making peace*, p. 118.

90. Smith, "British feminism", p. 47.

91. S. Bruley, *Leninism, Stalinism and the women's movement in Britain, 1920–1939* (New York: Garland, 1986).

92. Jarvis, "Mrs Maggs and Betty", p. 151.

93. *Ibid.*, p. 137.

94. Minnie Pallister, *Socialism for women* (London: Independent Labour Party, 1925), p. 5. See also Labour Party leaflets of the 1920s which appealed to women voters, Francis Johnson Collection, London School of Economics.

95. P. M. Graves, *Labour women: women in British working class politics, 1918–1939* (Cambridge: Cambridge University Press, 1994), p. 231. P. Thane, "Visions of gender in the making of the British welfare state: the case of women in the British Labour Party and social policy, 1906–1945", in *Maternity and gender politics: women and the rise of the European welfare states, 1880–1950*, G. Bock & P. Thane (eds) (London: Routledge, 1991), pp. 93–118, esp. p. 2.

96. Pugh, *Women and the women's movement*, p. 54.

97. Smith, "British feminism", p. 47.

98. *New Leader* (9 April 1929).

99. Jarvis, "Mrs Maggs and Betty".

100. Alberti, *Beyond suffrage*, p. 219.

101. H. Smith, "Sex vs class: British feminists and the labour movement, 1919–29", *Historian* **47**, pp. 19–37, 1984.

102. Thane, "Visions of gender"; P. Thane, "Women of the British Labour Party and feminism, 1906–45", in *British feminism*, Smith (ed.), pp. 125–43; P. Thane, "Women in the British Labour Party and the construction of state welfare, 1906–1939", in *Mothers of a new world: maternalist politics and the origins of the welfare states*, S. Koven & S. Michel (eds) (London: Routledge, 1993), pp. 343–77.

103. *New Leader* (21 June 1929); National Administrative Council of the Independent Labour Party, *Annual report* (1928).

104. H. Mitchell, *The hard way up: the autobiography of Hannah Mitchell, suffragette and rebel* (London: Virago, 1977), p. 189.

105. Alberti, *Beyond suffrage*, pp. 218–9.

106. *Ibid.*, p. 222.

107. E. Robins, *Both sides of the curtain* (London: Heinemann, 1940), p. 170, quoted in Alberti, *Beyond suffrage*, pp. 222–3.

108. Caine, *Victorian feminists*, p. 117.
109. I. O. Ford, "Woman as she was and is", *Labour Leader* **13** (May, 1904).

Suggestions for further reading

Useful overviews that cover some of the themes in the chapter are P. Levine, *Victorian feminism* (London: Hutchinson, 1987); O. Banks, *Faces of feminism* (Oxford: Martin Robertson, 1980); J. Lewis, *Women in England, 1870-1950* (Brighton: Harvester, 1986); and M. Pugh, *Women and the women's movement in Britain, 1914-1959* (London: Macmillan, 1992). The varied contributions made by women to nineteenth-century politics are covered in J. Rendall (ed.), *Equal or different. Women's politics, 1800-1914* (Oxford: Blackwell, 1987). P. Hollis, *Ladies elect: women in English local government, 1865-1914* (Oxford: Clarendon Press, 1987) is an invaluable guide to women's involvement in local politics. The complex ideas and political strategies of 19th century feminists are explored in B. Caine, *Victorian feminists* (Oxford: Oxford University Press, 1992), while S. S. Holton, *Feminism and democracy: women's suffrage and reform politics in Britain, 1900-1918* (Cambridge: Cambridge University Press, 1986) discusses the ideological tensions within suffragism and the relationship between the suffrage movement and the mainstream political parties. For an introduction to the issues and debates concerning interwar feminism, see J. Alberti, *Beyond suffrage: feminists in war and peace, 1914-1928* (London: Macmillan, 1989); S. K. Kent, *Making peace: the reconstruction of gender in interwar Britain* (Princeton, New Jersey: Princeton University Press, 1993); and H. Smith (ed.) *British feminism in the twentieth century* (Aldershot: Edward Elgar, 1990).

To understand the varied and complex ideas of nineteenth- and early-twentieth-century feminists it is important to read some of their writings and speeches. A selection of these can be found in collections of documents, e.g. P. Hollis, *Women in public, 1850-1900. Documents of the Victorian women's movement* (London: Allen & Unwin, 1979); C. A. Lacey (ed.), *Barbara Leigh Smith Bodichon and the Langham Place Group* (London: Routledge & Kegan Paul, 1987); and J. Lewis (ed.) *Before the vote was won: arguments for and against women's suffrage, 1864-1896* (London: Routledge & Kegan Paul, 1987). For the views of socialist feminists, see I. O. Ford, *Women and Socialism* (London: ILP, 1906); and Mrs. Wolstenholome Elmy, *Woman - the communist* (London: ILP, 1904).

Chapter Ten

ۏ

Ethnicity, "race" and empire[1]

Clare Midgley

What is "British" women's history?

Questions of ethnicity, "race" and empire in British women's history have
been subject to twofold neglect. In the first place, historians of British
women, preoccupied with the relationship between gender and class, have
paid little attention to questions of ethnicity and "race". Studies of "British
women" are often about English women to the exclusion of Scottish and
Welsh women,[2] and about white Protestant women to the exclusion of
women of Irish, Jewish, African or Asian descent. Secondly, general studies of
the politics of immigration, "race" and empire in Britain rarely address
gender issues.[3] Recently, however, scholars and activists have begun to
explore questions of ethnicity, "race" and empire in British women's history.
The first sections of this chapter draw upon this research to consider in
succession the histories of Jewish women, who originally came to Britain as
foreign immigrants; of Irish women, who migrated to Britain from within the
United Kingdom; and of black and Indian women, the majority of whom
were Britain's imperial subjects. The final section will explore white British
women's (particularly English women's) relationship to imperialism and to
racial politics.[4] The chapter as a whole aims to highlight the need to broaden
both the subject matter and the analytical base of British women's history.[5]

Before proceeding, a brief discussion of terminology is necessary. This is a
highly contested issue, with different terms associated with opposing political
perspectives. Ethnicity is here defined, following Anthias and Yuval-Davis, as
the sense of collectivity or community formed "around the myth of common
origin (whether biological, cultural or historical)".[6] Thus the white English
are as much an ethnic group as people from so-called ethnic minorities,

though they are rarely explicitly studied as such.[7] "Race" is identified when the supposed hereditary biological similarities of a population group are stressed. In Britain by the mid-nineteenth century all the groups selected for study in this chapter – Jewish, Irish, peoples of African and Asian descent, and white English – were seen in racial terms, that is as sharing "certain fundamental, biologically heritable, moral and intellectual characteristics with each other that they did not share with members of any other race".[8] This was not a value-free categorization but was associated with scientific racism: all "other" races were placed at points in a hierarchy below the white Anglo-Saxon English, who were seen as constituting the essence of the British nation and of being superior to both the "subject races" of the Empire and to Celts and Jews.[9] Placing the term "race" in inverted commas in this chapter is intended to emphasise that it is a changing social construct, rather than a fact of nature.

Jewish women in Britain

The lives and experiences of Jewish, Irish, black and Indian women in Britain need to be placed not only within the framework of women's history, but also in the context of the varied histories of immigration and settlement by different ethnic groups. In the case of Jewish women, the history of Jews in Britain can be traced back to the medieval period, but anti-Semitism led to the expulsion of the Jewish community in 1290, and Jews were not officially readmitted until 1656. The mid-seventeenth century onwards saw small-scale settlement by Sephardi Jews (whose ancestors had earlier been expelled from Spain and Portugal), and they were joined in the mid-nineteenth century by Ashkenazi Jews, from German and East European backgrounds. By 1880 some 50–60,000 Jews lived in England, including a group of wealthy and socially prominent Anglo-Jewish families. Numbers grew dramatically in the 1881–1905 period, when over a hundred thousand Ashkenazi immigrants, nearly half of whom were female, arrived from Eastern Europe as refugees from poverty and persecution in the Russian and Austro-Hungarian Empires. This influx, however, was followed by a new wave of anti-Semitism, and the Aliens Act of 1905 marked the first attempt by government to restrict immigration into Britain. Adolf Hitler's ascent to power in Germany in 1933 resulted in new pressure from Jews wishing to escape persecution, and some 50–75,000 refugees, over half of them female, managed to enter Britain. Following the outbreak of war, however, many refugees were sacked by employers or sent to internment camps as potential "enemy aliens".[10]

Women, while constituting around half of this developing Jewish community in Britain, have not been the subject of proportionate attention from historians. As Marks has pointed out, Jewish communal history has tended to present an idealized view of the "woman of worth", the hardworking and virtuous housewife and devoted mother, while ignoring the lives of single women and playing down women's economic contributions and organized activism.[11] Nineteenth-century Gentile stereotypes of the over-protective Jewish mother, the Jewish "princess", the exotic "Oriental" Sephardic Jewess, and the depraved immigrant prostitute have acted to further obscure the actual lives of ordinary Jewish women in Britain.[12] Only since the 1980s have oral history projects and archival research facilitated the creation of a clearer picture of Jewish women's lives.[13]

One topic of research has been the way in which immigration affected gender roles. Ricki Burman has studied a sample of over a hundred of the some 15,000 Ashkenazi immigrants from Eastern Europe who settled in Manchester in the 1881–1905 period, using oral history sources to reconstruct married women's contributions to the household economy and to religious life.[14] Male breadwinning activities, she argues, need to be placed "within the context of the family economy", to which women also made vital contributions, if we are to understand strategies for family survival and advancement.[15] Burman points out that around two-thirds of the immigrant women in her sample continued to engage in paid work after the birth of their children, and that around a third of them ran shops and other small businesses independently of their husbands. In this they followed the earlier pattern of their lives in Eastern Europe, where "proper" gender roles were marked not by the dominant British ideal of a division between the male public sphere of paid work and the female private sphere of the home, but rather by the divide between a spiritual male sphere of religious scholarship and a material female sphere of domestic life and economic activity. As the daughter of one Manchester immigrant couple stated: "My father was really, really no businessman to speak of at all . . . But mother was a sharp businesswoman".[16]

Men, however, as impoverished immigrants, were forced to shift their focus from religious study to paid labour. As had earlier happened with established Anglo-Jewry, economic success rather than religious scholarship became the key mark of status, and for the children of immigrants the withdrawal of wives from paid work marked the fulfilment of both middle-class aspiration and anglicanization. Prominent Anglo-Jewish author, Grace Aguilar, had promoted the ideal of the spiritual and dutiful Jewish wife and mother in her writing in the 1840s,[17] and by the 1930s Manchester oral history sources indicate that "It was a very rare thing for a Jewish girl to get married and go out to work."[18] Marks has identified a similar trend in the East End of London, where by the 1900s Jewish women were "far less likely to be working outside the home" than were English women in the same neighbourhood.[19]

Burman points out that as men's attention shifted from religious to economic affairs, women's roles in domestic religious practices were transformed "from a situation where they were viewed as relatively peripheral to the fundamental concerns of Jewish religion, to one where they emerged as core reference-points in the form and maintenance of Jewish identity".[20] In the "shtetl" culture of Eastern Europe, the foci of religious practice were the synagogue and study-house, both largely male preserves. In the British setting, these male preserves became less dominant in religious life, with many men forced to work on the Sabbath. Women, traditionally responsible for the observance of Jewish dietary laws and preparation for Sabbaths and festivals, became key definers of the Jewish identity of the household. Low levels of participation in male-led public worship contrasted with high levels of female-centred home observance, which was sustained by its deep roots in domestic routine. Mothers thus socialized their children into Jewish culture and, as Burman states, "associated with this pattern of strong domestic observance was a low rate of intermarriage, and a high degree of commitment among women to the transmission and preservation of Judaism."[21]

Jewish women's role as mothers has also been researched from the perspective of maternal and infant welfare. Marks has suggested that the unusually low infant mortality rate among the Jewish poor in late-nineteenth- and early-twentieth-century London can be attributed partly to the healthcare offered to mothers by Jewish welfare agencies in the East End.[22] The positive attitudes towards these "model mothers" contrasted with the special problems faced by unmarried Jewish mothers who, in common with Irish unmarried mothers, faced ostracism from their own ethnic community and the problem of coping alone in an unfamiliar environment. Their unwillingness to enter Protestant-run homes for unmarried mothers led both Jewish and Catholic community leaders to set up their own institutions.[23] As Marks points out, the care of both married and unmarried mothers in the East End in the late-nineteenth and early-twentieth centuries thus reflected the importance of religion and ethnicity in the provision of welfare.

The Jewish maternal welfare organizations were part of a network of organizations set up by middle-class Anglo-Jews to aid late-nineteenth-century immigrants. Fearful that the influx of these poor Yiddish-speaking immigrants would revive anti-Semitism, they attempted to promote assimilation and respectability as well as offering practical assistance. By the 1900s, revelations about the unfitness of Boer War recruits were inflaming imperialist anxieties about the physical deterioration of the British race, a degeneration blamed by some on contamination of the English stock by Jewish and Irish immmigrants. In this context, Jewish philanthropists were keen to demonstrate that Jewish women were good mothers and to keep prostitution in check, since it was viewed by the authorities as undermining both family and empire, and blamed by some on Jewish white slave traders.[24]

Jewish women's organized involvement in philanthropy, which can be traced back to around 1840, grew in scale from the 1880s onwards in response to the concerns outlined above. In 1885, for example, the Jewish Association for the Protection of Girls and Women (JAPGW), was set up in London in response to W. T. Stead's sensational exposés of child prostitution and the "white slave trade". It sought to rescue "fallen" Jewish women, whom it saw as the victims of the disruptions to community life caused by migration.[25] By 1902, the level of women's voluntary work was such that the Union of Jewish Women was created to act as a national umbrella organization for Jewish women's groups. Ambitiously, it aimed to be an "all-embracing sisterhood" forming a "bond between Jewish women of all degrees",[26] and to promote the social, moral and spiritual welfare of all Jewish women and foster co-operation among Jewish women workers. In practice, however, it was dominated by the Anglo-Jewish elite, and concentrated on providing educational and vocational training for middle-class women. It had strong international links and aspired to help the "scattered Jewish race" worldwide, while carefully stressing its loyalty to the British Empire in order to avoid attracting anti-Semitic accusations that it was part of an international Jewish conspiracy.[27]

Many middle-class Anglo-Jewish women also became involved in secular women's organizations in the late-nineteenth century, including those concerned with trade unionism. The founder of the JAPGW, Constance Rothchild Battersea, was active in the International Council of Women (ICW), and in 1901 she was elected president of the National Union of Women Workers (NUWW). Louisa, Lady Goldsmid joined the Women's Protective and Provident League (later the Women's Trade Union League) and persuaded the Jewish Board of Guardians to co-operate with its attempts to organize Jewish women garment workers, who were excluded by both English and Jewish tailors' unions and frequently worked in appalling conditions as "sweated" outworkers. Emily Routledge and May Abraham later became officials in the organizations, and in 1893 Abraham became one of England's first two female factory and workshop inspectors.[28]

Not all activists were well-to-do philanthropists and reformers. Millie Sabel and "Red" Rose Robins belonged to the circle around German anarchist Rudolf Rocker's Brenner Street Club, which fomented strikes among East End Jewish workers in the 1898–1914 period. Poor immigrant housewives joined in neighbourhood protests. In 1904, when the Jewish Bakers' Union went out on strike, Jewish women bought only bread approved by the union, forcing concession to union demands. In 1915, Jewish women living in the Gorbals took part in the Glasgow Rent Strike. Jewish women workers also joined in sporadic industrial action, including the 1886 strike of Leeds Jewish tailors, and the 1930s strikes by East-End trouser-makers under the leadership of Sarah Wesker.[29]

Jewish women also became involved in the feminist movement, and in the 1890–1914 period campaigned both for equality within the Jewish community and for national women's suffrage. Kuzmack's research has revealed their important contributions in both arenas, in the face of multiple obstacles "emanating from traditional Jewish attitudes toward women, the Christian bias of nineteenth-century feminists, anti-immigrant sentiment, and the anti-feminism that pervaded Jewish and secular culture."[30] Battersea's prominence in the ICW and NUWW linked English and Jewish feminism and, as Kusmack points out, "signalled the first crack in the monolithic Christian facade of English and international feminism".[31] Jewish women's input into feminism in Britain was further promoted by social worker Lily Montagu, who became the organizing force behind the development of Liberal Judaism in the 1900s. Within this progressive movement, Montagu promoted an end to the sexual double standard, and equal rights for women in religious marriage and divorce, and in religious life. Described as "the first official female religious leader in an organized Jewish movement",[32] in 1918 Montagu delivered the first sermon preached by a woman in any Anglo-Jewish synagogue. Preaching the connection between suffrage and feminism, Montague also became the spiritual guide to the Jewish League for Woman Suffrage.[33]

The League, founded in 1912, campaigned for both national and Jewish suffrage. As Kuzmack points out, for Jewish women, suffrage "became a vital symbol of their social acceptance as Englishwomen as well as of their political, religious and communal emancipation".[34] The League argued for the national vote for women, on the secular ground that it was a means of securing social reforms, on the religious basis of prophetic calls for justice, and on communal grounds with reference to the history of Anglo-Jewish men's suffrage campaign. Led by prominent members of the Anglo-Jewish "Cousinhood", it developed close links with secular women's suffrage societies at both national and international levels. The League also campaigned for women's rights within the Jewish community, calling for voting rights for female synagogue seatholders. It initiated a movement which led by the late 1920s to Anglo-Jewish women gaining the right to participate fully in the running of many synagogues and communal institutions. In 1930, another milestone in Jewish women's history was achieved: the election of Hannah Cohen as the first woman president of the Jewish Board of Guardians, a position from which she dominated communal welfare policy until the Second World War.

Women also payed an active part in the Zionist movement: in 1918, Rebecca Sieff founded the Federation of Women Zionists, to promote the creation of a Jewish homeland in Palestine. The movement gained added momentum in the aftermath of the Holocaust.[35] Jewish refugees from Nazi Germany, arriving from 1933 onwards, marked a new wave of Jewish immigration. Many were from middle-class backgrounds, but women were forced to take jobs as domestic servants as the only way to gain a permit to enter Britain. As Kushner has revealed, these women were subjected to enormous stresses caused by concern for relatives left behind in Nazi Europe, and by experiences of loss of status, linked to the need to take over as the main breadwinner in families where husbands and fathers could not obtain professional employment. These problems were exacerbated by unsympathetic and anti-Semitic treatment by employers and fellow domestics, and by

the threat of internment as "enemy aliens" on the outbreak of war in 1939.[36]
The women did, however, receive assistance from the Jewish community,
and in 1943 the League of Jewish Women was formed to co-ordinate
assistance to refugees.

Irish women in Britain

Whereas Jewish women came to Britain as foreign immigrants and refugees,
Irish women can be more accurately described as migrants, at least from 1801
(when Ireland became part of the United Kingdom under the Act of Union)
until 1922 (when the Irish Free State was founded). Irish migration was also
on a much larger scale than Jewish immigration. Indeed, at the time of the
1871 census, 566,540 Irish were recorded in England and Wales (2.5 per cent
of the total population) and 207,770 in Scotland (6.2 per cent of the
population).[37] While some Irish people came to Britain as temporary or
seasonal workers, the majority settled permanently. Initially, the Irish were
concentrated in Liverpool, Manchester, London and Glasgow, and indeed
within particular neighbourhoods in these cities, but by the late nineteenth
century they had spread more widely though urban areas, and residential
segregation had decreased. Large-scale emigration from Ireland had begun in
the 1780s, but it reached a peak during the Great Famine of 1845–9 caused by
the failure of the potato crop: over a million people died from hunger and
disease and a further one and a half million emigrated. Emigration from
Ireland continued on a large scale through the nineteenth century, and from
the 1900s Britain took over from the United States as the main destination for
Irish emigrants.[38]

Both prior to and during the Famine, migrants from Ireland were mainly
men or family groups, but after the Famine the proportion of children and the
old decreased and the proportion of unmarried women increased. By 1871,
50 per cent of the Irish-born population of England and Wales was female,
with a slightly lower figure of 47.8 per cent for Scotland, which mainly
attracted migrants from Ulster.[39] Between 1885 and 1920, slightly over half of
of all emigrants from Ireland were female, and these women were mainly
single and under the age of 24.[40] Union and free trade with Britain were
important factors behind the underdevelopment of the Irish economy and the
resultant pressure on people to emigrate, and research by Rossitor and Nolan
suggests that single women were particularly badly affected by declining job
opportunities, decreasing marriage rates and increasingly repressive social
norms.[41]

On arrival in Britain, men's and women's work patterns overlapped, and
until the 1870s at least both sexes tended to be concentrated in menial,
unskilled or semi-skilled work, providing a pool of cheap casual labour. Men
and women worked as seasonal agricultural labourers, travelling to Britain

annually, especially at harvest time. While men predominated, these temporary migrants included gangs of female potato-lifters. Some women worked in occupations often considered to be male preserves: in the iron furnaces of South Wales, and in mining. Other occupations were gender-specific, and job opportunities led to a predominance of male immigrants in some towns, and of female in others. Thus men joined the British army, or were attracted to ports and heavy industrial centres where they could obtain work as dockside porters and in the construction and transport industries, while women were drawn to the textile towns of Lancashire, Yorkshire and Scotland.[42]

Census records indicate that Irish women's employment patterns, and the extent to which they adhered to general patterns of female employment, varied regionally. In York in the 1851–71 period, for example, Irish women comprised almost all the females employed as field or general labourers, but only 3 to 5 per cent of female domestics.[43] In Bristol in 1851, the most common recorded female occupation was domestic servant, and the occupational spread was similar to the overall female workforce except for the rarity of Irish milliners or teachers.[44] In London, Irish women worked, like English women, mainly in domestic service and the clothing trades, but were disproportionately concentrated at the menial and sweated ends of these occupations.[45] In Scotland, Irish women were prominent in the textile industry in the mid-nineteenth century: in Greenock in 1851 they comprised 44.3 per cent of female workers in the textile mills.[46] The 1911, the Scottish census revealed that 30 per cent of the employed Irish women were in service, but a small proportion managed to obtain lower middle-class jobs, such as clerical work, and in the nursing and teaching professions.[47] Here the evidence shows greater social mobility among women than men, perhaps as a result of their greater literacy and numeracy.

Married women and widows tended to work within the home, taking in piecework, laundry or lodgers, while the poorest worked with their children as street hawkers. In London, both the milk trade and fruit-selling were largely in Irish women's hands. Irish families (in common with poor English families, and as was customary in rural Ireland) acted as economic units to which husband and wives, sons and daughters all contributed earnings and services.[48] As Davies points out, families were best off in places offering good employment opportunities for all family members, such as the Yorkshire cloth towns, where women and girls worked in the mills and men in the collieries and iron furnaces. Where female employment opportunities were particularly good, as in the Dundee jute industry, women acted as the main family breadwinners.[49] With fewer artisanal and commercial skills than Jewish immigrants, the Irish were less socially mobile, and as a result, married women's participation in waged work persisted longer following immigration than was the case among Jewish families. Forced to work, and subject to English stereotypes of the Irish as slovenly and alcoholic, married Irish women were often stigmatized as neglectful mothers, and contrasted unfavourably with Jewish housewives.[50]

As well as studying patterns of migration, settlement and employment, historians of the Irish in Britain have debated the extent to which people of Irish descent retained a sense of Irish ethnic identity. There are indications that women played a crucial and distinctive role in this regard. In the early- to mid-nineteenth century, when residential segregation fostered the development of close-knit communities in particular neighbourhoods, many Irish women offered lodgings to young Irish immigrants. A Glasgow commentator in 1913 lamented the demise of the "old-fashioned Irish landlady", who in the 1870s had provided immigrants with "a resting place and a certain amount of security among their own class".[51] By the late-nineteenth century, while residential segregation had broken down, a sense of Irishness continued to be fostered through family ties, through involvement in political, social and cultural immigrant organizations, and through the Roman Catholic Church. There were clear gender differences here: as Rossitor states, "men dominated virtually all the secular organizations whereas women formed the back-bone of church-based activities".[52] In contrast to Jewish women, Irish women were highly visible in the public forms of religious life: almost two-thirds of the Catholic adults counted attending mass on Census Sunday in 1903 were women. Women also seem to have been responsible for transmitting to Britain the folk beliefs associated with popular Catholicism in rural Ireland, while modifying them to suit an urban environment. Thus Saint Brigit, linked with agriculture and healing in Ireland, was honoured as a symbol of female virtue and chastity by a women's confraternity in London.[53] In common with Jewish women, Irish women also played a crucial role in transmitting culture within the home. Women not only brought up their children in the Roman Catholic faith but also spoke Irish to them, a language which, as Raphael Samuel points out, "might serve as a common bond of nationality and faith". Tom Barclay refers in his autobiography to his very religious mother reciting old Irish songs and poems in the Irish tongue to the children while their father was in the pub.[54] As was the case with Jewish settlers, when the children of such Irish mothers grew up they generally married within their own ethnic group.[55]

Important research remains to be undertaken into Irish women's public and political activism in Britain. In the arena of social and moral reform there is evidence that women were attracted in large numbers to Father Mathew's temperance crusade in London in 1843.[56] Evidence for Irish women's prominence in trade union activity comes from the Dundee jute industry, where women outnumbered men by four to one in the Mill and Factory Operatives Union.[57] The extent of Irish women's participation in the British feminist movement is unknown, but the dominance of middle-class Protestant women in the nineteenth-century movement may have made it seem unwelcoming to working-class Irish Catholic women. Frances Power Cobbe, a prominent feminist and anti-vivisectionist of Irish extraction, came from an upper middle-class Prostestant family.[58]

There are also indications of women's support for Irish nationalism. Campaigns for the amnesty of Irish Republican prisoners gained support on a family basis, and many women attended an amnesty meeting of 25,000 in Hyde Park in 1874. Women's role, however, seems to have been largely subordinate to their menfolk: the Home Rule Confederation of Great Britain, founded in 1873, was controlled by men-only organizations, and Irish women were confined to being auxiliaries at a time when many English women were playing equal roles to men in philanthropic and reforming organizations.[59] But while Irish nationalism was male-dominated it is important to remember that it was an Irish woman socialist who became the first woman to be elected to the House of Commons. Constance Markievicz was elected to Westminster in 1918, the year the British government gave women over the age of 30 the vote. However, as President of Cumann na mBan, the women's support organization for the Irish Volunteers, and a Sinn Fein member, she boycotted Westminster in favour of the Republican Dáil Éireann, the provisional Irish Parliament.[60]

Black and Indian women in Britain

While Irish women were migrants from within the United Kingdom, the majority of black and Indian women entered Britain as British subjects from its external areas of imperial control. Although the number of incomers involved was much smaller than in the case of Irish migration, black and Indian immigrants were a particularly visible minority, and the study of their histories has also provided an important corrective to beliefs that immigration from the Caribbean and the Indian subcontinent was an entirely post-Second World War phenomenon. In fact, the presence in Britain of people of African descent has been traced back to the Roman period; of Indians to the beginning of the eighteenth century. Discriminatory treatment of black settlers also has a long history, beginning with Queen Elizabeth I's attempts in 1596 and 1601 to deport "negars and Blackamoors". Increasing numbers of black people arrived as Britain became a major slave trading power from the sixteenth century; set up plantations dependant on African slave labour in the Caribbean from the early seventeenth century; gradually increased its control of the Indian subcontinent; and joined in the European powers' scramble for control of Africa in the 1880s.[61]

The precise number of people of African and Indian descent resident in Britain during the nineteenth and early-twentieth centuries is very difficult to estimate. It has been estimated variously that the black population in Britain around 1800 comprised some 10–20,000 individuals. Numbers probably fell off through the nineteenth century, but were boosted by the arrival of workers during the First World War, numbers again reaching around 20,000. The population of Indian descent in Britain was probably smaller: towards the end of the period under study, in 1932, the Indian National Congress survey estimated that there were 7,128 Indians in the United Kingdom. Some black and Indian people were temporary residents, and others permanent settlers. Low overall numbers masked particular concentrations, especially in the dockland communities of major ports such as London, Bristol, Cardiff, Liverpool, Newcastle, Southampton and Glasgow.[62] In such dockland communities, black and Indian incomers were mainly men, who arrived as sailors but settled and intermarried with white working-class women. Fryer argues that "the grandchildren of such unions no longer thought of themselves a constituting a distinct black community. They were part of the British poor."[63] While this may well have been the case for those living in isolation, concentrations of interracial families led, in the Pitt Street area of Liverpool and Butetown in Cardiff at least, to the creation of communities with a distinctive multicultural identity. In the Cardiff neighbourhood known as Tiger Bay or Butetown, a focus of black settlement from around the 1840s, Sinclair describes the creation of "an Afro-Celtic culture amidst its intra-cultural and multi-ethnic heritage", and of "a multi-national society upon a Celtic Matrix", in which Africans, Middle Easterners, Asians, Maltese, Portuguese and Greeks mingled with the native Welsh.[64] More research needs to be done into the part played by women in creating and sustaining such communities in the face of high unemployment caused by racist employment policies, negative outside perceptions of the neighbourhoods as centres of crime and immortality, and racist attacks which came to a head during the "race riots" of 1919 and 1948.[65]

Given that, in contrast to patterns of Irish or Jewish immigration, the majority of black settlers were male, the history of black women in Britain has proved particularly easy to ignore and especially difficult to reconstruct. Nevertheless, information about the nineteenth century can be pieced together using such sources as parish registers and gravestones; case histories in Anti-Slavery Society papers; Hogarth and Cruickshank's prints of London street life, and Henry Mayhew's 1850s survey of the London poor; newspaper advertisements for runaway slaves; the family records and portraits of prominent families who returned to Britain from the Empire accompanied by black and Asian slaves and servants; and from criminal court records and information about convicts deported to Australia.[66] For the twentieth century, oral history is an invaluable source, though most work has focused on the postwar period.[67] Overall, however, while a considerable amount of information has been assembled on a small number of individual women, a general picture of the history of black women in Britain has not yet been reconstructed.

While they lie slightly outside our timespan, it is important to note that the earliest group of black and Indian women who can be identified are those brought to Britain from the Empire as slave-servants. This situation continued right up to the passage of the Emancipation Act in 1834, and a rare personal insight into the impact of this process on an individual is provided by *The history of Mary Prince* (1831), the autobiographical account of a West Indian slave brought to Britain by her owners. Her plight indicates the limitations of Lord Mansfield's[68] judgment in the famous case of James Somerset in 1772, which historians used to take as marking the end of slavery in England.[69] For while her owners could not force Prince to stay working for them as their unpaid domestic, once they brought her to Britain in 1829 they were not obliged to pay her for her services or to manumit her formally, which meant that if she returned to the West Indies she would again be reduced to the status of a chattel. The *History*, however, is also indicative of the destruction of slavery in Britain by a process of self-emancipation.[70] Rather than return to a life of slavery, Mary Prince decided to leave her owners, risking destitution in London and permanent separation from her husband. Prince enlisted the assistance of the Anti-Slavery Society, presented a petition for her freedom to Parliament, and dictated an account of her life to publicize the suffering of her fellow slaves and arouse British action against slavery. She thus became a public anti-slavery campaigner, her initiatives challenging the dominant white abolitionist construction of enslaved black women as being silent and passive victims.[71]

Free black women faced considerable difficulty in obtaining employment in Britain. Mary Prince herself obtained employment as a servant with the family of the Secretary of the Anti-Slavery Society, and domestic service seems to have been the main occupation open to black women in both urban and rural areas from the late-eighteenth through to the early-twentieth centuries, just as it was for working class white women.[72] Black women faced the added problem of often being unable to obtain poor relief if they became unemployed, however, and some joined the very poor, eking out a living as street hawkers, beggars, prostitutes or petty thieves.[73] Forty-one women of African descent were among the 450 invididuals who were shipped to Sierra Leone in West Africa in 1787 under a scheme to resettle the London "black poor".[74]

Other women of African descent, however, came from more secure backgrounds. Alexander has identified a number of women, the offspring of West Indian planters and their black mistresses, who were sent to England or Scotland for education at fashionable boarding schools, dame schools or mission schools. At least one woman from this background became a prominent community activist. Frances Batty Shand, the Jamaican-born daughter of a Scottish landowner and a free black women, who was brought to Scotland as a child, went on to use money inherited from her father to found an Association for Improving the Social and Working Conditions of the Blind in Cardiff in 1865.[75]

Another Jamaican woman of mixed Scots and African ancestry, Mary Seacole (née Grant) (1805/1810(?)–1881), became the most famous black woman in Victorian England. A "doctress" who identified herself as a patriotic British subject, Seacole travelled to Britain at the outbreak of the Crimean War to offer her medical services to the military. She would have been an ideal recruit, given her experience of treating patients with dysentery, battle wounds and cholera, and her excellent references from British military doctors and surgeons she had worked with in the Caribbean. She was rejected, however, and was convinced that it was because her "blood flowed beneath a somewhat duskier skin". Undaunted, Seacole travelled independently to Sebastopol and there set up on the front line as a sutler, running a hotel where she fed and nursed British soldiers. She became loved by ordinary soldiers as a down-to-earth mother figure, her image in sharp contrast to the rather ethereal "lady of the lamp" image of Florence Nightingale, and on her return to Britain at the end of the war, Seacole received national recognition. She settled in London, wrote her autobiography, *Wonderful adventures of Mrs Seacole*, and undertook charity work among ex-servicemen, war widows and orphans, and nursed victims of the 1867 cholera epidemic. On her death in 1881 her obituary appeared in *The Times* and other newspapers but, in sharp contrast to Florence Nightingale, she sank in memory into historical obscurity until interest in her life was revived by black nurses and scholars in the 1980s.[76]

The positive public image of Mary Seacole that circulated in Victorian Britain acted as some counter to the increasingly negative views of black people that were developing in Britain in the second half of the nineteenth century. These were associated with the growth of polygenism (the scientific racist belief that Africans were a separate and inferior species rather than part of a common humanity), and fuelled by disillusion with the economic and social problems in post-emancipation Jamaica, which came to a head with the Morant Bay revolt of 1865.[77] Gross caricatures of people of African descent also circulated in popular culture, particularly in the musicals and comedies in the Victorian and Edwardian periods. Representations of blacks as stupid and lazy encouraged discrimination in employment, though some black women did manage to break though stereotyping to gain roles in more positive shows of African–American culture such as "In Dahomey". A few also succeeded in entering the classical music scene: Avril Coleridge Taylor, daughter of a successful black British musician and composer, Samuel Coleridge Taylor, became a conductor, while the daughter of black Shakespearean actor Ira Aldridge became a successful contralto singer.[78]

Small numbers of Indian women of varying backgrounds also came to Britain. The Indian maidservants who accompanied returning East India Company officials in the eighteenth century often had the indeterminate slave-servant status of their contemporaries of African descent. "Ayahs" (nannies) to the families of the British Raj arrived from the 1850s onwards, and an Ayah's Home was opened in Hackney for women discharged by their employers and unable to obtain employment on a return passage to India. By the 1930s women from more privileged backgrounds had begun to arrive: Indians formed the largest body of foreign students in Britain, and there were 100 female students, studying mainly medicine and education, out of around 1800 Indian students. In 1920, a women's hostel was set up in Highbury by prominent Indian women, and the Indian Women's Education Association offered scholarships to enable Indian women to study in Britain.[79]

Feminist periodicals such as *Englishwoman's Review* reported regularly on Indian women's activities and education in England. Women who gained particular prominence were the social reformer Pandita Ramabai, who studied at Cheltenham Ladies' College, and the lawyer Cornelia Sorabji. Sorabji (1866–1954) became the first woman law student at a British university and should be accorded a prominent place among the feminist pioneers of women's entry into higher education and the professions in Britain. Overcoming obstacles placed in her path as a woman in both India and Britain, Sorabji came to Somerville College in Oxford in 1889 and gained a law degree. She then returned to India and laboured in legal and welfare work on behalf of widows, wives and orphans. She was called to the Bar in London in 1923, after the legal profession had been fully opened to women, and on retirement she settled in Britain.[80] Another prominent individual was secret agent Noor Inayat Khan, daughter of the Indian founder of the Sufi religious order in Europe, who became the first woman wireless operator infiltrated from Britain into occupied France during the Second World War.[81]

A number of African–American women also came to Britain in the second half of the nineteenth century. Among them were fugitive slave Ellen Craft, who settled in Britain and was active in the anti-slavery movement in London, and Sarah Parker Remond, an important but neglected figure in the history of both British feminism and black political activism in Britain. Arriving in Britain in 1859, Remond attended Bedford College in London and became the first woman to conduct public anti-slavery lecture tours of Britain and Ireland, helping establish women's right to participate fully in public life and politics in Britain. As a member of a transatlantic network of reformers, she was a pivotal figure in forging links between feminists and abolitionists across both racial and national divides, and in articulating a black feminist perspective that encompassed a critique of slavery, racial oppression and the exploitation of women.[82]

While Remond was from a free Northern background, Ida B. Wells (1862–1931), who lectured in Britain some thirty years later, had been born into slavery in the American South. A journalist, Wells conducted lecture tours of Britain in 1893 and 1894 as part of her campaign against the lynching of black men in the American South. Like Remond, she attracted audiences of all classes and gained particular support from women, as will be discussed later in this chapter. Wells expanded on Remond's analysis of the sexual politics of racism: while Remond had highlighted white men's sexual abuse of black women under slavery, Wells drew on such evidence to expose the hypocrisy of arguments which justified the lynching of hundreds of black men in the South on the grounds that white women needed protection from their sexual advances.[83]

The period from the 1900s to the 1940s saw a ferment of anti-imperial political organization in Britain, and women played a part in these activities. Paris-based Bhikaji Rustom Cama (d. 1937) frequently visited London as one of the leaders of Indian revolutionary nationalism in Europe.[84] Women were also among the leadership of the succession of London-based pan-Africanist organizations, major political groups which promoted racial solidarity among peoples of African descent and emancipation from white Imperial domination. E. V. Kinloch, an African woman from Natal married to a Scotsman, became Treasurer of the African Association (founded 1897); Muriel Barbour-James, a Londoner of British Guianese background, was a leading supporter of the African Progress Union (founded 1918); Stella Thomas, one of the founder members of the moderate League of Coloured Peoples (founded 1931), went on to become the first woman barrister and first woman magistrate in West Africa.[85] Amy Ashwood Garvey, the estranged wife of leading black nationalist Marcus Garvey, was instrumental in the establishment of the Nigerian Progress Union in London in 1924, and became Treasurer of the International Association of the Friends of Abyssinia, formed in London in 1935. In 1945 she chaired the first session of the Fifth Pan-African Congress in Manchester, which attempted to forge cross-class connections by addressing the situation of poor black settlers. Garvey also made a speech to the Congress in which she criticized the movement's lack of attention to the multiple oppression of black women, pointing out that "Very much had been written and spoken of the Negro, but for some reason very little has been said about the black woman. She has been shunted into the social background to be a child-bearer".[86]

The fight against racial discrimination in Britain and the Empire was also fought by black and Indian women outside formal political organizations. One example of a successful fight was that waged by West Indian and black British women for their right to serve in the Auxiliary Territorial Service and the Women's Land Army during the Second World War. This was won in eventually 1943, in the face of War Office racism and of a more general "colour bar" that excluded black people from employment, from lodgings and from cafes and dance halls.[87]

White women, "race" and Empire

Standard histories of the British Empire have had little to say either about white women's involvement in Empire, or about the gender politics of imperialism. Early accounts of white women explorers, missionaries, reformers and settlers in the imperial context tended to be celebratory, and feminists are still struggling to find ways of writing about these women from analytical perspectives which acknowledge power relations based on race as well as gender within colonial society, and which do not render invisible the experiences of the colonized.[88] It lies beyond the scope of this book, however, to discuss the growing body of studies on white British women within the colonial setting. Rather, the aim here is to study white women's lives in Britain in the context of a period when, to quote MacKenzie, "the values and beliefs of the imperial world view settled like a sediment in the consciousness of the British people".[89]

While British women, as a disenfranchised group until women's suffrage was achieved in 1918/28, did not take a direct part in the exercise of imperial rule by the British government, they influenced both official policy and public opinion in a number of important ways. Some identified strongly with masculine ideologies of empire and with male imperial heroes. A key figure here is Flora Shaw (1852–1929), who herself came from a colonial background, and who became a leading pro-imperial propagandist, promoting British expansionism through her articles as first Colonial Editor for *The Times* from 1890 to 1900. According to Callaway and Helly, she helped "to shape the jingoistic discourse of a new and more aggressive imperialism rising in the 1890s".[90] She exercised tremendous influence through her journalism, which she described as "active politics without the fame". Writing for the newspaper of the national elite, she recognized that she was able not only to "rouse the British public to a sense of Imperial responsibility and an ideal of Imperial greatness" but also to shape imperial policy.[91] Her authority was based on her extensive firsthand investigations in South Africa, Australia, New Zealand and Canada, and on her close links with leading imperial politicians. Shaw eventually married Sir Frederick Lugard, High Commissioner of Northern Nigeria, and the couple were united by their commitment to serving an Empire "which is to secure the ruling of the world by its finest race".[92] Her belief in a hierarchy of races was clearly articulated in her book *A tropical dependency* (1905), in which she argued that black Africa needed to be governed by an "autocracy" of white administrators.[93]

Flora Shaw's belief in white racial superiority was in line with the dominant Social Darwinism of her day and was shared with other prominent late Victorian and Edwardian women such as explorer Mary Kingsley (1862–1900), author of *Travels in West Africa* (1897) and *West African studies* (1899), who campaigned for West Africa to be controlled by British traders rather than government administrators. As Birkett has pointed out, Kingsley took advantage of the almost masculine power her whiteness conferred on her in a colonial context.[94]

There is evidence that British women's differing responses to Empire played an important role in shaping their attitudes to women's suffrage. Those who, like Flora Shaw, supported a very masculist view of Empire, saw women's suffrage as threatening the Empire with "weakness at the heart", as the editors of the *Anti-Suffrage Review* put it.[95] In contrast, those who criticized aspects of current male imperial policy and developed a feminine vision of benevolent imperial social reform, tended to support women's suffrage.

The roots of this feminine reformist vision of empire may be traced to women's involvement in the anti-slavery movement. This reached its height in the 1825–38 period, but continued through to the 1860s, providing a training ground for feminist campaigners as well as a potent source of feminist rhetoric in terms of analogies made between the position of British women and African slaves.[96] The white middle-class women who founded ladies' anti-slavery associations adopted a "maternalistic" perspective. They professed sisterly concern for black women suffering from physical and sexual abuse by white men under slavery, and challenged colonial sterotypes of black women as being sexually promiscuous, but they also viewed enslaved women as passive and silent victims in need of the protection of white women who had the power to speak on their behalf. Their belief in black spiritual equality did not extend to a belief in cultural equality, and they developed a vision of a benevolent Christian imperialism in which emancipation would provide the foundation for the creation of a new form of colonial society based not only on a "free" (i.e. waged) labour economy but also on family life modelled on British middle-class ideals.[97]

In the 1860s, following emancipation in the United States, British women shifted attention from the sufferings of enslaved black women to the position of Indian women. Burton and Ware have both explored the imperial context in which the organized British feminist movement developed at this period. Their emphases are slightly different, however: Ware sees British feminists as struggling – if unsuccessfully initially – to develop "a vision of liberatory politics that connected the struggle against masculinist ideology and power with the stuggle against racist domination in the colonies".[98] In contrast, Burton argues that "liberal feminists . . . enthusiastically *claimed* racial responsibility as part of their strategy to legitimize themselves as responsible and imperial citizens".[99] Campaign literature and feminist periodicals, she claims, promoted a "feminist imperialism" which represented white women as being the prime agents of civilization, an approach that black feminists have also identified and criticized in the contemporary white women's movement in Britain.[100]

What is clear is that middle-class feminists felt it was their sisterly duty to aid Indian women, whom they represented as being helpless colonial subjects. They were concerned to promote Indian women's education, to cater for their medical needs, and to reform both indigenous Hindu practices and British imperial laws, which they considered to be harmful to women. Outrage was expressed over the seclusion of women, the practice of child marriage, "sati" (the ritual burning of Hindu widows on their husbands" funeral pyres), and the treatment of widows as outcasts. Between 1886 and

1915, Josephine Butler extended to India her feminist crusade against the Contagious Diseases Acts. Laws had been introduced there to control the spread of venereal disease among British soldiers through the detainment and forcible medical examination of Indian women identified as prostitutes. Butler and her supporters, Burton argues, desired to remould imperial power by moving from a reliance on masculine physical force to feminine moral influence. Their confidence was founded in beliefs in white racial and cultural superiority, beliefs which also underlay their view of themselves as leaders of an international sisterhood of women who would first secure rights for white women in Britain and then spread these to "backward" women of other races.[101]

Feminists saw the Empire as a field of opportunity not only for social reform activities but also for employment. Propaganda for female emigration to the British colonies developed from the mid-nineteenth century, linked to public debate over the gender imbalance in the British population and the presence of large numbers of single women. Anti-feminists such as W. R. Greg stigmatized single women as "surplus" or "redundant", and advocated emigration as the best solution to lack of marriage opportunities within Britain. In contrast, feminists, who set up the Female Middle Class Emigration Society in 1862, saw the problem as being one of limited employment opportunities for women in Britain and presented the colonies as potential arenas of middle-class female employment opportunity, freedom and self-fulfilment. In fact the demand from the colonies was mainly for working-class domestic servants and wives: to fulfil this need it is estimated that between 1862 and 1914 a succession of female emigration societies helped over 20,000 women to emigrate.[102]

Bush, focusing on the journal *The Imperial Colonist* and on the promotion of emigration to South Africa, has explored "the extent to which the female emigration societies reshaped the gendered contours of imperialist ideology", and provided a counterpoint to the "powerfully masculine myth of late Victorian empire" in the aftermath of the Boer War.[103] Women's propaganda stressed the impulse of "imperious maternity"[104] and described female emigrators as "the future nursing mothers of the English race to be",[105] whose destiny was to care for both husbands and children, and for the "lesser" races. In so doing it "succeeded in portraying an empire which both wanted and needed women".[106] Marriage and motherhood were brought to the heart of the imperial enterprise, providing women with an imperial role which was complementary, rather than subordinate, to men. Victorian domestic ideology was tied to imperial ideology: as one woman put it, "Englishwomen make homes wherever they settle all the world over and are the real builders of Empire".[107] Women would ensure the permanence of British imperial control by domesticating – settling and civilizing – their husbands, by producing the new white generation and rearing them to be loyal British subjects, and by exercising maternal care and control over the "natives".

The promotion of maternal imperialism affected white women of all backgrounds, in distinctive ways. A one end of the social spectrum, was Queen Victoria, who was proclaimed Empress of India in 1876, and transformed into the figure of imperial matriarch, the central symbol of maternal imperialism, her role as mother of her subject imperial children clearly commemorated by monuments erected throughout the Empire, most notably the Victoria Memorial in London itself.[108] At the other end of the social spectrum an ideal of "imperial motherhood" was promoted for working class women, as Davin has shown. Evidence for high infant mortality rates, population decline and unfit military recruits fuelled concern with maintaining a large and healthy white "race" which could populate Britain's colonies and maintain its imperial power in the face of increasing competition from other industrializing powers. Amidst fears of "race degeneration" among the urban poor, advocates of eugenics called for selective population control to prevent the "unfit" – whether poor, Irish or Jewish – from breeding. While no official policy of eugenics was adopted, there was increasing intervention in infant and maternal welfare by national and local government, the medical profession and voluntary societies. All focused on educating mothers as being the key to the future of the "race".[109]

In the late-Victorian and Edwardian periods popular support for imperialism was closely associated with patriotism. This link was fostered through such organizations as the Primrose League, the Tory organization which from 1884 organized large numbers of women through its Ladies' Grand Council; and the Women's Guild of Empire, founded at the time of the First World War by Flora Drummond and Lady Muriel Gore-Booth.[110] Women of all classes in Victorian and Edwardian Britain were thus implicated in Britain's imperial project in varied ways; imperial relations with colonized peoples were crucial to the construction of notions of white womanhood; and many middle-class liberal feminists saw the Empire as offering women enhanced opportunities for employment, adventure, status and influence, though further research is needed to determine the extent to which working-class women shared their views.[111]

While liberal women were generally pro-imperial, they did on occasion express opposition to racism, though generally in the context of the United States rather than the British Empire. Anti-racist activity by white British women in the second half of the nineteenth century was stimulated by contacts with leading African–American activists. In the 1880s, another Quaker woman, Catherine Impey (1847–1923), set up the periodical *Anti-Caste* and helped to form the Society for the Furtherance of Human Brotherhood, and in 1893 she and Scottish philanthropist and novelist Isabella Mayo organized the British lecture tour of Ida B. Wells, (discussed earlier in this chapter). This was followed by the foundation of the Society for the Recognition of the Universal Brotherhood of Man and of an influential Anti-Lynching Committee. As Ware has pointed out, lynching was a difficult issue for a "respectable" white woman to take up: defending black men against charges of assaulting white women was controversial given the taboo on sexual relations between black men and white women within the British Empire, and anxieties over the danger of black men assaulting white women settlers. Such anxieties had intensified following the Indian Rebellion in 1857 and the Morant Bay black uprising in Jamaica in 1865, and they contributed to the 1884 rejection of the Ilbert Bill in British India.[112]

Women's involvement in imperial issues assumed rather different forms in the interwar period. On the one hand, women's increasing access to positions of public authority enabled them to have a greater influence over imperial policy. The key figure here is Dame Margery Perham, who became a Reader in colonial administration at Oxford University, and published a number of influential studies of colonial policy in Africa, including *Native administration in Nigeria* (1937). On the other hand, the growth of Socialism, questioning of Empire in the aftermath of the First World War, and friendships with the growing number of London-based pan-Africanist activists encouraged opposition to imperialism among British feminists and socialists by the 1930s. Among them were Winifred Holtby, Eleanor Rathbone, Naomi Mitchison, Sylvia Pankhurst and Nancy Cunard. From the 1930s Pankhurst focused her energies on fighting Fascism and for Ethiopian independence. She supported the formation of the International Association of the Friends of Abyssinia (IAFA), founded in 1935 in response to the invasion of Ethiopia; edited the *New Times and Ethiopian News*, which developed into an anti-war and anti-fascist publication supporting self-determination for all black people; and became an associate member of the International African Service Bureau (IASB), founded in London in 1837 to support the demand of colonial peoples for democratic rights.[113] Nancy Cunard, a poet and journalist of aristocratic background who scandalized London society by cohabiting with African–American jazz pianist and composer Henry Crowder, was also a supporter of the IASB. She was active in the Scottsboro' Defence Committee, formed in London in 1932 as part of an international campaign to free nine young black men charged with the rape of a white girl in Alabama, and in 1934 she compiled the anti-racist *Negro Anthology*. At the outbreak of the Spanish Civil War, Cunard joined the International Brigade and went to Spain, where she wrote anti-fascist articles for both the *Manchester Guardian* and the Associated Negro Press.[114] For both Pankhurst and Cunard, anti-imperialism and support for pan-Africanism were thus closely associated with anti-Fascism.[115]

Conclusion

This chapter has pointed to ways in which a more comprehensive history of women in Britain might be created, one which explores the complex interaction of gender, ethnicity, "race", Empire and class in shaping the experiences and identities of *all* women in Britain. As has been shown, patterns of immigration and settlement, levels of community support, and racist ideologies evolving in the context of imperial expansion were some of the factors affecting Jewish, Irish, black and Indian women's employment opportunities, family relationships, cultural identities and political activities in Britain. White women in Britain were also affected by Britain's imperial expansion, which opened up new female opportunities in the colonial setting and which fostered a sense of the superiority of white womanhood. Seeking a voice in the running of both nation and Empire, liberal feminists developed a "maternalist" version of imperialism, and while some white Victorian women attacked racism it was only between the two world wars that any significant anti-imperialist activity emerged.

Many questions arise from this survey which remain to be fully answered. How, for example, did the lives of Jewish, Irish, black and Asian women in Britain compare? To what extent did women of the same class share a common experience regardless of ethnicity or "race"? On what occasions did women forge alliances across lines of ethnicity or "race", and on what occasions were their interests divided along these lines? To what extent did a sense of shared ethnicity or "race" bind together women of different classes? In what ways did women share experiences and perspectives with men along the lines of ethnicity or "race", and in what ways did gender differences lead to divergent experiences?

Further research is needed urgently before such questions can be answered. The study of such issues will be of crucial importance in opening up new ways of understanding the development of British society as a whole, and encouraging the creation of alternative national histories. I would suggest, however, that an exclusively national framework for women's history may in itself be limiting. How are we to understand Jewish and black women's histories outside the international context of the Jewish and African diasporas? How can we interpret white women's anti-slavery activities without acknowledging that they were part of a transatlantic abolitionist network? How can we comprehend black women's support of such an internationalist movement as pan-Africanism within a purely British framework?

In a contribution to debates on the school history curriculum, Paul Gilroy has contended that "It is clear that we cannot deal with the problem [of national history] by seeking to add 'Empire' into a pre-existing syllabus or by tacking on the supposedly discrete and distinct histories of 'minority' groups whose silenced and invisible presences can be shown to be dictating the hidden pattern of British national identity in the modern world".[116] His statement could provide the basis for a critique of this chapter, and indeed Gilroy argues convincingly for an alternative history that emphasizes "the decidedly trans-national character of modes of production, social movements and international exchanges".[117] I would argue, however, that national and transnational perspectives are not necessarily incompatible: transnational phenomena such as the slave trade and slavery, emancipation movements and the creation of diasporic communities take distinctive forms within particular nations and regions, and as historians one of our important roles is to explore such historical specificity. We need to continue to study the diverse and connecting histories of women in Britain, but also be willing to place these histories within an international framework.

Notes

1. As a synthesis this chapter is heavily indebted to all those scholars whose primary research and publications have opened up the area of study – it is hoped that they are adequately acknowledged in the footnotes. I would also like to acknowledge the very helpful comments made by Meg Arnot, Barbara Bush and Norris Saakwa-Mante on drafts of this chapter.
2. Scottish and Welsh women's history will not be considered in this chapter. Useful introductions are: A. John (ed.), *Our mother's land: chapters in Welsh women's history, 1830-1939* (Cardiff: University of Wales Press, 1991); and E. Breitenbach & E. Gordon (eds), *Out of bounds: women in Scottish society, 1800-1945* (Edinburgh: Edinburgh University Press, 1992).
3. Important general studies include: P. Panayi, *Immigration, ethnicity and racism in Britain, 1815-1945* (Manchester: Manchester University Press, 1994); J. Walvin, *Passage to Britain: immigration in British history and politics* (Harmondsworth: Penguin, 1984); C. Holmes, *John Bull's island: immigration and British society, 1871-1971* (London: Macmillan, 1988); C. Holmes (ed.), *Immigrants and minorities in British society* (London: Allen & Unwin, 1978); K. Lunn (ed.), *Hosts, immigrants and minorities, historical responses to newcomers in British society, 1870-1914* (Folkestone: Dawson, 1980); P. Rich, *Race and Empire in British politics* (Cambridge: Cambridge University Press, 1986); J. MacKenzie, *Propaganda and Empire: the manipulation of British public opinion 1880-1960* (Manchester: Manchester University Press, 1984); J. MacKenzie (ed.), *Imperialism and popular culture* (Manchester: Manchester University Press, 1986). See also the journal *Immigrants and Minorities*.
4. The term "black" here refers to peoples of African descent (African, African-Caribbean, African-American and black British-born).
5. The importance of such a project is stressed by L. Stanley, "British feminist histories: an editorial introduction", *Women's Studies International Forum* **13**, pp. 3-7, 1990. For an interesting sociological analysis of the connections between gender and race and ethnicity in the British context, see F. Anthias & N. Yuval-Davis, *Racialized boundaries: race, nation, gender, colour and class and the anti-racist struggle* (London: Routledge, 1992), esp. Ch. 4.
6. F. Anthias & N. Yuval-Davis, "Contextualizing feminism: gender, ethnic and class divisions", in *Defining women: social institutions and gender divisions*, L. McDowell & R. Pringle (eds) (Cambridge: Polity, 1992), p. 109.
7. C. Hall, *White, male and middle class: explorations in feminism and history* (Cambridge: Polity, 1992), pp. 25-6; 205-6. Part 3 of this book provides pioneering studies of the connections between gender and English ethnicity in the mid-

nineteenth century. See also C. Hall, "'From Greenland's icy mountains . . . to Afric's golden sand': ethnicity, race and nation in mid-nineteenth-century England", *Gender and History*, **5**, pp. 212-30, 1993.

8. K. A. Appiah, "Race", in F. Lentricchia & T. McLaughlin, *Critical terms for literary study* (Chicago: University of Chicago Press, 1990), p. 276. Note that current biological studies have displaced such definitions of race by showing that "human genetic variability between the populations of Africa or Europe or Asia is not much greater than that within those populations", A. Appiah, "The uncompleted argument: Du Bois and the illusion of race, in H. L. Gates Jr (ed.), *"Race", writing and difference* (Chicago: University of Chicago Press, 1986), p. 21. For a summary of the current scientific position see Steve Jones, *The language of the genes* (London: Harper Collins, 1993), Ch. 13. This scientific development, however, has failed to undermine the social salience of "race" in contemporary Britain.

9. For the history of scientific racism see N. Stepan, *The idea of race in science: Great Britain, 1800-1960* (London: Macmillan, 1982).

10. Recent general accounts of the history of Jews in Britain include: D. Cesarani (ed.), *The making of modern Anglo-Jewry* (Oxford: Basil Blackwell, 1990); and V. D. Lipman, *A history of the Jews in Britain since 1858* (Leicester: Leicester University Press, 1990). For anti-Semitism, see C. Holmes, *Anti-Semitism in British society, 1876-1939* (London: Edward Arnold, 1979). Precise numbers of Jewish immigrants are difficult to determine (records refer to country of origin rather than ethnic group), and historians vary in their estimates, while agreeing on the general pattern and scale of settlement.

11. L. Marks, "Carers and servers of the Jewish community: the marginalized heritage of Jewish women in Britain", in *Immigrants and Minorities* **10**, pp. 106-27, 1991.

12. F. Guy, *Women of worth: Jewish women in Britain* (Manchester: Manchester Jewish Museum, 1992), pp. 1-2.

13. For a fascinating published collection of oral history interviews, see Jewish Women in London Group, *Generations of memories: voices of Jewish women* (London: The Women's Press, 1989).

14. R. Burman, "Jewish women and the household economy in Manchester, c1890-1920", in *The making of modern Anglo-Jewry*, Cesarani (ed.), pp. 55-78; R. Burman, "'She looketh well to the ways of her household': the changing role of Jewish women in religious life, c.1880-1930", in *Religion in the lives of English women, 1760-1930*, G. Malmgreen (ed.) (London: Croom Helm, 1986), pp. 234-60.

15. Burman, "Jewish women and the household economy", p. 56.

16. Oral history interview in archive at Manchester Jewish Museum, quoted in Burman, "Jewish women and the household economy", p. 61.

17. See quotes from G. Aguilar, *The woman of Israel* (1845) in Guy, *Women of worth*, pp. 4, 14.

18. Oral history interview with Minnie C., Manchester (Manchester Jewish History Museum), as quoted in Guy, *Women of worth*, p. 7.

19. L. Marks, *Working wives and working mothers: a comparative study of Irish and East European Jewish married women's work and motherhood in East London 1870-1914*, PNL Irish Studies Centre Occasional Papers Series (London: PNL Press, 1990), p. 15.

20. Burman, "She looketh well to the ways of her household", p. 234.

21. *Ibid.*, p. 251.

22. L. Marks, "'Dear old mother Levy's': the Jewish maternity home and sick room helps society 1895-1939", *Social History of Medicine* **3**, pp. 61-88, 1990. For a fuller

discussion, see L. V. Marks, *Model mothers: Jewish mothers and maternity provision in East London, 1870-1939* (Oxford: Clarendon, 1994).

23. L. Marks, "'The luckless waifs and strays of humanity': Irish and Jewish immigrant unwed mothers in London, 1870-1939", *Twentieth Century British History* **3**, pp. 113-37, 1992.

24. Marks, "Carers and servers of the Jewish community", pp. 110-11.

25. Marks, "Carers and servers of the Jewish community", pp. 118-19; L. G. Kuzmack, *Woman's cause: the Jewish woman's movement in England and the United States, 1881-1933* (Columbus, Ohio: Ohio State University Press, 1990), pp. 53-62.

26. *Ibid.*, p. 48.

27. *Ibid.*, p. 82.

28. *Ibid.*, pp. 107-13.

29. *Ibid.*, pp. 114-16; Guy, *Women of worth*, pp. 7-8.

30. *Ibid.*, p. 188.

31. Kuzmack, *Woman's cause*, p. 62.

32. Kuzmack, *Woman's cause*, pp. 138-9.

33. For a full consideration of Montagu's achievements, see E. M. Umansky, *Lily Montagu and the advancement of liberal Judaism, from vision to vocation* (New York: E. Mellen, 1983)·

34. *Ibid.*, p. 142.

35. *Ibid.*, pp. 159-71.

36. T. Kushner, "Politics and race, gender and class: refugees, fascists and domestic service in Britain 1933-1940", *Immigrants and Minorities* **8**, pp. 49-58, 1989.

37. D. Fitzpatrick, "A curious middle place: the Irish in Britain, 1871-1921", in *The Irish in Britain 1815-1939*, R. Swift & S. Gilley (eds) (London: Printer, 1989), Ch. 1, table 1.1.

38. Recent general accounts of the history of the Irish in Britain include: Swift and Gilley (eds), *The Irish in Britain*; G. Davis, *The Irish in Britain, 1815-1914* (Dublin: Gill & Macmillan, 1991).

39. L. H. Lees, *Exiles of Erin: Irish migrants in Victorian London* (Manchester: Manchester University Press, 1979), p. 43; Fitzpatrick, "A curious middle place", table 1.1 and p. 12.

40. J. A. Nolan, *Ourselves alone: women's emigration from Ireland 1885-1920* (Lexington, Kentucky: University Press of Kentucky, 1989), p. 100, note 1; and Appendix, table A. 30.

41. For a thorough study of Irish women's motives for emigration see *ibid.*, Chs 1, 2 & 3; for an analysis which focuses specifically on emigration to Britain, see A. Rossiter, "Bringing the margins to the centre: a review of aspects of Irish women's emigration from a British perspective", in A. Smyth (ed.), *Irish women's studies reader* (Dublin: Attic Press, 1993), pp. 177-202.

42. Davis, *The Irish in Britain*, pp. 104, 109, 110 & 120; D. Fitzpatrick, "A curious middle place: the Irish in Britain, 1871-1921", in *The Irish in Britain*, Swift & Gilley (eds), pp. 18-19; C. Pooley, "Segregation or integration? The residential experience of the Irish in mid-Victorian Britain", in *ibid.*, pp. 66, 69.

43. F. Finnegan, "The Irish in York", in *The Irish in the Victorian City*, R. Swift & S. Gilley (eds), (London: Croom Helm, 1985), pp. 66-7.

44. D. Large, "The Irish in Bristol in 1851: a census enumeration", in *ibid.*, pp. 45-6.

45. L. H. Lees, *Exiles of Erin: Irish migrants in Victorian London* (Manchester: Manchester University Press, 1979), p. 95.

46. Davis, *The Irish in Britain*, p. 104.

47. Fitzpatrick, "A curious middle place", p. 23.

48. Lees, *Exiles of Erin*, pp. 96-115.

49. Davies, *The Irish in Britain*, pp. 108-10 & 120.

50. Marks, *Working wives and working mothers*, pp. 14-15.

51. Quoted in Swift and Gilley (eds), *The Irish in Britain*, p. 15.

52. Rossiter, "Bringing the margins into the centre", p. 193.

53. Lees, *Exiles of Erin*, pp. 184-5; R. Samuel, "The Roman Catholic Church and the Irish poor", in Swift and Gilley (eds), *The Irish in the Victorian city*, p. 267.

54. Samuel, "The Roman Catholic Church and the Irish poor", pp. 286-7.

55. M. A. G. O'Tuathaigh, "The Irish in nineteenth-century Britain: problems of integration", in Swift and Gilley (eds), *The Irish in the Victorian city*, p. 26; Lees, *Exiles of Erin*, p. 153.

56. Samuel, "The Roman Catholic church and the Irish poor, pp. 284-5.

57. Davies, *The Irish in Britain*, p. 110.

58. For co-operation between supporters of women's suffrage in Britain and Ireland, see M. Ward, "'Suffrage first - above all else!' an account of the Irish suffrage movement", in Smyth (ed.) *Irish Women's Studies Reader*, pp. 20-44. Ward highlights tensions caused by British feminsts" lack of interest in the Home Rule question and their attempts to direct Irish women's activities.

59. Fitzpatrick, "A curious middle place", pp. 34 & 37.

60. Ward, "'Suffrage first - above all else!'", pp. 41-2.

61. For general accounts of the history of peoples of African and Asian descent in Britain see esp. P. Fryer, *Staying power: the history of black people in Britain* (London: Pluto Press, 1984); and R. Visram, *Ayahs, lascars and princes: Indians in Britain 1700-1947* (London: Pluto Press, 1986). For a brief introductory account of Britain's invovlement in slavery, see J. Walvin, *Slaves and slavery: the British colonial experience* (Manchester: Manchester Univeristy Press, 1992). For general accounts of Britain's imperial expansion, see C. A. Bayly, *Imperial meridian: the British empire and the world 1780-1830* (London: Longman, 1989); B. Porter, *The lion's share: a short history of British imperialism 1850-1983*, 2nd edn (London: Longman, 1984); Ronald Hyam, *Britain's imperial century, 1815-1914: a study of Empire and expansion*, 2nd edn (London: Macmillan, 1993); C. C. Eldridge (ed.), *British imperialism in the nineteenth century* (London: Macmillan, 1984).

62. Fryer, *Staying power*, pp. 67-8, 295-6,; Visram, *Ayahs, lascars and princes*, p. 190.

63. Fryer, *Staying power*, pp. 234-6.

64. N. M. C. Sinclair, *The Tiger Bay story* (Cardiff: Butetown History and Arts Project, 1993), pp. 2, 4. For Liverpool see M. van Helmond & D. Palmer, *Staying power: black presence in Liverpool* (Liverpool: National Museums and Galleries on Merseyside, 1991), a souvenir of an exhibition held at the Merseyside Museum of Labour History in Liverpool in 1991.

65. P. Fryer, *Staying power*, pp. 298-316; 256-371.

66. Z. Alexander, "Let it lie upon the table: the status of black women's biography in the UK", *Gender and History* 2, pp. 22-3, 1990. For criminal and convict records which yield some information on black women, see N. Myers, "The black presence through criminal records, 1780-1830", *Immigrants and Minorities* 7, pp. 292-307, 1988; N. Myers, "'Servant, sailor, soldier, tailor, beggarman': black survival in white society 1780-1830", *Immigrants and Minorities* 12, pp. 47-74, 1993; Ian Duffield, "Skilled workers or marginalized poor? The African population of the United Kingdom, 1812-52", *Immigrants and Minorities* 12, pp. 48-87, 1993; Ian Duffield, "Identity, community and the lived experience of black Scots from the late eighteenth to the

mid-nineteenth centuries", *Immigrants and Minorities* **11**, pp. 105-12, 1992. Further research into criminal records is needed for the post-1850 period.

67. See B. Bryan, S. Dadzie, S. Scafe, *The heart of the race: black women's lives in Britain* (London: Virago, 1985); A. Wilson, *Finding a voice: Asian women in Britain* (London: Virago, 1978).

68. Interestingly, Lord Mansfield's own household included his black niece, Dido Lindsay, whose freedom he confirmed on his death, and to whom he granted a substantial annuity (see Gene Adams, "Dido Elizabeth Belle: a black girl at Kenwood", *Camden History Review* **12**, p. 10, 1984.

69. In Scotland, which has a separate legal system, the equivalent judgment was that in the case of Knight versus Wedderburn in 1778 (Fryer, *Staying power*, pp. 120-7).

70. See D. A. Lorimer, "Black slaves and English liberty: a re-examination of racial slavery in England", *Immigrants and Minorities* **3**, pp. 121-50, 1984.

71. M. Ferguson (ed.), *The history of Mary Prince, a West Indian slave, related by herself* (London: Pandora, 1987; new edition of the work first published in 1831). For a discussion of the significance of the text, see M. Ferguson, *Subject to others: British women writers and colonial slavery, 1670-1834* (London: Routledge, 1992), pp. 281-98. For women's resistance to British colonial slavery within the Caribbean, see H. McD. Beckles, *Natural rebels: a social history of enslaved black women in Barbados* (London: Zed, 1989); Barbara Bush, *Slave women in Caribbean soicety, 1650-1838* (London: James Currey, 1990).

72. Duffield, in "Skilled workers or marginalized poor?" identifies the occupations of the six women of African descent who were transported from the United Kingdom to Australia in the 1812-52 period as skilled needlewoman, plain cook, servant, laundress, housemaid and laundry maid (p. 71); Myers, in "Servant, sailor, soldier", states that three of the four females whose jobs were specified in the Newgate Calendars' record of crimes in the 1780-1830 period were servants; J. Green, "Some findings on Britain's black working class, 1900-1914", *Immigrants and Minorities* **9**, pp. 168-77, 1990 identifies black women domestic servants in London, Hampshire, Wiltshire, Hertfordshire and the Lake District.

73. For early evidence see D. Dabydeen, *Hogarth's blacks: images of blacks in eighteenth century English art* (Manchester: Manchester University Press, 1987), pp. 18-20, 37, 50, 62-4, 121.

74. Fryer, *Staying power*, pp. 195-202.

75. Alexander, "Let it lie upon the table", pp. 23-4, 28.

76. Z. Alexander & A. Dewjee (eds), *Wonderful adventures of Mrs Seacole in many lands* (Bristol: Falling Wall Press, 1984; original edn 1857); A. Josephs, "Mary Seacole: Jamaican nurse and doctress, 1805/1810(?)-1881," *The Jamaica Historical Review* **7**, pp. 48-65, 1991. A recent article on Seacole written by a staff nurse: Paul Crawford, "The other lady with the lamp", *Nursing Times* **88**, pp. 56-7, 1992, argues that historians' neglect of black women's contributions to nursing buttresses current discrimination against black nurses in Britain. See also A. Robinson, "Authority and the public display of identity: 'Wonderful Adventures of Mrs Seacole in many lands' ", *Feminist Studies* **20**, 1994.

77. See C. Bolt, *Victorian attitudes to race* (London: Routledge & Kegan Paul, 1971); D. A. Lorimer, *Colour, class and the Victorians: English attitudes to the negro in the mid-nineteenth century* (Leicester: Leicester University Press, 1978).

78. Z. Alexander, "Black entertainers, 1900-1910", *Feminist Art News* **2** (5), pp. 6-8.

79. Visram, *Ayabs, lascars and princes*, Ch. 2 & pp. 178, 181.

80. *Ibid.*, pp. 187-9.

81. *Ibid.*, pp. 139-43.

82. C. P. Ripley (ed.), *The black abolitionist papers, vol 1: the British Isles 1830-1865* (Chapel Hill, North Carolina: University of North Carolina Press, 1985) gives biographical information on Remond and the text of several of her anti-slavery lectures. For Ellen Craft, see R. J. M. Blackett, "Fugitive slaves in Britain: the odyssey of William and Ellen Craft", *Journal of American Studies* **12**, pp. 41-62, 1978.

83. V. Ware, *Beyond the pale: white women, racism and history* (London: Verso, 1992), Part 4, esp. pp. 178-82.

84. Visram, *Ayahs, lascars and princes*, p. 254, note 144.

85. Fryer, *Staying power*, pp. 280, 283-4, 293 & 327.

86. H. Adi, "The Nigerian Progress Union", in Association for the Study of African, Caribbean and Asian culture and history in Britain, *Newsletter* **9**, pp. 8-19, 1994; Fryer, *Staying power*, pp. 349-50.

87. B. Bousquet & C. Douglas, *West Indian women at war: British racism in World War II* (London: Lawrence and Wishart, 1991); Fryer, *Staying power*, pp. 356-67. See also Delia Jarrett-Macaulay, "National identity, race and gender - West Indian women in the frame", in *Nationalising femininity: culture, sexuality and British cinema in World War Two*, C. Gledhill & G. Swanson (eds) (Manchester: Manchester University Press, forthcoming).

88. See J. Haggis, "Gendering colonialism or colonising gender? Recent women's studies approaches to white women and the history of British colonialism", *Women's Studies International Forum* **13**, pp. 105-15, 1990, for a valuable critique of two key "woman-centred" approaches to the study of Empire: Helen Callaway, *Gender, culture, and Empire: European women in colonial Nigeria* (Urbana, Illinois: University of Illinois Press, 1987); and Claudia Knapman, *White women in Fiji 1835-1930: the ruin of Empire?* (Sydney: Allen & Unwin, 1986).

89. Mackenzie, *Propaganda and Empire*, p. 258. For the need to include a critical history of Empire in histories of British society, see S. Marks, "History, the nation and Empire: sniping from the periphery", *History Workshop Journal* **29**, pp. 111-19, 1990. For a fuller consideration of many of the issues raised in this section of the chapter, see Ware, *Beyond the pale*, parts 2, 3 & 4.

90. H. Callaway & D. O. Helly, "Crusader for Empire: Flora Shaw/Lady Lugard", in N. Chaudhuri & M. Strobel (eds), *Western women and imperialism: complicity and resistance* (Bloomington, Indiana: Indiana University Press, 1992), pp. 79-80.

91. *Ibid.*, p. 81.

92. *Ibid.*, p. 89.

93. *Ibid.*, p. 90.

94. *Ibid.*, pp. 92-4; D. Birkett, "The invalid at home and the Sampson abroad", *Women's Review* **6**, 18-19, 1986. See also D. Birkett, *Mary Kingsley, imperial adventuress* (London: Macmillan, 1992).

95. Callaway & Helly," Crusader for Empire", p. 93.

96. C. Midgley, "Anti-slavery and feminism in nineteenth-century Britain", *Gender and History* **5**, pp. 343-62, 1993. For a full consideration of the woman-slave analogy, see M. Ferguson, *Subject to others: British women writers and colonial slavery, 1670-1834* (London: Routledge, 1992).

97. C. Midgley, *Women against slavery: the British campaigns, 1780-1870* (London: Routledge, 1992), esp. Ch. 5. See also Ware, *Beyond the pale*.

98. Ware, *Beyond the pale*, p. 163.

273

99. A. M. Burton, "The white woman's burden: British feminists and 'the Indian woman', 1865-1915", in Chaudhuri & Strobel (eds), *Western women and imperialism*, p. 138.

100. *Ibid.*, p. 151; V. Amos & P. Parma•, "Challenging imperial feminism", *Feminist Review* **17**, pp. 3-19, 1984.

101. Burton, "The white woman's burden", pp. 139-45; A. Burton, *Burdens of history: British feminism, Indian women and imperial culture, 1865-1915* (Bloomington, Indiana: Indiana University Press, 1995).

102. A.J. Hammerton, *Emigrant gentlewomen: genteel poverty and female emigration, 1830-1914* (London: Croom Helm, 1979); C.J Macdonald, "Ellen Silk and her sisters: female emigration to the New World", in London Feminist History Group (ed.), *The sexual dynamics of history: men's power, women's resistance* (London: Pluto Press, 1983), pp. 66-86.

103. J. Bush, "'The right sort of woman'. Female emigrators and emigration to the British Empire 1890-1910", *Women's History Review* **3**, p. 386, 1994.

104. *Imperial Colonist* **2** (8) (August 1903), as quoted in Bush, "'The right sort of woman'", p. 385.

105. Poem by Dora Gore Brown entitled "To England's Daughters", in *Imperial Colonist* **3** (36), December 1904, as quoted in Bush "'The right sort of woman'", p. 386.

106. Bush, "'The right sort of woman'", p. 387.

107. *Imperial Colonist* **1** (6), June 1902, as quoted in Bush, " 'The right sort of woman' ", p. 399.

108. Mackenzie, *Propaganda and Empire*; C. Midgley & C. Gladys, "Public sculptures of women: whose heritage, whose future?", *Feminist Art News* **1.2** (2), pp. 6-9; D. Thompson, *Queen Victoria: gender and power* (London: Virago, 1990), esp. pp. 128-33.

109. A. Davin, "Imperialism and motherhood", *History Workshop Journal* **5**, pp. 9-65, 1978. For the history of eugenics, see D.J. Kevles, "In the name of eugenics: genetics and the uses of human heredity" (Berkeley, California: University of California Press, 1985). The founder of eugenics was Francis Galton, who first published his ideas in 1865; the Eugenics Education Society was funded in 1907, and eugenics was not finally discredited until revelations about the mass extermination of Jews and other supposedly "degenerate" groups by the Nazis in the name of racial purification.

110. MacKenzie, *Propaganda and Empire*, pp. 159-60.

111. See Ware, *Beyond the pale*, for a thorough exploration of the role of ideas about white women in the history of racism in Britain; for the relevance of such historically-based studies for contemporary feminist politics, see V. Ware, "Moments of danger: race, gender, and memories of Empire", in A. Shapiro (ed.), *Feminists Revision History* (New Brunswick: Rutgers University Press, 1994), pp. 217-46 (this essay first appeared in *History and Theory* **31**, December 1992.

112. Ware, *Beyond the pale*, part 4. The Ilbert Bill, by proposing to grant native Indian officials criminal juridiction of white British residents, was seen as leaving white women legally unprotected from the advances of lascivious Indian men (see Mrinalini sinha, "'Chathams, Pitts, and Gladstones in Petticoats': the politics of gender and race in the Ilbert Bill controversy, 1883-1884", in Chaudhuri & Strobel (eds), *Western women and imperialism*, pp. 98-116).

113. I. Bullock & R. Pankhurst (eds), *Sylvia Pankhurst, from artist to anti-Fascist* (London: Macmillan, 1992); P.W. Romero, *E. Sylvia Pankhurst, portrait of a radical* (New Haven, Connecticut: Yale University Press, 1987).

114. A. Chisholm, *Nancy Cunard, a biography* (London: Sidgwick and Jackson, 1979).

115. Valuable information on white women and imperial politics in interwar Britain is contained in B. Bush, *Britain and Black Africa in the inter-war years: metropolitan responses to the growth of race and political consciousness with specific reference to West and South Africa*, unpublished Ph.D. thesis, Sheffield University, 1986.

116. P. Gilroy, "Nationalism, history and ethnic absolutism", *History Workshop Journal* 30, p. 118, 1990.

117. *Ibid.*, p. 119.

Suggestions for further reading

No single book covers precisely the areas dealt with in this chapter, although a book edited by Joan Grant is forthcoming. For the history of women of Jewish, Irish, African and Asian descent in Britain, the best introductions are, respectively, L. Marks, "Carers and servers of the Jewish community: the marginalized heritage of Jewish women in Britain", *Immigrants and Minorities* 10 (1, 2), July 1991; A. Rossiter, "Bringing the margins into the centre: a review of aspects of Irish women's experience from a British perspective", in A. Smyth (ed.), *Irish women's studies reader* (Dublin: Attic Press, 1993), pp. 177–202; Z. Alexander, "Let it lie upon the table: the status of black women's biography in the UK", *Gender and History* 2 (1) Spring, pp. 22–33, 1990; and R. Vishram, *Ayahs, lascars and princes: the story of Indians in Britain 1700–1947* (London: Pluto, 1986). For white British women, "race" and Empire, see esp.: N. Chaudhuri & M. Strobel (eds), *Western women and imperialism: complicity and resistance* (Bloomington, Indiana: Indiana University Press, 1992); V. Ware, *Beyond the pale: white women, racism and history* (London: Verso, 1992); C. Midgley, *Women against slavery: the British campaigns, 1780–1870* (London: Routledge, 1992); and A. Burton & B. Ramusack (eds), "Feminism, imperialism and race: a dialogue between India and Britain", *Women's History Review*, Special Issue 3 (4), 1994. Moving beyond the scope of this chapter to the study of countries affected by British imperialism, M. Strobel, *European women and the second British Empire* (Bloomington, Indiana: Indiana University Press, 1991); and M. Strobel, "Gender and race in the nineteenth- and twentieth-century British Empire", in R. Bridenthal, C. Koonz, S. Stuard (eds), *Becoming visible: women in European history*, 2nd edn (Boston, Mass: Houghton Mifflin, 1987), Ch. 14, provide introductions to the nature of white women's presence in areas under British control; while the experience of colonized women is illuminated through a growing number of regional studies, including K. Sangari & S. Vaid, *Recasting women: essays in colonial history* (New Delhi: Kali for Women Press, 1989), which focuses on India.

Primary sources for Jewish women's history are located both in the London Museum of Jewish Life and the Manchester Jewish History Museum: these include oral history, and photographic and documentary archives that contain a large amount of relevant information on women. F. Guy, *Women of worth; Jewish women in Britain* (Manchester Jewish History Museum, 1992) is a useful booklet produced to accompany an exhibition of that name. Among valuable primary sources for black British history are Z. Alexander & A. Dewjee (eds), *Wonderful adventures of Mrs Seacole in many lands*, 2nd edn (Bristol: Falling Wall Press, 1984; original edn 1857); and M. Ferguson (ed.), *The history of Mary Prince, a West Indian slave, related by herself* (London: Pandora, 1987; original edn 1831); further resources are provided by the Black Cultural Archives, Coldharbour Lane, Brixton, London, and by the Association for the Study of African, Caribbean and Asian History in Britain, c/o Institute of Commonwealth Studies, University of London. For the multicultural roots of London society, see N. Merriman, *The peopling of London: fifteen thousand years of settlement from oversea*s (London: Museum of London, 1993). Unfortunately, published collections of primary sources for British women's history include little relevant material.

Chapter Eleven

ᐸ§

Women and the vote

Sandra Stanley Holton

Introduction

Sporadic calls for the enfranchisement of women were made from the time of
the 1832 Reform Bill, when women were for the first time expressly
excluded from this right. But no large-scale, organized demand arose until
1865, when a new Reform Bill was anticipated, and when John Stuart Mill,
the political philosopher, was elected to Parliament on a programme that
included women's suffrage.[1] By this time a women's movement was in
existence, and the vote was only one of a broad range of rights sought in the
following decades.[2]

In the early years of the twentieth century the suffrage campaigns took on
new colour and new urgency with the emergence of a younger generation of
leaders of charismatic power, and with the adoption of "militant" methods
far more sensational than those of earlier decades.[3] What remained a
constant, however, was the Parliamentary focus of the campaigns, for this
was the arena in which the question would be decided. Equally, the political
interests and reform goals of suffragists were rarely restricted to the gaining of
the vote for their sex. Many were also seeking an overall reform of the
political and social systems of Britain. For all these reasons, the internal
divisions within the suffrage movement often reflected party-political, and
sometimes even sectarian, struggles outside the movement itself, struggles
which in turn were often the outcome of class and regional tensions within
British society. The nature and course of the women's suffrage movement

277

cannot be understood, then, outside the broader settings of the women's movement, and of Parliamentary politics.[4]

The formation of a women's movement, 1840–65

Women's suffrage was part of the early programme of the Chartist movement in the 1840s, though this object was soon abandoned.[5] A middle-class Chartist, the Quaker Anne Knight, formed what was probably the first women's suffrage society, in Sheffield in 1851.[6] But in terms of the creation of a national demand with longstanding organizations, women's suffrage had to wait until 1865, when the promise of a second Reform Bill revived public debate on this question. By this time, a more broadly-focused women's movement provided both the social and intellectual capacity to mount such a campaign.[7]

Middle-class women had first gained valuable experience of political organization and political campaigning in the 1840s in the Anti-Corn Law League. The philanthropic efforts of such women grew during this period, and were also organized increasingly through national bodies that might take on something of a political cast. This was true, for example, of women's work for the abolition of slavery. Anti-slavery campaigning in Britain never politicized women to the extent that it did in the United States. Partly this reflected the different place of slavery in each society.[8] But there is some evidence that women from anti-slavery families in Britain began to link their abolitionism to the emancipation of their own sex in the years that followed the World Anti-Slavery Convention in 1840. And it was a visiting black abolitionist, Sarah Remond, who became the first woman to address mass mixed audiences in lectures that encompassed both anti-slavery and women's rights.[9]

Kinship and friendship circles among women were important to this process.[10] One group of friends who took a particular interest in the 1840 convention also went on to take a pioneering role in calling for women's rights. They included Anne Knight and Elizabeth Pease, both Quakers, and Harriet Martineau, Elizabeth Reid, Julia Smith, all Unitarians, together with a successful writer of the day, Anna Jameson. Anne Knight formed the first short-lived women's suffrage society some years later, as we have already seen. Harriet Martineau and Anna Jameson used their positions as established intellectuals and writers in support of women's rights over the next two decades, while Elizabeth Reid founded Bedford College in 1849, one of the first institutions to offer advanced education for women. Of this group, Julia Smith's role was perhaps the most indirect, in the influence she exercised over her niece, Barbara Leigh Smith. Aunt and niece were among the first students at Bedford College, while Barbara Leigh Smith was to pioneer organization on behalf of women's rights over the next few years.[11]

Together with her close friend, Bessie Rayner Parkes, also from a middle-class radical family, Barbara Leigh Smith began to rouse public debate in the mid-1850s over a range of issues concerning the rights of women: education, employment opportunities and family law. This last question led her to form a committee in pursuit of Parliamentary reform of the marriage laws, especially those laws that limited married women's rights to hold property. It seems she had been prompted to take up this question by the case of Anna Jameson, who had become something of a mentor to Barbara Leigh Smith. Anna Jameson had separated from her husband many years before, and had since maintained herself through her writing. While her husband had retained rights over all her property during this time, include the earnings from her professional work, he died leaving nothing to her in his will, and the law allowed her no claim on his estate.[12]

Barbara Leigh Smith made a detailed analysis of the state of the law, published her findings as a pamphlet, and organized a committee of women. These efforts also gained the support of leading male reformers, especially those involved with the National Association for the Promotion of Social Science, a forum in which issues of women's rights were raised continually from this time. In this way, a circle of women was established around Barbara Leigh Smith and Bessie Rayner Parkes who were concerned to improve the situation of their sex, and this was subsequently given a focus by the provision of meeting rooms in London, in Langham Place. Here various approaches to women's problems were pursued: a Society for the Promotion of the Employment of Women was formed; the Gentlewomen's Emigration Society encouraged middle-class women to venture abroad in search of a livelihood; and a vehicle for communication with women out of reach of London was established through the *English Woman's Journal*. These institutional structures ensured that such early attempts at organization were able to survive the marriage and removal overseas of Barbara Leigh Smith Bodichon. In the early 1860s a debating group was formed, called the Kensington Society, which provided women with experience in preparing papers and speaking before an audience.[13]

Though these initiatives had come out of radical and nonconformist reforming circles, they held an appeal also for a wide spectrum of women. This included, for example, the Conservative Anglican, Emily Davies, first attracted by the work of the Society for the Promotion of Employment for Women, and taking on an increasing leadership role after she came from Newcastle to live in London in the early 1860s. Over the next few years she took over editorship of the *English Woman's Journal*, and began the (eventually) successful campaigns to open up matriculation examinations to women, and to improve women's educational opportunities, most especially in terms of founding Girton College, Cambridge. She also helped her friend, Elizabeth Garrett, begin the campaign to open up the medical profession to women - one which took many years to win, so that Elizabeth Garrett had to complete her medical education overseas.[14]

The formation of the first women's suffrage committees, 1865–70

It was in a Kensington Society debate that the question of women's right to the vote was first raised among this circle, and the demand for women's suffrage was endorsed by a vote taken at the end of the debate. Emily Davies believed that it was too soon to raise such a challenge, and feared that it would attract extremists - "jumping like kangaroos" - to the movement.[15] But this period had also seen the election of a reforming government, and the return to Parliament of leaders of middle-class radical opinion such as John Stuart Mill. Barbara Bodichon and Elizabeth Garrett were among those who joined John Stuart Mill's election campaign in the seat of Westminster. After his election he agreed to take up the question of women's suffrage in the House of Commons if its supporters could organize the collection of a petition in support of this cause. The first suffrage committees were formed in London and Manchester in 1865 for this purpose. A corresponding member of the Kensington Society, Elizabeth Wolstenholme, a Manchester headmistress, undertook the work in that city, and the efforts of the provincial society soon proved more than equal to that of the metropolitan.[16]

The rest of the 1860s brought one disappointment after another for suffragists. The Reform Act of 1867 passed without the women's suffrage amendment moved by John Stuart Mill. Similarly, when a number of Lancashire women with the necessary property qualifications cast their vote in the election which followed, the returning officer ruled their votes invalid. Suffragists took a test case to the courts in Chorlton *v* Lings, and among their legal advisers was a young Manchester lawyer, Richard Pankhurst. Their case appealed to Brougham's Act of 1851, which declared that "in all Acts words importing the masculine gender shall be deemed and taken to include women unless the contrary be expressly provided", and that women were therefore legally entitled to vote under the franchise laws as they then stood.[17] This argument was not accepted by the court, and so this route to the vote was also closed.

In 1870, the first women's suffrage bill was drafted by Richard Pankhurst, and introduced as a private member measure by Charles Dilke and Jacob Bright. Both men were Radical–Liberals, a loose grouping within the Liberal party which drew especially on the ideas of John Stuart Mill, himself no longer in Parliament. Again, this measure was rejected by the House of Commons.[18] But this period did see one notable success for women's suffrage: Jacob Bright secured an amendment to the Municipal Corporations Amendment Act of 1869 which gave women with the appropriate property qualifications the right to vote in municipal elections.[19] In 1870 it was also established that women might both vote and serve on the local school boards formed by Forster's Education Act. This quiet advance marked the first formal entry of women into political life, and it was an advance on which women were to build in subsequent years.[20]

In contrast to the twentieth-century movement, the nineteenth-century campaigns have often been presented as being dull and staid, and nineteenth-century suffragists in general have been perceived as being less radical, or even conservative, in their approach to women's emancipation.[21] As a consequence, the varieties of opinion and approaches among nineteenth century suffragists to gaining full citizenship for women have only recently begun to receive analysis.[22] Yet these very earliest years of the movement revealed varying opinions among suffragists on a number of issues, the most divisive of which was whether or not to include married women in the demand. An analysis of these tensions reveals the presence of a significant Radical-Liberal current of thought. This put forward consistently an advanced account of women's wrongs, and a more challenging programme for change, most particularly over the issue of whether or not to include married women in the suffrage demand.[23]

This question arose because of a long-standing doctrine within the British legal system, that of coverture. By this doctrine, a married women was defined as a "feme covert", that is a woman whose legal personhood had been subsumed under that of her husband. In consequence of coverture, married women were unable, for example, to make contracts or to hold property in their own right, though wealthier families might protect a daughter's property by establishing a trust for her on marriage. It followed from this that married women were disabled from qualifying under any franchise system still based on the ownership of property, as was the case in Britain at this time. For this reason, many suffragists wanted expressly to limit their demand to the enfranchisement of the "feme sole", a status attaching only to unmarried women and widows.

For Radical-Liberals, however, coverture seemed as significant a bar to the citizenship of women as their disfranchisement.[24] They were unwilling consequently to accept any formulation of the demand which might appear to endorse the existing civil disabilities of married women. The leadership of the London suffrage society included initially Conservatives such as Emily Davies and Frances Power Cobbe, as well as Radical-Liberals such as Clementia Taylor, and it advocated the exclusion of married women from the demand. The Manchester society, in contrast, was far more firmly under the control of Radical-Liberals, who included Elizabeth Wolstenholme, Jacob Bright and his wife Ursula, and Richard Pankhurst, and who opposed the exclusion of married women from the demand.[25] This was also initially the position of Lydia Becker, who became an especially influential figure as both secretary of the Manchester society, and editor of the *Women's Suffrage Journal*, which began publication in 1870.[26] After a period of some tension, when John Stuart Mill and his stepdaughter, Helen Taylor, found it easier to work with the Manchester suffragists, a compromise formulation of the demand was agreed upon. This appealed strictly to the principle of sexual equality, and asked for the vote for women on the same terms as men. Though this effectively excluded married women – because of their standing as "femes covert" together with the property qualifications then required for the vote – it did not do so expressly. And at the same time, Radical–Liberal suffragists began to mount a parallel campaign for the reform of the laws relating to married women's property, so as to bring an end to this particular disability. Here again, the leadership of the Manchester society was much in evidence, and the headquarters of the Married Women's Property Committee were in Manchester, with Elizabeth Wolstenholme as its Secretary and Lydia Becker as its Treasurer.

Divided councils: the women's suffrage movement, 1870–97

A second source of disagreement among suffragists arose, however, in 1870 when a number of Radical–Liberal suffragists in the north-west also lent their support to the campaign for the repeal of the Contagious Diseases Acts. This legislation had been passed in the 1860s with the aim of reducing the extent of venereal disease within the armed forces. To this end it had introduced and extended gradually a system of medical surveillance of those designated by the police as prostitutes in naval ports and garrison towns.[27] The civil rights of these women over their own persons were abrogated by a requirement that they attend for medical examination, and spend a period in hospital if the medical officer concerned declared them to have a venereal infection, though there was no scientific method of diagnosis, and no certain cure available in this period.[28] Failure to comply with this regulation was punishable by a prison sentence with hard labour.

Though John Stuart Mill was an opponent of the Acts, he nonetheless believed that it was unwise to link the demand for women's suffrage with such a cause. The Radical–Liberals of the Manchester area, and in the other provincial societies which had come together in a loose federation by then known as the National Society for Women's Suffrage (NSWS), disagreed with him. They became Josephine Butler's firmest supporters and aides in the campaigns which followed, while the opinion of Mill prevailed in the London NSWS, and Radical–Liberals such as its one-time Secretary, Clementia Taylor, felt it necessary now to withdraw from its leadership to work with the Radical–Liberal suffragists in the provincial societies. There had always been considerable rivalry between London and the provincial societies, and resentment at the way the metropolitan body attempted to direct the movement nationally. At the time of this dispute the provincial societies established a Central Committee of the NSWS in which their voices might outweigh the previously dominant London society. Under Mill's sway, the

London society refused to become part of this Central Committee, and so for the next few years worked separately from the provincial societies.

These tensions were exacerbated when the Liberal party was defeated in the 1874 election, an election in which Jacob Bright lost his seat, and hence his leadership of parliamentary suffrage opinion. He was replaced by a Conservative MP, William Forsyth, who advised that suffragists limit their demand for the vote to unmarried women and widows. Mill had died in 1873 and so his considerable influence against such a limitation was no longer a factor in the debates that followed among suffragists. Lydia Becker, by this time a commanding presence in the suffrage movement, agreed reluctantly to accept Forsyth's advice. She went further and advised her colleagues on the wisdom of also suspending the work of the Married Women's Property Committee, and accepting for the time being the partial advance they had secured in the 1870 Married Women's Property Act.[29] Radical-Liberal opinion within the suffrage leadership was outraged by what appeared to be a damaging retreat from women's claims to full citizenship. The bitterness among suffragists was evident the following year when more moderate opinion among the leadership, including Lydia Becker, attempted to exclude Elizabeth Wolstenholme from the offices she held at that time in the women's movement, on the grounds of her premarital pregnancy.[30] Later married and as Elizabeth Wolstenholme Elmy, she continued to work closely with Radical-Liberal suffragists, most notably Ursula Bright. By their combined efforts, they secured the passage of a further Married Women's Property Act in 1882 which greatly extended the rights of married women, though it was so altered within the House of Commons as to leave intact the doctrine of coverture.[31] And so this question continued to be a source of dissension among suffragists for another decade and more.

With the return of the Liberal Party to power in 1880 came the expectation of a further Reform Bill to extend the franchise to those men, mostly agricultural workers, as well as miners in colliery villages, who at that time were unlikely to qualify for the vote. These years also saw suffragists beginning to try to build a more popular following. Priscilla Bright McLaren, with the help of another Radical suffragist from Leeds, Alice Scatcherd, organized a series of large demonstrations in a number of major cities, aimed at attracting working-class support. One of the great successes of this effort was the effect made on audiences by the first working woman to become nationally known as a suffrage speaker, Jessie Craigen, and popular support for the demand was evident. But once more the movement was divided by the proposal that married women be excluded explicitly from the claim. This was resisted by Ursula Bright and her supporters, who moved on to the offensive and demanded that they be expressly *included*.

More moderate counsels prevailed, however, and the women's suffrage amendment to the Reform Act of 1884 was again a compromise formulated in terms of sexual equality. Even so, the opposition of the Liberal Prime Minister,

William Ewart Gladstone, ensured its defeat.[32] The divisions among suffragists deepened in subsequent years as the Liberal Party itself split over Irish home rule. While the main body of Liberal women suffragists remained staunch Gladstonians, others such as Millicent Garrett Fawcett opposed home rule and became Liberal Unionists. Suffragists were also divided in this period over questions of moral reform. The more libertarian Liberal–Radicals, such as Elizabeth Wolstenholme Elmy, for example, opposed greater state intervention in areas of personal morality, especially the increasing harassment of prostitutes. "Social purity" advocates such as Millicent Garrett Fawcett, in contrast, supported greater intervention and restriction through local watch committees, and more repressive legislation, like the Criminal Law Amendment Act of 1886 which both raised the age of consent for girls and made homosexual relations between men a criminal offence.[33]

By the late 1880s the divisions and tensions among suffragists had become so great that the old NSWS split into two separate societies. Liberal Party women among its leadership had succeeded in changing the society's rules, and the new rules allowed the affiliation of other bodies, the aims of which included women's suffrage. Liberal Unionists, such as Millicent Garrett Fawcett, believed that this was simply a ploy to allow the take-over of the suffrage movement by the Liberal Party through the affiliation of the extensive network of Women's Liberal Associations formed since 1881, and brought together in the Women's Liberal Federation.[34] When she and her supporters failed to prevent the change of rules, she, together with Lydia Becker and Helen Blackburn, the Secretary of the NSWS, withdrew, and reconstituted a suffrage society under the old rules. The "new rules" society now called itself the Central National Society for Women's Suffrage (CNSWS), while the "old rules" society called itself, somewhat confusingly, the Central Committee of the National Society for Women's Suffrage (CCNSWS). Contemporaries soon found it more convenient to refer to each body by the address of its headquarters, and so the two were often referred to as the "Parliament Street society" (new rules, CNSWS) and the "Great College Street society" (old rules, CCNSWS).[35]

The Parliament Street society appears to have attracted the support of the majority of the existing branch societies, and to have been the significantly stronger body. Lydia Becker, in reporting this split, claimed that another source of dispute had been the formulation of the demand, and that the Parliament Street society supported the inclusion of married women. While it was the case that her own Great College Street society continued to argue for married women's exclusion, there was, in fact, a division of opinion in the Parliament Street society over this question. As a result, the latter attempted to hold its members together by deciding to support both suffrage Bills which excluded married women, and suffrage Bills framed in terms of equal rights. But it opposed the most radical formulation of the demand, which *expressly included* married women. This policy was challenged by Richard Pankhurst and other Radicals from the north-west, without success. As a consequence,

Elizabeth Wolstenholme Elmy, with the help of Alice Scatcherd and Harriet McIlquham, formed a third suffrage organization, the Women's Franchise League. This body was committed explicitly to include married women in the demand, as well as to work for a broad programme of civil equality for women.[36] Very soon, Ursula Bright moved into its leadership, together with Emmeline Pankhurst, wife of Richard Pankhurst. Over the next few years, the League maintained this radical programme, and prefigured twentieth-century developments in the links which it sought to build with the Labour and Socialist movements, and with working-class women's organizations, most especially the Women's Co-operative Guild.[37] Meanwhile, Elizabeth Wolstenholme Elmy, who had been ousted from its leadership, formed a new body, the Women's Emancipation Union, which went further still in attempting to improve the civil status of married women, most especially by campaigning against rape in marriage.[38]

The formation of the National Union of Women's Suffrage Societies, 1897

The 1890s proved to be far more successful for the women's movement on a number of fronts.[39] For suffragists, the early years of this decade saw tensions between the Parliament Street and the Great College Street societies ease. In 1894 the suffrage cause gained a most significant advance in the passage of the Local Government Act. By this Act, married women became eligible for *all* the local government franchises already open to single women and widows, and the issue of coverture, at least in relation to the franchise laws, was effectively dead. The Parliament Street and Great College Street societies had liaised and co-operated closely in the joint efforts to pressure the government for the inclusion of the relevant clause, while the Women's Franchise League had also lobbied hard on behalf of this advance, while failing to secure an even more extensive local government franchise for women.[40] The way was now clear for suffragists to work together for a measure which all societies could now agree upon – equal rights in the parliamentary franchise for women, both single and married. Suffragists from all sections of the movement helped to gather a large petition to present when the opportunity arose to introduce such a Bill. Work for the Special Appeal provided the foundation for the subsequent reunification of the suffrage movement in 1897 within the National Union of Women's Suffrage Societies (hereafter the National Union), under the leadership of Millicent Garrett Fawcett.[41] In that year, too, a women's suffrage Bill passed its second reading in the House of Commons for the first time. Though it was only a Private Member's Bill and lacked the government backing which would have been necessary for it to complete all its stages and become law, nonetheless it was the most hopeful sign suffragists had had for many years.

For the next few years, the North of England society, as the Manchester society was by this time known, once again moved to the fore in new developments in suffrage methods and policies. Its Secretary from 1894 was Esther Roper, a young graduate of the university there. Her father had been a child of the Manchester slums, who had died a missionary after gaining an education through the Church Missionary Society Sunday school. Esther Roper's lifetime companion, Eva Gore Booth, was, in contrast, from a landed family in Ireland.[42] She displayed her sympathies with the Labour movement in the role she played in these years as co-Secretary with Sarah Dickinson, a working-class suffragist and trade-unionist of the Manchester and Salford Women's Trades Union Council from 1900. From the mid–1890s, then, the North of England society emulated, with growing success, the work already begun by bodies such as the Women's Franchise League in organizing the support of working-class women for the suffrage cause.

The Manchester region was unusual in the extent of trade union organization among women, who over several generations had remained a significant presence in the textile factories there. This, together with the growing network of Women's Co-operative Guild branches, provided working-class women with valuable experience for public life and Labour movement politics. Their interest in the suffrage cause also grew alongside the movement for the independent representation of Labour in Parliament. The Independent Labour Party provided another body through which middle-class radicals and working-class activists might meet, and it was especially strong in Lancashire and Yorkshire in the late 1890s. Here was a new constituency to which the middle-class suffrage societies might appeal. Few did so, however, with similar success to the North of England society, with its forward-looking Secretary, and the established organization among working-class women there. The efforts of Manchester suffragists shifted in these years from the long-established pattern of drawingroom meetings and occasional set-piece public demonstrations in places such as the Free Trade Hall. Instead, open-air speaking was undertaken, often outside factory gates during dinner breaks, and petitions were collected from among women workers.[43] Some of the strongest supporters for the new development were to be found among the older generation of Radical–Liberal suffragists.[44] A third generation of suffragists now entering the movement was introduced to these new methods, including Christabel Pankhurst, the eldest daughter of Richard and Emmeline Pankhurst. Emmeline Pankhurst had withdrawn from political life for a period after her husband's sudden death in 1898. It was Eva Gore Booth and Esther Roper who, in these years, not only provided the initial training of Christabel Pankhurst in suffrage activism, but also encouraged their young protégée to follow in her father's footsteps and begin a law degree at the university in Manchester.[45]

For the years around the turn of the twentieth century, questions of domestic reform were put on "hold" while a Conservative government was in power, and war was waged against the Boers in South Africa. But from 1903 suffragists began to look to the next general election, when a Liberal Party victory was anticipated. Most local branch societies of the National Union remained dominated by middle-class women, and especially those with strong Liberal Party sympathies, such as Margaret Ashton, the foremost figure on the committee of the North of England Society. The daughter of a Lancashire industrialist, and active in local government, Margaret Ashton retained her faith at this time that her party would prove true to its principles, and that its return to government provided the best hope for securing equality in the franchise laws. Working-class women activists were likely to have a somewhat different perspective, however. Not only were they involved increasingly in the movement for the independent representation of Labour in Parliament, but it seemed that sexual equality in the franchise laws was likely to prove of limited value to them. Despite the three Reform Acts of the nineteenth century, a third of all adult men remained disfranchised, unable to meet its remaining property and registration requirements.[46] Working-class women could expect to meet with the same, or worse, difficulties.

Women's suffrage and the Labour and Socialist movements

It seems likely that it was such issues that explain why the textile workers, led by Esther Roper and Eva Gore Booth, broke away from the North of England society to form the Lancashire and Cheshire Textile and Other Workers Representation Committee (LCTOWRC). The very name of the organization indicated the close affiliation its members felt with the Labour Representation Committee that subsequently became the Labour Party. The LCTOWRC continued to build support for women's suffrage among the women workers of the north-west, but it demanded suffrage for all adult women. Its election policy also differed from that of the National Union. Whereas the larger body claimed a non-party policy of support for "the best friend" of the cause, the LCTOWRC helped to sponsor campaigns on behalf of Labour candidates who stood on a platform of womanhood suffrage. Wigan was the first constituency chosen by the LCTOWRC to run its own suffrage-Labour candidate.[47] This was work with which many in the National Union sympathised, and a number of its branch societies offered financial aid to the work of the LCTOWRC.[48]

In 1903 there was in Manchester the formation of yet another organization committed to linking Labour and suffrage campaigning: the Women's Social and Political Union (hereafter WSPU).[49] It was formed at the home of Emmeline Pankhurst, and attracted the support of local ILP women. Its early methods were similar to those of Esther Roper and Eva Gore Booth, emphasizing outdoor meetings in working-class areas, and building on the established role of the Pankhurst family in the ILP, both nationally and locally.

287

Its early membership was composed largely of working-class Labour and Socialist women.[50] The WSPU did not, however, follow the policies of the textile workers, but, at least to begin with, was intended rather as a "ginger group" within the Independent Labour Party (hereafter, the ILP). While some ILP leaders, notably Keir Hardie, were committed to the principle of sexual equality in the franchise, others, such as Bruce Glasier, were sceptical of the Pankhursts' new body, seeing it as a deflection of working-class energies and resources for a demand which he viewed as serving only middle-class interests. Many in the Labour and Socialist movements, especially the Marxist Social Democratic Federation, preferred to promote franchise reform in the form of adult suffrage. From 1904, women's suffragists found their resolutions at Labour and Socialist conferences increasingly under challenge, while formal support, at least, grew for adult suffrage.[51]

The WSPU first attracted national attention in October 1905, after a Liberal Party rally in the Free Trade Hall, Manchester. Christabel Pankhurst and Annie Kenney (a textile worker) determined to draw public attention to their cause by seeking arrest. After heckling the leading Liberal politician, Sir Edward Grey, and being ejected from the meeting, Christabel Pankhurst committed a technical assault on a police officer. The two women soon found themselves serving short prison sentences, and attracting press attention, which had been their aim. This occasion is generally taken as marking the beginning of suffrage "militancy", a departure that entailed both a new mode of suffrage campaigning and a new set of political policies.[52]

At its beginning, militancy drew on established practices of civil disobedience and passive resistance, forms of protest long adopted by dissenting religious groups against the payment of tithes and church rates, for example. These included tax resistance and non-co-operation with the police and prison authorities, and such methods had earlier been attempted by some individual suffragists in the 1870s and the 1880s.[53] Militancy as a political policy adapted the tactics of Josephine Butler in the campaigns against the Contagious Diseases Acts in the 1870s–1880s and the Irish Nationalists in the 1880s.[54] This adaptation involved active opposition to Liberal Party candidates during elections, whether or not those candidates were sympathetic to the suffrage cause as individuals. The aim was to pressure the Liberal leadership, who were expected to form the next government and who went to the country in 1906 as a party committed to an extensive programme of social reform. The WSPU sought, in this way, to secure a government measure of women's suffrage, another departure from the tactics of the National Union, which were focused on organizing the introduction and support of Private Members' Bills. Militant pressure was exerted, then, through the harassment of leading Liberal figures during major public meetings. In the general election of 1906, the militant policy was pursued in part by offering support for pro-suffrage Labour candidates such as Keir Hardie, because the electoral successes of Labour were already posing a threat to the Liberal Party. Those who rejected such an approach and remained loyal to the National Union, with its non-party policy that relied solely on the individual support of MPs, were dismissed as "non-militants".

Constitutionalists and militants

The National Union itself chose a positive form of identification in terms of "constitutionalism", one which also allowed it to suggest an equally strong, if varying, perspective on the demand.[55] The constitutionalist suffragist was one who maintained her faith in the existing political system to deliver reform. Hence her choice to continue with the old methods of petition and the organization of pressure from the constituencies by way of letters to the press, memorials from local notables to Members of Parliament, deputations, and the occasional large public meeting. The election activities of the National Union were directed at securing the election of as many "friends" of women's suffrage as possible, on whom pressure was then exerted to introduce a private member's measure of women's suffrage, and to support such measures when put before the House of Commons. The National Union claimed to be non-partisan in all its policies and activities, and to offer election support to the candidate considered "the best friend" of the cause. The dominance of women Liberals within its branches, and the sympathy for women's suffrage common among the rank and file of Liberal candidates meant that the National Union most often remained neutral, where it did not offer support for Liberal candidates, during elections.[56] It also meant that a formal breach between Esther Roper, and Eva Gore Booth and the North of England society, became inevitable in the context of the coming general election, although co-operative relations were maintained in other aspects of suffrage campaigning.[57]

As a consequence of these differing policies, militant and constitutionalist might on occasion find themselves running conflicting campaigns at a constituency level. And loyal Liberal suffragists were sometimes antagonized by militant attacks on their candidates, and the support offered to Labour. Others disliked the "unladylike" approach of the militants as they feared this might undermine the credibility of their cause, confirming the claims of anti-suffragists that women were unfit for public life. Members of the LCTOWRC and Women's Co-operative Guild especially, resented an assumption common among middle-class suffragists that militancy was a direct outcome of the growing presence of working class Labour and Socialist women in the movement.[58] But while class tension was a continuing fact of suffrage campaigning, it is an unhelpful generalization to suggest that the demand for the vote only appealed, or was relevant to, an elite of women.[59]

In the early years of militancy, Millicent Garrett Fawcett counselled against the hostility it aroused in some National Union members. While she did not herself feel that militant methods and policies were always wise, she admired the courage they often required. She also admitted frankly that the enormous growth in membership experienced by the National Union from 1906 onwards was due in large part to the increased notoriety that militancy had brought to their cause. When her old friend, Annie Cobden Sanderson, was among several WSPU demonstrators given two-month prison sentences late in 1906, it was Millicent Garrett Fawcett who arranged a banquet at the Savoy to welcome the prisoners on their release. Though the Pankhursts seem to have boycotted this event, other prominent WSPU members were more ready to acknowledge an important role for the National Union in educating public opinion, and in establishing a national base for the movement.[60]

For a time, then, the relationship between militancy and constitutionalism was essentially a symbiotic one, the activities of each wing serving to reinforce and bolster the efforts of the other, despite occasional clashes during specific election campaigns. Not surprisingly in such circumstances, joint membership was common, and, at branch level, National Union and WSPU societies were often able to work closely together. The national leaderships were somewhat less flexible, though Millicent Garrett Fawcett did listen carefully to those who argued for a unification of the two wings between 1906–8, and a degree of co-operation was evident in suffrage demonstrations and the preparation of suffrage literature.[61]

At this time, then, the distinction between "militant" and "constitutionalist" was not nearly as absolute as subsequent accounts sometimes suggest. There were a number of bodies that found it possible to work with both wings simultaneously, most notably perhaps those which drew on London's Bohemia for support. Groups of writers, artists and actors each formed their own particular suffrage societies in these years, and organizations such as the Writers' and Artists' Franchise League, and the Actresses' Franchise League remained neutral on the question of militancy versus constitutionalism. Though individually their members were most often in sympathy with militant methods, these organizations provided valuable aid to both wings of the movement, in terms of theatrical productions, novels, pamphlets, and the design and making of banners and posters. These years first saw the use of spectacle to attract public attention, especially in the staging of marches, demonstrations and pageants, and it was the Bohemian suffragists who provided much of the glamour that drew in many fresh recruits. These smaller, more specialized suffrage bodies also provided a link between the militant and suffrage wings that was valuable in itself.[62]

It is also the case that neither the militant nor the constitutional wing were as unchanging or as coherent as these categories suggest. Both wings of the movement experienced continuing internal tensions, and sometimes divisions. The WSPU especially was never a stable organization. Such coherence as was maintained rested on a combination of autocratic government from its self-appointed leadership at critical points, together with the large degree of autonomy allowed to its branch societies on a day-to-day basis.[63] Tensions among the original leadership of the WSPU began to emerge shortly after the election of a Liberal Government early in 1906. By the summer the WSPU had moved its headquarters to London, and had recruited, through the good offices of Keir Hardie, the considerable organizational and fundraising talents of Emmeline and Frederick Pethick Lawrence, wealthy radicals with Labour movement sympathies.[64] An inner circle formed around Emmeline and Christabel Pankhurst which was increasingly intolerant of any challenge to its dominance within the WSPU, and apparently jealous of such public attention and personal loyalty as might from time to time attach to other charismatic figures among its supporters.

Dora Montefiore was the first of the original leadership to be expelled, for reasons which remain unclear. There was some unsubstantiated suggestion of financial dishonesty, but of more significance almost certainly was the personal following she was building up within the London WSPU; the public attention she had attracted through her tax resistance; her unease at the growing physical violence that attended WSPU demonstrations; and her continuing insistence on seeing women's suffrage as part of the demand for adult suffrage. Other factors may have been "heterodox passages in her private life", especially a scandal surrounding her relationship with a married, working-class, man younger than herself, together with growing gossip about her taste for cocaine lozenges. Whatever was the truth, from this time on Dora Montefiore focused her energies on the Adult Suffrage Society, on offshoot of the Social Democratic Federation of which she was also a member.[65]

The next division within the leadership of the WSPU occurred the following year, when Emmeline Pankhurst expressed growing fears of disloyalty among previously close colleagues.[66] Christabel Pankhurst had introduced a change of policy without any consultation of the WSPU's membership in August 1906, one which caused some unease among Socialist suffragists, because it saw the WSPU attacking Labour and Liberal candidates equally in by-elections. Teresa Billington Greig, formerly a Manchester teacher, the first woman organizer of the ILP, and at that time the WSPU's organizer in Scotland, pressed for a more democratic constitution which would allow for greater rank and file participation in policymaking. She and Charlotte Despard, another socialist suffragist who had the previous year replaced Sylvia Pankhurst as Secretary of the WSPU, sought discussion of these issues at the annual meeting planned for October 1907. Emmeline Pankhurst and her supporters simply cancelled the meeting and established by fiat a new executive and set of officers for the WSPU.[67]

The dissidents, led by Teresa Billington Greig and Charlotte Despard, formed a second militant body, the Women's Freedom League (hereafter, WFL) which attracted the support of many socialist suffragists and a significant number of the WSPU's branch societies. But here again, at a branch level it is not uncommon to find women who belonged to both the

WFL and WSPU, and even to both of these as well as the National Union.[68] Similarly, the relationship between the WSPU and the ILP often remained much closer at branch level than might have been expected, given the growing antagonism between the leaderships of each body.[69]

The WFL, while formally non-party in its affiliations, remained close to the Independent Labour Party, and in general preferred methods such as tax-resistance, sometimes referred to as "constitutional militancy", in preference to the increasing violence attaching to WSPU demonstrations from the latter part of 1908 onwards. The WFL also encouraged the organization of male support in separate societies such as the Men's Franchise League, in which both militant and constitutionalist sympathizers were be found, and in which the men of London's Bohemia were again much in evidence. There was also a Men's Social and Political Union formed, though the WSPU remained ambivalent about the role of men in the suffrage movement, and by 1912 it was becoming increasingly hostile to men's influence in suffrage politics.

By the end of 1908, then, the term "militant" had become a complex category which might apply to members of any of the suffrage organizations. It encompassed those prepared to endure violence and to go to prison for the cause, but who were not themselves willing to commit acts of violence; those increasingly designated "fighting" or "warrior" militants who were prepared to throw stones, and worse; and those somewhat unkindly described by one sceptic as "clapping militants". These included many who were members of the National Union, but who also attended WSPU meetings and demonstrations, and contributed to its funds, while not themselves engaging in any direct confrontation with the authorities.[70]

"Democratic suffragists" and the National Union of Women's Suffrage Societies

Not surprisingly, then, the National Union itself was subject to many internal tensions, though its elaborate machinery for rank and file consultation, and the commitment of constitutionalists to democratic decisionmaking, meant that differences of view among its members were less disruptive. One source of increasing tension was the growing disillusion among many of its members with the Liberal Party, and a wish to develop a more assertive stance with regard to the Liberal Government. Pressure for such a change of direction grew as the cause of adult suffrage advanced after the new Liberal Prime Minister, Herbert Asquith, announced his party's commitment to this goal in 1909. Some suffragists throughout the movement feared, with good reason, that the ambitions of both the Liberal and Labour parties for franchise reform would be fulfilled by manhood suffrage, leaving the sex bar to the franchise in place. Many other Liberal and Labour women suffragists were also advocates of universal suffrage – the vote for all adults, male and female – and were prepared to trust that advocacy of adult suffrage would bring about this end. Working-class suffragists experienced more acutely, perhaps, the conflict of loyalties to which the demand for women's suffrage gave rise, for manhood suffrage promised to further the cause of independent Labour representation, while sexual equality would leave many working-class women, as well as men, disfranchised. It was the president of the Women's Co-operative Guild, who sought to unite the campaign for women's suffrage and the campaign for adult suffrage in an appeal to "democratic suffragists" in all classes and parties to work together for universal adult enfranchisement. She, together with other leading Labour and Liberal men and women, gave this approach organizational expression through the formation of the People's Suffrage Federation.[71]

Such an approach was regarded with considerable suspicion among the leaderships of both the militant and constitutional wings of the movement. But Margaret Llewelyn Davies was right to believe that there were women's suffragists in all parts of the movement who would prove responsive to such a call. Though this "democratic suffragist" current was not restricted to any one organization, it proved most effective within the National Union, and among those women who were now totally disillusioned with Liberalism, or who already had, or were shifting towards Labour and Socialist sympathies. Democratic suffragists were already a significant presence in the major National Union branch societies of Manchester, Newcastle and Edinburgh by 1909, and in the next few years they also began to move into influential positions within its national leadership.[72]

This group advocated, for a time unsuccessfully, an alliance between the National Union and the Labour Party as the best means of attacking the Liberal Government. Such a shift in policy was resisted initially by leading figures such as Millicent Garrett Fawcett, who preferred to hold to the existing non-party policy of the National Union. Hopes were high in the years 1910–12 for a successful outcome to a new initiative, the Conciliation Bill, a Private Member's Bill behind which the support of suffragist MPs of all parties had been organized. The WSPU agreed to a truce from militancy while this hope was kept alive, and the Bill's success in the House of Commons in 1910 and 1911 forced the Liberal Government to promise full facilities for its passage before the next election.[73]

Within months of this commitment, however, the Liberal Government completely undermined the all-party coalition behind the bill when Asquith announced, to a deputation from the Peoples Suffrage Federation, that his Government intended shortly to introduce a new Reform Bill. He also let it be known that his cabinet was so divided over the issue of women's suffrage that any successful measure threatened hopes for securing Irish home rule in the near future, and so important Irish Nationalist support for women's suffrage was lost. The WSPU ended its truce and now started a campaign of ever-increasing violence against property – the concerted smashing of shop-fronts in London's West End, the firing of empty buildings, and the burning of mail in pillar boxes. Not surprisingly, the Conciliation Bill of 1912 failed to secure its earlier majorities; and the National Union leadership was forced at last to rethink its political policies.

It was one of the chief proponents of the Conciliation Bill strategy, the radical journalist Henry Brailsford, who now advocated an alliance with the Labour Party as the best means of attacking the Liberal Government, and to bring the Labour Party to an unequivocal commitment to the inclusion of women in any future franchise reform. In this he was aided by a favourable vote at the Labour Party conference in 1912, which in turn brought a grateful letter from Millicent Garrett Fawcett to the Labour leader, James Ramsay Macdonald. In April–May 1912 the leadership of the National Union undertook protracted and delicate negotiations with a Labour Party leadership wary of selling its independence for the support of what remained a largely Liberal organization. The proposal that the National Union offer election support for Labour candidates committed to women's suffrage in three-cornered by-elections received support at a special Council meeting of the National Union in May 1912. For the remaining two years or so before the outbreak of the First World War the National Union was a significant force in helping to build the election machinery of the young Labour Party, while many formerly Liberal women began their transition to future Labour and Socialist commitments. Inevitably, the new policy alienated some of the most committed Liberals in the National Union, but it also made the constitutionalist wing a more attractive option for many Labour and Socialist women who sought a way of linking their suffragist commitments to their party political loyalties.[74]

Dissidents and freelancers within the Women's Social and Political Union

The Women's Freedom League, unsurprisingly, adopted a very similar approach to the National Union's in these years, working with the Socialist and Labour movements towards a "democratic suffragist" solution to franchise reform. Still within the WSPU, Sylvia Pankhurst sought to rebuild links with the socialist movement, most especially "rebel" organizations such as the Daily Herald League, and working-class leaders such as George Lansbury and James Larkin. She also advocated a return to the large, popular demonstrations of earlier years, and the building of working-class support, achieving both in the East End of London.[75]

The years of the Conciliation Bills had been difficult ones for the WSPU leadership. They had found it increasingly difficult to keep control of "freelance militancy" among those who had initiated the new departures in militant methods of protest in the previous few years, most notably in the resort to window-breaking and the hunger strike. An ethos of comradeship, which incorporated shared ideals such as Socialism, internationalism and animal rights, often bound these women together in intense friendships, and dangerously fearless loyalties.[76] Militancy had always embodied a view of historical process which emphasized the role of heroic individuals. It was by acts of will on the part of those rare authentics who remained ever constant to their personal values and view of events that true social progress was achieved.[77] And so it was not easy for the leadership to exert discipline regarding the truce, especially over its most committed and devoted of followers. Equally, the truce made it difficult for the WSPU to maintain the level of public interest and press notice essential to the success of its approach.

Many militants were in any case disenchanted by this time with parliamentary politics. They began to feel that the vote was a quite inadequate tool for the task of women's emancipation, which they saw increasingly in terms of the sexual and economic freedom of women. Some left the suffrage movement for syndicalist and anarchist groups which emphasized personal liberation. Others, especially among the intelligentsia, looked to new lifestyles and intellectual currents. They found a voice in *The Freewoman*, the founding editors of which were two former WSPU organizers, Dora Marsden and Mary Gawthorpe. The paper advocated sexual liberation; an end to monogamy; co-operative housekeeping; and economic independence for women.[78] In this it was appealing deliberately to a fresh generation to act as a vanguard for their sex.

The WSPU, in contrast, became ever more intransigent towards both Liberal and Labour politics. Following mass window-breaking raids, Emmeline Pankhurst and Emmeline and Frederick Pethick Lawrence were given lengthy prison sentences in 1912. The Liberal Government also began to censor the WSPU's weekly, *Votes for Women*, and to harass its financial supporters. The following year it also passed the Cat and Mouse Act which allowed for the continuing re-arrest of hunger striking prisoners released from prison. This was applied so as to allow hunger strikers just long enough to recover before being re-arrested, so that many now endured a continuing cycle of hunger strike, forcible feeding, release and convalescence, followed by re-arrest to begin the whole process once more.[79] At the end of 1912, the Pethick Lawrences sought a rethinking of WSPU tactics and a return to the large scale popular demonstrations of earlier years. Christabel Pankhurst, by now an exile in Paris, resisted any such change in favour of an increasingly underground organization dedicated to clandestine attacks on property and threats to public order. So, in their turn, the Pethick Lawrences found themselves expelled from the WSPU, subsequently helping to form in early 1914 a new body, the United Suffragists. This brought together both male and female militants within a single organization and attracted the support also of some leading "rebel" socialists such as George Lansbury. Meanwhile, Sylvia Pankhurst had also been summoned to Paris to be told that her following in east London might no longer form part of the WSPU, on the grounds of her close association with Lansbury and other Labour leaders. The East London Federation of Suffragettes continued to campaign independently, however, on similar lines to other dissident militants in the United Suffragists.[80]

Women's suffrage and the First World War

Despite such disunity – perhaps because of the very variety of approach it represented – the suffrage movement appeared to be in a relatively strong position in the months preceding the outbreak of war in August 1914. Liberal leaders were worried by the strengthening alliance between the Labour Party and sections of the suffrage movement, the continuing disruption of public order wrought by militancy, and the sharp decline of their own women's auxiliary, the Women's Liberal Federation. In the summer of 1914, leading members of the Cabinet, including Lloyd George, consequently began negotiations by which they hoped both to bring about an end to militancy and to restore the former loyalty of alienated Liberal suffragists. These negotiations were conducted through George Lansbury and Sylvia Pankhurst, and appear to have brought an agreement from this section of militants to call a truce. Christabel Pankhurst, however, refused any part in securing such a solution. At the same time, democratic suffragists within the National Union were pursuing a similar line with leading Liberals, promoting universal suffrage as the means by which the Liberal Party might best satisfy its suffragist membership, advance its own electoral interests, and attempt to stem the flow of support towards Labour.[81]

It seems, then, that suffragists had sound reasons for hoping for a succesful conclusion to their campaign before the next general election, when war broke out in August 1914. The fragmentation and demoralization evident among the WSPU in the months before the war only escalated after Christabel and Emmeline Pankhurst announced the end of militancy, and adopted the stance of super-patriots. Those who disagreed with this response to the war formed their own breakaway bodies, in which the freelance militants of the prewar years were a notable presence.[82] The National Union was similarly divided between patriots such as Millicent Garrett Fawcett and those democratic suffragists now to the fore of its leadership, most of whom were internationalist in outlook. For a time, a semblance of unity was maintained through the involvement of the National Union in efforts for the relief of distress occasioned by the war, both at home and among the soldiers and civilian populations in the battle areas.[83]

Meanwhile, the democratic suffragists consulted closely with similarly-minded women overseas, and sought to involve the National Union in the international conference of women convened at The Hague in 1915. In this they were defeated by Millicent Garrett Fawcett and her supporters, and most then resigned as officers of the National Union. But the National Union never altogether suspended its suffrage concerns and, together with the WFL, the East London Federation and the United Suffragists, it took up the campaign again as soon as the question of franchise reform returned to the political agenda in 1916. Democratic suffragists such as Helena Swanwick, Isabella Ford, Catherine Marshall and Kathleen Courtney meanwhile helped establish the Women's International League for Peace and Freedom which maintained an active advocacy of citizenship rights for women alongside the promotion in the future of international bodies to arbitrate in disputes between countries.[84] When the Representation of the People Act became law in 1918 it gave the vote to all women over the age of 30 who were on the local government register, or who were wives of men on the local government register. This was short of full equality, but it did enfranchise a broader range of women than previous mooted equal suffrage measures would have done.[85] Many of the organizations of the suffrage movement continued after this advance, either unchanged (like the Women's Freedom League) or with a broader platform (like the National Union, which now became the National Union of Societies for Equal Citizenship). The campaign finally came to an end in 1928, when sexual equality in the suffrage was at last enacted in Britain.[86]

Notes

1. For the early campaigns for the vote, see H. Blackburn, *Women's suffrage. A record of the women's suffrage movement in the British Isles with biographical sketches of Miss Becker* (London: Williams and Norgate, 1902); B. Mason, *The story of the women's suffrage movement. With an introduction by the Lord Bishop of Lincoln* (London: Sherratt and Hughes, 1912), Chs I and III; see also the early chapters in R. Fulford, *Votes for women* (London: Faber & Faber, 1957).

2. R. Strachey, *The cause. A short history of the women's movement in Great Britain* (London: Virago, 1978 reprint, first published 1928); P. Levine, *Victorian feminism, 1850-1900* (London: Hutchinson, 1987); S. K. Kent, *Sex and suffrage in Britain, 1860-1914* (Princeton, New Jersey: Princeton University Press, 1987). Each of these provides accounts of the nineteenth-century suffrage campaigns which set them within broader contexts. B. Caine, *Victorian feminists* (Oxford: Oxford University Press, 1992) provides a collective biography of four of the leading figures of the movement, Frances Power Cobbe, Emily Davies, Josephine Butler and Millicent Garrett Fawcett.

3. E. S. Pankhurst, *The suffragette movement* (London: Virago, 1977; first published 1931) provides perhaps the fullest account, and one written by a participant. For a more recent study, see A. Rosen, *Rise up women. The militant campaign of the Women's Social and Political Union, 1903-14* (London: Routledge & Kegan Paul, 1974).

4. See C. Rover, *Women's suffrage and party politics in Britain, 1866-1914* (London: Routledge & Kegan Paul, 1967); D. Morgan, *Suffragists and Liberals. The politics of woman suffrage in England* (Oxford: Basil Blackwell, 1975) for two of the most detailed accounts.

5. On Chartism and women, see B. Taylor, *Eve and the new Jerusalem. Socialism and feminism in the nineteenth century* (London: Virago, 1983), esp. pp. 265-85 for a discussion of the links between Owenism, Chartism and the early women's movement.

6. On Anne Knight and her circle, see G. Malmgreen, "Anne Knight and the radical subculture", *Quaker History* 71, pp. 100-12, 1982; C. Midgley, *Women against slavery. The British campaigns, 1780-1870* (London, Routledge, 1992), pp. 77-9.

7. O. Banks, *Faces of feminism* (Oxford: Martin Robertson, 1981) provides a helpful analysis of some of the intellectual, religious and political currents of thought on which the women's rights movement drew. It also provides a useful comparative perspective, as does C. Bolt, *The women's movements in the United States and Britain from the 1790s to the 1920s* (Amherst, Mass.: University of Massachusetts Press, 1993); R. Evans, *The feminists* (London: Croom Helm, 1977).

8. K. K. Sklar, "'Women who speak for an entire nation.' American and British women compared at the World Anti-Slavery Convention, London 1840", *Pacific Historical Review* 59, pp. 453-99, 1990 provides an especially stimulating comparative analysis of the role of anti-slavery in the creation of a women's rights movement in the United States and Britain; see also Midgley, *Women against slavery*, pp. 172-7.

9. Mason, *The story of the women's suffrage movement*, pp. 25-6; Midgley, *Women against slavery*, p. 143.

10. P. Levine, *Feminist lives in Victorian England: private roles and public commitment* (Oxford: Basil Blackwell, 1990); S. S. Holton, "From anti-slavery to suffrage militancy", in *Suffrage and beyond. International perspectives*, M. Nolan & C. Daley (eds) (Auckland, New Zealand: Auckland University Press, 1994), pp. 213-33 traces some of the kinship and friendship networks on which the women's movement was built. O. Banks, *Becoming a feminist. The social origins of first wave feminism* (Athens, Georgia: University of Georgia Press, 1987) provides an analysis of the family background of a sample of feminists.

11. S. Herstein, *A mid-Victorian feminist, Barbara Leigh Smith Bodichon* (New Haven, Conneticut: Yale University Press, 1985), pp. 18-19; and on this circle see also Midgley, *Women against slavery*, pp. 158-67.

12. Herstein, *Mid-Victorian feminist*, pp. 71-2. An even more notorious case of such injustice was that of Caroline Norton, who had mounted her own campaign in this period for reform of the marriage laws, while denying any concern for women's rights in general.

13. H. Burton, *Barbara Bodichon, 1827-1891* (London: John Murray, 1949), pp. 106-41; J. Rendall, "'A moral engine'? Feminism, Liberalism and the *English Woman's Journal*", in J. Rendall (ed.), *Equal or Different. Women's Politics 1800-1914* (Oxford: Basil Blackwell, 1987), pp. 112-38. For insightful discussions of the relationship between women's personal life and women's politics in this circle, see J. Rendall, "Friendship and politics: Barbara Leigh Smith Bodichon (1827-1891) and Bessie Rayner Parkes (1829-1925)", in *Sexuality and subordination*, J. Rendall & S. Mendus (eds) (London: Routledge, 1989), pp. 136-70; J. Matthew, "Barbara Bodichon: integrity and diversity (1827-1891)", in D. Spender (ed.), *Feminist theorists. Three centuries of women's intellectual tradition* (London, Women's Press, 1983, pp. 90-123).

14. B. Stephen, *Emily Davies and Girton College* (London: Constable, 1927); J. Manton, *Elizabeth Garrett Anderson* (London: Black, 1958). On middle-class women's education, see J. Purvis, *A history of women's education in England* (Milton Keynes: Open University Press, 1991), Ch. 5.

15. Emily Davies to H.R. Tomkinson (November, 1865), quoted in Stephen, *Emily Davies*, p. 109.
16. On Elizabeth Wolstenholme Elmy, see E. Ethelmer, "A woman emancipator: a biographical sketch", *Westminster Review* **CXLV**, pp. 424-8, (1894).
17. Mason, *The story of the women's suffrage movement*, p. 38.
18. *Ibid.*, pp. 31-44.
19. *Ibid.*, p. 42.
20. P. Hollis, *Ladies elect: women in English local government, 1865-1914* (Oxford: Clarendon Press, 1987) provides a detailed account and stimulating analysis of women's role in local government in this period.
21. See, for example, Rosen, *Rise up women*, p. 49.
22. Some of these early divisions are discussed in B. Caine, "John Stuart Mill and the English women's movement", *Historical Studies* **18**, pp. 53-67, (1982); B. Caine, "Feminism, suffrage and the nineteenth century English women's movement", *Women's Studies International Forum* **5**, pp. 537-50, 1982; A.P.W. Robson, "The founding of the National Society for Women's Suffrage", *Canadian Journal of History* **8**, pp. 1-22, 1973.
23. I examine this question in more detail in S.S. Holton, "Free love and Victorian feminism", *Victorian Studies* **37**, pp. 1-25, (1994); S.S. Holton, "'Educating women into rebellion': Elizabeth Cady Stanton and the creation of a transatlantic network of radical suffragists", *American Historical Review* **99**, pp. 1112-36, 1994; S.S. Holton, "From anti-slavery to suffrage militancy". See also M.L. Shanley, *Feminism, Marriage and the Law in Victorian England 1850-95* (London: I.B. Tauris, 1989), esp. pp. 52-8.
24. J. Rendall, "Citizenship, culture and civilization. The languages of British suffragists, 1866-1874", in *Suffrage and beyond. International perspectives*, M. Nolan & C. Daley (eds) (Auckland, Auckland University Press, 1994), pp. 127-50 provides a fine analysis of the range of arguments that liberalism offered the women's movement.
25. For further discussion of this current of opinion, see Shanley, *Feminism, marriage and the law*, pp. 58-68, 79; Holton, "Free love and Victorian feminism".
26. The career of Lydia Becker still awaits a detailed study, but see the sympathetic sketch in Blackburn, *Women's suffrage*, pp. 23-43; Pankhurst, *The suffragette movement*, pp. 34-52, which provides a more equivocal account; J. Parker, "Lydia Becker: pioneer orator of the women's movement", *Manchester Region History Review* **2**, pp. 13-20, 1991; A. Kelly, *Lydia Becker and the cause* (Lancaster: Centre for North-West Studies, University of Lancaster, 1992).
27. See J. Walkowitz, *Prostitution and Victorian society. Women, class and the state* (Cambridge: Cambridge University Press, 1980).
28. S.S. Holton, "State pandering, medical policing and prostitution. The controversy within the medical profession over the contagious diseases legislation, 1864-86", *Research in Law, Deviance and Social Control* **9**, pp. 149-70, 1988.
29. Lydia Becker to Dearest (Elizabeth Wolstenholme), 1 March 1874, in the E. Sylvia Pankhurst Archive, the Institute for Social History, Amsterdam.
30. Holton, "Free love and Victorian feminism", pp. 11-17.
31. Lee Holcombe, *Wives and property: reform of the married women's property laws in nineteenth century England* (Toronto:, Toronto University Press, 1983); Shanley, *Feminism, marriage and law*, pp. 125-7.
32. *Ibid.*, pp. 17-20.
33. J. Walkowitz, *City of dreadful delight: narratives of sexual danger in late-Victorian London* (London: Virago, 1992), pp. 22-4, 83-8, 102-5; L. Bland, " 'Purifying' the

public world: feminist vigilantes in late Victorian England", *Women's History Review* **1**, pp. 397–412, 1992; D. Gorham, "'The maiden tribute of modern Babylon' re-examined: child prostitution and the idea of childhood in late-Victorian England", *Victorian Studies* **21**, pp. 353–79, 1978.

34. S. S. Holton, "The strange death of Liberal feminism: Anna Maria Priestman and the origins of the Women's Liberal Federation", paper delivered to the Wollstonecraft 200 Conference, University of Sussex, December 1992; L. Walker, "Party political women: a comparative study of the Liberal women and Primrose League, 1890-1914", in J. Rendall (ed.), *Equal or different? Women's politics, 1800-1914* (Oxford: Basil Blackwell, 1987), pp. 165–91; C. Hirshfield, "Fractured faith: Liberal Party women and the suffrage issue in Britain, 1892-1914", *Gender and History* **2**, pp. 172–97, 1990.

35. Holton, "To educate women into rebellion".

36. Women's Franchise League, *Proceedings at the Inaugural meeting of the Women's Franchise League, 25 July 1889* (London, 1889); Women's Franchise League, Minute Book 1890-95, Special Collections Department, Northwestern University Library, Illinois, with my thanks to the Curator, R. Russell Maylone, for arranging a microfilm of this source.

37. Holton, "To educate women into rebellion".

38. Women's Emancipation Union, *Women's Emancipation Union. An association of workers to secure the political, social and economic independence of women* (Congleton, 1891). On this issue see also S. Jeffreys, *The spinster and her enemies. Feminism and sexuality, 1880-1930* (London: Pandora, 1985), Ch. 2; D. Rubinstein, *Before the suffragettes. Women's emancipation in the 1890s* (Brighton: Harvester, 1986), pp. 54–63; C. Dyhouse, *Feminism and the family in England, 1880-1939* (Oxford: Basil Blackwell, 1989), pp. 166–70.

39. D. Rubinstein, *Before the suffragettes* offers a significant reappraisal of this decade for the women's movement.

40. Holton, "To educate women into rebellion".

41. Millicent Garrett Fawcett remains a somewhat enigmatic figure, and her memoirs are unrevealing. Ann Oakley, "Millicent Fawcett and her 73 reasons", in Oakley, *Telling the truth about Jerusalem, a collection of essays and poems* (Oxford: Basil Blackwell, 1985), pp. 18–35 provides an insightful discussion of her career; see also the biography written by her admirer, R. Strachey, *Millicent Garrett Fawcett* (London: John Murray, 1933). D. Rubinstein, *A different world for women. The life of Millicent Garrett Fawcett* (Brighton: Harvester Wheatsheaf, 1991) provides a more recent full-length study.

42. G. Lewis, *Eva Gore Booth and Esther Roper, a biography* (London: Pandora, 1988), pp. 10–20, 28–31, 56–70; 69–72, 84–6, which also discusses their relationship in terms of a mutual rejection of "notions of sexual possessive love", and the "companionate love" which was a feature of women's close friendships in the suffrage movement, pp. 73–5, pp. 99–103.

43. On the role of middle-class women in the Independent Labour Party, see especially J. Hannam, *Isabella Ford* (Oxford: Basil Blackwell, 1989).

44. See, for example, the letters of Priscilla Bright McLaren to Esther Roper between 26 March and 11 July 1901, and to Miss Rowton, 25 March 1901, all NUWSS collection, Manchester Public Library Archives.

45. Lewis, *Eva Gore Booth and Esther Roper*, pp. 93–109; J. Liddington & J. Norris, *One hand tied behind us. The rise of the women's suffrage movement* (London: Virago 1978), pp. 170–5. Christabel Pankhurst left her own memoir, *Unshackled* (London: Hutchinson, 1959), and see also the sympathetic assessment in E. Sarah, "Christabel

Pankhurst. Reclaiming her power (1880-1958)'', in *Feminist theorists: three centuries of women's intellectual tradition* D. Spender (ed.) (London: Women's Press, 1983), pp. 256-84.

46. N. Blewett, ''The franchise in the United Kingdom, 1885-1918'', *Past and Present* **32**, pp. 27-56, 1965.

47. Liddington and Norris, *One hand tied behind us*, provides an excellent account of the working lives and politics of women textile workers as a context for understanding the work of Esther Roper and Eva Gore Booth and the emergence of the LCTOWRC. It suggests (p. 163) that the new organization may have been formed to avoid dividing the North of England society, of which Esther Roper remained as Secretary for a while longer; Lewis, *Eva Gore Booth and Esther Roper*, p, 89 sees it more as an attempt to exert greater pressure on local Labour MPs. The actual date of the formation of the LCTOWRC is not known, but it would seem that it was already under consideration in October 1903 - see Pankhurst *The suffragette movement*, p. 168. See also J. Liddington, *The life and times of a respectable rebel. Selina Cooper, 1864-1946* (London: Virago, 1984), for the biography of one of the working-class organizers associated with the LCTOWRC in these years.

48. S. S. Holton, *Feminism and democracy. Women's suffrage and reform politics in Britain, 1900-1918* (Cambridge: Cambridge University Press, 1986), pp. 33-4.

49. Again, the motivation remains unclear for the formation of a second Manchester body committed to suffrage-Socialist campaigning at the same time as the LCTOWRC was being planned, but Liddington & Norris, *One hand tied behind us*, pp. 174-5 emphasize the personal ambitions of Christabel Pankhurst (and her greater impatience, compared with the textile workers, with the ILP), while Lewis, *Eva Gore Booth and Esther Roper*, pp. 96-7 emphasizes Emmeline Pankhurst's jealousy of her daughter's then deep attachment to Eva Gore Booth. Possibly, Emmeline Pankhurst's wish to continue to distance herself from the North of England society and the moderate leadership of the National Union may also have been a factor, given her earlier association with Ursula Bright and the other Radical-Liberal suffragists of the Women's Franchise League.

50. See the autobiographical accounts of working-class and Socialist recruits to the WSPU in this period, in H. Mitchell, *The hard way up. The autobiography of Hannah Mitchell, suffragette and rebel* (London: Virago, 1978, first published Faber & Faber, 1968, ed. G. Mitchell); M. Gawthorpe, *Up hill to Holloway* (Penobscot, Maine: Traversity Press, 1962); A. Kenney, *Memoirs of a militant* (London: Edward Arnold, 1924); Pankhurst, *The suffragette movement*, pp. 164-70.

51. Holton, *Feminism and democracy*, pp. 53-75 discusses the debates over adult suffrage versus women's suffrage in greater detail.

52. Pankhurst, *The suffragette movement*, pp. 189-200. E. Pankhurst, *My own story*, (London: Virago, 1979, first published Eveleigh Nash, 1914), p. 43 claims, however, that militancy began with an impromptu demonstration at the House of Commons some months earlier, led by herself and Elizabeth Wolstenholme Elmy. This is an interpretation that emphasizes the spontaneous origins of militancy in ''a feeling of wild excitement and indignation'' that ''took possession of the throng'', not the rational calculations that preceded the Free Trade Hall demonstration. I explore this question more fully in S. S. Holton, '''In sorrowful wrath': suffrage militancy and the Romantic feminism of Emmeline Pankhurst'', in H. L. Smith, *British feminism in the twentieth century* (Aldershot: Edward Elgar, 1990), pp. 7-24.

53. Holton, ''From anti-slavery to suffrage militancy''.

54. Pankhurst, *The suffragette movement*, p. 243.

55. More detailed accounts of the National Union, and its policies and campaigns, are to be found in Holton, *Feminism and democracy*; L. P. Hume, *The National Union of Women's Suffrage Societies, 1897-1914* (New York: Garland, 1982).

56. More detailed comparison of constitutional suffragism and militancy may be found in Holton, *Feminism and democracy*, pp. 29-52.

57. Liddington and Norris, *One hand tied behind us*, pp. 194-6.

58. Esther Roper to Millicent Garrett Fawcett, 25 October 1906, Manchester Public Library Archives, M50/2/1/230. See also Liddington & Norris, *One hand tied behind us*, pp. 205-7.

59. I look at this issue in more depth in S. S. Holton, "The suffragist and 'the average woman'", *Women's History Review* 1, pp. 9-24, 1992. For the perspectives of some working class women on the suffrage movement, see *Ada Nield Chew, the life and writings of a working woman*, collected by Doris Nield Chew (London: Virago, 1988); T. Thompson (ed.), *Dear girl. The diaries and letters of two working women 1897-1917* (London: The Women's Press, 1987).

60. Holton, *Feminism and democracy*, pp. 37-8. The table plan of the Savoy banquet, held in the Fawcett Library, the London Guildhall University, suggests that all three Pankhurst sisters were invited, with a guest of their choice. There was no place nominated by the organizers especially for Emmeline Pankhurst, and Christabel was not allocated a place on the top table, unlike Sylvia and Adela.

61. *Ibid.*, pp. 39-40. The educational effect of participation in WSPU campaigns should also not be ignored: see J. Purvis, "A lost dimension? The political education of women in the suffragette movement in Edwardian Britain", *Gender and Education* 6, pp. 319-327, 1994.

62. L. Tickner, *The spectacle of women. Imagery of the suffrage campaign 1907-14* (London: Chatto & Windus, 1987) provides a most stimulating analysis of the role of writers and artists in the suffrage movement; see also J. Holledge, *Innocent flowers. Women in the Edwardian theatre* (London: Virago, 1981); S. Oldfield, *Spinsters of this parish. The life and times of F. M. Mayor and Mary Sheepshanks* (London: Virago, 1984); S. Stowell, *A stage of their own. Feminist playwrights of the suffrage era* (Manchester: Manchester University Press, 1992).

63. The WSPU's leadership also had great difficulty keeping control of policymaking, and many new developments in militancy were introduced by the rank and file, see Holton, "Feminism and democracy", pp. 41-2, 46-7. L. Stanley with A. Morley, *The life and death of Emily Wilding Davison. A biographical detective story* (London: Woman's Press, 1988) provides further confirmation of this point.

64. Pankhurst, *The suffragette movement*, p. 206. See also E. Pethick-Lawrence, *My part in a changing world* (London: Victor Gollancz, 1938); F. W. Pethick-Lawrence, *Fate has been kind* (London: Hutchinson, 1943). **Note:** The couple did not hyphenate their names during their time in the suffrage movement, and I have followed them in this.

65. D. Montefiore, *From a Victorian to a modern* (London: E. Archer, 1927), pp. 89 & 108-12, and compare with Frances E. Rowe to Mrs McIlquham, 26 October 1905, 9 January 1907, 13 May 1907, all in the Harriet McIlquham papers, part of the Fawcett Library Autograph Collection, London Guildhall University. C. Collette, "Socialism and scandal: the sexual politics of the early Labour movement", *History Workshop Journal* 23, pp. 102-11, 1987 discusses aspects of the controversy within the Labour movement over Dora Montefiore's private life.

66. E. Pankhurst to S. Robinson, 22 June 1907, Hannah Mitchell papers, Manchester Public Library Archives, M 220/1/2/4; also printed in Mitchell, *Hard way up*, Appendix, p. 247.

67. Pankhurst, *The suffragette movement*, pp. 187-8, 208, 263-6. For Teresa Billington Greig, see C. McPhee & A. Fitzgerald (eds), *The non-violent militant. Selected writings of Teresa Billington Greig* (London: Routledge & Kegan Paul, 1987); B. Harrison, *Prudent revolutionaries. Portraits of British feminists between the wars* (Oxford: Clarendon, 1987), pp. 45-72. For Charlotte Despard, see A. Linklater, *An unhusbanded life: Charlotte Despard. Suffragette. Socialist. Sinn Feiner* (London: Hutchinson, 1980); M. Mulvihill, *Charlotte Despard. A biography* (London: Pandora, 1989).

68. Holton, *Feminism and democracy*, p. 39. L. Garner, *Stepping stones to women's liberty: feminist ideas in the women's suffrage movement, 1900-1918* (London: Hutchinson, 1984) provides a comparative study of the main suffrage organizations in this period.

69. More detailed studies of the suffrage movement in specific regions and localities are badly needed, but see L. Leneman, *A guid cause. The women's suffrage movement in Scotland* (Aberdeen: Aberdeen University Press, 1991); C. Murphy, *The women's suffrage movement and Irish society in the early twentieth century* (London: Harvester, 1989).

70. H. Swanwick, *I have been young* (London: Victor Gollencz, 1935), p. 225; J. Purvis, "'Deeds not words': the daily lives of militant suffragettes in Edwardian Britain", *Women's Studies International Forum* **18**, pp. 91-101, 1995 examines the bonds of sisterhood among the disparate groups that made up the WSPU.

71. See The People's Suffrage Federation, *Annual Report, 1910-12*.

72. Holton, *Feminism and democracy*, pp. 65-9 traces the gradual change in National Union leadership and policies. Helena Swanwick, of the Manchester Society, for example, became founding editor of the National Union's weekly, *The Common Cause*, in 1909. Kathleen Courtney, for a time Secretary of the Manchester society, for a short time became Secretary of the National Union. Catherine Marshall, from the Keswick society, became acting parliamentary Secretary in 1911, a post she retained until 1915. The executive committee of the National Union also gradually became dominated by democratic suffragists, such as Margaret Ashton of the Manchester society; Isabella Ford of the Leeds society; Ethel Bentham and Ethel Williams of the Newcastle society; Maude Royden, who eventually replaced Swanwick as editor of *The Common Cause*; and Alice Clark of the Street society. Swanwick, *I Have Been Young* is the only full autobiography left by any of this circle, but see Hannam, *Isabella Ford*; Sheila Fletcher, *Maude Royden* (Oxford: Basil Blackwell, 1989); J. Alberti, *Beyond suffrage. Feminists in war and peace* (London: Macmillan, 1989); S. Oldfield, *Women against the iron fist. Alternatives to militarism, 1900-1989* (Oxford: Basil Blackwell, 1989); J. Vellacott, *From Liberal to Labour with women's suffrage. The story of Catherine Marshall*, (Montreal and Kingston, Ontario: McGill-Queen's University Press, 1993) for helpful individual and collective biographies of members of this current of suffrage opinion.

73. See Holton, *Feminism and democracy*, pp. 69-75; Hume, *The National Union of Women's Suffrage Societies*, pp. 61-142.

74. Holton, *Feminism and democracy*, pp. 76-115.

75. Pankhurst, *The suffragette movement*, pp. 416-35.

76. Stanley with Morley, *The life and death of Emily Wilding Davison*, suggests this terminology, see for example, p. 118.

77. For further discussion of the meaning and nature of militancy, see Holton, "'In sorrowful wrath'"; M. Vicinus, *Independent women: work and community for single women, 1850-1920* (Chicago: Chicago University Press, 1985), esp. Ch. 7; B.

Harrison, "The act of militancy", in Harrison, *Peaceable kingdom: stability and change in modern Britain* (Oxford: Clarendon Press, 1982), pp. 26-81.

78. Garner, *Stepping stones to women's liberty*, pp. 61-77, provides a useful short account of *The Freewoman*; see also L. Garner, *A brave and beautiful spirit. Dora Marsden, 1882-1960* (Aldershot: Avebury, 1990) and L. Bland, "Heterosexuality, feminism and *The Free Woman* Journal in early twentieth-century England", *Women's History Review* 4, pp. 5-23, 1995.

79. See J. Purvis, "The prison experience of the suffragettes in Edwardian Britain", *Women's History Review* 4, pp. 103-133, 1995.

80. Pankhurst, *The suffragette movement*, pp. 411, 516-18 & 520.

81. Holton, *Feminism and democracy*, pp. 124-30.

82. Stanley with Morley, *The strange death of Emily Wilding Davison*, p. 181.

83. Holton, *Feminism and democracy*, pp. 116-32. Garner, *Stepping stones to women's liberty*, pp. 94-103 provides a thoughtful analysis of the impact of war on the suffrage movement. Compare with M. Pugh, *Women and the women's movement in Britain 1914-1959* (London: Macmillan, 1992), pp. 6-42.

84. Holton, *Feminism and democracy*, pp. 134-9; J. V. Newberry, "Anti-war suffragists", *History* 62, pp. 411-25, 1977; J. Vellacott, "A place for pacifism and transnationalism in feminist theory: the early work of the Women's International League for Peace and Freedom", *Women's History Review* 2, pp. 23-56, 1993; A. Wiltsher, *Most dangerous women. Feminist peace campaigners in the Great War* (London: Pandora, 1985).

85. Holton, *Feminism and democracy*, pp. 143-50.

86. Alberti, *Beyond suffrage*, pp. 135-63; Pugh, *Women and the women's movement in Britain 1914-1959*, pp. 43-71.

Suggestions for further reading

There is as yet no comprehensive history of the women's suffrage movement in Britain from its beginnings in the 1860s to its successful conclusion in 1928. E. Sylvia Pankhurst, *The suffragette movement. An intimate account of persons and ideals* (London: Virago, 1977, first published 1931) remains perhaps the most readable introduction, though it needs to be remembered that it was written from one particular perspective. It is instructive to compare this with the very different account of the nineteenth-century movement found in Helen Blackburn, *Women's suffrage. A record of the women's suffrage movement in Britain* (London: Williams and Norgate, 1902), and a different perspective on the twentieth-century campaigns provided in Helena Swanwick, *I have been young* (London: Victor Gollancz, 1935), and to note especially the absences evident in each. The development of suffrage history, and the nature of suffragist memoirs, is now beginning to receive more detailed analysis; see, for example, K. Dodd, "Cultural politics and women's history writing. The case of Ray Strachey's *The Cause*", *Women's Studies International Forum* 13, pp. 127-37, 1990; H. Kean, "Searching the past in present defeat: the construction of historical and political identity in British feminism in the 1920s and 1930s", *Women's History Review* 3, pp. 57-80, 1994; J. Marcus (ed.), *Suffrage and the*

Pankhursts (London: Routledge & Kegan Paul, 1987) for her Introduction to this collection of primary sources, pp. 1–17. Further useful collections of primary sources are P. Hollis, *Women in public: documents from the Victorian women's movement, 1850–1900* (London: Allen & Unwin, 1981); J. H. Murray (ed.), *Strong-minded women and other lost voices from nineteenth century England* (New York,:Pantheon, 1982); J. Lewis (ed.), *Before the vote was won* (London: Routledge & Kegan Paul, 1987). Much of the periodical and pamphlet material from the women's movement is now available in facsimile or on microfilm, and contains relevant items for further work on the suffrage movement. See, for example, *The Englishwoman's Review of social and industrial questions* (New York: Garland, 1985: facsimile reprint); *The social and political status of women in Britain. Radical and reforming periodicals for and about women* (Brighton: Harvester Microfilms, 1983–6); *Helen Blackburn's pamphlet collection, from Girton College, Cambridge* (Brighton: Harvester Microfilms, 1987); *The Common Cause* (New Haven, Connecticut: Research Publications, n.d.).

Chapter Twelve

ఆన్

Women and war in the twentieth century

Penny Summerfield

Many accounts of twentieth-century British history assume that the two World Wars inaugurated significant changes for women. The wars are seen as turning points or watersheds bounding well-recognized historical periods and redirecting the course of women's lives. They were special because, unlike the numerous colonial wars of the previous century, they involved a large proportion of the British people directly, either as combatants, in support roles, or as the victims of the bombing, shortages and disruption characteristic of "total war". This has given rise to two kinds of historiography. In one, the wars are understood to have had profound effects on women's lives, but because the focus of the historical work is elsewhere, the changes are assumed and not explored.[1] In the other, the wars are subject to close scrutiny, and different interpretations of the changes are hotly debated.[2]

This chapter draws on the second kind of historiography, to address the question of what differences the wars made to women, in the hope that the uninformed assessments found in the other kind of history-writing will not be repeated endlessly. But first it is important to clarify the parameters of the debate. Would anyone pose the question "What difference did the wars make to men?" without appearing to be both simplistic and reductionist, since "men" are obviously a diverse group whose members experienced changes of many different sorts? Yet the terms of the debate about war and women insist on such generalization. The question about the effects of the wars on women only makes sense in relation to the understanding of "change" that has been used.

Conceptualizations of women and social change fall into two groups, relating to equality on the one hand and to difference on the other. Since the rebirth of the women's movement in Britain in the 1970s, interest in women, war and social change has focused mainly on the issue of war's stimulus to equality. Within this problematic, one possibility is that wartime change promoted equal rights for women, and another is that war required women to cross gender boundaries, either temporarily or permanently. But in the 1950s and 1960s, debate concerned the wars' impact on women within the separate sphere. Titmuss believed that women's status as dependants of men was enhanced by war, and Myrdal and Klein thought that women received recognition for a specifically feminine wartime contribution, made both at work and at home.[3] Such writers made an essentialist identification of women with their socio-biological functions as wives, mothers and home-makers, and conceptualized change within this category, whereas feminist critics later asked whether the wars loosened the grip upon women of their socio-biological roles.

Gender difference

Women as dependants

I shall start this enquiry by exploring the ideas current in the 1950s, that war raised the status of biologically defined women within their feminine sphere, conceived of as an existence centred exclusively on the home, separate from involvement in paid work and, in wartime, from military service. In 1955, Titmuss celebrated the wars' stimulus to the support of women as dependants in a way that would be improbable among present-day feminists:

> In no particular sphere of need is the imprint of war on social policy more vividly illustrated than in respect to dependant needs – the needs of wives, children and other relatives for income-maintenance allowances when husbands and fathers are serving in the Forces . . . The more in fact that the waging of war has come to require a total effort by the nation the more have the dependant needs of the family been recognized and accepted as a social responsibility.[4]

Two questions arise from Titmuss's observation: What did this recognition amount to in each war as far as women were concerned; and Was it permanent? Titmuss was referring to the allowances paid for the support of servicemen's wives and their children, which were introduced in the First World War and repeated in the Second.[5] Four points can be made about them. First, as Titmuss stressed, the allowances were based on the principle that when a male breadwinner was removed from home to fight for his country, the state had to take over his role in providing for his family. This implied that in wartime the state upheld conventional patriarchal economic relations and recognized the socially useful labour of wives in the families of combatants. Secondly, the allowances guaranteed wives a weekly cash payment which represented a distinct improvement for many women on their peacetime economic situation.[6] But was it permanent? The feminist, Eleanor Rathbone, and the Family Endowment Society campaigned during and after the First World War for the state to pay the housewife a wage embodying a child allowance, to put an end to the vagaries of male practice and to keep wives and children out of poverty.[7] But servicemen's wives' allowances lasted only for the length of time a man was in the Armed Forces, so for most women they ceased at the end of each war, and the idea of a wife's wage was not embodied in interwar social policy or, more surprisingly, in the legislation that established the "Welfare State" after the Second World War. Family Allowances, introduced in 1945, started with the second child in the family and although at Rathbone's insistence they were paid to the mother and not the father, these did not include wives' benefits.[8] The idea that a wife should receive an allowance when her husband could not perform as a breadwinner because he was sick or out of work was presented as an important new principle by William Beveridge in his *Report on social insurance and allied services* published in 1942. But in the social insurance legislation of 1946, "married women remained totally dependent on their husbands' contributions and the benefits husbands received on their behalf".[9] So, contrary to the impression given by Titmuss, the wartime model of the cash payment made directly to wives to provide for their maintenance as well as that of their children, did not become a permanent part of social policy.

The third point to make in respect of servicemen's wives' allowances is that though they may have been welcome as an economic contribution, in the First World War they were accompanied by less acceptable moral intervention. Before the war, charitable doles had been conditional on what was seen by the donors as "appropriate behaviour", which was monitored by intrusive systems of "visiting". Early in the First World War this principle was applied to separation allowances. The Home Office asked police to exercise surveillance over servicemen's wives "to ensure that relief shall not be continued to persons who prove themselves unworthy to receive it", through, for instance, being drunk, disorderly or in general "unwifely". An outcry against this unwelcome interference led to a modification of the regulation, so that allowances would only be stopped if a woman was convicted of an offence.[10] But these arrangements suggest that the state was not only taking on the breadwinner role with respect to providing for "the dependant needs of the family", but also assuming the disciplinary function of the absent husband over his wife. Such blatant leverage was not apparently exercised in the Second World War, but that is not to say that the attitudes underlying it had disappeared.

The fourth and final point about servicemen's wives' allowances is that although they may have been a welcome source of regular payment to wives, the money did not stretch far. Rents rose fast during the First World War, especially in large towns where there was an influx of workers to the

munitions industries, swamping the available accommodation. When land-
lords evicted tenants for non-payment of rent, servicemen's wives on their
fixed incomes were particularly vulnerable. The 1915 Glasgow rent strike was
triggered by outrage over evicted service wives.[11] It struck a chord with
women all over the country[12] and led directly to the introduction of the Rent
Restriction Act of 1915, controlling increases on rents of under £30 a year.[13]
This was a wartime rather than a permanent measure, repeated at the start of
the Second World War, but it eased a difficult situation for women, who were
responsible traditionally for paying for housing.[14] However, even if rents
were not allowed to soar in the Second World War, servicemen's wives had
difficulties with respect to housing. One sign that their allowances were
insufficient is the evidence that they were frequently not wanted as tenants.[15]
Another is evidence that they were chronically in debt. A 1942 survey
showed that wives of servicemen living alone with children in Leeds owed on
average nearly half their weekly allowances.[16] A third sign of the inadequacy
of the allowances concerned nutrition. The *Lancet*, journal of the medical
profession, reported in 1940 "in the case of the soldier's wife . . . the
Government allowance is not sufficient to give mothers and their children a
diet which is not lacking in some of the essentials for good health".[17]

In view of the slight and impermanent improvement in the position of
wives as dependants in the wars it is really quite surprising that Titmuss was
as optimistic as he was about the acceptance, as a result of the wars, of
"dependant needs" as a "social responsibility". The traditional response of
wives who were short of money was to seek paid work, and married women
in the two world wars did so in exceptionally large numbers. It was estimated
that, in 1917, 40 per cent, and in 1943, 43 per cent of women in paid
employment were married, compared with 14 per cent in 1911, and 16 per
cent in 1931. War work paid considerably better than most kinds of work
married women could get in peacetime. The causes of health improvements
are much disputed, but it seems more probable that the higher wages wives
could earn in war work, rather than servicemen's wives' allowances alone,
account for the improved wartime rates of morbidity and mortality of adult
women and of school-age children.[18] Infant mortality, widely recognized as a
sensitive indicator of the health of the nation, rose at the start of both wars
and then fell dramatically.[19] However, in spite of the coincidence of
remarkable infant survival rates with a high proportion of married women
working, both wars were times when attention was directed to advocating
that mothers should devote themselves exclusively to motherhood.

Women as mothers

The wartime preoccupation with motherhood arose in part from the loss of
life in each war. In the First World War this involved mainly the deaths on the
battle front of young male soldiers, 744,000 of whom died between 1914 and

1918. In the Second World War, in addition to 264,000 military deaths, over 60,000 civilians, women as well as men, were killed in bombing raids.[20] During and after both wars, there was a concern to replenish a depleted population. But each war also inherited a set of concerns about motherhood specific to its own period.

Before the First World War, attention focused on whether the quality of the population was adequate for an imperial power. Members of the eugenics movement argued that Britain was being overpopulated with debased stock, as a result in part of inadequate working-class mothering.[21] Two kinds of solution were advocated: one was reform of the physical conditions in which women had children, and the other involved the education of working-class women, who were assumed to be ignorant and insanitary. A number of working women's organizations, which did not share the eugenicist perspective, capitalized on wartime concern to press home long-standing demands for paid maternity leave, a midwifery service and extra food for expectant and nursing mothers.[22] The other "solution", opposition to mothers who did paid work, was more popular with moralists and conservatives. At the hysterical exteme of this position, a journalist, Margaret Hamilton, wrote in July 1915 that the typical woman war worker was "the woman who, driven from her home is forced to work in the factories and the workshops while her baby lies dead", and Dr C.W. Saleeby stated in 1918 that working women committed "a sin against the laws of life".[23] National Baby Weeks were organized in 1917 and 1918, to educate women in devotion to motherhood and teach them how to "save every savable child".[24]

Were the outcomes of these wartime concerns positive for women as mothers? The moralising campaigns were designed to induce guilt in mothers who did paid work, many of whom, as we have seen, had little choice if they were to maintain themselves and their children above the poverty line. But, in this atmosphere, the reformists' concerns also led to policy changes. The Maternity and Child Welfare Act passed in 1918 enabled local authorities to set up maternity homes, infant welfare centres and crèches, and to provide salaried midwives and health visitors as well as milk and food for mothers and children.[25] These provisions must have been welcomed by many mothers. However, the WCG and other women's organizations argued that what mothers needed above all, in order to improve their health, was contraception. In spite of evidence of the appalling effects of too many births too close together on both women and children, the postwar clinics were not allowed to offer a contraceptive service.[26] The limitations of the wartime improvements in the conditions of motherhood are suggested by the fact that the rate of maternal mortality (that is, the death of mothers as a result of childbirth) remained stubbornly high throughout the interwar years.[27]

In the Second World War, concern about motherhood stemmed not so much from anxieties about the *quality* of the population, as panic about the *quantity*. The birthrate fell steadily during the interwar years, and reached a

311

low point in 1940. It was anticipated that the dwindling and ageing population to which this would give rise would be inadequate to ensure national prosperity and defence in the second half of the twentieth century. A stream of books was published during and after the Second World War, with titles such as *Parents' revolt* (1942) and *Britain and her birthrate* (1945), which discussed the decline in family size.[28] Four main explanations were offered, two of which: the material disadvantages of having large families; and the "cosmic anxiety" induced by the use of the atomic bomb on Japan in August 1945, applied to both men and women. But the other two reasons focused on women as a category. Changes in marital styles were said to mean that women expected more equality with their husbands in terms of, for example, the right to have outside interests and not to be household drudges. Solutions such as local authority babysitters and holiday homes for tired mothers were mooted, but did not become part of postwar social policy.[29] Women were believed to be worried about the effects of childbearing on their health, understandably in view of the maternal mortality rates mentioned earlier, and of evidence published as late as 1939 about the high levels of ill health among working-class married women.[30] The establishment in 1948 of the National Health Service, which provided health care free of charge to the entire population, was particularly valuable to working-class wives, most of whom had not been covered by health insurance before the war.

The "pronatalist" debate of the 1940s was overtaken by a dramatic increase in births at the end of the Second World War, leading to the highest birthrate ever recorded: 20.7 births per thousand of the population, in 1947. The baby boom is likely to have been caused at least partly by couples deferring births because of wartime separation. We cannot tell how many births were the result of the campaigns proclaiming the joys of motherhood,[31] but family size did not increase to the recommended minimum of four children after the Second World War; it settled down to an average of two children born close together early in a marriage.

It is often assumed that pronatalism, and particularly the contributions of psychologists such as John Bowlby, who recommended that mothers should devote themselves to motherhood to the exclusion of other activities including paid work, for the sake of the mental health of their children, was engineered to coincide with the end of the Second World War and the removal of women from war work.[32] In fact, Bowlby did not publish *Maternal care and mental health* until 1952. On the other hand, as we have seen, the belief that the physical health of children and the future of the race depended on devoted mothering enlightened by the strictures of middle-class experts, went back to the First World War and before. During the 1930s and the Second World War, the new discipline of psychology suggested that the emotional stability as well as the physical health of young children depended on the constant presence of the mother. During the Second World War, the establishment of wartime nurseries to take the children of women prepared to do war work was constantly impeded by the objections of the Ministry of Health and its local representatives, the Medical Officers of Health. In the 1940s, as in the 1910s, these authoritative individuals argued that "a mother's place is in the home where she should look after her own children".[33] Diametrically opposed views of women's social role in wartime were held by the Ministry of Labour's local representatives, desperate to increase the labour supply and therefore to establish nurseries, and the Medical Officers, who opposed them in the name of epidemics and disturbed children. The outcome in terms of nursery provision was that even at the height of the war there were places for only about a quarter of the children aged under five of women war workers.[34] Official policy recommended that childminders should look after the others, in spite of half a century of official suspicion of the minder as a potential infanticide expert and the difficulty for mothers of finding one, when women up to the age of 50 were being recruited for war work. Even this level of childcare was seen as being temporary. The state subsidy was halved at the end of 1945, and wartime nurseries were phased out, as individual localities struggled to meet the numerous demands on their social spending after the war.

Even if there was no concerted state policy to meet the reservations that women evidently felt about it, motherhood was constructed powerfully as the norm for women at the end of each war. In the last years of the First World War, discussion of motherhood was framed in terms of national need. Basil Worsfold spoke for many in a book published in 1919: "it cannot be emphasised too strongly that the service which the State most requires from the generality of women is motherhood and the maintenance of the family in purity and happiness".[35] In the Second World War, more emotional language was used in the construction of a discourse of desire for an idealized family that the war was supposed to have fractured. For example, the tone of a parliamentary debate on the demobilization scheme in 1944 was set by a male MP quoting a constituent: "We cannot think the scheme just which fails to take into account these empty, wasted years, sacrificed in war: years deprived of husband, often of home, and of the children we long to have."[36]

Women as wives

The reconstructed postwar family was, of course, to be based on marriage. The wars are often thought to have stimulated changes in marital styles, because women were coping alone while servicemen husbands were away, and were combining paid work (and independent incomes) with responsibility for households. It is difficult to find firm evidence of such changes. After both wars, returning soldiers were encouraged to re-establish themselves as heads of households and chief wage earners. Wives may have found that coping with the after effects of the injuries and traumas their husbands had suffered on the battlefield took priority over altering the distribution of tasks and responsibilities between them.[37] Harold Smith argues that marriage did not change as a result of the Second World War, and that women in the 1940s wished themselves back to the 1930s.[38] But autobiographical evidence indicates that at least some women believed that the war had changed marriage for them.[39] The idea that women were gaining status as wives was strong. After the First World War, those over the age of 30 had the vote, and a growing proportion of women experienced paid work before marriage. In the interwar years, the concept of "companionate marriage" was advocated in the United States and the idea of marriage as teamwork based on some sort of sharing gained authority in Britain in the 1940s.[40] Even if marriages based on equal partnership were hard to achieve in the postwar years, it is likely that the war contributed to aspirations for them.

Did the increase in divorce that accompanied each war indicate women's dissatisfaction with marriage? During the First World War, the divorce rate was stable at 0.2 per 10,000 population, but rose immediately after the war, to 0.8 per 10,000 in 1920.[41] (The rise represents relatively tiny numbers, because divorce was expensive and hard to obtain.) Liberalization of the divorce laws in 1923 and 1937 had little to do with the First World War.[42] But during and after the Second World War, an increasing number of couples made the most of the changes, and of the financial help that was available through the Forces Welfare Service, as a matter of morale, to end unsatisfactory marriages. The rate rose from 1.5 per 10,000 in 1938, to 3.6 in 1945, and then peaked at 13.6 in 1947.[43] No doubt the rises at the end of each war in part reflect the hastily arranged "khaki weddings" of their early months. But, rather than dissatisfied wives divorcing errant husbands, the majority of petitions at the end of the Second World War were filed by husbands on the grounds of wives' adultery.

The rising divorce rates did not coincide with a decline in the popularity of marriage. In the First World War, aggregate marriage statistics showed a slight rise in the incidence and a fall in the age of marriage.[44] This trend was much more marked in the Second World War. After a relatively low marriage rate in the interwar years, a record 22 people per thousand were married in 1940. The figure fell in 1943, but rose again at the end of the war to 19 per thousand in 1945, including 80,000 marriages to American servicemen, known as GIs. A quarter of brides in that year were under 21.[45] Members of a small sample of women who had worked in the Auxiliary Territorial Service in their early twenties during the Second World War, emphasized in letters written in the 1980s that they had strong, if ambivalent, expectations that they would marry at the end of the war, an impression confirmed by other data.[46]

Sexuality

The rise of divorce in each war was blamed on an increase in sexual activity among women, and the appearance of war babies appeared to bear testimony to women's immorality. But, aside from the double standard embodied in such a view, the figures present a more complex picture. In the First World War there was a 30 per cent rise in the proportion of illegitimate babies per thousand births. But in fact the birthrate fell so dramatically during the war that this higher proportion was achieved without an increase in the number of illegitimate births.[47] In the Second World War there was an absolute increase. In 1939, 4.4 per cent of all live births were illegitimate, compared with 9.1 per cent in 1945. But calculations undertaken in the office of the Registrar-General showed this did not necessarily mean that there was an increase in extramarital sex as such, rather that during the war fewer extramarital conceptions were legitimized by marriage.[48] The Second World War offered unprecedented opportunities for temporary liaisons. Fifty-two per cent of the British male population aged between 19 and 40 were in uniform, and there were in addition 1.5 million allied, dominion and colonial troops stationed at British camps in 1944.[49] This was also a war of immense mobility and lengthy separations. In such a context, traditional ways of neutralizing the results of illicit sex melted away.

Attitudes to unmarried mothers were punitive in the First World War. In contrast, there was some sympathy for the mothers of illegitimate children in the Second World War, especially for older and married women, including those married early in the war to servicemen whom they then did not see for years. Social agencies noted a new spirit of independence among some unmarried mothers, who were resistant to traditional "moral welfare" messages that they should do penance for their sins, and who wanted to keep their babies.[50] But the double standard of sexual morality was still strong. The woman, and not the man, had to pay the price of sexual transgression. Indeed, women's sexuality in wartime was constructed as being problematic, by a range of commentators in both world wars.

In the First World War, fears were expressed that a rising tide of immorality would result from women working long hours alongside men, travelling to and from work at night, and mixing with soldiers in barracks near large towns. In the Second World War, anxieties focused particularly on women in uniform. Whereas there were just over 60,000 women in the armed forces and Women's Land Army in 1918, there were 460,000 women in the three women's military services and a further 80,000 in the Land Army in 1944.[51] Women in uniform were suspected of every kind of (contradictory) sexual transgression, including vampishness, sluttishness and lesbianism.[52]

Feminists in both wars saw these reactions as attempts to hold women back from participation in the war effort. Robust resistance to the idea that war work undermined women's morals was offered by the suffragist and socialist Sylvia Pankhurst commenting on the First World War, and by the feminist MP, Edith Summerskill, in the Second.[53] Their responses suggest the strength of the dominant discourse which, by focusing on women's sexual deviance, may have effectively legitimized predatory male behaviour. How did individual women respond to wartime pressures and opportunities? Oral history testimony suggests that in both wars many women suffered various forms of harassment at work: some turned the tables on men, like the First World War women at Greenwood and Batley's munitions factory in Leeds, who "debagged" any man who dared step into "their" territory. Others experienced sexual exploitation, although some found ways of resisting, such as the diminutive Stella Banfield who tells of repelling an attempted rape in the Second World War by calling upon the sturdy protection of her Land Army uniform and her newly-developed agricultural muscles.[54]

There were divided views about male and female sexuality among feminists in the First World War. In 1913 Christabel Pankhurst warned of the dangers for women of sexual intercourse inside and outside of marriage, and urged chastity for both sexes, on the grounds that the widespread use of prostitutes meant that a high proportion of men was infected with VD. The social purity movement of which she was a part stressed the vulnerability of women and children to predatory male behaviour and urged the protection of women, pioneering the women's police force for this purpose in 1914.[55] The women police were taken over, however, by non-feminists, who wished to use them to patrol and control rather than to protect women. Other feminist groups were developing alternative views of female sexuality, notably the idea that women might take an active part in sexual intercourse, which would be enjoyable both to themselves and to their partners. These new ideas were advanced by Marie Stopes, the birth control campaigner, in her marriage manual *Married love*, published in 1918. They have been criticized subsequently as being hostile to the spinster, who was conceptualized as being "repressed" because she was apparently not participating in hetero-sexual activity; and to the lesbian, who was "inverted" in her desire for other women. They have also been shown to be based on the view that masculine sexuality was predatory and unbridled, whereas the social purity argument was that the masculine sex urge was well within a man's control.[56] By the Second World War, the idea that women should enjoy sex, coupled with the prevalence of the view that a man once aroused could not be restrained, presumably compromised many women, even if some, such as Joan Wyndham, made the most of wartime opportunities for sexual relationships.[57] And the prevailing homophobia must have been oppressive to women whose same-sex affection and desire was stimulated within the all-women friendship networks of the women's services and the war factories.

Equality

Equal rights

Wartime is popularly thought to have stimulated the formal equality of the sexes, through equal rights legislation. Above all, the passage of the

Representation of the People Act in February 1918, before the ending of the First World War in November of that year, is seen as a symbol of women's gains from the war.[58] It enfranchised women aged over 30 who were (or were married to) local government electors. However, historians have disputed the idea that women were granted the vote because of their roles in the war. In favour of it, there is evidence that politicians such as Herbert Asquith, Prime Minister until 1916, and Earl Grey, Foreign Secretary in 1914, both spoke of the vote as a reward for women's participation in the war. Asquith referred to women's war work, and Earl Grey to their roles as housewives and mothers. But Martin Pugh suggests that Asquith's eulogies were no more than "a reasonably dignified expedient" allowing him to reverse long held opposition, and that they were contradicted by the misogynistic views he expressed about women electors after the war.[59] Earl Grey's advocacy can be seen in the context of the preservation of the principle of difference within this apparently egalitarian measure, namely the denial of the vote to women under the age of 30. Older and married women were less likely to rock the political boat than were younger women, who had formed the majority of war workers and who might use the vote to insist on further equal rights legislation.[60] It took ten more years of campaigning by the National Union of Societies for Equal Citizenship before the vote was gained for women on equal terms with men.

If women were not granted the vote in 1918 as a reward for their war work, how do we account for the timing of this piece of legislation, long sought after by women? Pugh argues that it was bound to happen once the need for wartime franchise reform to enable ex-servicemen to vote was accepted in Parliament in 1917. It was inevitable, he argues, because the pre-war suffrage movement had prepared the ground so that the majority of MPs sitting in 1914 were in favour of the inclusion of women in the franchise. In addition, Pugh asserts, the strident wartime patriotism of the Women's Social and Political Union as well as the participation of women generally in the war effort, removed the last grounds for opposition, namely that women were all pacifists and could not contribute to the defence of their country.[61] This point should not be exaggerated. Pugh fails to note that there was a vocal women's peace movement during the First World War, led in Britain by women such as Helena Swanwick, Maude Royden and Catherine Marshall, which split the National Union of Women's Suffrage Societies and drew upon itself much unfavourable publicity. Women pacifists shared the view that women were in a special position to urge that political disputes should be settled by reason rather than physical force, because an essential difference between the sexes was women's moral superiority.[62] This was not a point which those who granted some women the vote in 1918 appear to have conceded.

In contrast to Pugh, Holton emphasizes the persistent wartime lobbying by the non-militant women's suffrage societies in 1916 and 1917 which ensured that, if a franchise measure was drawn up, women would not be left out.[63] It also demonstrated that the suffrage movement had not been killed by the war. At least one politician, Walter Long, President of the Local Government Board and a long-term anti-suffragist, was motivated to seek a compromise for fear of the disruption of a revived suffrage movement after the war.[64] It makes sense that politicians wanted to avoid renewed suffrage militancy, when they faced the potential revival of prewar industrial unrest and Irish Home Rule agitation, with, in addition, the prospect of thousands of servicemen returning from the horrors of the trenches to an uncertain future, against the backdrop of the Socialist revolutions of 1917 in Russia.

In the Second World War there was no single legislative measure that could be regarded as an equal rights "reward" for women. Marwick has presented equal pay as the Second World War's equivalent to the vote.[65] Equal pay was certainly promoted with more vigour than before, but the case for regarding it as a significant gain rests on how far it was in fact achieved, which I shall now explore, looking first at political and then at industrial attempts to secure equal pay.

Feminist MPs made three major parliamentary attempts to secure equal remuneration for women during the Second World War. In December 1941 they tried to prevent the passing of the National Service (Number Two) Act, which made certain groups of women liable for conscription, unless a guarantee of equal pay was included.[66] Their attempt was unsuccessful. The government was far from being prepared to reward women equally for their participation in the war effort, and principles of difference permeated the apparently egalitarian decision to conscript women as well as men. First, no mother of a child under 14 could be called up or directed to work. Secondly, conscription (involving direction away from home) applied only to single women aged between 19 and 30. Although married women could volunteer it was felt to be dangerous for men's morale to conscript them. Thirdly, a woman's housework could exempt her from full-time war work, though from 1943 such women up to the age of 50 could be directed into part-time work.[67]

In spite of the failure to obtain equal pay for conscripted women, parliamentary feminists campaigned successfully for equal compensation for war injuries for women. Under the 1939 Personal Injuries Act a woman received seven shillings a week less than a man if she was incapacitated by a bomb. Mavis Tate, MP, made the case for equal treatment in Parliament: bombs were not "chivalrous"; they did not discriminate between men and women; and the lives of both sexes were precious.[68] In this instance, campaigners received considerable support from the national press, civil defence organizations and trade unionists. The arguments for equal compensation were in part egalitarian: that women deserved it as a matter of justice; and in part related to difference. For example, the TUC argued that a woman's chances of marriage or remarriage would be reduced by her injuries, so she could not be treated as a dependant with respect to compen-

318

sation. The government was defeated on the issue, and equal compensation for war injuries was introduced in April 1943.[69] Its intrinsic war-relatedness, however, meant that its long-term implications were limited.

One of the reasons for the government's opposition to equal compensation was fear that it would open up the issue of equal pay, and to some extent it did. An amendment to the Education Bill of 1944, proposing equal pay for teachers, introduced by Thelma Cazalet Keir, MP, was passed by one vote.[70] However, Winston Churchill caused it to be withdrawn by forcing a vote of confidence in his government on the issue, and then deflected the rising head of steam behind equal pay by referring the matter to a Royal Commission. After sitting from 1944 to 1946, the Commission made disappointing recommendations, restricting the possibility of equal pay to the "common classes" in the civil service: that is, those in which men and women worked at the same jobs, which were few in an organization that had virtually pioneered gender segregation.[71] The Commission's report upheld some traditional views based on gender difference to justify refusing equal pay to the majority of women workers, notably that women were less efficient than men in industry, commerce and the professions; that their primary orientation was to home and family, either in prospect if they were single, or in practice if they were married; and that in consequence men must be paid more than women to enable them to support families.[72] In the event, the postwar Labour Government did not implement even the moderate equal pay measure that the Commission had suggested, on the grounds that the nation could not afford to do so in the context of the postwar economic crisis. Only after another decade of campaigning were women in public service granted equal pay.

Equal pay and "men's work"

Equal pay was an issue for workplace negotiators in both world wars before it became one for legislators in the Second World War. It appeared in this context not primarily because of feminist agitation, but because of male trade unionists' traditional desire to protect men's jobs and wage rates. The issue for men was as follows: if women were employed during wartime in jobs formerly done by men, at women's rates of pay, employers might be tempted always to pay for that job at the women's rate and to continue to employ women in it after the war. Trade unionists argued during both wars that women should not be given men's jobs, even in the exceptional circumstances of war; if however this was unavoidable, women should be paid the same rate as men. These attitudes had a profound effect on the possibility of women being employed on equal terms with men in wartime.

In the First World War, the trade union view of women as an unwanted rival workforce, whose proper place was in "women's work" or at home, gave rise to industrial unrest when employers started to take on women, and it led to government intervention in capital–labour relations in order to limit the damage to the war effort.[73] In the crisis year of 1915 the government secured two agreements with employers and with trade unions, which were embodied in a Munitions Act of June 1915. The Act was designed to speed up the production of munitions by removing the right to strike, and by obtaining a promise from the unions that they would not prevent women doing some parts of a skilled man's job, in return for a guarantee that women fully replacing skilled men would receive the men's rate. This heralded increasingly rapid "dilution" and "substitution", terms of immense significance for women workers. Dilution meant the employment of less-skilled workers on skilled work which had been simplified by the breaking down and mechanization of processes. Substitution meant the direct replacement of men by women on skilled work. The unions were assured that the changes were for the duration of the war only, and that they would be reversed at its end, a point reinforced by the passing of the Restoration of Pre-War Practices Act in 1916.[74] Women could not be members of craft unions, such as the Amalgamated Society of Engineers, and were not invited to participate in the negotiations: these arrangements so crucial to their chances of equality in the workplace were made exclusively by the government, employers and male trade unionists.[75]

In the Second World War, the Minister of Labour, Ernest Bevin, himself an former trade union leader, persuaded the two sides of industry to agree to similar principles regarding the "extended employment of women" and the "relaxation of pre-war practices", without direct government intervention. Following the lead of unions and employers in engineering and transport, agreements covering a long list of trades were made between 1940 and 1943. The usual formula embraced both dilution and substitution, as defined above. A woman who replaced a man could start by earning a proportion of the men's rate and graduate to the full rate in stages over a probationary period. But she only received the men's rate if she was a full substitute able to do the work of the man she replaced "without additional supervision or assistance". If she was a dilutee rather than a substitute, the rate would be negotiable "according to the nature of the work and the ability displayed".[76] The right to strike was again withdrawn, and in 1942 another Restoration of Pre-War Practices Act was passed promising to reverse wartime changes at the war's end. But in contrast to the First World War agreements, an exception was made for "women workers engaged on work commonly performed by women in the Industry". This clause acknowledged the expansion of women's employment following the First World War in exclusively women-employing sections of a wide range of industries, as well as in white collar work, where women were increasingly appointed to clerical and commercial jobs.[77] Women employed in such "women's work" were not to be regarded as temporary; nor were they seen as having a claim to equal pay, since their work was defined as intrinsically inferior to that which men did.

Did these arrangements mean, in either war, that women war workers did "men's work" and received equal pay? There are two issues to consider: first, the extent of women's substitution for men and of the prevalence of "women's work"; and secondly, whether the dilution agreements were honoured by employers and trade unionists.

The first issue is surprisingly opaque. Published figures of the numbers of women recruited to war work vary, and few authors distinguish between women doing men's work, and others. Woollacott depicts an increase in the industrial labour force between 1914 and 1918 of 1,590,000 women, of whom one million worked in munitions. But although she lists the numbers in different types of munitions work, she cannot be more specific about the gender identification of their work than to say that "women entered areas of work that were strictly male preserves before the war, and many became skilled or semiskilled workers".[78] The Second World War presents similar problems. Janet Hooks, a US government observer, and Peggy Inman, official historian of labour in the munitions industries, went into the matter in detail. Hooks wrote that 1,500,000 more women worked in "essential industries" in 1943 than in 1939.[79] But Inman found that only a very small proportion of these women were in the highly skilled grades.[80] Hooks perceived that "Much of the work undertaken by women since the war was formerly classified as women's work in certain plants or certan sections of an industry, and lower rates were the rule for women on women's work." This applied to 75 per cent of the women in the engineering industry in 1942.[81] While it is impossible to be precise about the numbers of women who did "men's work" in either war, these observations suggest that its extensiveness has been exaggerated. But assuming that at least some women were given men's jobs in each war, I will now address the second question, concerning whether or not the agreements governing women's employment were honoured by the employers and trade unionists who had made them.

In spite of the protection that the agreements were supposed to offer, there is evidence of union hostility towards women war workers throughout the First World War. A case which encapsulates union views is the objection of the Leeds branch of the Amalgamated Society of Engineers in March 1917 to women maintaining or repairing trams. The men demanded that these women should receive equal pay, but in response the employers removed women completely from this type of work, an outcome that was celebrated in the ASE journal as "more satisfactory than any award could have been".[82] There are other examples of male resistance: railwaymen opposed women ticket collectors, tramway workers objected to women drivers, and dockers took action against women labourers. Repeatedly, trade unionists justified their actions on the grounds that the work would be detrimental to women's health or morals.[83]

The idea of the agreements was that men would drop their opposition in return for guarantees that they would not be undercut by women employed at lower rates. But cases in which women received the full male rate appear to have been rare. Employers argued that women could not be doing the work of fully skilled tradesmen in engineering, and evaded paying equal piece- and time-rates, on the grounds that processes had been altered or that women could not do all aspects of the work. Even when employers paid women an equal basic rate, they usually gave them a lower war bonus. In August 1918, workers on the London buses and trams went on strike in support of women's demands for equal war bonus. The unions were frank about their motivation. Women were good bus and tram conductors, and were likely to be kept on after the war if they were cheaper to employ, but not if employers had to pay them as much as men. However, to many unionists, the idea that women deserved or needed the same wages as men was anathema. They were either working (before marriage) for pin money, or they should be supported by their husbands. The solution, above all, was to ensure the removal of women from men's trades at the end of the war.[84]

The story of women's pay in the Second World War is similar. Employers used the clause of the agreements referring to "additional supervision or assistance" to claim that women could not do equal work to men. The other loophole that employers exploited was the clause excluding "women's work" from the terms of the agreements. If employers could claim that the work they gave to women in wartime was "commonly performed by women in the industry" they could deny women the men's rate, even if they had, in fact, replaced men. Unions resisted this because it could mean the reclassification of men's work as women's work, with subsequent permanent job losses for men. There were impassioned arguments between union and employer representatives about whether jobs such as sweeping up, core-making, crane driving, welding and inspection had been "commonly performed by women" in the 1930s. Trade unionists tried to convince employers that women's work before the war was confined to simple, light, repetitive work. But employers replied that any work that was shown in wartime to come within the limited competence women were assumed to possess, should be regarded as women's work. The insecurity of this position for men suggested to some unionists, for example, George Woodcock of the TUC, that arguments based on women's competence were too weak to protect men, and that the classification of work by gender would have to go.[85] Other union leaders, notably Jack Tanner of the AEU would not drop from wage negotiations arguments based on difference. He said that men should be paid a breadwinner's wage large enough to support a family, but that women should be paid as much as men, both as a matter of justice and to stop women being employed at a lower rate in preference to men.[86] Justice to women was a relatively new concept for the Amalgamated Engineering Union, but men's need for a family wage and to prevent undercutting had a long history.

When trade unionists were successful in their claims that work women were doing during the Second World War was not "women's work", but should come under the dilution agreements, they achieved substantial pay rises (if not equal pay) to the satisfaction of the women affected. On some occasions, women took matters into their own hands. A dramatic equal pay strike took place at a Rolls Royce engineering factory at Hillington, near Glasgow, in 1943. Women and men, equally lacking in experience of engineering, were recruited to the factory to work on new machines, but the men were paid at higher rates than the women.

Women went on strike in October 1943, taking with them most of the men in the plant.[87] The solution was an agreement in which each machine was named, and placed in one of four grades. However, since the grading system was gender related, it was not quite the victory for "the rate for the job" that has been assumed.[88] And the support of the men working at Hillington was not a straightforward victory for egalitarian solidarity either. A union broadsheet purporting to speak for the striking women put the traditional union viewpoint: "Rolls Royce workers are determined to achieve their demands and in doing so realise that they are defending the wages of their husbands, brothers and sweethearts and other workers in the armed forces."[89] Accounts which claim that equal pay was achieved in the Second World War are interpreting the attention paid to the issue of equality at work as an indicator of practical outcomes for which there is little evidence.

In spite of the seemingly unbreachable nature, in both wars, of the gender divide in paid work, many women appreciated the chance to do work they had not thought of doing before, in which women were a novelty, and in which the pay was a great improvement on rates in traditional women's work.[90] Women in the new women's auxiliary services in the First World War, and their successors in the Second World War, in particular, seemed to have crossed gender boundaries. Like men, they wore military uniforms, and, free from the constraints of the labour–capital relationship, they learned to do the same skilled work as servicemen. However, they did not receive equal pay for it in either war.[91] And a fundamental difference remained: women were not allowed to handle lethal weapons - propriety would not relax this far. An experiment with using women to fire anti-aircraft guns in the Second World War was shortlived, because Churchill himself objected.[92] Women were socially constructed as life-givers not life-takers: they could service those employed to kill but not do the killing themselves.

Demobilization

At the end of each war, women were reminded forcibly that they were employed in "men's work" on a temporary basis. Following the Armistice in November 1918, women munition workers were mostly laid off, though some women in general engineering and aircraft work managed to stay on for a few months. In other industries, such as the leather trade, sawmills and brewing, they found their way into jobs formerly regarded as boys' (but not men's) work. More stayed in offices and shops, in work that was becoming identified as women's work.[93] The government assumed that when women lost their wartime jobs they would return quietly to women's trades or stay at home, but nearly half a million had registered as unemployed by March 1919. They were not prepared to surrender their claim for work similar in terms of pay and conditions to their war work. Determined to restore conventional gender divisions, the government, the press and the labour exchanges mounted a campaign to force women back into trades such as domestic service, laundry work and dressmaking. Women who refused such work and continued to claim unemployment benefit were lambasted in the press as "slackers with state pay" trying to take the bread out of the mouths of ex-servicemen, when only a year previously they had been celebrated as heroines. In the second half of 1919, Employment Exchanges cut women's benefit if they refused to take domestic or laundry work. These pressures were effective. By November 1919, the number of women registered as unemployed had dropped to only 29,000.[94] The economic slump of 1920, and the soaring levels of male unemployment, finally undermined women's chances of reinstating themselves in work that would use their wartime skills, and the number of women in domestic service rose from 1.8 million in 1921 to 2.1 million in 1931. But it is misleading to assume that women were content with the re-establishment of gender boundaries at work at the end of the First World War.

Not surprisingly, after the experiences of women in 1918–19, many women did not expect to get fair treatment at the end of the Second World War. But demobilization was not as abrupt for most women in 1945–6 as it had been in 1918–19. Lay-offs started earlier, in some cases such as filling factories, during the war itself. On the other hand, some women stayed on for several years, if their factory had full order books and their names were not on the union's list of dilutees. When the latter was the case, women were powerless, as a former Yorkshire weaver, Barbara Davies, discovered. She appealed to her union representative against redundancy from Armstrong Whitworth's aircraft factory in Coventry in 1945, but she was on his list of dilutees: "He said that the jobs were for the men coming out of the forces and that we had to leave the job for them . . . no matter how we tried to pressure him, there was nothing that we could do at all. In fact I think really we were quite an embarrassment to him. It was all decided, and so we just had to leave the premises and that was that."[95] Women protested collectively against redundancy at several engineering factories during 1945, but to no avail.

However, the economic aftermath of the Second World War was very different from that of the First World War. The new Labour Government, elected between the surrender of Germany in May and that of Japan in August 1945, launched an export drive to try to correct the balance of payments, and maintained controls such as rationing. It was a period in which, although there were not many goods to be bought, there was a lot of work to be done. The government was establishing the framework of the "Welfare State", which involved the reform of the health and education services, as well as the generation of masses of paperwork. Women were in demand as nurses, teachers and clerical workers, and the marriage bars that had operated in the 1920s and 1930s formally were dropped from these occupations. Women were also wanted in the women's sectors of the textiles industries and other types of factory work, as well as in institutional cleaning.

The buoyant demand for women's labour in the 1940s, supported by a government campaign in 1947 to attract women who had left work at the end of the war, is often forgotten because attention focuses on the "back to the home" rhetoric of postwar pronatalism, and the apparent evidence of the marriage and baby booms of 1945 and 1947 that women wanted to go home and settle down. Undoubtedly there was a strong expectation that young women would marry, have children and stay at home. The pressures against mothers working during the war were reinforced afterwards. But the Second World War had changed the expectations of a significant group of women about their involvement in the labour market. A small proportion of older married women had done paid work in the interwar years. In the 1940s and 1950s they became more numerous than the young, single women who had once dominated women's employment. They included women with school-age children, and many were offered and took part-time work, which had been pioneered on an organized basis during the war, to "mobilize" such women for the war effort.[96]

Conclusion

What does this review of women and war in the twentieth century tell us about change, either in terms of gender equality or within the separate sphere? Enfranchisement in the First World War is undoubtedly significant, even if it was not a direct reward for women's war work. Without the vote, and the accompanying legislation that permitted women to stand for Parliament, there would have been no women MPs; and, without them, it is improbable that equal compensation for war injuries would have been achieved in the Second World War, or that the question of equal pay would have been opened up for public debate. However, clinching arguments for both the enfranchisement of women and equal compensation were couched in the language of gender difference. This might suggest that the status of women within the separate sphere was rising. But it is hard to find concrete wartime gains for women as wives and mothers, apart from the relatively small and shortlived servicemen's wives' allowances and the more important Maternity and Child Welfare legislation of 1918 and National Health Service of 1948.

Even though they were not responsible directly for increasing the crucial availability of divorce and contraception, the wars appear to have contributed to changes in the concept of marriage. But a material difference to wives and mothers was made above all by their participation in the labour market. While this was emphatically temporary in the First World War, the contrasting conditions at the end of the Second World War ensured the continuing participation of older and married women in paid work afterwards. Nevertheless, in both wars and their aftermath, women were under pressure to conform to the ideal of the domestic wife and mother, both directly through maternalist rhetoric, and indirectly, through the suspicion with which the sexuality of women in transgressive wartime roles was regarded. Above all, gender divides at work were obdurate. The idea that women in general did "men's work" in the wars is a myth. Women in the Armed Forces took over masculine servicing roles, but their work was by definition temporary. And women in industry either came and went as dilutees, patrolled by unions intent on preserving male privilege, or did work defined in terms of gender difference as "women's work".

The indicators of change examined here suggest that the wars did not cause profound changes, defined in relation to equality or difference, to women as a category. However, the personal accounts of individual women suggest that the wars were important to them subjectively, even if it was other aspects of their lives than their gender identities that were being transformed. Such testimony awaits systematic exploration.

Acknowledgements

I should like to thank Gail Braybon and Linda Walker for helpful discussions and correspondence concerning aspects of this chapter.

Notes

1. This is true of some otherwise exemplary feminist historical writing on the "interwar years", which relegates both world wars to a hazy zone outside the scope of consideration. See M. Glucksman, *Women assemble: women workers and the new industries in inter-war Britain* (London: Routledge, 1990); A. Light, *Forever England: femininity, literature and conservatism between the wars* (London: Routledge, 1991).
2. Some recent volumes devoted to the debate, all of which include essays on women and war if they are not entirely devoted to the topic, include B. Brivati & H. Jones (eds), *What difference did the war make?* (Leicester: Leicester University Press, 1993); M. R. Higonnet et al., *Behind the lines: gender and the two World Wars* (New Haven, Connecticut: Yale University Press, 1987); A. Marwick (ed.), *Total war and social change* (London: Macmillan, 1988); H. Smith (ed.), *War and social change:*

British society in the Second World War (Manchester: Manchester University Press, 1986); S. Constantine, M. Kirby, & M. Rose (eds), *The First World War in British history* (London: Edward Arnold, forthcoming).

3. R. M. Titmuss, *Essays on "the welfare state"* (London: Unwin, 1958); A. Myrdal & V. Klein, *Women's two roles, home and work* (London: Routledge & Kegan Paul, 1956).

4. Titmuss, *Essays on "the welfare state"*, p. 84.

5. In 1915 these were worth 17s 6d (87p) per week for the wife of a private soldier with three children and they rose with the cost of living to £1 11s 7d (£1.57) in 1918, when the average male labourer's weekly wage was £2 8s (£2.40). See J. Lewis, *Women in England 1870-1950: sexual divisions and social change* (London: Harvester Wheatsheaf, 1984), p. 26; J. M. Winter, *The Great War and the British people* (London: Macmillan, 1985), p. 234. In the Second World War, a wife with two children received £1.18s in 1942, rising to £3 in 1944, at a time when the average weekly earnings of men in the engineering industries were £6 16s (£6.80). S. M. Ferguson & H. Fitzgerald, Studies in the social services (London: HMSO, 1954) p. 22; P. Inman, *Labour in the munitions industries* (London: HMSO, 1957), p. 330.

6. Evidence about the amount that husbands allowed wives from their wages before, during and after both wars shows a wide diversity of practices. But Jane Lewis draws on pre-1914 and 1930s documentation to suggest that "the vast majority of husbands kept back a proportion of their income for their own use" as well as keeping their wives in ignorance of what they earned, which led in many cases to the "maldistribution of resources within the family". Lewis, *Women in England*, p. 26. And a survey of saving and spending in seven British towns, undertaken by Charles Madge during the Second World War, emphasized that husbands typically did not enlarge wives' allowances as their own incomes went up, or as the family expanded and grew up. C. Madge, *War-time patterns of saving and spending* (Cambridge: Cambridge University Press, 1943), pp. 53-9.

7. J. Lewis, "Models of equality for women: the case of state support for children in twentieth-century Britain", in *Maternity and gender policies: women and the rise of the European welfare states, 1880s-1950s*, G. Bock & P. Thane (eds) (London: Routledge, 1991) pp. 82-7.

8. J. Macnicol, *The movement for family allowances* (London: Heinemann, 1980), pp. 185-9.

9. Lewis, *Women in England*, p. 49.

10. G. Braybon & P. Summerfield, *Out of the cage: women's experiences in two world wars* (London: Pandora, 1987), pp. 108-9.

11. J. J. Smith, "Rents, peace, votes: working-class women and political activity in the First World War", in *Out of bounds: women in Scottish society 1800-1945*, E. Breitenbach & E. Gordon (eds) (Edinburgh: Edinburgh University Press, 1992), p. 179.

12. Lewis, *Women in England*, p. 27. In Leeds, women also went on rent strike, and in London Sylvia Pankhurst linked suffrage and housing in her campaign slogan "No Vote No Rent".

13. Smith, "Rent, peace, votes", p. 179.

14. The Rent and Mortgage Interest Restrictions Act was introduced in September 1939. See W. K. Hancock & M. M. Gowing, *British War Economy* (London: HMSO, 1949) p. 166.

15. R. M. Titmuss, *Problems of social policy* (London: HMSO, 1950), p. 414, n.1.

16. Madge, *Wartime patterns*, pp. 17 & 39 (15s out of £1 18s).

17. *Lancet* **11**, p. 569, 1940.

18. Winter, *The Great War*, p. 117; J. M. Winter, "Aspects of the impact of the First World War on infant mortality in Britain", *Journal of European Economic History* **11**, pp. 713–38, 1982; J. M. Winter, "The demographic consequences of the war", in *War and social change: British society in the Second World War*, H. L. Smith (ed.) (Manchester: Manchester University Press, 1986), pp. 163–5. Lewis, *Women in England*, p. 26, suggests that the allowances caused the difference in the First World War.

19. Winter, *The Great War*, p. 141; Ferguson & Fitzgerald, *Studies in the social services*, p. 172.

20. Braybon & Summerfield, *Out of the cage*, p. 2.

21. A. Davin, "Imperialism and motherhood", *History Workshop Journal* **5**, Spring 1978; C. Dyhouse, "Working-class mothers and infant mortality in England 1895–1914", *Journal of Social History* **XII** (2), 1978.

22. See, for example, the Women's Co-operative Guild, *Maternity: letters from working women*, M. Llewelyn Davies (ed.) (London: Virago, 1978; first published London: G. Bell & Sons, 1915).

23. G. Braybon, *Women workers in the First World War* (London: Routledge, 1989), pp. 118–19.

24. Braybon & Summerfield, *Out of the cage*, p. 107.

25. D. Dwork, *War is good for babies and other young children: a history of the infant and child welfare movement in England 1898–1918* (London: Tavistock, 1987), p. 214.

26. There is some evidence that wartime military service introduced men to the condom, and that its use became more widespread, but this method was under male rather than female control: D. Gittins, *Fair sex: family size and structure 1900–1939* (London: Hutchinson, 1982), pp. 112–13.

27. Winter, *The Great War*, pp. 136–7.

28. For a discussion of this writing, see D. Riley, *War in the nursery: theories of the child and mother* (London: Virago, 1983).

29. J. Finch & P. Summerfield, "Social reconstruction and the emergence of companionate marriage, 1945–59", in *Marriage, domestic life and social change: writings for Jacqueline Burgoyne (1944–88)*, D. Clark (ed.) (London: Routledge, 1991).

30. M. Spring-Rice, *Working-class wives* (London: Penguin, 1939).

31. The popular press published articles with alluring pictures of babies growing into little children, like Anne Scott James' feature "Why women won't have babies", *Picture Post* (November 1943).

32. J. Mitchell, *Psychoanalysis and feminism* (London: Penguin, 1974).

33. Summerfield, *Women workers*, p. 94.

34. *Ibid.*, p. 84 and n. 53.

35. Quoted Braybon, *Women workers*, p. 120.

36. Hansard 404 HC Deb 5s, 2034.

37. Braybon & Summerfield, *Out of the cage*, pp. 270–1.

38. H. Smith, "The effect of the war on the status of women", in *War and social change: British society in the Second World War*, H. Smith (ed.) (Manchester: Manchester University Press, 1986), p. 225.

39. See P. Summerfield, "Women, war and social change: women in Britain in World War II, in *Total war and social change*, A. Marwick (ed.) (London: Macmillan, 1988), pp. 109–11.

40. Finch & Summerfield, *Social reconstruction*, pp. 26–8.

41. Braybon & Summerfield, *Out of the cage*, p. 110.

42. After 1923 a husband, and not just a wife, could be divorced for adultery, and in 1937 cruelty, insanity and desertion became grounds for divorce.

43. Braybon & Summerfield, Out of the cage, pp. 212-13 & 272.

44. Winter, *The Great War*, pp. 261-3.

45. Braybon & Summerfield, *Out of the cage*, p. 267.

46. D. Sheridan, "Ambivalent memories: women and the 1939-45 War in Britain", *Oral History* (Spring 1990), p. 34.

47. Braybon & Summerfield, *Out of the cage*, p. 110. This is demonstrated by the fact that the proportion of "unmarried mothers" was lower at 7.6-7.7 per cent in wartime than in 1911, when it had been 8 per cent.

48. Ferguson & Fitzgerald, *Studies in the social services*, pp. 90-91. One in three mothers conceived their first child extramaritally in 1938, but 70 per cent of these women married before the child was born, whereas in 1945 only 37 per cent did so.

49. P. Summerfield & N. Crockett, "'You weren't taught that with the welding': lessons in sexuality in the Second World War", *Women's History Review* **1** (3), p. 436, 1992.

50. Ferguson & Fitzgerald, *Studies in the social services*, pp. 95-6.

51. Central Statistical Office, *Statistical digest of the war* (London: HMSO, 1951), tables 9 & 18.

52. Summerfield and Crockett, "'You weren't taught that with the welding'", pp. 435-41.

53. S. Pankhurst, *The home front* (London: Hutchison, 1932) p. 98. "Alarmist morality mongers conceived most monstrous visions of girls and women, freed from the control of fathers and husbands who had hitherto compelled them to industry, chastity and sobriety, now neglecting their homes, plunging into excesses, and burdening the country with swarms of illegitimate infants", E. Summerskill, "Conscription and women", *The Fortnightly* **CLI**, pp. 209-10, March 1942. A feminist MP, Edith Summerskill drew parallels between the moral panic about women in uniform in the Second World War and attitudes towards women in public throughout the previous century: "There is a certain type of individual who is always ready to suspect the morals of women who indulge in activities outside the home and who is obsessed with the idea that a girl in uniform attracts certain undesirable characters." Referring to attitudes to Florence Nightingale in the Crimean War, by that time an icon of feminine propriety, Summerskill wrote "no doubt the grandfathers of those who whisper about the morals of the woman in the Services to-day opined that no respectable woman could become an army nurse and still preserve her chastity".

54. Braybon & Summerfield, *Out of the cage*, p. 78; Summerfield & Crockett, "You weren't taught that with the welding", p. 449.

55. P. Levine, "'Walking the streets in a way no decent woman should': women police in World War I", *Journal of Modern History* **66**, March 1994.

56. M. Jackson, *The 'real' facts of life: feminism and the politics of sexuality c1850-1940* (London: Taylor and Francis, 1994).

57. J. Wyndham, *Love is blue, a wartime diary* (London: Heinemann, 1986)

58. A. Marwick, *The deluge: British society and the First World War* (London: Bodley Head, 1965) pp. 102-3.

59. M. Pugh, *Women and the women's movement in Britain 1914-1959* (London: Macmillan, 1992), p. 40.

60. Pugh, *Women and the women's movement*, p. 42.

61. *Ibid.*, p. 11-12.

62. A. Wiltsher, *Most dangerous women: feminist peace campaigners of the Great War* (London: Pandora, 1985); J. Alberti, *Beyond suffrage: feminists in war and peace*

1914-28 (London: Macmillan, 1989); J. Vellacott, "Feminist consciousness and the First World War", in R. Roach Pierson (ed.) *Women and peace: theoretical, historical and critical perspectives* (London: Croom Helm, 1987). Thanks to Linda Walker for the third reference.

63. S. S. Holton, *Feminism and democracy* (Cambridge: Cambridge University Press, 1987), pp. 134-50.

64. Pugh, *Women and the women's movement*, p. 38.

65. A. Marwick, *Britain in the century of total war: war, peace and social change 1900-1967* (London: Bodley Head, 1968), p. 293.

66. E. Summerskill, "Conscription", p. 209.

67. See Summerfield, *Women workers*, Ch. 3. As well as upholding gender differences, British mobilization policy discriminated racially; see B. Bousquet & C. Douglas, *West Indian women at war. British racism in the Second World War* (London: Lawrence & Wishart, 1991).

68. V. Douie, *The lesser half: a survey of the laws, regulations and practices introduced during the present war which embody discrimination against women* (London: Women's Publicity Planning Association, 1943), p. 49.

69. Braybon & Summerfield, *Out of the cage*, p. 182; Summerfield, *Women workers*, pp. 175-6.

70. H. Smith, "The problem of 'equal pay for equal work' in Great Britain during World War ll", *Journal of Modern History* **53**, p. 668, December 1981.

71. M. Zimmeck, "We are all professionals now: professionalisation, education and gender in the civil service 1873-1939", in *Women, education and the professions*, P. Summerfield (ed.) (Leicester: History of Education Society, Occasional Publication 8, 1987).

72. Summerfield, *Women workers*, p. 103.

73. Braybon, *Women workers*, p. 51.

74. *Ibid.*, pp. 51-3; Braybon & Summerfield, *Out of the cage*, pp. 35, 120.

75. Braybon & Summerfield, *Out of the cage*, p. 37.

76. P. Inman, *Labour in the munitions industries*, pp. 441-2; Summerfield, *Women workers*, pp. 193-4.

77. See C. E. V. Leser, "Men and women in industry", *Economic Journal* **62** (246), pp. 326-44, 1952. Leser argued that the increasing proportions of women in a range of industries, including engineering and national and local government, meant "not so much that women took men's jobs as that women-employing sections of the industries concerned gained at the expense of men-employing sections", p. 330. See also M. Glucksman, *Women assemble: women workers and the new industries in inter-war Britain* (London: Routledge, 1990).

78. A. Woollacott, *On her their lives depend: munitions workers in the Great War* (Berkeley, California: University of California Press, 1994), pp. 17-18; table 2, p. 31; pp. 30-1.

79. J. M. Hooks, *British policies and methods of employing women in wartime* (Washington, DC: United States Government, 1944), p. 24. In terms of mobilisation, 1943 was the high point of the war effort. "Essential industries" included engineering, chemicals, vehicles, transport, the energy industries and shipbuilding.

80. Inman, *Labour in the munitions industries*, pp. 78-80.

81. Hooks, *British policies*, p. 29; Inman, *Labour in the munitions industries*, p. 354.

82. Braybon & Summerfield, *Out of the cage*, p. 48.

83. *Ibid.*, pp. 48-51.

84. *Ibid.*, pp. 48-51.

85. Royal Commission on Equal Pay, Minutes of evidence, 27 July 1945, para. 2930.

86. *Ibid.*, 3 August 1945, paras 3406–12 & 3380.
87. R. Croucher, *Engineers at war* (London: Merlin, 1992), pp. 285–95.
88. For example, by A. Calder, *The people's war, Britain 1939–45* (London: Panther, 1971), p. 466. Pay for work in the higher grades was related to the rates for skilled and semi-skilled (men's) work in engineeering, and in the lower grades it was related to the women's rates. There was a differential of about a pound between them: in 1944 the women's national minimum time-rate in engineering was £2 16s (£2.80) compared with male labourer's minimum of £3 15s 6d (£3.78); Inman, *Labour in the munitions industries*, p. 354.
89. Summerfield, *Women workers*, p. 172.
90. Braybon & Summerfield, *Out of the cage*, pp. 281–2.
91. P. Summerfield, "The patriarchal discourse of human capital: women's work and training in the Second World War", *Journal of Gender Studies* **2** (2), pp. 189–205, November 1993. Women joined various military nursing organizations in both wars. The most famous are the Voluntary Aid Detachments and the First Aid Nursing Yeomanry. In 1917, the Women's Royal Naval Service, Women's Army Auxiliary Corps and Women's Royal Air Force were formed. In the Second World War, all three were revived, the last two being renamed the Auxiliary Territorial Service and Women's Auxiliary Air Force. The Women's Land Service Corps, renamed Women's Land Army, was also started in 1917 and revived during the Second World War. Members of the Women's Voluntary Service for Air Raid Precautions, formed in 1938, also wore uniform.
92. D. Parkin, "Women in the armed services 1940–45", in *Patriotism: the making and unmaking of British national identity*, vol. II, R. Samuel (ed.) (London: Routledge, 1989), pp. 158–70.
93. Braybon & Summerfield, *Out of the cage*, p. 120.
94. *Ibid.*, pp. 120–5.
95. *Ibid.*, p. 260.
96. See P. Summerfield, "Companionate marriage and the double burden: women in Britain since 1945", in J. Obelkevich & P. Catterall (eds), *Understanding postwar British society* (London: Routledge, forthcoming).

Suggestions for further reading

G. Braybon, *Women workers in the First World War*, and P. Summerfield, *Women workers in the Second World War*, both reissued by Routledge in 1989, investigate in greater depth many of the issues discussed here. The book we wrote together, G. Braybon & P. Summerfield, *Out of the cage, women's experiences in two world wars* (London: Pandora 1987) covers women in Britain in both wars and draws extensively on autobiographical sources. A. Woollacott, *On her their lives depend: munitions workers in the Great War* (Berkeley, California: University of California Press, 1994) provides a wealth of detail on women in munitions work in the First World War. Denise Riley, *War in the nursery: theories of the child and mother* (London: Virago, 1983) is a fascinating analysis of pronatalist thinking and social policy during and after the Second World War. For an international perspective readers should consult the collection edited by M. R. Higonnet et al., *Behind the lines: gender and the two world wars* (New Haven, Conneticut: Yale University Press, 1987). C. Tylee, *The Great War and women's consciousness* (London: Macmillan, 1990) is a path-breaking study of images of militarism in women's writing; and C. Gledhill & G. Swanson are currently editing a major collection on cultural constructions of femininity in the Second World War: *Nationalising femininity* (Manchester University Press, forthcoming). For pioneering work on black women in the Second World War, see B. Bousquet & C. Douglas *West Indian women at war. British racism in the Second World War* (London: Lawrence & Wishart, 1991). There are now numerous collections of essays on various aspects of the debate about women, war and social change, some of which are indicated in Note 2 on page 321.

Index